Morocco

Marvine Howe

Morocco

The Islamist Awakening

and Other Challenges

CANCELLED

UNIVERSITY PRESS

2005

OXFORD
UNIVERSITY PRESS

Oxford University Press, Inc., publishes works that further
Oxford University's objective of excellence
in research, scholarship, and education.

Oxford   New York
Auckland   Cape Town   Dar es Salaam   Hong Kong   Karachi
Kuala Lumpur   Madrid   Melbourne   Mexico City   Nairobi
New Delhi   Shanghai   Taipei   Toronto

With offices in
Argentina   Austria   Brazil   Chile   Czech Republic   France   Greece
Guatemala   Hungary   Italy   Japan   Poland   Portugal   Singapore
South Korea   Switzerland   Thailand   Turkey   Ukraine   Vietnam

Published by Oxford University Press, Inc.
198 Madison Avenue, New York, New York 10016

www.oup.com

Oxford is a registered trademark of Oxford University Press

Library of Congress Cataloging-in-Publication Data
Howe, Marvine.
Morocco : the Islamist awakening and other challenges / by Marvine Howe.
    p. cm.
Includes bibliographical references and index.
ISBN-13 978-0-19-516963-8
ISBN 0-19-516963-8
1. Morocco.   2. Islam and politics—Morocco.   I. Title.
DT305.H69 2005
964.05—dc22   2004018891

9 8 7 6 5 4 3 2 1

Printed in the United States of America
on acid-free paper

For my Moroccan friends,

past and present—

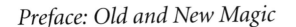

Preface: Old and New Magic

*T*he storied land of *kasbahs* and palaces, mosques and *marabouts*, veiled women and hooded men, Islamic rituals and feudal intrigue is in the midst of upheaval. From the remote hamlets of the High Atlas to oases on the edge of the Sahara, from the halls of the medieval Karaouyine University in Fez to the grimmest shantytowns around Casablanca, there's an urgent hunger in Morocco for the good things of modern times, as flaunted daily on television and the Internet.

Moroccans are deeply aware of their identity as descendants of the great Muslim empires that ruled Iberia and much of northern Africa in the Middle Ages. They are for the most part devoted to their monarchy, which has ruled for more than 1,200 years. There are, however, a growing number of voices in the independent press and human rights organizations, among scholars, businesspeople, professionals, and politicians, that are calling for representative government, accountability, and other democratic reforms.

There is also an Islamist awakening on university campuses, in some political circles, and among ordinary Moroccans, much like that which has taken place elsewhere in the Muslim world, including Iran and even secular Turkey. Muslim activists are looking to political Islam as an alternative to Western-style politics, which have failed to satisfy many people's aspirations for basic dignity, justice, and well-being.

In general, the Islamist movement in Morocco has chosen to express itself through nonviolent means. There have been, however, angry *fetwas* by a few exalted Islamic preachers against Western secularism, fiery audiotapes and articles denouncing Western immorality, and street demonstrations in solidarity with Muslim victims of Western terrorism. But Moroccans have always prided themselves on their relaxed and tolerant interpretation of Islam and what has come to be known as "the Moroccan exception."

The resurgence of Islamic activism in Morocco has been reinforced by sharpened divisions between Muslim countries and the West over the long-festering Palestinian question and the war against terrorism that many Muslims perceive to be a war against Islam. Still, as the westernmost Muslim nation, Morocco has looked primarily to Europe and the United States to propel it into the global economy, while preserving strong spiritual ties to Islam's heartland in the Middle East. To maintain this delicate balance as a Western-oriented Muslim nation is the most daunting challenge facing the inexperienced King Mohammed VI, who succeeded his redoubtable father, the late Hassan II, in 1999.

Since coming to the throne at age thirty-five, King Mohammed has initiated drives against slums and poverty, illiteracy, corruption, and the abuse of human rights, but even the monarch admits the problems persist. He has expressed his attachment to the principles of democracy and continued his father's cautious easing of the tightly controlled regime but taken no steps to share his power. As a result, political leaders on the Left and the Right have lacked the authority to carry out the necessary social and economic reforms, and their credibility has suffered. The Islamist movement has benefited from liberalization to become the main organized opposition to what often appears to be an inept and corrupt political system.

Morocco's first relatively free elections, in the fall of 2002, constituted a serious warning to the establishment. Disenchanted with politicians and impatient for change, the people said so at the polls. None of the mainstream parties won a majority; the numbers of abstentions and invalid ballots were unusually high; and the Islamist opposition tripled its seats in parliament. The king named a trusted technocrat as prime minister, but his unwieldy six-party coalition was characterized by continuity and stability rather than change.

Then on May 16, 2003, fourteen Moroccan suicide bombers attacked foreign and Jewish targets in Casablanca, killing forty-five persons, including twelve of their own. It was the first time that Islamic zealots had resorted to this type of martyrdom in Morocco, although radical preachers had raised the level of verbal violence in recent years. Before May 16, Moroccans had felt insulated from radical Islamic fundamentalism, which has taken root in other Muslim countries, including neighboring Algeria. Most Moroccans believed in the much-touted "Moroccan model," that of a moderate Muslim society, led by the Commander of the Faithful and moving toward Western democracy and progress.

The terrorist attacks shocked the kingdom—much in the same way that the assault of September 11, 2001, on the World Trade Center and the Pentagon traumatized the United States. Suddenly Morocco's moderate Muslims were confronted with the fact that their country was no exception but part of the global struggle with Islamic fanaticism. A national debate has ensued in Morocco on the underlying causes of this appalling tragedy and how to respond without jeopardizing the country's newborn and still-faltering democratic gains.

But it was the March 11, 2004, terrorist attacks on Madrid's commuter trains, killing 191 people and wounding some 1,800, that catapulted Morocco to center stage of the clash of civilizations. Spanish investigations showed that mostly Moroccans were implicated in the planning and execution of the bombings. The suspects were not Casablanca slum dwellers desperate to escape their hopeless lives but Moroccan immigrants living relatively well in a thriving Spain. They were Moroccans with links to that shadowy worldwide movement of Islamic radicals who have claimed responsibility for terrorist acts from the United States to Saudi Arabia and Indonesia.

Why, I asked myself, were so many Moroccans found in the ranks of the international *jihad*? What had happened to the gentle, fair-minded people I had come to know in the struggle for independence?

I had first discovered this exotic kingdom in the early 1950s—when it had become essentially a French colony, flanked by Spanish and international zones. It was the same time that Paul Bowles immortalized Morocco in *The Sheltering Sky*. I was fresh out of the Rutgers School of Journalism and had come to Fez as an *au pair* in a French military family to perfect my French. At that time, the North African independence movements were taking off, and I was beginning my career as a freelance journalist. Over the next decade, I worked for Radio Maroc, wrote my first book, *The Prince and I*, and became a stringer for the *New York Times* and *Time-Life*, covering the conflict in Algeria and the debut of Moroccan independence. But the Moroccan dream of freedom soon became tarnished. The modern Prince Hassan turned into a feudal monarch. Thousands of people were jailed for their beliefs. An old nationalist friend of mine, Mehdi Ben Barka, who led the opposition to the dictatorial regime, was kidnapped and probably murdered. I severed my relations with what was no longer a fairytale kingdom, but remained in touch with Moroccan friends.

This book is the story of my return to Morocco and my rediscovery of this wondrous and troubling land. It is an introduction to today's Morocco, with its 30 million inhabitants, many of whom still cling to ancient traditions, while some have adopted a modern Western lifestyle, and others have chosen a contemporary Islamic identity. It is a personal view of an ancient country engaged in the transition to modernity, a tolerant, Western-oriented

Muslim nation confronted by the surge of political Islam sweeping the Muslim world.

Morocco is much more than old and new; it is a fascinating, complex, many-layered land. Most Moroccans are friendly and wonderfully diverse. I have sketched portraits of some outstanding Moroccans I have met, like the late King Hassan, a brilliant statesman for all of his flaws and cruelty; the dynamic opposition leader Mehdi Ben Barka, whose disappearance was a national tragedy; and former Socialist prime minister Abderrahmane Youssoufi, who did much to restore public freedoms but failed to keep his promises of social and economic reform. My gallery includes the dedicated human rights activist Sion Assidon; the articulate rebel Prince Moulay Hicham; the irreverent satirist Ahmed Sanoussi; the persistent choreographer Lahcen Zinoune; and the dauntless journalists Aboubakr Jamai and Ahmed Reda Benchemsi. There are also many courageous women: Khadija Rouissi, a leader of the movement for truth and justice; Meryam Demnati, the Berber *passionaria*; Nadia Yassine, the militant and eloquent daughter of the Islamist leader Sheikh Abdessalam Yassine; Nouzha Skalli, pharmacist and member of parliament in the vanguard of the struggle for women's rights; and sociologist and author Fatema Mernissi, whose long fight for the emancipation of women has led her to the cause of forgotten rural communities.

In these pages, I explain why Morocco matters. Strategically positioned in northwestern Africa at the Atlantic gateway to the Mediterranean, Morocco has had a long and complex relationship with its European neighbors. During World War II, the Allies launched their North African campaign, landing on Morocco's Atlantic coast and Algeria's Mediterranean shore. Although the Vichy government of France was nominally in control of French Morocco, Sultan Mohammed V supported the Allies from the outset and rejected Vichy's anti-Semitic decrees targeting the Jewish minority. After the war, the United States remained at the naval airbase at Port Lyautey (now Kenitra) and concluded an agreement with the French, in late 1950, for the establishment of five military bases in Morocco. Leading Morocco to independence in 1956, Mohammed V forged an independent foreign policy by getting rid of the foreign troops, joining the Non-Aligned Movement and the Arab League, but discreetly remaining in the Western camp.

Under the autocratic King Hassan II, who succeeded his adored father on his death in 1961, Morocco consolidated its economic and cultural ties with its former colonial masters, France and Spain. In Cold War politics, King Hassan openly sided with the United States and, in return, received military and diplomatic support in the bitter conflict with Socialist neighbor Algeria over Western Sahara. One of King Hassan's main achievements was to maintain cordial relations with both Israelis and Palestinians and thereby play an active role as intermediary in the peace process. More recently, the kingdom negotiated an association accord with the European Union, which accounts for two-thirds of its trade.

King Mohammed VI has pursued his father's pro-Western policies, upgrading relations with the European Union to a strategic partnership. The monarch also agreed to establish a free trade association with the United States, despite local and French criticism. An early supporter of the United States in its war against terrorism, Morocco was the only Arab country to hold a memorial service for the victims of September 11, 2001—an action denounced by radical Islamists as a grave sin. Although the kingdom opposed the U.S. wars in Afghanistan and Iraq, it has won a place on Osama Bin Laden's list of "impious" Muslim countries because of its firm clamp-down on Islamic radicals.

This book addresses the central question: can an absolute Muslim monarchy embrace Western-style democracy in an era of growing confrontation between the Islamic world and the West? The authorities must tread carefully because the Moroccan public, like much of the Muslim world, is profoundly opposed to American policies in the Middle East.

Closely related is the dilemma of how to combat Islamic extremists without jeopardizing the country's tortuous progress toward democracy. Can the security services be made to distinguish between those who peacefully seek to restore Islamic rule and those who advocate violent change? Is the Moroccan establishment prepared to reach an accommodation with the nonviolent Islamists, and in turn, are mainstream Islamists willing to come to terms with the establishment?

Mohammed VI continues to articulate the vision of a democratic and modern Morocco. The question remains: is he ready and able to take the necessary steps to relinquish some of his absolute powers to create an equitable state of law, accountable to the people? This would be a powerful response to radical Islamic ambitions.

Contents

The Kingdom of Morocco and the disputed territory of
Western Sahara

Return to Morocco

I

Commander of the Faithful

1

Enveloped in a white hooded robe and seated on a gilt and plush throne, King Mohammed VI greets one by one the members of the royal family, Islamic theologians, and high officials from around the country. They in turn bow deeply and embrace the royal hand.

This annual rite is a renewal of the *beia*, the act of allegiance on which Moroccan sovereigns base their legitimacy, a ceremony that has changed little in the past 300 years. The Moroccan king, who claims direct descent from the Muslim Prophet Mohammed, bears the distinguished title of *Amir al Mouminine*, or Commander of the Faithful, and is both spiritual and temporal ruler of this ancient North African kingdom.

When the boyish Crown Prince Mohammed took over the reins of power in 1999, Morocco was caught up in a royal whirlwind. It was the most exciting time since independence, nearly a half century before. The nation believed that an era of reform had begun, that springtime had come at last. The new king appeared determined to correct the cruel abuses of a despotic state and lead the country firmly on the path to a modern democracy.

King Mohammed belongs to the younger generation of Arab leaders, who came to power at the turn of the century on the deaths of their fathers, all towering figures of contemporary Middle Eastern politics: King Hussein of Jordan, Syrian president Hafez al-Assad, and Morocco's King Hassan. The sons, respectively, King Abdullah II, President Bashar al-Assad, and King Mohammed, are Western-educated and known as political moderates and have brought with them immense hope for change in the Arab world.

The thirty-five-year-old King Mohammed was an unknown element for most people. Few journalists, politicians, or diplomats could claim familiarity with Morocco's new monarch. As crown prince, he had been a reserved

3

King Mohammed VI, wearing a ceremonial while djellaba, receives his first beia as Commander of the Faithful on July 23, 1999, after the death of his father, King Hassan. The king is seated, with Socialist prime minister Abderrahmane Youssoufi standing on his right. In the background stand the king's brother, Prince Moulay Rachid, and next to him, the king's rebellious first cousin, Prince Moulay Hicham. (Moroccan Ministry of Communications)

figure, remaining quietly in the shadow of his father, Hassan II. The late sovereign had ruled Morocco with a steel grip for nearly four decades and gained international renown as one of the leading statesmen of the Middle East and Africa.

Early in his reign, Mohammed VI demonstrated by words and acts that he was prepared to distance himself from his father's oppressive rule and forge a more open command. Yet as time goes by, King Mohammed, who has always spoken with deference toward the late King Hassan, has generally favored continuity over change.

One event, in particular, has threatened the king's declared aim to gradually democratize the autocratic regime. In the spring of 2003, fourteen suicide bombers struck at the heart of Casablanca, killing thirty-three Moroccans and foreigners and twelve of the terrorists, in the name of Islam.

Who Is Mohammed VI?

In the summer of 1999, the Moroccan press and *souks* were flooded with photos of the new king. In some portraits, His Majesty wore sleek Armani suits or modern sports gear to appeal to his contemporaries; in others he wore flowing white robes for his elders and the devout. Effusive articles appeared at home and abroad on "the king of the poor," "the royal jet-skier," "King Charming," "the modern monarch," "the M-6 generation," and "the king and the revolution."

The poised young man with closely cropped hair and dark sunglasses, wearing jeans and a leather jacket on the cover of *Jeune Afrique*, was a world away from the timid crown prince, raised in a medieval court under the stern watch of King Hassan. In his memoirs, Hassan II had told how his father beat him with a stick until he was ten or twelve years old, adding that he had shown the same severity with his own children and so "didn't have any problems with them at school."[1]

In the past, palace life was strictly private. There had been no announcement, no public ceremony at the time of Crown Prince Hassan's wedding. It was later learned that prior to his accession to the throne, the prince had married Fatima, the daughter of *Caid* Amharoq, a Berber tribal leader. As Fatima bore him no heirs, he took a second wife, her cousin Latifa. Her existence was acknowledged only when she gave birth to two sons, Princes Mohammed and Rachid, and three daughters, Princesses Meryem, Hasna, and Asma. Latifa was given no royal title and almost never appeared in public until after King Hassan's death, but remained cloistered in the royal harem.

There were two other princes in the palace, Moulay Hicham, who was the same age as Crown Prince Mohammed, and the younger Moulay Ismail, and their sister, Princess Zeineb. These were the children of King Hassan's brother, Moulay Abdallah, who had died of cancer in 1983. In Arab tradition, the king became their second father.

In her bestselling book *Stolen Lives*, Malika Oufkir gives a glimpse into the medieval world of the royal palace, where she spent her childhood as a companion to King Hassan's youngest sister. Oufkir was the daughter of the powerful interior minister, General Mohammed Oufkir, who was accused of plotting against the king and summarily executed in 1972. The focus of her book is the two decades of harsh punishment in various prisons that she, along with five siblings and their mother, suffered for the alleged sins of the father.

Oufkir provides a vivid account of palace life, a world of magic potions, curses, and cruel punishments (she recalls receiving painful whippings by the king for bad report cards). Hassan II possessed some forty concubines, in addition to forty inherited from his father, each of whom had a special task: washing the monarch's feet, dressing him on holidays, bearing incense, or keeping the palace keys. There were also slaves, whose ancestors had been bought from African slave traders and who had served in the royal palace for generations. The women slaves cared for the kitchen and housework and sometimes became "third class concubines," while the men waited on table, took care of the royal garage, and acted as the king's spies.[2]

This portrait of King Hassan as an Oriental potentate is corroborated by Jean-Pierre Tuquoi, a correspondent of the Paris daily *Le Monde.* In his book *Le Dernier Roi,* published in Paris in 2001, Tuquoi recounts secrets of King Hassan's palace, including the rivalries of the concubines and devotion of the slaves. He also describes the incredible opulence, the elaborate meals left untasted, the vast wardrobes of French designer clothes, and the garage filled with Rolls-Royces, Jaguars, Mercedes—but no BMWs, which the king detested. Tuquoi, who is known as a specialist on African affairs, does not cite his sources. Needless to say, *Le Dernier Roi* was banned in Morocco.

Crown Prince Mohammed hated the feudal aspects of his father's lifestyle and escaped whenever he could, according to sources familiar with palace life. *Sidi* (a title of respect) Mohammed attended the Collège Royal (secondary school) in the palace compound, which had been set up for his father and a select group of the best students in the kingdom. The school was run along the French *lycée* system, with additional courses in Arabic and Moroccan history. The crown prince was also given advanced studies in the Koran, as befits a descendant of the Prophet. His associates recall that he preferred arts, literature, and sports to mathematics and the sciences. When Sidi Mohammed passed his *baccalauréat,* King Hassan gave him a villa of his own, "Les Sablons," with a park and stables, across the river from Rabat and at considerable distance from the royal palace. The crown prince loved his retreat so much that he insisted on living there after he became king rather than moving into the palace, which still resonates with his father's memory.

Although he had wanted to pursue advanced courses in fine arts, Sidi Mohammed was forced by the king to study law at Rabat's Mohammed V University, and he obtained a master's degree in 1983. That year, the crown prince was named to his first official post as coordinator of the Royal Armed Forces' General Headquarters in Rabat. In 1988, he was able to evade the constraints of his father's presence by serving an internship with Jacques Delors, president of the European Commission in Brussels. There, the crown prince was known as a serious, attentive student, but on weekends, he was another person, according to Tuquoi. The French correspondent notes that Sidi Mohammed and his band of friends openly enjoyed themselves in the cafes, nightclubs, and castles that flourish on the outskirts of the Belgian capital.

At home, the crown prince spent his private time more discreetly, although he and his companions could be encountered partying in fashionable restaurants and nightclubs, speeding in the latest sports cars on the highway between Rabat and Casablanca, or jet-skiing on the Atlantic coast. Meanwhile, Sidi Mohammed worked on his doctoral thesis: "Cooperation between the European Union and the Countries of the *Maghreb*." In 1993, he obtained his doctorate in law with very honorable mention from the Sophia Antipolis University in Nice, under the sponsorship of his father's influential minister of the interior, Driss Basri. A close companion of that period remembers the crown prince saying that he did not believe he would ever accede to the throne because his father would never relinquish it.

As King Hassan's health deteriorated, he was increasingly accompanied by the crown prince on ceremonial occasions. But the king did not include his son in policy making, probably because Sidi Mohammed did not hide the fact that he wasn't really interested in politics, according to sources in his entourage. This gave rise to a certain tension between the king and the crown prince.

There was another problem between father and son: the king's insistence that Sidi Mohammed marry and sire an heir. Although he obeyed his father in almost everything, the crown prince had balked at marriage, say palace sources. He preferred his bachelor lifestyle and saw no reason to change it. But King Hassan's primary preoccupation was for the continuation of the Alaouite Dynasty.

The ailing monarch was also concerned over Morocco's deepening political and economic stagnation, according to close associates. King Hassan had tried various political formulas with meager results and had concluded it was necessary to bring the left-wing opposition on board to ensure an orderly succession. Thus the king called on Abderrahmane Youssoufi, leader of the Socialist opposition, to head a government of *Alternance* (alternative to the previous conservative or technocratic cabinets) in February 1998. The appointment of Youssoufi, a respected human rights lawyer, as prime minister was widely welcomed as a guarantee of the king's pledge to introduce real democratic rule at last. The trouble was that the king retained all of his prerogatives and direct control over the key ministries of sovereignty, like interior, foreign affairs, and Islamic affairs. Powerless to respond to the country's expectations, Youssoufi's mainstream coalition soon became the target of national frustrations.

Moroccan Springtime

After a prolonged absence, I returned to Morocco shortly before King Hassan's death. The country's mood was a mixture of apprehension over an uncertain future and hope for change. Youssoufi's multiparty government had ostensibly put an end to flagrant abuses of human rights and opened the way to much greater freedom of expression. But there had been no structural changes. The palace and its security apparatus remained pervasively in control, under the pretext of concern over restive tribes and festering problems in Western Sahara. The easing of restrictions on the press and other public freedoms had served to highlight the overwhelming social and economic problems and the government's incapacity to resolve them. The Islamist opposition grew increasingly militant and was the main beneficiary of the erosion of the country's political institutions.

Although the country was relatively quiet, Moroccans seemed haunted by the specter of troubles in neighboring Algeria. Everyone I met went out of his or her way to reassure me that Morocco would not follow in Algeria's steps. When Algerian Islamists had triumphed at the polls in 1991, the election was canceled by the military-dominated regime. This electoral fraud led to what amounted to an Islamist insurrection followed by brutal military repression, propelling Algerians into a spiral of violence that has taken some 150,000 lives.

Hassan II died of a heart attack on July 23, 1999, after a long illness, and the nation appeared stricken along with him. More than 2 million Moroccans were said to have attended the royal funeral in Rabat to express their pain and loss. That the country did not erupt into chaos, after nearly four decades of autocratic rule, is to the credit of Hassan's vision, Prime Minister Youssoufi's prestige, and widespread hope in the youthful king.

When the timid Prince Mohammed acceded to the throne, he firmly asserted himself, astonishing everyone with his bold and swift actions. From the outset, Mohammed VI differed radically from his father in style. Barely three months after coming to power, he met with governors, other regional administrators, and elected officials and announced "a new concept of authority" based on the defense of public services, freedoms, security, and stability. It sounded almost revolutionary.[3] The young monarch adopted a more democratic image than King Hassan, who was always the aloof autocrat. Where the father cultivated a formal, ceremonial presence, the son was more relaxed and casual. For most of his reign, Hassan had ruled as an enlightened despot, but Mohammed VI early on showed populist tendencies, enjoying crowd contacts and presiding over charitable works.

While King Mohammed has retained the traditional rituals of state, close associates say the young monarch is more at ease skiing or water skiing, dressing in the latest sportswear rather than ceremonial robes, and in the company of his old school friends rather than the political and religious dignitaries of the realm.

Unlike his worldly, articulate father, Mohammed VI does not like the press and has rarely granted interviews—and almost never to Moroccan journalists, which is a sore point with the national media.

During his first year of grace, however, the monarch said and did almost all the right things. In his debut Throne Speech, King Mohammed pledged to support the Socialist prime minister and the coalition government, named by his father. Defining his own role as an "arbiter," the king said: "We are devoted to the constitutional monarchy, a multiparty system, economic liberalism, regionalization and decentralization, the construction of a state of law, the safeguard[ing] of human rights and individual and collective freedoms, and the preservation of security and stability for all."[4] A few weeks later, the king gave additional insights into his program. He pledged to pursue his father's defense of the unity of the kingdom in its authentic frontiers, a reference to Moroccan claims to Western Sahara. He also spoke of his own commitment to the plight of the rural poor, to helping jobless youths, and to equal rights for women.

Some of these principles, like the multiparty system, economic liberalism, security, and the integrity of the Saharan territories, were a direct legacy from King Hassan's rule. There was, however, new emphasis on freedom, human rights, a state of law, and social issues, although there was no reference to a separation of powers.

Prime Minister Youssoufi, a courtly, soft-spoken nationalist, whom I had known since the struggle for independence, spoke favorably of the new king. "From the outset, King Mohammed gave the impression of a man conscious of his responsibilities and ready to assume the succession, take decisions, and not to hesitate," Youssoufi told me. At their first working session, the monarch had assured his prime minister: "You must know I am a democrat."[5]

Initially, the king's words were accompanied by decisive acts. Moving swiftly to correct his father's sorry record on human rights, Mohammed VI granted amnesty to more than 46,000 prisoners. On August 20, 1999, he announced the establishment of an arbitration commission linked to the state Human Rights Council to provide monetary compensation to past victims of arbitrary detention. "We are fully aware of the extreme importance of moral and humanitarian compensation to close this dossier definitively," King Mohammed said.[6] By the end of 1999, the Human Rights Council had received about 6,000 claims for compensation from former prisoners and their survivors for physical and moral injuries. It was believed thousands more had not taken advantage of the reparation process.

Mohammed VI had hardly settled on the throne when he shook the kingdom with a series of gestures that may not have brought substantive change but showed a desire to get rid of some feudal trappings. One measure was given no publicity but was significant for those involved: the decision to close down the palace harem. Some forty women, several dating from the time of the monarch's grandfather, were dispatched to their families or other destinations.

King Mohammed also reached out to political opponents of the regime. The most prominent political exile was Abraham Serfaty, a 1970s Marxist, who had been imprisoned for seventeen years for championing self-determination for Western Sahara and was subsequently deported to France. King Hassan had adamantly refused Serfaty's request to return to his homeland. But Mohammed VI sent a close aide to Paris to inform Serfaty that he could return "without conditions or concessions." On September 30, 1999, Serfaty and his wife, Christine, flew to Rabat to a royal homecoming.

Next, the family of the missing opposition leader Mehdi Ben Barka returned to Morocco. It was a powerful signal of what people hoped would be a new era of reconciliation under Mohammed VI. Thirty-five years after Ben Barka had been kidnapped and presumably killed by King Hassan's aides accidentally or on purpose, his wife and four children were welcomed home by representatives of the new king and government. At a reception of some 200 of Ben Barka's old friends, disciples, and relatives, his fifty-year-old son, Bachir, a teacher in France, acknowledged that despite countless investigations, he still did not know what had happened to his father, but he was determined to learn "the truth."[7]

In another conciliatory move, Mohammed VI made a triumphal tour of the neglected northern regions and the intractable Rif Mountains. King Hassan had refrained from visiting the area since 1956, when the Royal Armed Forces, under his leadership, had brutally crushed a tribal rebellion. During the ten-day visit to the Rif, King Mohammed was received as a national hero and pop star combined. He plunged into the crowds of adoring fans and shook all of the outstretched hands, much to the consternation of his bodyguards.

At the king's side, Minister of the Interior Driss Basri, generally held responsible for Hassan's repressive regime, was openly vilified. An unassuming figure with dark penetrating eyes, the taciturn Basri was reputed to be the most powerful man in the country after the king. Coming from a modest family, Basri had dropped out of school to become a policeman and later put himself through law school. By diligence and cunning, he worked his way up through the ranks to become head of the Bureau of Territorial Surveillance (local equivalent of the FBI) and, in 1979, was named minister of the interior.

In public, Basri was "His Majesty's faithful servant," but behind the scenes he built up an extensive security network, which enabled him to control much of the political life of the country.

Undoubtedly the single most important act of the first year of Mohammed VI's reign was the removal of the omnipotent minister of the interior. Many Moroccans believed that Basri, who had run Hassan's security systems for twenty years, was untouchable because he knew everyone's secrets. But King Mohammed carefully stripped Basri of his powers in what was popularly called "the artichoke operation." First, the Bureau of Territorial Surveillance was put under a *gendarmerie* officer. Next, the delicate mission to manage Moroccan claims to Western Sahara was transferred from Basri's control to a former diplomat. Then, Basri's men were removed from the head of the state television and national news agency (Basri had also served as minister of information). Finally, the sovereign decorated the interior minister with the kingdom's highest award, and then dismissed him. In a few weeks, the man who was feared and detested like another Lavrenti Beria, the dreaded head of the Soviet Union's secret police, was reduced to nothing. His successor was a former governor and critic of Basri, Ahmed Midaoui. He was seconded by the king's trusted former classmate Fouad Ali el-Himma as secretary of state for the interior.

Shortly afterward, King Mohammed announced the replacement of forty-four governors and other senior officials, who had been the backbone of the Basri network. There was no revolution, not even a whimper of protest. Basri's cohorts who were removed were apparently glad to leave the scene without charges brought against them, and those who remained chose to comply with the new regime and preserve their privileges. Basri himself dropped out of sight for a while and then reappeared threatening to go into politics, but few persons took him seriously.

In the spring of 2000, the king freed his father's foremost adversary, Islamist leader Abdessalam Yassine, after eleven years under house arrest. Sheikh Yassine had dared to question King Hassan's legitimacy as Commander of the Faithful and, more recently, had urged Mohammed VI to use his father's fortune to pay the national debt. Ignoring this advice, the king ordered the release of the impenitent sheikh, who was now free to receive visitors and travel around the country, but remained under surveillance. The Islamist leader was the last of the prominent political prisoners. An unknown number of Saharan dissidents remained in detention, but officially they were considered to be separatists, and so didn't count as political prisoners.

Another sign of the freer atmosphere was the creation of the Moroccan Forum for Truth and Justice in November 1999. This volunteer association aimed to set up a South African–type Truth and Justice Commission. Talks with the Interior Ministry dragged on, with wide divergences over the nature and powers of the commission. But the mere existence of the Truth and Justice Forum was considered a major step forward.

Palpable evidence of the new opening was the appearance of books published in Morocco, which revealed horror tales of torture and arbitrary imprisonment during the repressive period of Hassan's reign, from the mid-1960s to 1990. Ahmed Marzouki, a former military officer implicated in the failed plot against King Hassan in 1971, wrote his story of eighteen years of hell in the desert prison of Tazmamart. His memoir, *Tazmamart: Cellule 10*, became a national bestseller. Salah El Ouadie, a poet and leader of the Truth and Justice Forum, described with humor and irony the tortures he suffered during ten years' imprisonment in *Le Marié*. After three editions in Arabic, it came out in French and could be found in the main bookstores in the country. Fatna el Bouih, a student activist, has written in Arabic a devastating personal account of torture and five years' incarceration in *Imraa Ismuha Rached* (A Woman Named Rachid).

The Moroccan press, which flourished with newfound freedoms, soon became the main voice of opposition, denouncing the authorities openly for inertia and inefficiency. The fiercely independent weeklies raised such sensitive subjects as Western Sahara and Islam. It seemed that the only remaining taboo was the monarchy and, by implication, the Royal Armed Forces.

The general public waited patiently for more fundamental changes. Early on, King Mohammed declared that one of his main goals was to modernize the economy to enable it to meet the challenges of globalization. To undertake this mission, he named international-minded cadres to key posts in the administration and public enterprises in what amounted to a shadow government. But it was clear to all that King Mohammed's program for social and economic reform would require time.

By the end of 2000, there was some good news. After two disastrous years of drought, the rains came, which meant a significant boost to agriculture and the economy in general, a blessing widely attributed to the new king. Also, the country received an unexpected windfall when the French holding company Vivendi-Universal bought a 35 percent interest in the Moroccan state telecommunications company for a record $2.2 billion, a deal largely credited to the king's economic adviser André Azoulay.

In social matters, King Mohammed reinvigorated an organization he had headed as crown prince, the Mohammed V Foundation, which had run an annual campaign for the poor and underprivileged. As king, he turned the foundation into a permanent instrument for his social policy. The foundation continued to distribute food and clothing to the poor, but its main activity was to support government social centers and provide funds to private organizations working with the urban poor and uneducated rural inhabitants. In other words, the royal agency was now going out into the field where Islamist charitable organizations had made serious inroads.

By most accounts, the king had made a positive start. His first anniversary on the throne was marked with confidence and hope. He had gotten rid of unpleasant baggage left over from his father's regime. He had established a good working relationship with the Socialist prime minister and his broad coalition government. And everywhere there were signs of affection for the young monarch.

The international press gave King Mohammed generally high marks for his first year. But none were as rapturous as *Time*, which devoted four pages to the Moroccan monarch, with a banner headline: "The King of Cool: Hip. Charming. Mod. Mohammed VI is the Beatles of Arabian Royalty." Reporter Scott Mac Leod found the king to be "confident yet modest, part regal, part ordinary guy," and concluded: "Combining a common touch with strategic vision, he may be the most impressive of the new generation coming to power in the Middle East."[8]

Even the *Washington Post* wrote effusively of "Morocco's King of Hearts" at the time of his first official visit to Washington, D.C., calling him "the Middle East's most eligible bachelor." The *Post* reported that the Clintons threw "the largest state dinner in White House history" (435 guests) for the Moroccan king and quoted the president's toast: "No foreign guest is more deserving of a warm welcome here than King Mohammed."[9]

In barely a year, the king had succeeded in transforming Morocco's image from the remnants of an autocratic police state to an open society moving toward democracy. Nowhere else in the Arab world had the atmosphere changed so dramatically in so short a time.

First Frosts

It's difficult to say when the king's period of grace came to an end. For most Moroccans, the honeymoon lasted well into the second year. The king continued to be cheered by adoring crowds long after political, journalistic, and diplomatic circles began to question the direction of the kingdom.

By early 2001, however, ordinary citizens were grumbling about the monarch's frequent, costly visits abroad, not always for affairs of state. Peo-

King Mohammed, often dressed in the latest French fashions when receiving visitors, sometimes appeared ill at ease on his throne during the second year of his reign as criticism began to mount. (Moroccan Ministry of Communications)

ple could not, for example, understand why the king was skiing in the Alps when, as president of the Jerusalem Committee, he was expected to attend an Arab summit on the Palestinian *intifada* in Cairo.

Moroccans also expressed indignation that King Mohammed VI had given a huge piece of prime farmland to athlete Hicham El Guerrouj, the world champion of the 1500-meter race, even though he is a national hero. The weekly *Maroc-Hebdo* said such practices harked back to the old days, a reference to King Hassan's tendency to reward his favorites with state lands.

After King Mohammed's first exciting year, it became clear that getting rid of the minister of the interior was not enough. The arbitrary security system remained intact. Democratic freedoms of press and assembly had their limits. Despite all the good intentions, the administration seemed paralyzed, and social and economic disparities widened.

There were several unfortunate incidents in 2000 that showed that the security forces were having difficulties adapting to the changes and gave rise to the question, who was in control? That summer, Sheikh Yassine's Islamist movement was refused authorization to organize religious retreats at the beach. Defying the ban, they tried to hold seaside prayer meetings, but the security forces intervened with force to prevent them from gathering together. Subsequent demonstrations by the Islamist opposition, the Association of Unemployed University Graduates, and even the Moroccan Association for Human Rights were banned and the militants forcefully dispersed.

The authorities did agree to let human rights activists hold a vigil at the infamous desert prison of Tazmamart, and the news of the pilgrimage appeared in the local press. But a French television team covering the event was arrested and detained for forty-eight hours allegedly for filming military installations, and their film and videocassettes were seized.

Other measures against the press followed, apparently taken at the discretion of the king, who is directly in charge of the Ministry of the Interior and the security forces. The correspondent of *Agence France Presse* was ordered to leave the country within forty-eight hours for showing "hostility to Morocco and its institutions." In fact, the expulsion seemed linked to the agency's reporting of the case of Mustapha Adib, an air force captain who had denounced officers in his unit for corruption. Adib had been proven right but was sentenced to two and a half years in prison for talking to the French press and human rights organizations. The authorities also closed down three independent Moroccan weeklies for publishing a 1974 letter implicating Prime Minister Youssoufi in the 1972 abortive military coup against King Hassan, which Youssoufi categorically denied. After strong protests at home and abroad, the newspapers reappeared several weeks later under new titles.

The most serious example of backsliding occurred over women's rights. Shortly after taking office, the Socialist-led government had introduced the Plan for the Integration of Women, which aimed to correct inequities in the *Moudawana*, or civil code, such as obligatory male guardianship, repudiation, and polygamy. But when religious scholars, Islamists, and other conservatives joined forces in a vociferous campaign against the plan, Youssoufi's government backed down. The delicate problem was turned over to the king, who set up a commission to study the matter. The Islamists had won this round. The plan was not revived until the clamp-down on radical Islamists in the wake of the May 16, 2003, terrorist attacks.

In the economic domain, the king and his government committed a grave error, which hurt their credibility. On his thirty-seventh birthday, King Mohammed announced the discovery of oil and gas at Talsinnt in eastern Morocco. Thanking God for "this divine grace," the sovereign said the discovery would favor an economic take-off and accelerate social development. Lone Star Energy, the Texas company which made the find, estimated the reserves at Talsinnt and an offshore concession to be between 10 and 12 billion barrels. Taking these estimates for reality, the minister of energy and mines, Youssef Tahiri, declared that Morocco, heavily dependent on oil imports, would soon enter the club of the world's oil producers. For a few days, the public spoke elatedly of the king's *baraka*, divine luck. Officials talked of ambitious development plans. The Casablanca stock market soared.

One of the first persons to throw a damper on the oil mania as premature was former political exile Abraham Serfaty. A mining engineer, Serfaty pointed out that Lone Star had made only a single test drilling, which would cover only three months of Morocco's oil needs. The overly optimistic minister of energy resigned. Worse, it was disclosed that Lone Star was short of funds, even though members of the royal family were among the financiers. No one came out well from this affair, except Serfaty, who was named consultant to the new minister of energy, Mustapha Mansouri.

The Talsinnt fiasco followed other major disappointments, including the return of the drought and the failure of Morocco's third bid to host the World Soccer Cup, in 2006. The public didn't blame the king, but they did hold his government responsible.

The most serious challenge to the king's authority came from an unexpected source, a group of *oulema* (Islamic theologians) who protested his expressions of solidarity with Americans after the September 11, 2001, tragedy. King Mohammed had been one of the first Arab leaders to condemn the terrorist attack and express his sympathy for the victims. As Commander of the Faithful, the king presided over prayers that emphasized the peaceful and tolerant nature of Islam and its prohibition of violence and terrorism. The monarch sent special representatives to a ceremony honoring the victims in the Rabat Cathedral and attended by the prime minister, members of his government, and Christian and Jewish leaders. A royal envoy delivered the sovereign's personal message renewing "our firm condemnation of this cowardly aggression and our unequivocal solidarity with our American friends," according to the Moroccan Press Agency of September 16, 2001.

In a belligerent *fatwa* (opinion in Islamic law), sixteen *oulema* proclaimed that it was illegal to join a coalition against any Muslim community or state; that Muslims were barred from holding prayers in a church or synagogue, which constituted "a great sin"; and it had been wrongful to alter Friday prayers in the wake of the attacks on Washington and New York. In conclusion, the *oulema* expressed their "consternation" over the catastrophe that the Americans had suffered but urged the U.S. government "to seek out the reasons of hatred" directed against it and to review its international policy. After considerable pressure from the king's minister of Islamic affairs, seven of the sixteen *oulema* said they had signed the *fatwa* "in error," but the damage had been done. A few days later, 244 theologians, preachers, and other Islamists publicly expressed solidarity with the original *fatwa*. The inviolability of the royal minister of Islamic affairs had been questioned and, indirectly, the king.

By early 2001, midway into King Mohammed's second year, some foreign newspapers, particularly in France and Spain, had published severe assessments of his rule, accusing him of ignoring his official duties and following his father's dictatorial policies. There was however little echo of these negative judgments in Morocco, even in the antigovernment press, because criticism of the monarchy is banned by the constitution and punishable by imprisonment.

The Rebel Prince

One Moroccan voice (besides the Islamist opposition leader, Sheikh Yassine) dared to criticize the monarch openly, and he is the king's first cousin, Moulay Hicham ben Abdallah el Alaoui. Prince Moulay Hicham called for the establishment of a genuine constitutional monarchy in statements to leading French, Spanish, and Arab newspapers. The independent Moroccan press has reprinted some of the prince's controversial declarations and published interviews with him, despite the taboo on any discussion of the monarchy.

I first met the rebellious prince in Princeton, New Jersey, in the winter of 2002, shortly after he had retreated there with his family. Moulay Hicham received me in the handsome, spacious, gray stone house that he had bought some twenty years before, when he was a student at Princeton University. Now thirty-eight, the prince, dressed in jeans and sport shirt, appeared relaxed and sure of himself and could have passed for an American graduate student rather than the protagonist of a Byzantine tale of intrigue. His wife, Malika, who comes from an old Moroccan nationalist family, helps her husband at the computer and cares for their two young daughters. Independently wealthy, the prince does not receive a salary from the royal palace. His business enterprises include a 3,000-acre citrus farm and a venture in renewable energy in Morocco and a fish farm in the Gulf of Sharja, off southeast Arabia.

Moulay Hicham is not a revolutionary and certainly not a republican, as some Moroccan circles claim. In his writings and in several lengthy conversations, the prince has shown himself to be a convinced monarchist but in favor of major reform of the Moroccan monarchy and Arab monarchies in general. He believes that a king should be a symbol of national unity and an arbiter, not engaged in running the daily affairs of the kingdom, "along the lines of the monarchies in Thailand or Spain."[10]

The nonconformist prince is clearly ambitious and would like to play a role in the new Morocco but will not accept being a royal flunky—and there does not seem to be any other position open.

During King Hassan's funeral and the first few days of King Mohammed's succession, Moulay Hicham recalls, he may have overstepped the bounds. "I was very assertive in my suggestions, thinking it was my duty to help guide what was sometimes a confusing situation of transition." He took charge of the American delegation, led by President Bill Clinton, and advised the new king on protocol and press questions, urging him to do away with "archaic" habits like the hand-kissing ritual. "I thought it was necessary to define a break with the past that would confirm the intention to reform," the prince explained later. But Mohammed VI was determined to be his own man and soon declared his strong-minded cousin to be persona non grata in the palace.

Banishment was not new to Moulay Hicham. For his independent views, and daring to express them in the foreign press, the prince had been excluded from the palace by his uncle King Hassan in 1995. They were reconciled the following year, however, when it became apparent that the monarch was seriously ill. From the outset, Moulay Hicham refused to bow to royal rules. "I wanted to be something else, not just a space in the palace protocol; I wanted my own independence," he explains.

The prince attributes his free spirit to his independent upbringing. He grew up in the palace compound under the indulgent care of his Lebanese mother, Princess Lamia El-Solh, and his father, Prince Moulay Abdallah, King Hassan's younger brother. But Moulay Hicham managed to escape the Collège Royal and went to the American School in Rabat. Unlike the other princes, who studied law under the French system, Moulay Hicham took degrees in social sciences from the American universities of Princeton and Stanford.

Moulay Hicham came into open conflict with his uncle King Hassan in 1994 over the plan to establish a research institute at Princeton's Center of International Studies to honor the memory of his two grandfathers, King Mohammed V and Lebanese prime minister Riad el-Solh. Originally the institute was to bear the names of the two Arab leaders, but the palace issued a statement prohibiting the use of Mohammed V's name, apparently because the prince had neglected to get the king's permission. Moulay Hicham went ahead with his project, providing Princeton with a generous endowment, but the research institution was named the Institute for the Transregional Study of the Contemporary Middle East, North Africa, and Central Asia.

It was, above all, the prince's articles in the foreign press that led to his strained relations with King Hassan and, later, King Mohammed. No member of the royal family was allowed to speak out publicly, except for the king or his representatives. In a piece published by *Le Monde Diplomatique* in July 1995, Moulay Hicham opens with the provocative statement: "Not a single democratic regime, not a single State of law in the entire Arab World. This scandalous situation exasperates Arab public opinion, at a time when democracy is making advances everywhere on the rest of the planet, in Latin America, Africa and Asia."[11] The prince was more explicit in September 1996, denouncing the evils of poverty, inequality, and corruption in Morocco, again in *Le Monde Diplomatique*. He spoke of the need for the monarchy to adapt to changing times, redefine its role, and pull back from trying to manage the country's day-to-day problems.

Barred from the palace, Moulay Hicham looked to new horizons. The Carter Foundation sent him with a mission to observe elections in Palestine in 1996 and, later, in Nigeria. After King Hassan's death, Moulay Hicham was named by UN secretary general Kofi Annan as an aide to Bernard Kouchner, who was charged with looking out for human rights and minorities in Kosovo.

The wandering prince did not, however, abandon his crusade for reform. In May 2001, Moulay Hicham delivered a speech entitled "The Monarchic Pact" at the prestigious French Institute of International Relations in Paris. It was a sober review of the state of the monarchies in the Arab world, those that had fallen victim to coups, like Egypt and Iraq, and those that had survived coup attempts, such as Morocco and Jordan. The prince also spoke of present challenges: the collapse of Arab nationalism, the decline of the Left, and the upsurge of Islamic movements. And he suggested the need for a new pact, whereby monarchies would withdraw from daily governance to become symbols of national identity, uniting different regions and social groups.

An independent Moroccan weekly, *Demain Magazine*, dared to publish the entire text of Moulay Hicham's speech. The newspaper also reported unsuccessful attempts by the Moroccan authorities to persuade the French institute to postpone the lecture and to get France's television network TV5 to cancel an invitation to the prince to appear on one of its programs. Clearly, the palace was running out of patience.

Not heeding the warning signals, the unrepentant prince published a devastating piece in *Le Monde* on the political crisis in Morocco. Commenting on growing criticism that the kingdom suffered from a deficit of authority, Moulay Hicham wrote, "In reality, none of our traditional institutions—not Parliament, nor the political parties, not even the monarchy—has seriously engaged in the urgent task of restoring the political structures."[12]

There followed several strange incidents involving the outspoken prince: the detention of a close friend, the kidnapping and interrogation of his former chauffeur, and allegations that Moulay Hicham was plotting with a group of officers to create a principality in the Sahara and also was conspiring with certain Spanish persons against Morocco.

At this time, the Paris-based weekly *Jeune Afrique l'Intelligent* published a cover story on "Moulay Hicham: The Man Who Would Be King" (January 22–28, 2002). The reporter quoted an unidentified member of the royal family as saying that Moulay Hicham had gone too far and become completely uncontrollable. "His ego," the royal source said, "has made him lose his head."

The prince, who was in the United States at the time, laughed at the allegations, but said he had decided to "take his distance to avoid further escalation." Insisting that he was not going into exile, he expressed concern for the security of his family "in this unhealthy atmosphere."[13] In early spring, he flew to Morocco to get his wife and daughters and brought them to their new home in Princeton.

The academics and politicians I talked to in Morocco regretted this open split in the royal family. Some faulted Moulay Hicham for irreverence toward his cousin; others spoke of ominous machinations by the secret services against the prince. But most people generally agreed that the schism was a pity because the palace could put to use a man of the prince's experience and vision.

Royal Wedding

Marrakech seemed depressed during those warm sunny days in the fall of 2001, still in the doldrums from the indirect effects of the September 11 terrorist attacks on Washington and New York. It was to have been a boom year for international tourism, but that fall, virtually all of the American and British groups and individuals had canceled their reservations, and nobody knew when they would return. Upscale hotels and restaurants that cater to American tourists suffered terrible losses, and some businesses were concerned about the possibility of bankruptcy.

Then overnight, the atmosphere changed in Marrakech and around the country. The palace announced on October 12 that a ceremony marking the engagement of King Mohammed to Salma Bennani had taken place that day in the royal palace in Rabat. The wedding was set for early the following year, but no details were given. Marrakchis (residents of Marrakech) were convinced that only their city could handle such an important event. People cited as proof of their expectations the recent planting of gardens along the city walls, the repaving of streets in the old city, and work almost completed on the king's new palace.

Political circles and ordinary citizens alike expressed joy and relief over the news. Although the issue had not been raised publicly, this conservative society was not happy with the prolonged bachelorhood of its king. Under Islam, a man is not considered complete until he is married. By age thirty-eight, good Moroccans are expected to be married, if they can afford it, and all the more so, a king should produce heirs. It was often pointed out that by his second year in office, King Hassan had two children.

Moroccans were also pleased that the news of the engagement had been made public. This was interpreted as another sign that Mohammed VI was prepared to modernize antiquated practices. Women especially were elated that their king's fiancée was not some anonymous figure from the harem. She had a name, an identity. The news spread rapidly that Salma Bennani was modern, well educated, a professional in computer sciences, and had worked for the Moroccan holding Omnium Nord Africain. She had friends and colleagues, who soon circulated photographs of the beautiful auburn-haired royal fiancée in fashionable Western dress. Activists in the national women's movement were optimistic: here would be a powerful ally in their fight for equal rights.

On March 18, 2002, the palace held a press briefing to announce that the marriage ceremony—the signing of the contract—would take place three days later in the royal palace in Rabat, with the presence of only the two families. The wedding celebrations were set for April 12–14, at Marrakech. Two hundred couples from around the country would be invited to share in the festivities.

For the first time in Moroccan history, the press was given biographical information and photographs of a king's fiancée. Salma Bennani appeared a radiant beauty in the traditional silk caftan with her long, dark red hair uncovered. The twenty-four-year-old bride-to-be was born in Fez, the daughter of Hadj Abdelhamid Bennani, a school teacher. Her mother had died when she was three, and she was raised by a grandmother in Rabat. Bennani graduated from the Advanced School for Communications and System Analysis, where she was known as a hard-working student with a strong personality. She had met the crown prince at a private party in April 1999. The following year, she was employed by Omnium Nord-Africain as a computer expert and remained there until shortly before the engagement. She had already been seen in public with the king at his thirty-seventh birthday party.

A palace communiqué announced on March 21 that the act of marriage had taken place between King Mohammed VI and "the chaste pearl," Lalla Salma. Morocco's Socialist press called the wedding and the publicity around it "a real revolution" in palace traditions. There were some private complaints among left-wing academics about the expense of the projected three-day wedding party. More serious grumbling came from Islamist circles which charged that it was unseemly for a Muslim country to hold elaborate celebrations when their Palestinian brothers were under siege in Ramallah and Jenin.

Bowing to public pressures, the palace called off the wedding celebrations because of the Palestinian crisis. A communiqué said the festivities would take place "when the situation in Palestine permits." Marrakchis were grievously disappointed, but most Moroccans applauded the king's decision. This time, he had undercut the Islamist opposition with a double blow: taking a modern bride and sacrificing his wedding party for the Palestinian cause.

The three-day celebration finally happened in July in Rabat, but it was a relatively low-key affair by Moroccan standards. The official guest list was cut in half to 1,500, mostly Moroccan dignitaries. Prominent foreign guests included President Bill Clinton and his daughter, Chelsea; the brother of the king of Saudi Arabia; several other Arab princes; the president of Senegal; the son of Libyan leader Mouammer Qadhafi; the foreign minister of Afghanistan; and some European notables.

For the fortunate guests, the pageantry was memorable. The main event was the *hedya*, the traditional gift-giving ceremony on the palace parade ground, presided over by the king, with his brother, Moulay Rachid, at his side—not the bride. It was a joyous procession, led by the Royal Guard in red and green uniforms on horseback, followed by official dignitaries, *oulema*, and students from Koranic schools. Small groups in colorful dress from the sixteen regions performed their local dances and songs and presented to the king symbolic offerings of sculpted candles, rose petals, henna, sandalwood, and Oriental perfumes.

After the procession, the royal guests were escorted into the palace for refreshments: almonds, dates, sweets, fruit juices, and mint tea. At this time, the bride appeared, completely covered by a pale-green silk veil, seated on a carved-wood palanquin. The king, dressed in a fine white and gold *djellaba* and red fez, sat on another palanquin. Moulay Rachid and members of the court carried the litters with the bride and groom on their shoulders, bouncing them as they went around the huge wedding cake seven times for good luck. And the entire proceedings were shown on national television.

Other strictly private events included a post-midnight supper for fifty close friends in the king's villa, Les Sablons, a grand buffet dinner of lobster, foie gras, and Moroccan specialties for 800 special guests in the royal palace, and a banquet for 500 friends in the beachside palace of Skhirat to the rhythms of an American jazz band flown in from New York for the occasion. Meanwhile, the general public was treated to four days of fireworks and *fantasias* with 1,500 horsemen from around the country.

The royal wedding won general approval. A left-wing newspaper hailed the event as "a triumph of tradition and progress." The general public admired the ritual and costumes, which were just like any other Moroccan marriage, albeit on another scale. Most people applauded the innovations, the televised ceremonies, the pictures of the handsome couple on the front page of all the newspapers and in European magazines. Women in particular were happy that the bride was given the official title of Her Royal Highness Princess Lalla Salma. In the past, the wife of the king was known simply as "the mother of the princes." Even the Islamists had little to criticize, although Nadia Yassine, daughter of the Islamist leader, did make a wry comment to me after the wedding: "Just because Princess Salma was photographed with her hair uncovered doesn't mean advancement for the cause of women."[14]

The Islamist Challenge

The glow of this bright interlude was short-lived and could not conceal a widespread malaise. After the euphoria of the first year of King Mohammed's reign, the country seemed stricken by a kind of paralysis and unable to grapple with any of the national problems.

The king's declared intentions—to fight against poverty, unemployment, and corruption, to promote literacy and decent housing, and to modernize the economy—seemed overwhelmed by harsh reality: insufficient public funds, entrenched interests, and a bumbling bureaucracy. Youssoufi's coalition government was diminished by internal dissension and a lack of authority to achieve its basic program of reforms, such as an overhaul of the justice system and equal rights for women. Meanwhile, social pressures continued to build: new revelations of scandals in public agencies, demonstrations by unemployed college graduates demanding jobs, an increase in strikes for higher wages, and relentless waves of Moroccan boatpeople seeking a better future in Europe.

Only the Islamist opposition prospered amid the general public disaffection. Sheikh Yassine's movement proved its mobilizing strength with mass rallies over popular causes like Palestine and Iraq, which inevitably turned into antigovernment demonstrations. With greater freedom of expression, radical *oulema* became more vehement in their diatribes against the Left and the West. Islamist zealots openly preached violence and confessed to committing cruel acts of punishment against "the ungodly." The Islamic-rooted Party of Justice and Development did unusually well at the polls in the fall of 2002, thanks in part to a substantial protest vote. These Islamist gains sent shivers through the establishment, which nonetheless retained its parliamentary majority.

Initially, the palace and its security forces reacted to these challenges much as they had under King Hassan, by banning demonstrations that might get out of hand, jailing protesters, seizing or closing irreverent newspapers, and unveiling dark conspiracies. Although national elections were far more transparent than in the past, it was widely rumored that the results had been embellished in favor of the establishment parties, although this was firmly denied on all sides.

Nevertheless, Mohammed VI was proving to be more concerned than his father about the country's democratic image. Repression was less brutal and not systematic as in King Hassan's time. The press enjoyed much greater latitude although journalists were still being jailed for expressing their opinions. Elections were freer if imperfect. To all appearances, King Mohammed had heeded the increasingly outspoken press and the human rights associations that continued to denounce official abuses. Aladdin's bottle had been opened. Moroccans had gotten a taste of democratic freedoms. It would not be easy to force the genie back into the bottle.

Then the terrible blow occurred. The May 16, 2003, suicide attacks against "un-Islamic targets" in Casablanca shook the nation's confidence in itself, the monarchy, and the country's faltering progress toward democracy. In the crack-down that followed, security forces resorted to the familiar past practices of sweeping arrests, kidnappings, torture, and flawed trials. Only this time, the victims were Islamic activists, not left-wing militants, and the number of suspects and alleged plots seemed unlimited.

The independent press warned that a return to the indiscriminate repression of the past would be counterproductive, stirring new resentment, hatred, and desire for vengeance. In an editorial on "The Fight against Terrorists," Ahmed Benchemsi, publisher of the weekly *TelQuel*, wrote that torturing terrorist suspects would not make them change their views: "On the contrary, this will convince them that the system is not only impious but barbaric and must be fought until death."[15]

King Mohammed was confronted with the impossible dilemma of whether to return to his father's harsh security policies, which ensured the kingdom's stability, or pursue the democratic reforms that have emboldened Islamic fanatics and enabled them to strike against what had become known as the most open society in the Arab world.

Tour of Morocco.

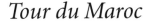

Tour du Maroc

2

*T*he land is much as I remembered: majestic, exotic, and incredibly diverse.

I have tried to fathom what it is about Morocco that has appealed to so many foreign artists and writers over the years: the dazzling light and colors, heady sounds and smells, mysterious rites and ceremonies, the impression of impunity, and perhaps, the sense of living in another time. The late Paul Bowles, whose name is indelibly linked to Morocco, once told an interviewer that he chose to live in Tangier because "it's changed less than the rest of the world and continues to seem less a part of this particular era than most cities."[1]

The same can be said today for much of the Moroccan countryside. Ethereal mountain peaks tower over inaccessible stone hamlets and rocky plateaus. Green terraced slopes are dotted with mud and thatch villages and squat whitewashed saints' tombs. Isolated adobe compounds rise on the parched plains. Grandiose canyons are lined with commanding crimson *kasbahs*, and refreshing palm oases give way to stony desert expanses. Along the wild Atlantic coast, ancient Portuguese fortifications stand guard against lost illusions.

Rural life continues to revolve around subsistence farming, weekly markets, Islamic customs, and a male-oriented social code. Some village women peek furtively at the world from behind voluminous shrouds. Others, with uncovered faces and bright floral-print dresses, wash laundry in streams and carry huge piles of firewood on their backs. Country men wear white tunics and turbans, dark hooded *djellabas*, or the dashing *burnous* and drive heavily laden donkeys to market. Children tend sheep and goats and peddle rocks and other treasures along the road.

It is the cities that have changed. To be sure, the glories of the ancient imperial capitals of Fez and Marrakech have been preserved to a large extent; their powerful walls, innumerable palaces and mosques, hidden gardens, and lively markets are still there. But the center of gravity has moved from the *medinas*—the traditional neighborhoods—to the *villes nouvelles*, modern residential and shopping districts laid out under the French protectorate and greatly expanded since independence. The coastal cities especially have come of age, with new apartment and office buildings, palatial villas, seaside promenades, industrial zones, and sprawling shantytowns.

Nearly a half century has passed since Morocco won its independence; the population has tripled to 30 million. But the dichotomy between rural and urban lives seems more irreconcilable than ever, as if the inhabitants belong to two separate countries, two different eras. Part of the population is on the move, ready to leap into the twenty-first century and beyond, while the rest remains trapped in the Middle Ages. Many Moroccans in cities and towns have embraced a modern way of life for themselves or at least for their children. On the other hand, 45 percent of the population inhabits remote mountains, deserts, and other rural reaches of the kingdom, and many country people live rudimentary existences very similar to those of their ancestors.

In the last few years, however, new ideas and new technology have begun to penetrate even the poorest and most isolated regions. In an obscure town on the edge of the Sahara, Moroccan youths clad in jeans and irreverent T-shirts pass their evenings at cybercafes. At a bustling *souk* in the Middle Atlas, a shepherd pulls out his cell phone to advise a colleague on a nearby peak of the going price of mutton. The owner of a derelict *kasbah* proudly shows off a solar energy panel. In a tin shack on the outskirts of Casablanca, headscarved women meet regularly to pay interest on small business loans. In the hall of the great Karaouyine Mosque in Fez, religious students sit crosslegged on straw mats, learning English.

In 2001, I traveled the length and breadth of Morocco (except for Western Sahara, which I visited later) with two old friends, to observe the changes since independence—and to measure the distance that must be covered to reach the twenty-first century. The following passages are highlights from my journal.

Moroccan Tangier

Our journey begins at Tangier, that once international city overlooking the Strait of Gibraltar, which has been coveted by foreigners since the Phoenicians in the eighth century B.C. I remember that the nationalist leader Abderrahim Bouabid hated Tangier's special status, which gave foreigners more rights than Moroccan citizens. Ruled by a consortium of foreign powers from 1923, Tangier was incorporated into the kingdom after independence in 1956 and, for a while, continued under a liberal regime. But when Bouabid was named minister of the economy in 1958, Tangier's fate was sealed, and it progressively became Moroccanized.

There is of course more to Tangier than its former role as an international tax haven and smugglers' paradise. The city's essence is unchanged—first of all, its strategic position as an African outpost at the gateway to Europe and the Mediterranean. And it still possesses a special magnetism, which over the years has seduced foreign artists, musicians, writers, and celebrities like Delacroix and Matisse, Samuel Beckett and Jean Genet, and Brian Jones, Catherine Deneuve, Barbara Hutton, and Malcolm Forbes.

An early visitor, Mark Twain writes in *The Innocents Abroad*: "We wanted something thoroughly and uncompromisingly foreign—foreign from top to bottom—foreign from center to circumference—foreign inside and outside and all around—nothing anywhere about it to dilute its foreignness—nothing to remind us of any other people or any other land under the sun. And lo! In Tangier we have found it."[2]

Gertrude Stein first suggested to Paul Bowles that he go to Tangier in 1931, because the sun shines every day—which isn't quite true. Bowles remained there with occasional sorties until his death in 1999, because he felt he was watching "a huge drama" all around him. When asked by an interviewer, why Tangier? Bowles said quite simply: "I loved it. And I still love it. Less, naturally. One loves everything less at my age; also it's a little less lovable than it was 40 years ago."[3]

Not everyone shared Bowles's enthusiasm. William Burroughs, whose *Interzone* and *The Naked Lunch* were inspired by Tangier, was fascinated by the sleaze. "There's an end-of-the-world feeling in Tangier with its glut of nylon shirts, Swiss watches, Scotch and sex and opiates sold across the counter. . . . something sinister in this complete *laissez faire*," Burroughs wrote to Allen Ginsberg in June 1954.[4]

Returning to Tangier now, I find the attraction still there, the special African-Atlantic-Mediterranean light, which performs miracles with colors; the Oriental shapes and sounds and odors of the *medina* overlooking the bay; the luxurious palaces in the *kasbah*; and the flower-framed villas on the mountain.

We drop by the American Legation, which I had known in its heyday as the seat of the U.S. diplomatic mission to the international city. Located just inside the old walled *medina* near the former Jewish quarter, the Legation was a gift to the United States in 1821 from Moroccan Sultan Moulay Sliman.

The original eighteenth-century stone building has been enlarged to form a handsome complex with thick walls, arches, a Moorish Pavillion, and a tiled patio and is the only historical landmark the United States owns abroad. After Moroccan independence, all the foreign embassies moved to Rabat, but the Legation served as a consulate for several years until a new one was built. Then it was used as an Arabic language school for American Foreign Service personnel and later a training center for the Peace Corps. By the mid-1970s, the Legation had been deserted and was badly in need of restoration. At this point, a group of Americans formed a nonprofit organization, the Tangier American Legation Museum Society, to save the historic building.

Now the American Legation has been transformed into a vibrant cultural center and frequently hosts seminars and lectures. In the museum, hundreds of paintings, prints, sketches, photos, and maps trace Tangier's history from the seventeenth to the twentieth centuries. The research library, in a separate building, contains an important collection of books and other documents on Morocco and North Africa, with a pleasant reading room. I came away with the feeling that this is what has to happen to the city. The citizens must get together and give it a new raison d'être.

The desperate poverty is there too, worse than in the old days, with all of the would-be illegal emigrants hovering around the port and certain cafes, hoping to find a way to flee the country. Tangier has become the main point of departure for a new generation of boatpeople from Morocco and other African countries, who are seeking a better life in Europe.

There is an indefinable sadness about Tangier these days, nostalgia for a lost golden age, something I do not feel in Marrakech or other Moroccan cities. Tangier's cosmopolitan lifestyle faded when the old diplomatic missions left. After Tangier lost its special financial status, the banks and the big speculators and the petty shysters moved on. Tangier was no longer the refuge of permissiveness and excess that had prevailed during the lax international interregnum and after. Most of the celebrities who used to attract friends and disciples to Tangier are gone, and Paul Bowles's death in 1999 marked the end of an era.

But Tangier has an important ally. King Mohammed VI is enamored of the city on the strait, enough to spend part of his summer there each year. And he believes in the Tangier zone enough to be sponsoring the first major development project of his reign: a new commercial and industrial port and duty-free zones, the Tangier-Mediterranean Port. Tangier-Med, as the project is known, aims not only to relieve the busy harbor but to create from scratch another pole of development in northern Morocco. Originally, the authorities planned to locate the new port on the Atlantic, south of Tangier, near the main north-south highway and railroad. Then the king got involved and decided the port should face the Mediterranean. Tangier-Med is to be located at a site about forty miles east of Tangier and a stone's throw from the Spanish enclave of Ceuta.

The ambitious billion-dollar project is not just another Moroccan pipe dream. After my visit to the area, Morocco signed a contract with the French firm Martin Bouygues for the construction of the new port, which is to be completed in 2007. Financing has been secured from the Kuwaiti Development Fund, the Abu Dhabi Development Fund, the Hassan II Fund, and private investors. The location of the new port next to Ceuta seems to have been a political choice. The Spanish presidio of Ceuta has long been an abscess on the Moroccan coast, the center of smuggling, illicit drug trading, and illegal immigration. Moroccan planners have concluded that if Spain won't relinquish Ceuta, they will suffocate it with competition from Tangier-Med.

I wonder, can Tangier-Med resuscitate the former international mecca from the doldrums? With the king's personal backing, the battle is half won, but it will require substantial follow-through, a quality that is often missing in Morocco.

The Indomitable Rif

East of Tangier, my traveling companions and I set forth on the *Rocade*, a 300-mile coastal highway which runs parallel to the Rif Mountain chain and has been under construction forever, it seems. At present, the road goes about 60 miles, skirting Tetouan, the sprawling, congested capital of former Spanish Morocco, past a hodgepodge of luxury resorts, popular holiday developments, and simple fishing villages. Palatial hotels, a Club Med, and gated residential communities are interspersed with ugly, hastily built apartment buildings and many abandoned projects. "Drug money" and "money laundering" are the local explanations for the haphazard development along the Rif coast. Marijuana, which had long been disdained as a shameful remnant of feudal times by young Moroccans, is now grown in huge quantities in the Rif and sold to international traffickers, who smuggle it to Europe just across the strait.

The Rif Mountains resonate with rebellion and contraband. Here, the nationalist hero Abdelkrim el Khattabi and his Berber tribesmen defeated General Francisco Franco's army in 1921 and set up the short-lived Republic of the Rif. From bases in the Rif, the Moroccan Liberation Army launched a guerrilla assault against French military posts in 1955 in a decisive action in the war for independence. After independence in 1956, the Rifains rebelled against the urban nationalists of the Istiqlal party, who dominated the government, and were firmly quelled by Crown Prince Hassan and his Royal Armed Forces.

Another Rif uprising occurred in 1984, when the authorities tried to curtail the trafficking of cannabis, the principal cash crop of the area. The Rif with its cheap, accessible marijuana had been discovered by hippies, tourists, artists, and other foreigners in the 1960s. As the demand increased, marijuana and its concentrate, known as *chira*, became big business and an important if clandestine export. Morocco gained the dubious reputation of the world's number one producer of marijuana.

Moroccan and European authorities seize about 500 tons of Moroccan hashish a year, but nobody knows how much gets through to the world market. Official policy since the 1960s has been to phase out the cultivation of marijuana and replace it with other crops. The problem is that substitutes like almond and fruit trees take too long to grow and are less lucrative than marijuana. In 1992, King Hassan acknowledged that some 50,000 hectares (125,000 acres) in northern Morocco were devoted to marijuana plantations and launched a campaign to eradicate the plague, making many arrests. At the same time, he stated it was up to consumer countries to do their own policing. But there has been no let-up from either producers or consumers, and the trade has continued to prosper.

Wary of the potentially explosive situation, the government eschewed any move to ban marijuana production and revived plans for crop substitution and tourism. By the time of our visit to the Rif, however, there was still no evidence that the authorities had made a dent in the cannabis culture.

Chaouen is an idyllic mountain village with whitewashed houses, orange tile roofs, and iron balconies, built by refugees from Muslim Spain in the sixteenth century. The town has retained its Hispano-Mauresque profile and relaxed atmosphere, but is now part of the Mediterranean tourist circuit. We are greeted by hustlers who offer to escort us to our hotel and get us anything we want—code language for hashish, the processed cannabis resin. "It's simple," confides a retired Englishman whom we meet in a small *couscous* restaurant. "Foreigners come here because hashish is accessible and Moroccans are generally tolerant."

Early the next morning at a cafe on Makhzen Plaza, we see Moroccan men openly smoking *kif*, as marijuana is known locally, in long reed pipes with tiny clay bowls. At our hotel, we are told that it is illegal to grow, sell, or consume the narcotic plant. But as a rule, cultivation, possession, and use are tolerated, while dealing is treated as a crime.

The Rif has different faces. The western hills are covered with olive trees and cork oaks and look like an extension of the Iberian peninsula. On the higher slopes, the landscape is composed of dense pine and cedar forests. In the background, bare peaks are clearly marked in geological layers, and some are often wrapped in snow. The natural beauty has altered little since independence.

Change, however, is noticeable around the town of Ketama, the heart of *kif* country. In late February, marijuana plantations are not yet detectable, but pushers are out on the highway aggressively plying their wares. Planting takes place in mid-May and harvest at the end of August, according to friendly locals, who discuss the subject openly in the central cafe. Marijuana grows on the plateaus and in the valleys of the northern and southern slopes, behind walls of corn or fig and almond trees, or sometimes in open fields like any other crop. What is visible is all of the new money in the traditionally poor region. Men walk about with mobile telephones. Numerous palatial stone and brick houses are going up in town. The smallest hamlets nearby boast satellite dishes, and everywhere are showy Mercedes automobiles and Japanese four-wheel drives.

On the outskirts of Ketama, a dense curtain of fog falls over the narrow winding mountaintop road that runs parallel to the sea. A Mercedes looms in the fog and gives us chase, the occupants waving excitedly to get us to stop. We head south, losing our pursuers and the fog. High along the crest are more newly constructed mansions with three-car garages. The views of the Sra River valley are spectacular; some plantations are terraced, others nearly vertical. At the weekly market center of Ikaouen, we run into a monstrous traffic jam. Donkeys, bicycles, and wheelbarrows, trucks and Mercedes automobiles line the road. Stands offer local produce, piles of oranges, apples, potatoes, and onions, as well as the latest fashions in children's jeans, European-style men's pants, shoes, sneakers, and plastic flowers.

In the spring of 2003, the prime minister was to declare the development of this region "a national priority." To emphasize the importance accorded to the zone, the king named Driss Benhima, the dynamic governor of Casablanca, to head the Agency for the Promotion and the Development of the North. A few months later, several middle-level drug traffickers and local officials were arrested and charged with corruption. Then, silence, and the drug dealers and smugglers resumed business as usual. As in the past, the clamp-down halted before reaching the powerful interests behind the lucrative trade. At year's end, the United Nations warned that cannabis production was expanding and threatening the ancient forests of the region. The UN Office on Drugs and Crime reported that 134,000 hectares (335,000 acres), or one-fourth of the farmland in the Rif, is devoted to cannabis, and two-thirds of the population depends on the crop for their livelihood.[5]

The question of marijuana in the Rif seems to be as intractable as that of cocaine in the Andes. Similarly, it's the drug lords and intermediaries who make the big money and buy immunity. The producers and much of the population of the region depend on the marijuana business for their modest, if better-than-average livelihood. Any attempt to stamp out this resource could provoke yet another Rif uprising.

Arab Fez

I had been reluctant to return to Fez, like meeting a first love after many years. I was afraid that either the city had developed, become modernized, and lost its medieval mystery; or that it had not developed but stagnated to become a crumbling museum. It was at Fez in the early 1950s that I had been introduced to Moroccan politics and culture and began my career as a freelance reporter.

Fez then was the most exotic city I had ever seen (even more exotic than my birthplace of Shanghai), clinging to its history as a defense against the intruding colonial culture. Moulay Idriss, a holy man who claimed direct descent from the Prophet Mohammed, had founded Fez in the year 789, as the capital of Morocco's first Muslim dynasty. His son Idriss II turned the small Berber town into a flourishing religious and cultural center with the help of Muslim, Jewish, and Christian refugees from Cordoba and Kairwan, the major hubs of Arab civilization at the time. Over the centuries, Fez alternately shared the role of imperial capital with Marrakech, until the 1912 Treaty of Fez, which divided the country into French and Spanish protectorates. France's first resident general, Marshal Louis Hubert Lyautey, preferred to build his modern administrative capital at the Atlantic port of Rabat, while Spain established the seat of its protectorate in the ancient city of Tetouan on the edge of the Rif Mountains.

It was the Fassis—the people of Fez—who took up the torch of nationalism after the defeat of Abdelkrim el Khattabi and his Rif tribesmen by the French and Spanish colonial forces in 1926. That same year, a young nationalist, Allal el Fassi, founded the Reform party, which became the Istiqlal, or Independence, party in 1944 and led the struggle to liberate the country from colonial rule. After independence in 1956, Moroccans retained Rabat as their capital, perhaps to avoid the rivalry between Fez and Marrakech. But throughout its political vicissitudes, Fez remained the heart of Arabic art and learning in Morocco.

From a distance, Fez is still that breathtaking, sensuous, sand-colored city sprawling along the river valley. Crenellated ramparts encircle the old city with its maze of alleys, mosques, and towering rectangular minarets; *medersas*, or religious schools, with green tile roofs; tiny shops and workshops;

and tall terraced residences, with the occasional palm tree or pine peering from a patio. Completely separate, the *ville nouvelle* is a pleasant French colonial creation, with broad tree-lined boulevards, villas with gardens, and modern apartment buildings.

Yet, Fez has undergone tremendous change in the past half century and suffers monumental problems of both growth and decay. Many of the old merchant families and scholars have moved to Rabat and Casablanca, where they continue to play an influential role in politics, trade, banking, and industry. Some migrant sons still have property here, and they return for wedding receptions or other significant events. Aissa Benchekroun, a retired Moroccan diplomat, who left the city long ago but comes back whenever he can, boasts, "Everybody knows that the cuisine and the music, the lifestyle, not to mention the women of Fez, are the finest in the country."

At the same time, Fez has been inundated with country people, who cram three or four households into a single-family home or have moved to the new slums on the outskirts of the city. "If the people of the periphery aren't given jobs, they will explode; the king and the government have to do something soon," warns Khalid Taouil, a journalist for a Socialist daily newspaper. In a surprisingly sharp tirade, the Moroccan journalist faults all of the governments since independence for failing to live up to the people's expectations. He emphasizes that most of Fez's modern infrastructure—the three hospitals, roads, schools, railroad, slaughterhouse, and even the soccer field—was the work of the French colonialists. It's true, he concedes, that several new industrial quarters have been built since independence, but only with the help of Swiss, Germans, and Italians.[6]

Taouil introduces me to a senior government official, who prefers to speak off the record. What Fez needs most is investments in small and medium enterprises to create jobs, he emphasizes. Traditional industries, like textiles, have moved to the coast. At present, three-quarters of the 250,000 inhabitants of the *medina* make their living from handicrafts—leather goods, copper, wood, embroidery. The city has high hopes for increased tourism, but there are not enough hotels, and at present many tourists just pass through. In sum, there are not enough decent jobs to keep young people from leaving.

Taouil, his wife, and most of their friends live in the *ville nouvelle*, but his mother still lives in the *medina*, where she feels more at home. The journalist takes me for a tour of the former French quarter, which has grown into a real city, a Moroccan city, not the sleepy colonial outpost I once knew. The downtown area is bustling with traffic and shoppers, pastry shops and pizzerias. But everywhere, there are idle young men on street corners, at crowded cafes, because, as Taouil points out, they have nothing else to do. I am surprised to see so many young couples, wearing jeans and strolling hand-in-hand in this supposedly conservative religious city. There also seem to be fewer veiled women than in other Moroccan cities.

We pass the French *lycée*, where I gave English lectures so many years ago. It looks a little run-down, but is said to be very popular with Moroccans. Another foreign school much in demand these days is the American Language Center, which was opened in a charming old villa in 1998. Mohamed Baghdadi, the supervisor of English teachers, talks to me about the Fassis' fascination with English. He points out that while Arabic is the national language, the Moroccan elite usually prefer to send their children to French schools, since French is still widely used in business and government. "But now with globalization, the Internet, the explosion of cybercafes, Moroccan students believe the key to jobs and a better future lies in English and computer sciences," remarks Baghdadi, himself a graduate of the University of Manchester.[7]

From the Hotel Batha, on the edge of the *medina*, my traveling companions and I set out to explore the old city. I am struck by how much cleaner the streets are, although this might not be apparent to a first-time visitor. I learn that Fez—like New York and other big cities—has hired a private firm to clean the streets. The upper part of the *medina* has been repaved with large flagstones, much easier on the feet than the old pebbles and mud holes, and many sewers have been covered. Some ancient palaces have been restored and opened to the public as luxury guesthouses and restaurants. The Nejjarine, or carpenters' *caravansary* or hostel, has been converted into an exquisite Museum of Wood Handicrafts. To be sure, the main form of transport in the steep narrow alleys is still the donkey. Tanners, coppersmiths, and weavers still live and work under archaic unsanitary conditions, except that they now have televisions and their children go to school. Another sign of the times, discreetly placed in some of the minuscule shops, are photos of Osama Bin Laden.

Even that bastion of Islamic tradition, the Karaouyine Mosque and University, has changed. The Karaouyine was built around 860 by Fatma bent Mohammed el Feheri, for her fellow refugees from Kairwan. Subsequently, it was enlarged to hold 20,000 worshipers and became one of the foremost centers of Islamic studies in the world. It was the French resident general Lyautey who barred the Karaouyine and other Moroccan mosques to non-Muslims, to avoid incidents between his soldiers and devout Muslims. This ban has been followed since independence, except for the new Hassan II Mosque in Casablanca, where nonbelievers can pay to get in.

Now, for the first time, I enter the Karaouyine discreetly, and no one makes any objection. The students sit on straw mats in groups of twenty to a class; the only teaching tools are chalk and a blackboard. It's the way they have been studying for centuries. But at present, in addition to courses on the Koran and Arabic history, they are learning French and even English. "Most of them hope to go to Europe to find work," a young teacher explains.

An American provides insights on what is happening in old Fez. David Amster, director of the American Language Center and its affiliate, the Arabic Language Institute, came to Fez in 1997 to teach at the new English-language University of Al Akhawayn, at a mountain resort nearby. Al Akhawayn was too elitist for his tastes, however, and he joined the staff at the American Language Center. Amster, who is interested in urban renewal, decided to buy an old house in the *medina* and fix it up and has learned a lot about Moroccan life in the process.

For a long time, Moroccans tended to move out of the *medina* because their children wanted to live in the modern world, according to Amster. Now, people, including foreign students, are moving into the *medina* because it's warmer, friendlier, and more affordable. But Amster notes that there's an underside to the gentrification story. Restoration funds have disappeared into people's pockets; some fountains have been shoddily restored; a beautiful palace was declared unsafe and sold in pieces; antique gates, doors, windows, and ceilings have been ripped out and exported to Europe. "All this is public knowledge but nothing is done about it," he notes sadly.[8]

Friends in Rabat had recommended that I look up Asmae el Mahdi, a founder of the Initiative for the Protection of Women's Rights in Fez. A philosophy professor with three children, El Mahdi and a group of academics set up the volunteer association in 1998 to fight all forms of discrimination against women. She talks to me passionately about a traditional problem that only lately has become public: the violent treatment of young female maids, which she calls "a modern form of slavery." I remember that, in the old days, child maids were routine appendages in many wealthy Fassi homes. They were perhaps not violently mistreated but made to scrub floors and dishes and other heavy-duty tasks, with no hope of schooling or escape.

El Mahdi tells me of three recent cases of abused ten-year-old girls that have attracted national attention. The children showed up separately at a Fez hospital; two had scars and burns around their genitals and one was the victim of collective rape. Most cases involve unschooled village women, often widows, who sell their daughters to intermediaries who promise to find them better homes. The girls will then be placed with sterile couples or as maids in well-to-do families.

"Such incidents happened in the past, but they were usually covered up," El Mahdi notes, showing me press clippings about the scandals. "Nowadays, at least hospitals are reporting these practices and the media is talking about them."[9]

I learn by chance about a conference on "The Moralization of Public Life," sponsored by the Regional Association of Young Lawyers, and decide to drop in. Prominent speakers tell the assembly of lawyers, judges, and magistrates that King Mohammed and his government are determined to "combat corruption at all levels." When someone lists the well-known people who have been taken to court on corruption charges, the audience breaks into enthusiastic applause. This kind of meeting could not have taken place even five years before. Until recently, both foreign and local experts have held that graft and bribery were endemic to Morocco and nothing could be done. Yet here are young professionals in the country's most traditional city who clearly believe that corruption is not necessarily a way of life.

Fez leaves me with mixed feelings. The mystery is still there although it's threadbare in places and being cleaned up in others, but that is not so bad. What's good is that feudal mentalities are beginning to change. What troubles me is all those hapless young people lazing on street corners or in cafes, whose only ambition is to get away.

Stirrings in the Atlas

Across the fertile Fez plain, the road begins the climb into the Middle Atlas Mountains. There are three parallel Atlas ranges that cross the center of the country diagonally, forming a barrier between the coastal cities and the Sahara. The French classified the fertile Atlantic plains and accessible mountains as *le Maroc utile* and the higher peaks along with the desert as *bled as siba*, or the dissident lands.

Barely fifty miles south of Fez, the Middle Atlas hill stations of Immouzer and Ifrane, with quaint chalets, cedar and pine groves, lakes, and snowy peaks in the background, still exude a French alpine atmosphere. I recall coming here many years ago on delightful promenades with my French colonial family to escape from the torrid summers of Fez. There are no foreign visitors in sight, but government ministries send personnel to vacation colonies in the region. The Casablanca-Rabat business crowd flocks here for winter sports on weekends, and many new townhouses are going up. King Mohammed, who owns a vast new European-type castle at Ifrane, often shows up with his entourage during skiing season. It is striking how the Moroccan elite has so wholeheartedly adopted certain aspects of the colonial legacy.

We pause on the outskirts of Ifrane to see Al Akhawayn University, modeled on the U.S. university system and specializing in advanced technologies and scientific research. But it might have been Fort Knox. The guards wouldn't let us set foot on the wooded campus "without a prior appointment."

At the market town called Rich, on the border between the Middle and High Atlas mountain ranges, we meet a high school student, who says a new paved road has transformed life in his mountain village of Imilchil. We invite the French-speaking student to join us at a cafe to learn what has become of Imilchil.

The French used to call the place "Little Tibet," because of the forbidding, bare, stony plateaus and severe climate. The big event of the region was the *Fête des Fiançailles*, the Aït Hadiddou tribal marriage market, every September. According to the local legend, two lakes nearby were formed from the tears of two lovers, whose marriage was forbidden by their rival tribes. In the 1960s, it used to take a long day's trip to reach Imilchil, struggling over dirt tracks and fording mountain streams. There were no hotels or cafes, and we slept in huge goatskin tents with other visitors. It was like a big fair with thousands of visitors and animals milling about. Young men would seek out their brides from the crowd of girls, who were sometimes only twelve years old, flaunting tattoos and brash makeup, traditional silver jewelry and brightly colored gowns. The novelty of the occasion was the fact that the young women, particularly widows and divorcees, could also choose their grooms, without parental negotiations.

Does the marriage *souk* still take place? I ask the student, over mint tea and brochettes.

Yes indeed, the *Fête des Fiançailles* is held regularly, and there are more visitors than ever, responds the young man, who introduces himself as Haddou Ohdouch. It's much easier to get to Imilchil now, just a two-hour ride from Rich by the new asphalt road. Unfortunately, he adds, there weren't many weddings last year because of the drought; nobody had much money.

Ohdouch's father owns ten sheep, but Ohdouch isn't interested in raising sheep. When he finishes his studies, he hopes to work with a French friend as a guide. His family lives in a *ksar*, an old fortified village near Imilchil. They have a mud house with electricity from a generator but no running water, heat, or television. In fact there are only two television sets in the entire area; one belongs to the town's rich man and the other to the *imam*'s daughter. Ohdouch's seventeen-year-old sister goes out early every morning with the mule to get firewood for cooking. No, she never went to school. "When I am ready to get married, I'll choose a girl from Imilchil because they know how to work," Ohdouch said emphatically. "The city girls go to school and don't want to work any more."[10]

From our brief foray into the High Atlas, it is difficult to imagine the lives of those in this region of steep naked cliffs and ravines, jagged snow-capped summits and gorges, bleak stretches of naked plateaus. Life appears virtually unchanged since independence, or in the past thousand years for that matter. On the rocky slopes, shepherds watch the flocks, still their main source of livelihood. Men till patches of grain with wooden plows. Women still weave their own wool and do the washing in streams. The adobe hamlets perched along the steep cliffs show no sign of modern conveniences. These *ksour* are constructed in the traditional manner: flat-roofed houses with tiny windows, a central patio, and a community silo, surrounded by a defensive wall.

But change is coming even to the High Atlas, as I was to see firsthand in later visits.

The Pre-Sahara

The rim of the Sahara follows the valley of the Ziz, which wends its way from Rich at the base of the High Atlas south through deep red gorges, along the ancient caravan route from Fez to the Sahara. It's a land of dreams and nightmares, with its lineup of splendid ocher *ksour*, or fortified villages, old French Foreign Legion forts, and more recent Moroccan military prisons. Here are the palm oases that once dominated the trans-Saharan desert trade and stretches of the Sahara, which Morocco shares uneasily with Algeria. Unlike their neighbors, Moroccans have found neither oil nor natural gas in commercially exploitable quantities on their side of the desert.

A few miles east of Rich on the bank of the Ziz River stands Tazmamart, the military base and former concentration camp, and visitors are not welcome. It's not on any map, but Moroccans know that this is where the military men accused of plotting against King Hassan in the 1970s were incarcerated. For a long time, the authorities denied the existence of Tazmamart. But on the eve of an official visit to the United States in 1991, King Hassan freed the surviving inmates of Tazmamart and proclaimed the desert prison closed.

South of Tazmamart, the road follows the Ziz River through spectacular gorges that resemble the Grand Canyon, arriving at the nondescript administrative and military town of Er Rachidia. Built at the beginning of the twentieth century as a base for the French Foreign Legion, this outpost was used by the French forces from Algeria for their incursions into Morocco, prior to the establishment of the protectorate.

Today, Er Rachidia, 220 miles south of Fez and 300 miles east of Marrakech, is an important commercial center and crossroads. This is the gateway to the Tafilalet oasis region, cradle of the ruling Alaouite Dynasty and an increasingly popular tourist destination. In a family-type restaurant recommended by our hotel, a solicitous waiter asks us where we are from. When I say America, he welcomes us as long-lost cousins.

"Shimon Peres is my relative," he announces with pride and produces a scrap of paper with a telephone number, which he says is that of the former Israeli Labor party leader. There are only four Jews in the Er Rachidia area and fewer than 5,000 in all of Morocco, mostly in Casablanca, he says, pointing out that there were 300,000 at independence. No, he and his family do not have any special problems, but they are worried about the increasing strength of the Islamic fundamentalists, especially since recent demonstrations of solidarity with the Palestinian *intifada* in Casablanca and Rabat. He is in regular telephone contact with other Jewish communities and has a passport so he can leave the country whenever he has to.

We set off early the next morning for the desert. The Ziz valley route passes through rose-colored hills, dense palm groves, and handsome mud-brick *ksour*, some with metal doors, television antennas, and satellite dishes. At the old French garrison town of Erfoud, a few miles from the Algerian border, we are astonished to find a number of large, luxurious *kasbah*-like hotels and a flotilla of tour buses and Land Rovers, all packed with tourists headed for the dunes of Merzouga, thirty-five miles into the desert. We decide to abstain.

Instead, we drive twelve miles south to Rissani, the market center for the vast Tafilalet oasis, which the early Arab conquerors considered a new Mesopotamia. On the outskirts of Rissani, a few crumbling adobe walls and two once-handsome gates are all that remain of the legendary city of Sigilmassa. Some historians claim that Sigilmassa dates back to Roman times, but by most accounts, it was founded by Arab settlers at the end of the seventh century. At its height in the fourteenth century, Sigilmassa had about 100,000 inhabitants and rivaled Fez and Marrakech as a center for Saharan caravans, importing gold, ivory, and slaves from the Sudan and Guinea and exporting salt, textiles, and metals. By the seventeenth century, medieval Sigilmassa had been replaced by Rissani as capital of the Tafilalet. The ruling Alaouites, who came to Morocco from Arabia, first settled in the Tafilalet in the thirteenth century. The founder of the Alaouite Dynasty was Moulay Ali Cherif, whose son Moulay er Rachid conquered Fez and northern Morocco in the 1660s.

As infidels, we are barred from the handsome Moorish-style mosque and mausoleum of Moulay Ali Cherif, rebuilt after surprise floods washed away the original shrine in 1955. But we are allowed to wander around the ruins of *Ksar* Abbar, a vast nineteenth-century royal palace with fortifications, monumental gates, and courtyard. Here the Alaouite sultans were said to have stored part of the royal treasury under the watch of 600 members of the Royal Guard. Here too is a huge harem—now empty—where the sultans' widows and wives out of favor used to be kept. Local residents tell us proudly that King Mohammed VI has shown keen interest in the birthplace of his ancestors and visited the mausoleum several times.

The desert around Erfoud has become known as one of the world's richest sources of trilobites—fossilized sea creatures—but it is also home to a thriving trade in fake fossils. The government tourism office at Erfoud recommends a visit to the fossil workshop/showroom of Moulay Idrissi Madani, a proud descendant of the Idrissids, who established the first Muslim dynasty in Morocco in the eighth century.

Moulay Idrissi recounts how a French geologist, doing his military service in the 1950s, had first noted traces of fossils during a trip from Erfoud to Taouz near the Algerian border. He had been accompanied by a *goumier*, a Moroccan soldier serving with the French army, named Moha Ohamou. After Moroccan independence, the former *goumier*, who transported marble for a factory in Casablanca, told people in the industry about the fossil site. By 1970, a French-Moroccan company was excavating fossils and sending the blocks to Italy to be refined and marketed. Then a Moroccan firm from Marrakech acquired the license to exploit a marble quarry. Moulay Idrissi, who ran a small handicraft shop, saw how interested the public was in the stones. He got some craftsmen to work with the fossil rock, at first making small objects like ashtrays, and later opened his workshop.

In a dusty patio behind the showroom, one craftsman uses a saw to cut huge blocks of marble into manageable parts. Another slices marble with a drill to find precious fossilized sea creatures. Other workers polish pieces of rock to bring out the myriad fossil shapes. Moulay Idrissi shows us his prize trilobites, grotesque petrified shrimp and crabs, evil-looking snails and scorpions perched on rocks, which he says are more than 300 million years old. I admit that I wouldn't let a trilobite into my home, even though these fashionable fossils can command thousands of dollars on the American market.

Maybe Moroccans haven't found oil in their slice of the Sahara, but the many fossil quarries and massive golden dunes rising from the black, rocky Erg Chebbi have spawned increasingly important desert tourism, bringing hope to a region that had nothing.

From this fossil town, we head west and find that tourism has already brought progress, or at least change, to *kasbah* country. At first glance, those fiery red desert fortresses and their inhabitants look like holdovers from medieval times. But when we pause to photograph a flock of camels and goats at a fountain, children appear from nowhere demanding in French: "Money please, candy, lipstick?" In towns and villages along the *route des kasbahs*, many modern houses have been built of traditional stone or sun-dried brick. Some girls have shed the customary leggings, shawls, and turbans for skirts, blouses, and headscarves and can be seen carrying backpacks to school.

The ancient oasis of Tinerhir has become a busy, prosperous town with hotels galore. This is a popular base for tourists to explore the steep red-orange Todra gorges and the even more spectacular Dades gorges, both of which are lined with magnificent rock formations and *kasbahs*. No billboards yet, but there are cafes with souvenir stands. We are astonished at the number of sports utility vehicles and motor homes with European and Moroccan license plates winding through the gorges headed for the rough tracks of the High Atlas, a newly popular destination for trekkers.

The pre-Sahara region has been discovered not only by tourists but by the movies, the other flourishing local industry. From the early days of the French protectorate, French movie makers have been attracted by exotic Morocco—the veiled women and harems, desert caravans, Berber warriors, the French Foreign Legion. Ouarzazate, the gateway to the High Atlas, *kasbah* country, and the southern oases, was a natural center for film companies. Built by the French as a military outpost and administrative center in the late 1920s, Ouarzazate's main sights were the grandiose rose-colored *kasbahs* belonging to the Glaoui, the fabled *pasha* of Marrakech and staunch ally of the French colonial authorities. After independence, many of the Glaoui's *kasbahs* were confiscated and transformed into film sets, a museum, a hotel, a restaurant, and even a disco. Nowadays, Ouarzazate has an airport with regular flights to Casablanca and Paris and an increasing number of luxury hotels and restaurants. In fact, it isn't easy to find a room at Ouarzazate because there are usually several big-budget movies on location in the area. Three large film studios have been established here, and there is talk of a film school.

"We have the natural scenery, the technicians and craftsmen, 320 days of sunshine a year, and wages are five times less than in most places," Souheil Ben Barka, the head of the Moroccan Cinema Center, told me later in Rabat. "Our only problem is that when we call for 5,000 extras, 10,000 show up."[11] Ben Barka (no relation to the political leader) was production manager for Martin Scorsese's 1997 film, *Kundun*, about the Dalai Lama. Scorsese moved the location of *Kundun* to Morocco after China put pressure on India to not allow the filming there. And so the Tibetan landscapes were recreated at Aït Benhaddou.

Aït Benhaddou, twenty miles north of Ouarzazate, is Morocco's Hollywood. The adobe Berber village with its crenellated towers has been totally restored and has appeared in numerous films, including *Lawrence of Arabia*, *Jesus of Nazareth*, and *Sodom and Gomorrah*. When there are no movie peo-

The crimson kasbah *of Aït Benhaddou, known as "Hollywood of the Atlas," has served as the backdrop for films like* Jesus of Nazareth *and* Kundun. *(Moroccan Ministry of Communications)*

ple around, life reverts pretty much to normal. Women do their laundry in the river, girls mind the cattle, and boys sell amethysts and other rocks to the occasional tourist. The reconstituted *ksar* has been marred by souvenir stalls and is better viewed from afar. Most of the inhabitants moved out of the village to a crumbling old *ksar* nearby. One of the ubiquitous guides shows us the marketplace, which served as the arena in *The Gladiator*. The guide's father raises goats, while his mother stays home weaving carpets. His sister went to grade school and got married. He completed seven years of schooling and hopes to become a movie star.

African Marrakech

Marrakech is living theater, with its intense light, spectacular backdrop of snowy peaks, palm groves, magnificent walls, and an exotic cast of characters. It never ceases to astonish me that those medieval warriors, the ascetic Almoravids and Almohads, would choose this sensuous, easy-going city as their capital.

They call it the Red City, but the magic of Marrakech is that it changes from ocher to gold to crimson, old rose, and burgundy, depending on the light and the eye of the beholder. The great adobe ramparts, monumental gates, and 200 towers, which stretch for eleven miles around the old city, were first constructed in 1126. They have been restored innumerable times and look as if they are here to stay. The elegant Koutoubia Mosque, which also dates back to the twelfth century, was a model for the Giralda in Seville, and has recently undergone much-needed repairs. The ruins of the sixteenth-century Badia palace, with its romantic gardens, tiled patio, and pool, is a natural setting for the Popular Arts and International Cinema festivals.

Marrakech has matured, grown more cosmopolitan and yes, more touristy, but it retains the magnetism of an African marketplace. Djemaa el-Fna, the vibrant Meeting Place of the Dead, has always been the heart of the city. In recent times, efforts have been made to spruce up and sanitize this incredible spectacle. While the storytellers, healers, musicians, acrobats, snake charmers, and magicians still draw crowds, the atmosphere is more subdued. The strict clamp-down on hustlers and other low life may have something to do with it. Attempts have been made to reorganize the popular food stalls, setting up stands with stools, where one can eat a traditional Moroccan meal for a reasonable price. Of late, Djemaa el-Fna has been turned into a pedestrian area but motorcycles and bicycles are still a menace. It seems nothing can overcome the square's free spirit.

Foreign visitors have not always been enthralled with Marrakech. Edith

Wharton, who journeyed to Morocco in 1917 as the guest of French resident general Lyautey, seems to have disliked the southern city vehemently. "Dark, fierce and fanatical are these narrow *souks* of Marrakech. All these many threads of the native life woven of greed and lust, of fetishism and fear and blind hate of the stranger," she notes. While she admires the refinements of the palaces, she castigates "the megalomania of the great southern chiefs."[12]

One of the last great feudal lords was Si Thami el Glaoui, the *pasha* of Marrakech. This powerful Berber chieftain of the High Atlas had thrown his lot in with the French at the beginning of the protectorate. In return, the *pasha* was given free rein to extend his rule and collect taxes throughout the south. He also commanded a private army of several hundred thousand Berber tribesmen. In fact, it was the Glaoui, backed by hard-line French colonials, who led the movement to overthrow Sultan Mohammed V in 1953. It is said that the Glaoui died of humiliation, shortly after his hated rival returned to the throne in 1955.

For all of the Edith Whartons, Marrakech has attracted a host of eminent admirers. Some came for a visit and returned. Winston Churchill first visited Marrakech in 1935 and stayed at the luxurious Mamounia, which he considered one of the best hotels he knew. He would spend time on the balcony painting the scene of orange and olive trees, red ramparts, and snow-topped Atlas in the distance. The Churchill Suite is still there and available to guests for a price. The shah of Iran and his entourage also stayed at the Mamounia, when he was forced into exile by Islamic revolutionaries in 1979. I had the enviable assignment of covering his stay in the luxury hotel, while negotiations (ultimately unsuccessful) were under way to obtain a visa for his medical treatment in the United States.

Others have chosen to settle in Marrakech, though they may spend the summer months in cooler climes. In the 1920s, French painter Jacques Majorelle set up his studio in a magical garden, which was later purchased and restored by Yves Saint Laurent. In the 1980s, Patrick Guerand-Hermes bought Ain el Quassimou, a thirty-acre estate built by descendants of Leo Tolstoy and once owned by the late Barbara Hutton, which now includes the Polo Club de la Palmeraie. Frederick Vreeland, a former U.S. ambassador to Morocco and son of the legendary fashion editor Diana Vreeland, was one of the first foreign residents in the *palmeraie*, where he and his wife, artist Vanessa Somers, built a fantasy home in 1980.

Vreeland recalls that in 1991, the U.S. Agency for International Development (USAID) was involved in a program to clean up the *bidonvilles* around Tetouan in the north. "I told them they must do something in the mountains because if they didn't, all of the mountain would come down to the city," he says, adding that in those days USAID didn't have money for rural investment because it wasn't proven that this would stop urbanization. Nor did the Moroccan Ministry of Agriculture have any program to help the countryside at the time. Over the next seven or eight years, however, both the United States and Morocco changed and began to focus on rural development. When Vreeland's term was up in 1993, King Hassan suggested that he retire in Morocco. The ambassador promised the king he would stay on to try to do something useful for the rural population.[13]

In 1996, Vreeland set up the Maison d'Energie, a society to bring solar energy to villages. His project, called Noor Web, has backing from E and CO, an energy investment service affiliated with the Rockefeller Foundation. Noor Web's franchises are concentrated in the province of Taroudant, a 17,000-square-kilometer area in the High Atlas and Anti-Atlas mountains, south of Marrakech. It took time to work out arrangements with the National Energy Office and Al Amana, a private microfinance organization. By 2001, Noor Web was serving 2,200 customers and acquiring 200 new households a month.

"There's a huge potential for solar energy in Morocco," emphasized Amine Bennouna, who is in charge of Noor Web's head office in Marrakech. He notes that even if the National Energy Office realizes its development program by 2010, there will still be about 20 percent of the population living in villages, farms, and mountain hamlets just too small to be connected to the grid.[14]

Marrakech's light has captivated an eclectic gallery of admirers that includes painter Eugène Delacroix, fashion designers Giorgio Armani and Donna Karen, actors Robert De Niro, Roman Polanski, and Alain Delon, to mention a few.

"There's something impalpable that transcends the landscape and has to do with the purity of the air, the lack of pressure, the quality of the colors, the gentleness of the people," reflected Adolfo de Velasco, antique dealer, friend of the royal family, and host par excellence, who has since passed away. We met Velasco at his antique shop in the Mamounia, and he invited us to his home in a corner of the luxuriant Majorelle Gardens. Spanish-born Velasco recalled that Diana Vreeland discovered Oriental fashions in Morocco back in 1965 and introduced them to the world: "Now, all the designers and photographers come here; we're à la mode again."[15]

Velasco said Marrakech went through a difficult time from 1991 to 1995, at the time of the first Gulf crisis, when some foreigners sold their properties and pulled out. "But at last people have understood that Morocco is totally

Luxury living in the Marrakech palmeraie *at the* Palais Rhoul.
Sylvia Rhoul rents out her palace with immense pool, rotunda,
and colonnaded terrace to celebrities like Roman Polanski,
who come to Morocco to find privacy.

different from the Middle East . . . that the only thing in common is the religion," he emphasized. "There's a lot of new investment now, new hotels and convention tourism," he continued. "More foreigners are buying winter homes here and people are staying longer. Hollywood has discovered Marrakech is an ideal film location, with desert, sea, mountains, everything in less than two hours' drive."

"It's also about the new king and the new generation," Velasco added. "Some people thought Mohammed VI would be a pushover, but I know him and he's tough as nails. He's enthusiastic and daring, makes his own decisions, and encourages new ideas. More important, the country loves him."

That conversation took place in early 2001, when Morocco was still aglow from the accession of the young king, who had brought with him exciting perspectives for a freer, fairer, more progressive Morocco. That was before the new challenges by Islamic radicals.

Atlantic Cities

From Marrakech, we head for the Atlantic coastal cities, which have changed tremendously since independence. Agadir is my first shock, completely new and unrecognizable, except for the magnificent bay. For the *New York Times*, I had covered the 1960 earthquake, which took at least 15,000 lives, three-quarters of the population, and razed most of the old city. I never had any desire to go back.

New Agadir is Morocco's pride, the most modern, the most international resort and a major fishing and commercial port, with construction sites everywhere. It has a population of about 150,000 and receives some 500,000 tourists a year, mostly from Germany, Sweden, and France. As we stroll along the beachfront, with its luxury high-rise hotels full of charter groups, expensive restaurants, bars, and nightclubs, I feel that this could be a resort anywhere in the world, except Morocco. In an exciting new development, however, Agadir University has become a pole for Berber cultural activities and fervor.

Heading north, we drive past a string of increasingly popular seaside cities, still dominated by massive Portuguese fortifications established in the fifteenth and sixteenth centuries to guard the important trade routes to India and China. The fishing village of Essaouira had been revived as Morocco's main center of foreign trade in the latter part of the eighteenth century by Sultan Mohammed III, who had it largely rebuilt by a French architect. An important Jewish community settled here and, with royal backing, controlled much of the country's imports and exports.

In modern times, Orson Welles discovered the enchantment of Essaouira and its fortress and shot most of his 1949 masterpiece *Othello* there. Moroccan movie people tell how Welles, who was operating on a very tight budget, used local artisans, carpenters, ironmongers, and ceramicists whenever possible. When advised by Essaouira's Jewish tailors that it would take ten days to make the costumes, Welles decided that the only place he could shoot scenes without costumes was the *hammam*, or Turkish bath.

It was probably Welles's cult film that drew the hippies to Essaouira in the 1960s. Legendary musician Jimi Hendrix visited the Berber village of Diabat in the sand dunes at Cap Sim south of town and wrote "Castles Made of Sand." Cat Stevens and waves of hippies followed, and Essaouira became a legend. After trouble with some junkies, the police cleaned up the place in the mid-1970s, and Essaouira began looking for a new image.

Gradually, the modest fishing port has developed into a center for art and music. Danish art patron Frederic Damgaard opened a gallery here in 1988 and has promoted the flamboyant works of the local self-taught artists. At the same time, native son André Azoulay, an adviser to the king, has almost single-handedly put Essaouira back on the world map, this time for its international music festival featuring the popular drumbeats of the *gnaoua*, who are descendants of African slaves.

The townspeople now talk excitedly of plans to turn this walled town of whitewashed houses, superb sandy beaches, and mild Mediterranean climate into a major tourist resort. We had encountered similar ambitions in other coastal towns, but we take Essaouira's dreams seriously because of Azoulay's influence. Early in 2004, King Mohammed would preside over the signing of a convention with European developers for the creation of the Mogador Seaside Resort, just south of Essaouira. The half-billion-dollar project is to include thirty-two hotels and guesthouses, two golf courses, a horseback-riding center, and a beach club and will give new energy to tourism on Morocco's Atlantic coast.

Modern Morocco

If most Moroccan cities tend to dwell on past glories, Casablanca is resolutely turned to the future. This is not just another modern metropolis with skyscrapers and slums. Casablanca is the heart of new Morocco, home to the stock exchange, banks, industries, trade unions, and a vocal political press. Here is a modest replica of the Twin Towers (one tower, owned by Libyans, has never been occupied and is a monument to the underbelly of the economy). This is the center of a wide range of nongovernmental organizations, which defend single mothers and battered women, fight against corruption and illiteracy, demand truth and justice.

Casablanca is really a French creation, but Moroccans have propelled it into the twenty-first century. From a modest fishing village and pirates' lair, French planners built a modern economic center, with broad boulevards and elegant residential quarters, handsome neo-Moorish public buildings, a huge artificial port, and industrial areas, accompanied by the inevitable *bidonvilles*, shantytowns that have invaded most of the industrial quarters. The city has since spread upward and outward, with a population today of some 5 million—up from 600,000 at independence.

This is above all the engine that drives the country's economy. Here are the new glass and steel headquarters of Omnium Nord Africain, better known as ONA, Morocco's largest holding company, with interests in mining, fishing, agriculture, and the new hypermarkets and supermarkets around the country. The royal family is an important shareholder of ONA, which represents 60 percent of the capitalization on the Casablanca Stock

Exchange. The other giant corporation is the Benjelloun Group, with holdings mainly in banking, insurance, and telecommunications. Méditel, a joint venture between Benjelloun and a Spanish-Portuguese consortium, has become a significant player in the new booming business in mobile telephones.

The labor unions are concentrated in Casablanca. A major actor in the struggle for independence, the labor movement has since splintered into different politically oriented federations, but is still a force to be reckoned with. Most of the media is also based in Casablanca, although it was largely quiescent under the late King Hassan's authoritarian rule. When Socialist leader Abderrahmane Youssoufi was named prime minister in 1998, his government introduced greater freedoms, and the press has been flexing its muscles.

In Casablanca, more than elsewhere, the gap between rich and poor is glaring and growing. The residential quarter of Anfa is overflowing with opulent villas and mansions (some of the walled palaces belong to Arab notables from the Gulf). The Boulevard de la Corniche, with private beach clubs, expensive discos, and restaurants, is one massive traffic jam on summer evenings. Yet in the El Hank neighborhood across the way, families squat in slums without minimal conveniences, like running water and sewers, and live by begging. King Mohammed shocked the nation in the summer of 2001 when he announced that some 4 million Moroccans live in *bidonvilles*—half of them in the developed cities along the coast.

Overlooking the Atlantic, the Hassan II Mosque with a 200-meter-high minaret, completed in 1993 for the king's sixty-fourth birthday, is said to be the third largest mosque in the world, after those of the Muslim holy cities of Mecca and Medina. This marble testimony of Morocco's faith can hold 25,000 worshipers and 80,000 more on the esplanade and is said to have cost some $800 million, paid for by public contributions, not always voluntary. The nation was shocked some time ago to learn that the foundations of this proud monument are threatened. Studies are under way to see how to shore up the grandiose mosque against the force of the waves.

Ironically, this modern metropolis is home to religious zealots like Sheikh Abdelbari Zemzmi, who has openly called for the restoration of *Sharia*, or Islamic law. It is in Casablanca's poorer neighborhoods that the Islamist Justice and Development party has made substantial inroads, largely replacing left-wing parties. And it was here that a group of fanatic suicide bombers struck in the spring of 2003, reminding Moroccans that they are not immune to Islamic violence in this era of globalization.

Rabat, the sedate, flowering capital, is much as the French left it, only more so. Attractive colonial-style government buildings are a legacy from the protectorate, as is the walled neo-Moorish royal palace—although the parade ground has been spruced up with landscaped gardens. There are more

The new symbol of Casablanca is the grand Hassan II Mosque, said to be the largest in the world outside of Saudi Arabia. This majestic monument, with marble floors, intricately carved arches, cedar cupolas, and huge Venetian chandeliers, was built by (not always) voluntary contributions from the Moroccan people. (Moroccan Ministry of Communications)

wealthy suburbs now and many more low-to-medium-income neighborhoods, where villas have been replaced by apartment buildings and farmland swallowed by concrete blocks.

The capital's most spectacular monument is the ruins of the twelfth-century Hassan Tower, an immense ocher-colored minaret built by the Almohad sultan Yacoub al Mansour. Intended to be the largest mosque in the world after that of Mecca, Al Mansour's shrine was left unfinished at his death in 1199. Today the majestic columns have been partially restored, and beside them stands a modern, white, sculpted mausoleum. Here lies the tomb of Mohammed V, the father of Moroccan independence, and beside him, his two sons, Moulay Abdallah and Hassan II.

The royal palace, a sprawling group of low-lying buildings in the center of town, remains the seat of authority—not the French-designed government ministries and parliament nearby. The prime minister's office is next to those of the king and his counselors, and the Ministry of Islamic Affairs is adjacent. The government implements royal directives, carries out day-to-day policies, and serves as a convenient foil for the palace. All good things come from Allah and the king. Any missteps, failures, or unpopular gestures are the responsibility of the government.

Although Morocco is legally a constitutional monarchy, in fact everything revolves around the king. The late King Hassan fashioned this all-powerful role for himself and ruled by skillful manipulation, political astuteness, *baraka*, and a robust security service. King Mohammed VI has taken his father's mantle and seems reluctant to forgo any of his political prerogatives but is gingerly introducing economic and social reforms.

The only declared challenger to the monarchy, Sheikh Abdessalam Yassine, an emaciated Islamist leader with a wispy beard, lives in a walled villa in the whitewashed old pirate city of Salé, across the river from Rabat. Long years of persecution have only increased the Sheikh's popularity. Nor has he wavered in his refusal to recognize the king as Commander of the Faithful and his objective to come to power peacefully, by persuasion and education.

As we head back to Tangier, I feel that I have only skimmed the surface of this multilayered land. There have been immense changes since independence nearly five decades ago, changes for better and worse. The most obvious transformations are the creation of a substantial middle class, a growing number of nouveaux riches, and a dramatic increase in the urban poor and jobless. The warning signs are clear; anyone venturing into the *bidonvilles* can feel the pent-up desperation, which drives thousands of young Moroccans to flee the country illegally each year and provides fertile terrain for recruitment by Islamic radicals.

At this point, I decide to return to Morocco to examine the multiple challenges facing this strategic, enigmatic, and endearing country as it emerges from the Middle Ages into modernity.

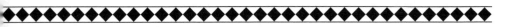

The Ever-Present Past

II

Protectors, Wards, and Rebels

3

When I first came to this bewildering kingdom in 1950, there were essentially two Moroccos: a modern, prosperous land inhabited by a European minority intersecting an undeveloped country whose inhabitants were mostly poor, uneducated Moroccans. The sultan retained nominal sovereignty but did not rule. Administratively, the country was divided into French and Spanish protectorates and the international zone of Tangier, with France in control of the main cities and natural resources.

American political scientist John Waterbury succinctly sums up the ambiguous legacy of the French colonial experience in the kingdom: "During their brief sojourn in Morocco, the French set up a modern administrative apparatus geared to an expanding economy based on commercial agriculture, mining, industry and trade. However, Moroccans were at best marginal participants in this endeavor." He adds: "There was practically no sustained attempt made by the French to familiarize or, more important, to associate Moroccans with the new structures."[1]

Yet Morocco had once been a powerful Muslim empire. Reminders of a great civilization were everywhere: splendid palaces with elaborate mosaics and enclosed gardens; grand mosques with arches, domes, and tall square minarets; *medersas* (religious schools) decorated with elaborate tiles and carvings; ancient walled cities; and desert fortresses. Proud, insular, unruly Morocco was one of the last African countries to fall in the early twentieth century to the overwhelming power of European colonialism with its greed, brutality, modern technology, and ideals of human rights.

I found that, even subject to colonial rule, the Moroccans had a strong sense of national identity. The most sophisticated professional and the illiterate housemaid shared a common pride in being Moroccan, as distinct from European or Algerian or Tunisian. They knew who they were and where they came from although it was unclear where they were going.

In the Beginning

Morocco's original inhabitants were the *Imazighen*, or free people, known for their strong spirit of resistance. Their history has generally been told by the occupiers, who referred to the *Imazighen* as Berbers, from the Latin word *barbarus*, meaning "primitive and foreign." Most historians agree that at the end of the second millennium B.C. all of North Africa was inhabited by Berbers, east as far as the Nile Valley, west to the Canary Islands, and south to include the Sahara and Mauritania. Little is known about early Berber history, according to Abdallah Laroui, a leading Moroccan historian, who points out that Berber grave inscriptions and rock carvings are still a mystery.[2]

Through the centuries, the Berbers were overrun by foreign invaders: Phoenicians, Carthaginians, Romans, Vandals, Byzantines, Arabs, and Europeans, who have left their marks to varying degrees. But the *Amazigh* (Berber) identity remains indelible.

Recorded history in this westernmost corner of North Africa begins with the arrival of the Phoenicians, who sailed from Tyre, in today's Lebanon, around 1100 B.C. The Phoenicians are known to have established coastal trading posts at Lixus, near today's Larache, Tangier, and as far south as Essaouira. Their main quest was gold from the desert caravans, but they also traded in wheat and corn, grapes and fish—pictured on coins with Punic inscriptions found in the area. In return, the Phoenicians and their descendants from Carthage taught the Berber population the use of plants and iron.

It is generally held that Jews first came to North Africa along with the Phoenician traders. While the Phoenicians eventually disappeared, the Jews stayed, becoming part of the North African community until the exodus to Israel in the mid-twentieth century. French authority André Chouraqui says it was the fundamental similarities between the Punic language and Hebrew that "enabled Judaism to spread and flourish in Africa to attract Berber masses."[3] When the Romans arrived, they found some Berbers worshiping local divinities and nature cults and some communities that had embraced Judaism.

The fall of Carthage in 146 B.C. marked the beginning of the Roman occupation of North Africa, which was to last more than four centuries. The kingdom of Mauritania—as Morocco was known—appears to have been

Rome's stepchild. Archaeologists have found few reminders of Roman glory in Morocco, aside from the monumental remains of a triumphal arch, a basilica, and numerous wealthy homes at Volubilis near Meknès in the center of the country. There is nothing, however, like the impressive Roman ruins in Algeria, Tunisia, and Libya, and no evidence even of Roman roads between the main towns of Tangier, Salé, and Volubilis. Rome's interest in Morocco was essentially as a source of wheat for the empire, not settlement, according to French historian Charles-André Julien. He emphasizes that the Romans never tried to administer the population directly but ruled through Berber chiefs and community organizations.[4]

By the fifth century, North Africans had largely rid themselves of foreign rule. The Maghreb, as northwest Africa is known in Arabic, was divided into a number of independent principalities, some followers of the Punic religion, some of Christianity or Judaism, others of Donatism or Manichaeanism.

The Arab conquerors arrived in northwest Africa in the mid-seventh century, bringing with them their most powerful weapon, Islam. It is generally agreed that in the beginning, the Arab incursions were not part of a deliberate plan of conquest mapped out by the Umayyad caliphate in Damascus, but rather raiding parties launched by Arab military chiefs from Egypt in search of prestige and booty. The Arab governor, Musa ibn Nusair, is credited with establishing Arab rule over all of North Africa by 710, although fighting continued in Ifriqiya—today's Tunisia—for some time. It is said that the Arab army occupying North Africa at the time did not exceed 50,000 men. From his base at Tangier, Musa dispatched his forces to Spain, under the command of a Berber, Tariq ibn Ziyad. This Muslim army, made up largely of Berber recruits, conquered most of the Iberian peninsula and reached as far as Poitiers in France before being forced to retreat in 732 A.D.

Historians have been at a loss to explain the rapid spread of Islam across North Africa, which had proved so resistant to earlier invaders. Nevill Barbour compares the Arab conquest of North Africa to the Spanish conquest of Central and South America, in that they shared an "intense devotion to the propagation of their faith" and a "ruthless assertion of their military superiority."[5] North African Islam was an occidental Islam; it assumed Berber characteristics—egalitarianism, austerity, and a certain mysticism—and soon declared its independence from Oriental Islam. Although there were various sectarian revolts, Moroccans generally looked for spiritual guidance to the western centers of Islamic orthodoxy at Cordoba and Kairwan, not Baghdad or Damascus, a religious autonomy they were to retain even after the decline of Muslim Spain.

Great Muslim Dynasties

Morocco's first Muslim dynasty, the Idrissids, were said to be descended from the Prophet Mohammed through his son-in-law Ali. After taking part in an unsuccessful revolt against the caliph of Baghdad, Idriss ibn Abdallah sought refuge in central Morocco at the end of the eighth century. This Arab *sherif* (descendant of the Prophet) soon gained the respect of the Berber population, who acclaimed him as their *imam*—religious leader—and military chief in the region of Fez and Meknès. When word of Idriss's successes reached Baghdad, Caliph Haroun al Rachid sent an emissary to Morocco, who poisoned the rebel *sherif*. His son with a Berber concubine, Idriss II, laid the foundations of his capital at Fez and established the first independent Muslim kingdom in Morocco.

The three great dynasties that presided over Morocco's golden age from 1093 to 1465 were of Berber origin: the Almoravids, who were Saharan Islamic missionaries; the Almohads, who were Islamic reformers from the High Atlas; and the Merinids, who were nomads from eastern Morocco. At its height in the twelfth and thirteenth centuries, the Moroccan empire stretched from Spain across North Africa to the shores of Tripoli and south to include today's Mauritania. From the forced marriage between Christian Spaniards and Muslim Moroccans was born the rich Hispano-Mauresque culture, a zenith in the life of the two peoples. Historians agree that under the Berber dynasties, the process of Arabization and Islamization continued, and was even accelerated.

After being driven from the Iberian Peninsula in the fifteenth century, Moroccans were on the defensive. Their Christian neighbors, Spain and Portugal, signed the Treaty of Tordesillas, dividing the world between them. The kingdom of Fez was declared a Portuguese preserve, and Spain was free to occupy territories to the east. Portugal established trading posts along the Atlantic coast, while Spain occupied Melilla and Peñon de Velez on the Moroccan Mediterranean, which it still holds, as well as Oran and other ports in today's Algeria. In an attempt to drive out the Spanish occupiers, Algiers' leadership appealed for help to fellow Muslims, the Ottomans, only to find themselves under Ottoman occupation.

In this troubled time, another *sherifian* family, also claiming descent from the Prophet Mohammed, which had settled in the thirteenth century near the southern oasis of Zagora, assumed power in southern Morocco. The Saadian Dynasty, backed by *marabouts* (holy men), established an independent kingdom with Marrakech as its capital. The Saadians enhanced their prestige by capturing several Portuguese posts, including the bastion of Agadir in 1541. The turning point in the Saadian struggle to liberate the kingdom is known as the Battle of Three Kings and took place in 1578. The Moroccan king, Abdel Malik, died from an illness early in the battle, but his army routed the combined forces of his predecessor, former king Moulay Mohammed, and his ally, the Portuguese king Sebastião, who had hoped to regain a foothold in Morocco. The late King Abdel Malik's brother Ahmad was proclaimed sultan and given the title "Al Mansour," the Victorious, the name by which he is remembered.

A prodigious builder, Al Mansour revived Marrakech with such works as the vast Badia Palace; the richly decorated Ben Youssef Medersa (formerly a theological boarding school, now a museum); and the Saadian Tombs, whose grandeur is still visible. His most notable achievement, however, was to halt the advance of the Ottoman Turks, who had taken over the rest of North Africa. Historian Jamil Abun-Nasr notes that Sultan Ahmad defended Morocco against the Ottoman invaders by reorganizing his army on the Ottoman model, with Turks providing technical skills. With this professional force led by Christian renegades and Andalusians (Muslim exiles from Spain), Al Mansour preserved the stability of his reign. He also made important incursions into the Sahara as far as the kingdom of Gao on the Niger, where a Moroccan protectorate was established, bringing to the Saadian throne riches of gold, slaves, ebony, and rhinoceros horns.[6]

After Al Mansour's death in 1603, the Saadian dynasty disintegrated over family quarrels, and Morocco split up into several independent principalities. During this period, when the central authority was weakened, people turned for guidance to local *sheikhs* and *marabouts*, who had long played an important role in the education and moral life of the country. While the position of the sultan was not disputed, the tribes with their religious leaders and holy men retained considerable autonomy in the countryside.

The Ruling Alaouites

By the middle of the seventeenth century, yet another *sherifian* family emerged from the desert to rule Morocco. The Alaouites were descendants of the Prophet Mohammed through his daughter Fatima. As we have seen, they had come from Arabia in the thirteenth century and settled at the important caravan center of Sigilmassa. The first member of this Arab dynasty to achieve prominence was Moulay Rachid who, with the help of local Arab tribes, captured Fez and was proclaimed sultan in 1668.

Moulay Rachid's controversial younger brother, Moulay Ismail, consolidated the kingdom and ruled for a half century, until his death in 1727. Moulay Ismail is generally portrayed by Moroccan historians as a great leader, unifier, builder, and the creator of the formidable Black Guard, an elite corps composed of descendants of African slaves. European scholars, however, write of his barbaric cruelty to Christian prisoners, his megalomania, and his philandering; it is said that he fathered as many as 1,000 children. It is not clear how much of Moulay Ismail's legend is fantasy.

It is true that with his slave army, Moulay Ismail drove the Spanish out of Morocco, recovered Tangier from the English, kept out the Ottomans, and annexed Mauritania. He also ruled with a firm hand, bled the country with exorbitant taxes to pay for his military endeavors and public works, and even promoted piracy to swell his coffers. An ardent admirer of Louis XIV, Moulay Ismail urged the Sun King to convert to Islam and asked for his daughter's hand in marriage. The French monarch refused both suggestions, but the two courts maintained diplomatic relations. The imperial city of Meknès was actually inspired by Versailles. While the palace has fallen into ruins, the monumental adobe walls, gateways, prison, and stables are an impressive reminder of the sultan who succeeded in pacifying the country during his long reign.

After Moulay Ismail's death, the country fell into anarchy. His sons tried to rule by force but were at the mercy of warring clans, the Black Guard, and the Arab militia. Taking advantage of the confusion, Berber tribes of the Middle Atlas Mountains, backed by Muslim brotherhoods, rose up against the central government. In this vacuum of authority, Moulay Ismail's grandson Mohammed ben Abdallah restored a semblance of order. Known as Mohammed III, he moved the slave army out of the capital, bought off tribal leaders, and recruited his own army from Arab and Berber tribes. A follower of the rigid Wahhabi reform movement from Arabia, the sultan tried to reduce the authority of the brotherhoods without much success. The influence of these religious orders, which often played an important political role, is said to be an important factor in countering the penetration of Wahhabi fundamentalists today.

European Rivalries

The nineteenth century is largely the story of heated rivalries among European powers—namely France, Spain, Germany, and England—to obtain mining concessions, trade advantages, and influence in this unruly kingdom. Wary of the foreign interest, successive sultans tried to play one power off against another, accepting loans and military assistance while preserving nominal independence.

It was France's occupation of neighboring Algiers in 1830 that first shook the Alaouite throne. In his final stand against the French, the Algerian hero Abdul Kader appealed to Morocco for assistance. But the Moroccan army was routed by French forces in the border area near Oujda, and for good measure, the French fleet shelled the ports of Tangier and Essaouira. The sultan was forced to pledge to expel the Algerian leader if he sought refuge in Morocco.

Moroccan rulers had been made painfully aware of their country's vulnerability and concluded that their only hope to remain independent was to acquire a protector. The natural choice was Britain, which already controlled 75 percent of Morocco's foreign trade. In 1856, Sultan Abdul Rahman signed a treaty granting Britain trade privileges, and in return, the British obtained guarantees from the French that they would not occupy Morocco. When Spanish troops invaded northern Morocco in 1860, occupying Tetouan, they were prevented from taking Tangier by British diplomatic intervention.

Hassan I, who reigned from 1873 to 1894, was the last Moroccan sultan to retain a degree of independence. He managed to keep order but was plagued by dissident tribes and encroaching European powers. His son Abdelaziz was only fourteen when he came to the throne, and he depended heavily on an entourage of European profiteers and unscrupulous businessmen. The young sultan became known for his passion for gadgets like cameras, phonographs, and mechanical birds, and for his extravagances, such as importing bicycles and coaches to a country with no roads. Initially Abdelaziz tried to pursue his father's reforms, but these only angered the privileged landowners, *caids* (tribal chiefs), and religious orders, who resented the sultan's foreign advisers. One of the most influential members of the royal court was a former British navy officer from Gibraltar, Harry Maclean, known as "Caid" Maclean. He had come to Morocco as a military instructor twenty-five years before and became the sultan's confidant and chief aide on foreign affairs.

Restive Berber tribesmen undermined national stability with sporadic uprisings and attacks on foreigners. Much has been written about Ahmad Raisouni, a Robin Hood figure, who terrorized northern Morocco with acts of banditry. Raisouni kidnapped prominent foreigners for ransom, among them, the sultan's military adviser, Sir Harry Maclean; the London *Times*'s correspondent Walter Harris; and American millionaire Ion Perdicaris. Alarmed at this lawlessness, the Europeans pressured Abdelaziz to control Raisouni. But the sultan responded by naming the rebel to be governor of northern Morocco. Even today, Moroccan rulers tend to prefer to buy off their adversaries rather than make martyrs of them and enemies of their followers.

Citing increasing disorder, the French made incursions into eastern Morocco from Algeria. Morocco was now deeply in debt and forced to levy harsh taxes, which stirred new resentment. As the situation grew more chaotic, Britain abandoned its role as Moroccan protector. The kingdom's independence was progressively eviscerated through a series of international accords in 1904: the British accepted French intervention in Morocco in exchange for a free hand in Egypt; the Italians recognized France's "rights" in Morocco for freedom to act in Libya; the French and Spanish carved out their respective zones of influence. Only Germany's Kaiser Wilhelm II visited Tangier, in 1905, in support of Moroccan rights.

Encouraged by German backing, Sultan Abdelaziz called for an international conference to preserve Moroccan sovereignty and territorial integrity. On April 7, 1906, eleven European powers meeting in southern Spain signed the Act of Algeciras, which upheld the sultan's sovereignty but granted France and Spain control of the police and finances in Moroccan coastal towns. It also internationalized the Moroccan question by giving all of the treaty countries a voice in economic matters. Notwithstanding the guarantees, French military intervention became inevitable after the murder of a French doctor at Marrakech and several port workers at Casablanca.

In a last-ditch effort to save his country's independence, Moulay Hafid rose against his brother Abdelaziz and declared himself sultan. Later, however, Moulay Hafid was forced to call on the French for help when tribesmen laid siege to Fez. Taking advantage of the growing confusion, Spain dispatched troops into its zone of influence in northern Morocco, occupying Larache and Alcazarquivir. Again Germany intervened, sending the gunboat *Panther* to Agadir in July 1911, raising Moroccan hopes for a savior. This time, however, the German action was not a show of support for the embattled sultan but a move to persuade France to open diplomatic negotiations. In a much-criticized accord, Germany recognized France's right to pacify Morocco in return for land in the French Congo.

Faced with no alternative, Moulay Hafid signed the Treaty of Fez on March 30, 1912, establishing the French protectorate and laying the groundwork for a Spanish protectorate—and thereby ending eleven centuries of Moroccan independence.

Armed Resistance

Subduing the Moroccans—the French called it "pacification"—was no picnic. Europeans were well aware of Morocco's long history of resistance to foreign occupation, starting with the Romans. But there was that persistent myth that Morocco had been the granary of the Roman Empire and could again become a source of agricultural and mineral wealth, under enlightened European management. More important for the French, a defiant Morocco remained a permanent threat to French Algeria and the missing link in France's African empire. After all, the French had won approval for their Moroccan enterprise from the world powers meeting at Algeciras.

Under the Treaty of Fez, the French government pledged to safeguard the spiritual status, respect, and prestige of the sultan; guarantee the exercise of the Muslim religion and all religious institutions; and support His Majesty against all dangers to his person or throne. But in reality, France had imposed its rule over Morocco, except for several minor Spanish possessions and the international city of Tangier. France assumed the right to occupy the territory militarily and preserve order, handle Morocco's foreign relations, and initiate administrative, judicial, educational, economic, financial, and military reforms.

It came as no surprise that as soon as the Treaty of Fez was signed, armed rebellions broke out in different parts of the country. Tribal resistance in the High Atlas Mountains and the southern desert regions was not overcome until 1935. This violent rejection, however, only served to justify the French contention that their intervention was necessary to restore order to this strategic Mediterranean country. From the outset, France dominated the resistance with its modern armaments and political maneuvers.

In Fez, Moroccan troops revolted against the sultan, who had succumbed to French pressures, and were joined by some 20,000 tribesmen. The French army reacted with force, bombarding Fez and the region. Some seventy-five French military and civilians died in what is still remembered as *les journées sanglantes*—the days of blood. There is no reliable estimate of the Moroccan casualties, said to be in the thousands.

The next sustained armed resistance came from Al Hiba, a Saharan tribal chieftain whose father, Ma el Ainin, a holy man, had recognized the Moroccan sultan's sovereignty at the turn of the century. Like earlier Berber leaders, Al Hiba succeeded in uniting the desert tribes and then moved against the French and occupied Marrakech.

It was this threat that induced the French resident general, Louis Hubert Gonzalve Lyautey, to seek help from other Berber tribal chiefs, like the Glaouis, known as the lords of the Atlas. The Glaouis' tribesmen defeated Al Hiba's forces and drove them back to the Sahara, where they continued their resistance for several years. In exchange for their services, the Glaouis were rewarded with lucrative posts. The most prominent of these "French friends" was Si Thami el Glaoui, the *pasha* (governor) of Marrakech, who was given free rein to exact tribute in southern Morocco. Lyautey's strategy of tribal alliances became a cornerstone of France's pacification policy.

The most serious armed uprising came from the Rif and was directed against the Spanish protectorate. In the end, it took the forces of France and Spain to defeat the ragtag Rif Liberation Army. The Rif leader, Abdelkrim al Khattabi, generally known by his first name, was not just another rebellious tribal chieftain. He is considered by Moroccans today as the father of the nationalist movement, and his victory over the Spanish at the Battle of Annoual in July 1921 is still celebrated each year. After defeating the Spanish forces, Abdelkrim proclaimed the Republic of the Rif in 1923, assuming the post of president. This was the first open challenge to the Moroccan monarchy and would explain in part the ruthless repression of a new Rif rebellion in the early years of independence.

Abdelkrim had deliberately tried to keep the French out of his war to liberate the Spanish protectorate, and Lyautey reciprocated by maintaining cordial relations with the Rif leader. But by May 1925, border skirmishes broke out between the French troops and Rif tribesmen. France removed Lyautey, considered too soft on the natives, and dispatched Marshall Henri Philippe Pétain to coordinate military operations with the Spanish dictator, General Primo de Rivera, who had taken charge of the Rif front. The 60,000 Rifains put up a valiant fight but in the end were no match for 325,000 French troops, backed by tanks and aircraft, and the 100,000-man Spanish army. On May 25, 1926, the Rif leader surrendered to the French, who deported him to the island of La Reunion. After twenty-one years' exile, Abdelkrim was transferred to France, but jumped ship at Port Said. He was given asylum in Egypt, where he headed a liaison office for the North African nationalist movements, which had all achieved independence by his death in 1963.

Lyautey's Vision

If anyone could have made a success of the French protectorate, it was Marshall Lyautey, distinguished soldier and administrator, who served as resident general until 1925. Monarchist and visionary, Lyautey had a clear plan for Moroccan society, which would retain its identity while advancing under the benevolent guidance of France. Defining his concept of a protectorate, Lyautey said in 1920: "It is a country keeping its institutions, its government and managing its affairs with its own governing bodies, under the control of a European power."[7]

Thanks to Lyautey, Morocco's monumental cities have been largely preserved with entirely new urban areas built alongside. Likewise, Lyautey laid the groundwork for a modern administration and economic and social infrastructure, while safeguarding Moroccan traditions and Islamic institutions. The basic trouble was that no attempt was made to modernize these outmoded institutions.

It is not sure that Lyautey's dream ever had a chance of materializing in an age when the winds of decolonization were sweeping the continents. Furthermore, his idealistic policies were rapidly undermined by activist French settlers, diehard colonial administrators, powerful business and banking circles, as well as less enlightened officials in Paris. Soon the protectorate was transformed into direct colonial administration.

"Efforts to erect some sort of legal façade for the protectorate seem irrelevant, for it was inevitable that the technocratic invasion which Morocco witnessed after 1912 would reduce the outmoded *makhzen* [royal establishment] to a subservient role," Waterbury writes in *The Commander of the Faithful.* "Lyautey's plans for indirect administration and the revivification of traditional institutions were pipedreams. . . . In fact, all the tangible aspects of the sultan's power were done away with, while certain ludicrous trappings were conscientiously maintained."[8]

Political Resistance

When it became clear to Moroccans that freedom could not be regained by military struggle, they turned to political resistance. Initially, political action was cloaked in Islamic reform, but soon it evolved into a broad nationalist movement. The nationalist leadership was essentially bipolar at the start, emanating simultaneously from pan-Arab, Islamic students at the Karaouyine led by Allal el Fassi, and from French-educated students like Ahmed Balafrej, who were imbued with European ideals of human rights.

"Since armed resistance had proved ineffectual, we had to learn to fight foreign occupation with ideas," the charismatic El Fassi told me much later.[9] Born in 1910, El Fassi came from an elite family of Fez—his father was grand mufti and a professor at Karaouyine University—and from an early age, he engaged in social protest. The young El Fassi became a disciple of Muhammad Abduh, an Egyptian scholar, who introduced the *Salafi* message of Islamic modernism and anticolonialism to North African students, through his teachings at Al Azhar University in Cairo and a secret society in Paris. This is El Fassi's description of the birth of political nationalism in Morocco:

> The Moroccan youths found in the *Salafiyah* movement a field for action and a training center for disciplined service and sacrifice. They formed centers in Fez, Rabat, and Tetuan for participation in public affairs. Opposition to the *sheikhs* who had benefited from the pro-

tectorate regime was foremost in their program of action. Small study groups sprang up for investigating outstanding public issues and enlightening public opinion in regard to them. The Karaouiyine University at Fez was a meeting place for students from all parts of the land, and we considered it our duty to instill into them the spirit of the *Salafiyah* and the nationalist creeds.[10]

The French protectorate authorities soon gave the budding nationalist movement a rallying cry: the Berber *dahir* (decree). The first major error of the post-Lyautey administration was the 1930 ruling which established a double standard: the Arab population would continue to fall under Islamic law, but Berbers (who are also Muslims) would be subject to French law in criminal cases and tribal customary courts for other matters. It was clearly a divide-and-rule maneuver, which reinforced nationalist sentiments and angered the rest of the Islamic world. Arabs and Berbers joined together in strikes, protest demonstrations, and rallies at Fez, Rabat, and other towns. In response, the protectorate authorities made widespread arrests and declared a state of emergency.

The battle over the Berber *dahir* marked a new chapter in the nationalist struggle. The nationalists formed an organization called the National Action bloc, and its first cause was to defend national unity against the moves to divide Arabs and Berbers. In Paris, Ahmed Balafrej, the leader of the bloc's French-educated wing, directed a magazine called *Maghrib*, which aimed to win over liberal circles in France to the nationalist cause. The bloc also sent delegates to Cairo and Jerusalem to alert the Muslim world to "the colonial conspiracies against Islam and Arabism." In the following months, the nationalists spread their message through posters, songs, lectures, and new French-language and Arabic newspapers in Morocco. Finally the protectorate authorities were forced to amend the *dahir*, in what was seen as the first victory of the Moroccan nationalists. Their campaign was so successful that long after independence, any move to revive a Berber identity was denounced as antinational, anti-Arab, and anti-Islamic.

Unwittingly, the young sultan, Mohammed ben Youssef, had signed the controversial Berber decree. The French had chosen seventeen-year-old Sidi Mohammed as sultan in 1927, over his two older brothers, because it was assumed he would be more docile. Aware of the importance of the monarchy as a national symbol, the nationalists decided it was essential to win over the shy, inexperienced sovereign to their cause. In 1933, the nationalists proclaimed November 18, the day Mohammed V acceded to the throne, as a national holiday. Nationalist leader El Fassi met with the sultan early in 1934 and called him "a great monarch," who had promised to recover the Moroccans' lost rights.

Over the next few years, Paris named a succession of representatives to Morocco with orders to initiate reforms, which were always blocked by events on the ground. Demonstrations of any kind—whether over reforms, water or union rights, or press censorship—would be followed by a crackdown on the nationalist leadership, with arrests and expulsions.

In early 1937, the nationalists formed a political party whose undeclared aim was to prepare the country for self-government. El Fassi was elected president of the National party. Alarmed over the spread of nationalism, the French authorities accused El Fassi of plotting an insurrection with the aim of becoming king. Despite nationalist denials, El Fassi was arrested and deported to Gabon in French West Africa. Balafrej, who had been named secretary general of the party, fled to the international zone of Tangier. With the Moroccan nationalist movement decapitated, France could concentrate on impending problems in Europe.

World War II: Political Truce

At the outbreak of World War II, the National Action bloc reassured the French resident general of its support, and French Morocco for the most part remained quiescent. In the Spanish zone, however, nationalist leader Abdelkhalek Torres showed sympathy for the Nazis, although his Reform party reiterated its loyalty to the sultan. After the defeat of the Rif hero Abdelkrim in 1926, Madrid had recruited many Rifains into the Spanish army. In fact, General Francisco Franco had launched his national movement from northern Morocco in 1936, and his success in the Spanish Civil War was due in part to Moroccan troops. As a result, Spanish policy toward its protectorate was more lenient than that of the French.

At this time, the gentle sultan became an unexpected hero. When the Vichy government tried to force the monarch to impose anti-Jewish laws in Morocco, Mohammed V said no. He told the resident general that Moroccan Jews were like all other subjects, and it was his duty to protect them. After the Allied landings in 1942, the sultan urged Moroccans to join the campaigns against the Axis in North Africa and Europe. In recognition of Moroccan valor and the sultan's role, General Charles de Gaulle named him *Compagnon de la Libération*.

What cannot be overestimated is the American influence in Morocco during World War II. With the arrival of American forces in Casablanca, the

Vichy rule evaporated, clearing the way for liberation. A French colleague, Bertrand Bellaigue, a boy at the time, recalls the scene:

> The Americans arrived perched on their floating tanks and their little open cars they called jeeps, sporting brand new uniforms and netted helmets and looked like an army of Martians. On the beach north of Rabat, they were met by French and Moroccan *spahis* from a light cavalry regiment, who charged them with drawn swords. The Americans were so astonished that they held their fire and stopped to take pictures of the exotic pagentry.
>
> Meanwhile their planes were dropping thousands of leaflets over Casablanca with the American flag and President Roosevelt's picture that said "Message from the President of the United States." Addressed to the people of French North Africa, the message said: "We come to your country to free you from the grip of the conquerors who seek to deprive you of your sovereign rights, your religious freedom and the right to lead your own way of life in peace." . . . The message did not specify who were "the conquerors" in Morocco—the Axis or France.
>
> It was a sad paradox that, because of the Vichy regime's order to resist, it took the allies three days of combat and cost the lives of more than 1,000 French troops and 2,000 wounded in addition to 1,500 American forces killed or missing.[11]

The meeting between President Franklin D. Roosevelt and Mohammed V at Anfa, a suburb of Casablanca on January 22, 1943, changed history. President Roosevelt had invited the sultan and Prince Hassan to dine with him and Churchill. There were no journalists present, but Roosevelt's son Elliot recalls the president's private assurances to the sultan that Morocco should belong to Moroccans. In his book *As He Saw It*, Elliot Roosevelt quotes the president as saying:

> Why does Morocco, inhabited by Moroccans, belong to France? Anything must be better than to live under French colonial rule. Should a land belong to France? By what logic and by what custom and by what historical rule? . . . When we've won the war, I will work with all my might and main to see to it that the United States is not wheedled into the position of accepting any plan that will further France's imperialistic ambitions.[12]

Historic meeting between U.S. president Franklin Roosevelt and King Mohammed V, with Prime Minister Winston Churchill looking on, at Casablanca in 1943. The boy standing in fez and white djellaba is future King Hassan. This was a landmark in the North Africans' struggle against French colonial rule. (Moroccan Ministry of Communications)

The Independence Party

Although the United States had made no public commitment, Moroccan nationalists were encouraged by the new focus on the principle of self-determination, the Atlantic Charter, and the United Nations. Early in 1944, Balafrej, who had assumed the leadership of the nationalist movement in El Fassi's absence, announced the formation of the Istiqlal, or Independence, party. The Istiqlal's manifesto, which had been worked out with the palace, demanded full independence. The French were so hostile to the manifesto that the Istiqlal leadership issued a clarification, emphasizing that they would not jeopardize the war effort and that they were opposed to violence. The nationalists also reassured the sultan of their loyalty, emphasizing that in a future independent state, the monarch would exercise complete control over the administration.

Allal el Fassi, head of the Istiqlal party, which led the movement for Moroccan independence.

Moroccans greeted the Istiqlal party with peaceful demonstrations of support in the main cities. The local French authorities responded firmly by arresting a score of nationalist leaders on charges of collaborating with the "enemy," that is, Nazi Germany. The mild-mannered Balafrej was arrested and shipped off to Corsica under house arrest. These arrests were followed by disorder, violence, deaths, and more detentions. Deprived of its leadership, the Istiqlal turned to younger militants to reorganize the party and pursue the campaign to win international support for the nationalist cause.

France, typically, tried to resolve the crisis by naming a new representative to Morocco. Resident General Eric Labonne initiated a more liberal policy, freeing the nationalist leaders, including El Fassi. Labonne also introduced a plan for economic reforms, providing for rural modernization and Moroccan participation in public corporations. These liberal concessions were rejected by conservative French settlers and by the Istiqlal, which now would accept nothing less than independence.

The Sultan Speaks Out

French hopes in the soft-spoken sultan were dashed after his visit to Tangier in 1947—the first since the establishment of the protectorates. Encouraged by the nationalists to play an increasingly active role, Mohammed V had persuaded the resident general to allow him to travel to the international city, passing through the Spanish zone. The French put stringent conditions on the expedition, including that residency officials should accompany the monarch at all of his receptions and review all speeches beforehand. The royal visit was a triumph for the sultan and the nationalists. In his public declarations, Mohammed V spoke of national unity and the desire to attain full rights. He stressed Morocco's attachment to the Muslim world and the Arab League and omitted any reference to French-Moroccan cooperation.

France reacted sharply to what was seen as an open challenge by the sultan and again changed the resident general. The new French envoy was General Alphonse Juin, a World War II hero, born in Algeria, and a known hardliner, who arrived with a plan for French-Moroccan municipal elections. The nationalists denounced Juin's plan as a move toward co-sovereignty, not envisaged under the protectorate treaty. Wary of this strategy, the sultan refused to sign decrees presented to him by the resident general. The monarch's strike resulted in a major crisis for Paris.

To resolve this impasse, French president Vincent Auriol invited Mohammed V for a state visit to Paris in October 1950. Amid a lavish show of hospitality, the sultan presented a memorandum, calling for an end to the protectorate regime as the way to improve relations. Although the sultan returned home empty-handed, the Moroccans gave him a hero's welcome, and it was clear he had become the symbol of nationalism, both for his people and the French government.

In the French Camp

When I first arrived in French Morocco in the fall of 1950, the country was ostensibly peaceful and enjoying a postwar economic boom, but it was divided into two hostile camps. Clearly dominant was the French residency's governing apparatus, including French banks, businesses, settlers, and military, which were allied with some Moroccan tribal chiefs and religious leaders. In opposition, the sultan and the nationalists were united in an undeclared pact and seemed to have the support of at least the urban masses.

An aspiring journalist, I was inadvertently thrust into the French camp because of my position as an *au pair* in a French military family. In light of the growing independence movements, I had thought Morocco would be a good place to begin as a freelance reporter. Besides, North Africa had come into American focus in the wake of World War II and the establishment of American bases. People back home at least had heard of Morocco now, and there was increased interest in news from the area.

Despite the exotic setting of Fez, my life was uneventful. I was restricted by an unwritten code to the French community and its routine of social gatherings and school events, like life in any French provincial town. There was virtually no contact with Moroccans, except servants and orderlies.

My only brush with history was as an observer of what became known as "the bombardment of Fez"—alarmist reports in the foreign press of an assault by Berber tribesmen on the former Arab capital. One weekend in February 1951, Berber horsemen had in fact camped around the walls of Fez, and the local French garrison went on the alert, but nothing happened. I went with my French family and many other French residents to take photos of the tribesmen with their magnificent steeds and gold and silver saddles and watch them prepare their evening feast of roast mutton. The next day, the tribesmen paraded through town, waving French flags, then disappeared as surreptitiously as they had come, and life returned to normal—except that I was inundated with mail from family and friends asking about the massacres at Fez and urging me to come home.

Seizing the chance to begin my freelance career, I contacted the French army's headquarters for its explanation of the events. A military spokesman referred me to the accounts of the colorful demonstration which had appeared in the local press. I was even more frustrated when, at the suggestion of army headquarters, journalists from *Paris Match* contacted me as "the only American witness" to the siege of Fez. At this point, I rebelled against the confines of my position. Without quitting my French family, I took a part-time job as a lecturer at the Fez *lycée*. There I met other members of the French community—civil servants, businesspeople, and intellectuals.

My new French friends told me that the so-called tribal movement against Fez was part of an operation aimed "to tame" the recalcitrant sultan, worked out by conservative colonial circles and Resident General Juin. Reluctant to attack the popular sovereign frontally, the resident general tried to force him to break with his main supporters, by accusing the Istiqlal party of Communism. In December 1950, General Juin expelled all nine Istiqlal members from the government council. A few weeks later, Juin issued an ultimatum to the sultan to sign all outstanding decrees and denounce the Istiqlal—or abdicate. At the same time, Juin ordered armed troops to surround the palace and threatened to unleash the tribes against the cities. As a last resort, the sultan called on the French government in Paris for help.

At this point, General Juin's main Berber ally, the *pasha* of Marrakech, had ordered his tribesmen to march on Fez. The "invasion" of the stronghold of nationalism had been an act of intimidation to force the sultan to disavow the Istiqlal and to persuade Paris to give free rein to Resident General Juin.

As anticipated, the French government, concerned over troubles in Indochina, ordered the sultan to yield to the resident general's demands, to avoid a bloodbath. Mohammed V had no alternative but to sign the protocol disavowing the methods of "a certain party"—the Istiqlal—and to dismiss a number of high officials known to be nationalists. The Glaoui's menacing tribesmen were promptly ordered home.

Undaunted, the depleted Istiqlal leadership met with other nationalist groups in Tangier in April 1951 and formed the National Front to fight for full independence and a constitutional and democratic monarchy. France reacted by sending a new resident general to replace Juin. From the outset, General Augustin Guillaume dashed any hopes of easing tension by his speeches, which denounced the nationalists and threatened to crush them. Positions had hardened on both sides, and violence seemed inevitable.

The View from Radio Maroc

My year's tour of duty with the French military family in Fez was nearly up. I had published several features and was beginning to understand the complexity of the situation. But there was still much to learn, and I wanted to remain in Morocco. Then I heard that Radio Maroc, the French protectorate's broadcasting station, planned to start an English-language program for the new American bases and was looking for a journalist. The salary was a pittance, but it was a chance to go to Rabat and follow the colonialist-nationalist struggle at close range.

Rabat looked like a flower-bedecked, whitewashed French town on the Côte d'Azur, encircled by medieval Moorish ramparts. Life in the Moroccan capital had the same dual quality. For the most part, the colonial lifestyle was very pleasant and moved at a relaxed pace. Yet just beneath the surface lay competing nationalist emotions ready to erupt. Despite the appearance of a firmly entrenched colonial society, backed by local feudal collaborators, Morocco in the mid-twentieth century was a key participant in the revolution of colonized people around the world, a struggle sharpened by Cold War rivalries.

My job at Radio Maroc was limited to reporting international news and local cultural events—no Moroccan politics. But I came into contact with the diverse society around me through colleagues from Radio Maroc's French, Spanish, Arabic, Berber, and Hebrew programs.

The American program was an anomaly in this country, which could not permit neutrality. The director was Catherine Tolliver, the American widow of a senior French protectorate official. Her assistant, Elinor Canedy, was a radio and television professional and wife of a U.S. Navy commander stationed at the American naval base at Port Lyautey, and I was the house journalist. We were counseled to avoid "controversial subjects" and complied since our program was a "friendly gesture" from the French to Americans living in Morocco.

Radio Maroc, however, turned out to be a good base for freelance work. To supplement my meager salary, I wrote a column in *Maroc Presse*'s American Edition, again with a taboo on local politics. But I soon became a regular contributor to the BBC's Arabic program and was obliged to concentrate on local politics. I developed a broad range of Moroccan contacts, which inevitably caused problems with the French protectorate authorities.

I soon found that even in the cosmopolitan capital of Rabat, there was a kind of social apartheid. Members of the royal family and senior Moroccan officials were usually included at official French galas, and the European colonists—mostly French—were permitted to attend official Moroccan feasts. But Europeans and Americans were expected not to socialize with ordinary Moroccan citizens, even those with positions in the protectorate administration.

One of the most popular Moroccan officials with the foreign community was the *pasha* of Marrakech. When he was not mobilizing his tribesmen against the sultan, the Glaoui was serving the French protectorate as genial host to the likes of U.S. defense secretary Charles Wilson, General Matthew Ridgeway, and other prominent personalities. Besides the constant round of elaborate banquets in his palace or hunting parties in the Atlas, the Glaoui offered his private golf course to the U.S. Air Force for the Fifth Air Division's annual invitational tournament. During the 1952 tournament, I accompanied my boss, Catherine Tolliver, who had obtained an audience with the Glaoui. I was disappointed in the legendary lord of the Atlas, who looked at us with a stony, rude gaze and showed no warmth, not even common courtesy.

We had wanted to get the *pasha*'s views on the French-American agreement to construct four American bases in Morocco, which had been negotiated without consulting the Moroccans and had angered the sultan. The Glaoui replied like a spokesman for the protectorate: "The bases have been allowed by the French government. I am always pleased by the very real friendship between the French people and the American people. That is why I am in full agreement with what the Americans are doing in connection with the French authorities."[13]

As a reporter for Radio Maroc, I was given easy entrée to the French residency and invited to attend innumerable inaugurations of French works:

ports and dams, hospitals and schools. There was no doubt in my mind but that the French were making an important contribution to the modern development of Morocco. It was just as obvious that the companies, the equipment, and financing were mostly French, and the main beneficiaries were French corporations and colonials, who were determined to remain in Morocco, and their staunch Moroccan friends like the Glaoui.

Royal Contacts

Ironically, it was easier to contact the Moroccan royal family than the nationalist leadership. I proposed doing a feature on the sultan and his family and how they lived for Radio Maroc, and my French superiors did not say no. I supposed it was because the French felt they could still reason with the sultan, whereas the Istiqlal was treated as a band of outlaws.

I had gotten to know Prince Moulay Abdallah shortly after my arrival through a mutual friend, a Moroccan-Jewish real estate agent. The tall young prince, who had his father's handsome features, was completing his studies in the Royal College. A relaxed, fun-loving boy, Moulay Abdallah preferred sports to politics. Occasionally he invited me to go dancing or hunting with his group of French and Moroccan friends, but I had little time for such pastimes.

I had also met Princess Lalla Aicha at informal gatherings in the home of her cousins Zeineb and Shedlya Rachid, close friends of mine. I admired the courageous princess, who drove her own car, wore a bathing suit on public beaches, and flaunted Muslim traditions. But no matter how hard I tried, Lalla Aicha rejected my friendly overtures. The Rachids suggested the princess might be envious of my freedom.

It was the older prince, Moulay Hassan, who interested me the most. The twenty-two-year-old prince had a lively sense of humor and quick repartee; he was a keen sportsman and enjoyed a good time, but was also deeply involved in politics. He used to brag that the Istiqlal activist Mehdi Ben Barka had been his mathematics professor at the Collège Royal. Moulay Hassan had obtained his master's degree in French law from Rabat's Institute of Juridical Studies, and was working for his degree in public law. I saw quite a bit of the prince socially, but he usually spoke guardedly in public. And so I welcomed the chance for serious talks when he offered to give me horse-riding lessons.

Moulay Hassan had a brilliant analytical mind and readily answered my questions on political events and their implications. He was thoroughly familiar with French politics and politicians and could predict their moves like a champion chess player. But he acknowledged that he did not understand Americans and would like to know them better. I introduced the prince to my colleague Elinor Canedy and her husband. In those tense times, Moulay Hassan seemed to take pleasure escaping from the palace to drop in at the Canedys' comfortable flat, and over hamburgers and soft drinks, ask questions about the United States. It was clear he enjoyed the American informality.

On one such occasion, I asked the prince about his father's meeting with President Roosevelt. Pointing out that he was only fourteen at the time, Moulay Hassan recalled that the American president had predicted "drastic change" in colonial affairs after the war. Privately, Roosevelt had assured the sultan that in recognition of his efforts for peace, Morocco would be independent "within ten years." Mohammed V had responded that he would call on the United States for help in the struggle for independence. But before the war's end, Roosevelt had died. Moulay Hassan said he could not understand why the United States had forgotten the president's promises and given free rein to France in postwar Morocco.[14]

Later, I learned that the protectorate authorities considered that, behind his playboy appearances, Moulay Hassan was his father's chief political adviser and link with the Istiqlal. This may have been so at the time, but the prince's relationship with the Istiqlal cooled considerably after independence, and their mutual distrust was one of the main problems facing the new Morocco.

Nationalists under Fire

It was more difficult for me, as an employee of the French protectorate, to meet the Istiqlal, many of whose leaders had been imprisoned or forced into exile. But with my BBC hat, I got to know Abderrahim Bouabid, the editor of the Istiqlal's French-language newspaper, early in 1952. Bouabid and Mehdi Ben Barka were the youngest founders of the Istiqlal and representatives of a new generation of nationalists who had brought a democratic dynamic to the movement of Islamic scholars and sons of notables. I would not meet Ben Barka until 1954 because he had been sent into political exile in the Sahara for three years.

Bouabid, thirty-two, was an impassioned spokesman for the nationalist cause—in impeccable French. With lanky good looks and an infectious smile, he had a natural sophistication combined with down-to-earth common sense. Son of a poor carpenter from Salé, Bouabid had completed high school while in prison for nationalist activities and then went on to study law in Paris.

For Bouabid, the fight against colonialism was essentially economic, a struggle against colonial financial groups that maintained a stranglehold over the economy, draining its natural resources. He emphasized that nationalism was only "a first step" to necessary social and economic changes; the main battle was yet to come against foreign and national vested interests, to establish a new and just order.[15]

Among his tasks, Bouabid had been delegated by the Istiqlal to help Moroccan union leaders take over the French Communist-dominated confederation. Their decision to call a general strike in December 1952, to protest the assassination of Tunisian trade union leader Ferhat Hached by French extremists was followed by fierce repression that changed the nature of the Moroccan struggle. French troops and police fired on unarmed Moroccan demonstrators, and French mobs freely lynched nationalists. A *New York Times* correspondent reported several hundred victims. *Agence France Presse* wrote of a vast political roundup with the arrest of 400 nationalists, Communists, and unionists. *Maroc Presse* called the operation a "rat trap."

What remained of the nationalist leadership went underground. The new young militants, who appeared in the vacuum, rejected the Istiqlal's political strategy and called for violence. At the same time, French colonials and their Moroccan feudal associates felt that with the Istiqlal out of the way, the time was ripe to get rid of the nationalist sultan once and for all.

As political passions rose to a feverish pitch that winter of 1952–1953, I turned to my Arabic teacher, M'hamed Douiri, to put the events in perspective. This well-groomed young man was assistant director of mines, one of the highest posts held by a Moroccan in the French protectorate administration. He was eager to practice his English, and I wanted to learn conversational Arabic, and so we had agreed to an exchange. But of course we talked more of politics than grammar. I appreciated his cool analytical reasoning.

Douiri was a French-Moroccan success story. Morocco's first mining engineer, he was a graduate of the French Ecole Polytechnique and the Ecole des Mines. Born in a modest family of Fez artisans, Douiri had won one of ten scholarships to a French university offered by the sultan in 1945. Douiri had planned to go into medicine but Mohammed V had persuaded him to study engineering because of the urgent need for technical cadres. A fervent nationalist, he told me he could best serve his country by doing his job. Only after independence did I learn that, with the decimation of the nationalist leadership at the end of 1952, Douiri had been named a member of the Istiqlal's secret Executive Committee.[16]

What was clear to me at the time was that the situation had become so polarized that most Moroccans had joined the nationalist movement, except for some notables and their unschooled followers.

There were ominous rumblings from the *caids* and religious brother-hoods in the countryside during the winter of 1952–1953. Douiri warned me that this was no spontaneous revolt against the palace. It was, in fact, a new phase in the plan initiated by General Juin and the colonial lobby to get rid of the independent-minded sultan. When the Glaoui toured the country, collecting signatures of *pashas* and *caids* to remove the sultan, it was obvi-ously with the encouragement of the French residency, Douiri pointed out. Likewise, he noted, the congress of North African religious brotherhoods or-ganized by the sultan's sworn enemy, *Sherif* Abdelhai Kittani, at Fez in April was done so with the blessings of French officials.

The Palace under Fire

In late May, the Glaoui and 270 *pashas*, *caids*, and other dignitaries formally presented a petition for the dethronement of Mohammed V because of al-leged links with "extremists," a euphemism for the Istiqlal party. I asked the French Information Department about France's response to this open act of rebellion against their protégé, the sultan.

"Our policy is one of total neutrality," a residency official said. "This is a Moroccan affair among Moroccans." At the radio, I was told to announce that "the *rapports* between Morocco and France will remain unchanged, whatever the outcome of the tribal revolt."

When I questioned Prince Hassan about the tribal rebellion, he said the problem was "a French matter." Under the protectorate treaty, he told me, the French government had pledged to support the Moroccan sovereign against any danger to his person or throne. The *caids* were civil servants of the palace and obliged to obey orders or resign. The sultan had received many petitions of loyalty and support from the *oulema* and other dignitaries, the prince stressed, adding that these declarations had not been reported by the French-controlled press—and the Moroccan press had been closed down.

It was clear that the palace was counting on Paris to intervene to end this mutiny. The sultan had sent his personal representatives to France to explain his position directly to French cabinet ministers, religious leaders, and press circles. French liberals, who opposed their country's colonial policies in North Africa, were working through a nongovernmental organization, the Comité France-Maghreb, to mobilize opinion in France against the attempts to de-pose the sultan.

In July 1953, the Canedys organized a small dinner for the prince's twenty-third birthday and my forthcoming trip to the Middle East. I had misgivings about leaving the country at that time but had been offered a rare opportunity to accompany a group of Moroccan pilgrims by bus across North Africa as far as the Islamic holy sites in Saudi Arabia. Moulay Hassan seemed genuinely dismayed when I told him of my plan and asked if I would arrange a contact to the foreign press, which couldn't be censored by the French, "if worse comes to worse."[17]

I was taken aback by his sober mien and the fact that he thought he might need foreign help. After all, the palace had survived similar crises. I gave him the name of a friend at the Associated Press, and the Canedys said they would be there to provide moral support. Moulay Hassan soon recovered his good spirits, agreed to give me an interview on palace life, and promised to introduce me to his father and mother when I returned from the Middle East.

That didn't happen. I was in Beirut when I learned that the sultan and his family had been exiled to Corsica on August 20, 1953, and replaced by an unknown, elderly cousin, Mohammed Ben Arafa. I was shocked by the news and felt like a traitor for not being in Morocco to report the events. When I returned a month later, I found everything had changed. The country looked like an armed camp, with detachments of French troops and police around the main cities. The French press reported acts of terrorism, retaliatory raids, arrests, and reprisals. People in the streets appeared glum, suspicious, and vengeful.

The exiled Sultan Mohammed ben Youssef and his family, who were later transferred to Madagascar, were now taboo. Most of my Moroccan friends had been arrested or gone into exile. Even Douiri had been interrogated at length and resigned in protest against the sultan's banishment. How, I wondered, had the monarch's enemies succeeded in ousting him when it was clear that he had the support of the majority of his people and important friends in France?

French colleagues filled me in on the events leading up to the royal ouster, even though they had not been permitted to report the facts in the local press. I learned that most Europeans believed the official line that Mohammed V had been "a tool of Istiqlal extremists," that is, Communists, and had been overthrown by a popular movement of tribal leaders and religious brotherhoods.

When Paris refused to act on the petition of 270 *pashas* and *caids* to oust the sultan, a Casablanca newspaper close to the colonial lobby decided to force the issue. It published a menacing statement attributed to the Glaoui, warning the French government that there was "not one more minute to lose" and the revolution would take place in Morocco "with or without" France. This threat, which was eventually retracted by the *pasha*, had the desired effect. Persuaded that the Glaoui and his tribes were prepared to massacre the French population, Paris had no choice but to give the resident general carte blanche to depose the sultan.

In his authoritative account, *The Franco-Moroccan Conflict*, Stephane Bernard writes that the French cabinet had two choices: keep Mohammed on the throne and use force against tribal chiefs and notables loyal to France, or exile the sultan and risk protests from the Istiqlal and the Arab world. The resident general was instructed to go to the sultan and urge him to abdicate, since the tribes were rising on all sides. Mohammed V refused to abdicate but agreed to leave the country with his family.[18]

Other details came from Elinor Canedy, who had kept in close contact with Moulay Hassan. The palace was practically under siege that final week and the prince was a virtual prisoner, unable to leave the palace grounds without a guard. She noted that the prince had not realized the gravity of the situation until the end. He continued to expect that the foreign missions in Rabat—if not the French, then the Americans, or British, or Russians—would intervene and put an end to the hard-liners' machinations. "Why don't they say something or do something?" he asked her over and over again. "They see what's happening."[19]

The New Resistance

Following the exile of the royal family, several developments changed the political scene entirely. Almost overnight, the quiet, retiring Sultan Mohammed V became a hero in the struggle against colonialism throughout the Third World. The nationalist movement, with its political leadership silenced, turned to violence, and the Moroccan resistance was reborn. There were also new French players on the Moroccan stage: a vocal liberal movement and a vicious counterterrorist organization. Then there was Spain, the co-protector, which had not been consulted by France over the decision to oust the sultan. Annoyed by France's unilateral action, Spain refused to recognize Mohammed V's replacement. What's more, Spanish colonial authorities discreetly provided bases and aid to the Moroccan resistance.

Probably no leader in Moroccan history has commanded such adoration and loyalty as Sultan Mohammed ben Youssef. The more the French press attacked the deposed sultan for alleged excesses—concubines and illicit affairs, a proliferation of horses and automobiles, shady business deals—the more beloved he became to Moroccans. Despite official French attempts to blot out the memory of Mohammed V, Moroccans seized every opportunity to march through the streets chanting the sultan's name and brandishing portraits of the royal family. In a kind of mass hysteria, citizens around the kingdom claimed to see the monarch's face in the full moon. Even the mosques were empty because people refused to say prayers in the name of the usurper, Ben Arafa.

For the first time in the long nationalist struggle, the country was wracked by terror. In the past, the Istiqlal had come under pressure from militants to react to French violence with Moroccan violence. But the Istiqlal leadership had firmly opposed any form of terrorism. With the exile of Mohammed V and the disbanding of the Istiqlal, militant nationalists were left to act on their own. As Douglas Ashford writes, "The French clique who virtually ruled Morocco from 1953 on had destroyed the one device at their disposal for preventing the bloodshed and destruction that followed"—the Istiqlal party.[20]

The terrorist acts began right after the exile of Mohammed V with isolated cases of arson, sabotage, stonings, knifings, shootings, and bomb explosions. At first the campaign didn't attract international attention because the victims were mostly pro-French Moroccan informers—shopkeepers, water carriers, petty officials, policemen. Later, resistants organized several unsuccessful attacks on "the puppet sultan" and his master, the Glaoui. Almost daily, trains were derailed, French farms burned, and French shops, cafes, and cinemas boycotted. The climate of insecurity was widespread.

The resistants generally came from the ranks of the Istiqlal and were mostly obscure workers, shopkeepers, peasants, and unemployed people convinced that nothing could be gained by the political struggle and the only solution was direct action. They began as small isolated cells and later formed two clandestine armed groups: the Secret Organization in urban areas and the Liberation Army in the countryside.

Allal ben Abdallah, an unknown house painter from Rabat, became the first martyr of the resistance when he attacked "the French sultan" Ben Arafa with a kitchen knife, as Ben Arafa rode on horseback to Friday prayers on September 11, 1953, only weeks after Mohammed V's exile. The startled Ben Arafa fell from his steed but escaped unharmed, while the assailant was shot and killed by a member of the French guard.

The first devastating act of terrorism claimed by the resistance was the explosion in Casablanca's central market on Christmas Eve 1953, which killed twenty-six people. Mohamed Zerktouni, a carpenter, former Istiqlal militant, and head of the Secret Organization, was arrested and accused of planning the attack. Zerktouni committed suicide by poison at the Casablanca police station rather than disclose secrets of the organization. The resistance had taken over the nationalist movement and seemed out of control.

French Repression and Counterterror

The French protectorate authorities reacted to the nationalist attacks with force, establishing a state of siege. Army squads patrolled the countryside and police forces cordoned off volatile neighborhoods in the cities. I recall that on the first anniversary of the sultan's exile, there were peaceful demonstrations in the cities calling for the return of Mohammed V. In Fez, the situation got out of hand when some students threw stones at the Moroccan security forces, who responded by firing on the demonstrators. Moving to stifle the nationalist agitation once and for all, the French sealed off the quarter of a million inhabitants for two weeks. Once again, Berber tribesmen were ordered to surround Fez, while French troops with machine guns were stationed at the gates to the city and Foreign Legion marksmen were posted on rooftops. During this show of force, Moroccans shouted, "*Vive* Sidi Mohammed ben Youssef!" and "*Vive* Mendès-France!"—a sign they still hoped that France would intervene to curb its colonial hard-liners.

By 1954 the situation in Paris had changed dramatically. Socialist premier Pierre Mendès-France had taken steps to end the war in Indochina and open negotiations with Tunisia for internal autonomy. A Ministry of Moroccan and Tunisian Affairs had been set up to negotiate with the nationalists. A civilian resident general was named to Rabat, with the mission to restore order and lead Morocco to self-government.

I had met French liberals in Morocco, particularly among my colleagues at *Maroc Presse*, who were very critical of colonial abuses, but they were isolated voices, drowned out by the conservative majority of French colonials. Only after the removal of Mohammed V did the liberals come together and make themselves heard. Their first public stand was the Letter of the Seventy-five, which was sent to French president René Coty on May 8, 1954. Highlighting the *cycle de violence*, the petitioners demanded a change in French policy, the liberation of political prisoners, and the implementation of necessary reforms. Among these unsung heroes were Antoine Mazella, editor in chief, and Henri Sartout, director of *Maroc Presse*, who published the letter in defiance of a ban by protectorate authorities. Signatories included a few brave journalists like Bertrand Bellaigue, lawyers, professors, engineers, and entrepreneurs. A wealthy Casablanca businessman, Jacques Lemaigre-Dubreuil, had taken over *Maroc Presse* after the sultan's exile, and he used it to express the views of French and Moroccan liberals, who went so far as to call on Paris to restore Morocco's sovereignty.

But the French government's new liberal approach to colonial issues had a reverse effect in Morocco. Colonial extremists, alarmed by Mendès-France's conciliatory gestures and moves to grant autonomy to Tunisia, decided to take matters into their own hands. In 1954, European counterterrorism made its appearance with underground groups like the Organization for Anti-Terrorist Defense, linked to the powerful settler lobby, Présence Française. These vigilantes acted with broad impunity and were known to have sympathizers in the police force. Their main targets were liberals, who were trying to find some kind of solution to the cycle of violence. The counterterrorists gunned down a few wealthy Moroccans for supporting the Istiqlal and, on several occasions, attacked the offices of *Maroc Presse*. There was as yet no question of restoring Mohammed V to his throne. But the resident general, Francis Lacoste, did free many Istiqlal leaders and unionists, among them Mehdi Ben Barka.

Ben Barka, a slight figure with lively dark eyes and bushy eyebrows, was like no other Moroccan I had met. He was very "American" in temperament, with boundless energy and a capacity to absorb new ideas rapidly, coupled with a natural optimism and an indomitable spirit. During his three years under house arrest in the Sahara and High Atlas, Ben Barka had taken correspondence courses in English and political economics, perfected his Arabic, and learned Berber. He had also organized Istiqlal cells in the desert region, until the authorities got wind of this activity and deported him to Imilchil, where he was completely isolated. Nevertheless, he managed to get messages out to the Istiqlal and to Arab delegations at the United Nations.

On his release in October 1954, Ben Barka's main task was to reorganize the Istiqlal, badly weakened by the waves of arrests. He also became official spokesman for the nationalist movement with the English-language press since few Istiqlal leaders spoke fluent English. In my work for the BBC, I saw quite of bit of the nationalist spokesman, and we soon became friends. Ben Barka's home in a modest working quarter of Rabat was like a dentist's office. There were always visitors waiting in the small rooms off the central patio. French officials from Paris, foreign correspondents, trade union representatives, and Roman Catholic priests rubbed shoulders with Istiqlal militants, unionists, and clandestine resistants. Ben Barka was also the chief liaison between the Istiqlal and the resistance movement.

The resistance had grown up separately from the Istiqlal and had its own clandestine organizations, although many militants were former Istiqlal members. After the death of Zerktouni, chief artisan of the terrorist attack on the Casablanca market, Fqih Basri, a fiery Arabic scholar, assumed leadership of the Secret Organization, an urban resistance group. When the budding urban terror provoked brutal repression, the resistance changed tactics, forming the Moroccan Liberation Army in the Spanish zone. Links were established with the Algerian Liberation Army, which had launched its own guerrilla war in 1954.

That spring of 1955, a new opposition organization appeared on the scene, the Union Marocaine du Travail, which became a powerful ally of the Istiqlal in the fight for independence. Mahjoub ben Seddik, a forceful Istiqlal militant and railroad union man, had formed the Moroccan labor federation in defiance of protectorate laws, which allowed only French unions. He had the backing of the U.S.-supported International Confederation of Free Trade Unions, which was engaged in a fierce struggle for influence in Africa against the French Communist-dominated Confédération Générale du Travail. This was the Cold War in all its ambiguity. American labor unions were giving open support to Moroccan nationalist unions against French Communist unions. But American government officials, allies of France in NATO, could not contact the Moroccan nationalists of the Istiqlal party, because they had been labeled by the French as Communists.

Although my French superiors at Radio Maroc warned me against Moroccan contacts, they were reluctant to take action against an American journalist. I was careful to abide by the radio station's unwritten taboos on local politics. Nevertheless as things deteriorated after the exile of the royal family, I became increasingly frustrated and began to work on a book about the Moroccan struggle for independence.

When I told Ben Barka about the book, he urged me to focus on the palace and the Moroccan people, not the Istiqlal. The French ultras, he stressed, had succeeded in tainting the image of the Istiqlal with charges of Communism, terrorism, Islamic extremism, and all kinds of base crimes. Writing about the Istiqlal at that point could damage the national cause. Ben Barka insisted that it was urgent to alert American public opinion to the dangers of civil war and the need to restore King Mohammed V, as the only means to bring stability and calm to the country. There would be time to write about the Istiqlal later, he promised.[21] I had to agree with my pragmatic friend. It was clear that the nationalist movement's hopes now depended on the return of the exiled sultan.

The Cycle of Violence

On June 11, 1955, the owner of *Maroc Presse*, Lemaigre-Dubreuil, was shot down by machine-gun fire in front of his apartment building in Casablanca, apparently by colonial extremists. Conscious they had lost a friend, thousands of Moroccans gathered at the Casablanca cathedral for the funeral. The murder of the liberal French publisher shocked Paris. Mendès-France's successor, Premier Edgar Faure, sent a new representative to Rabat, with instructions to clean up the Moroccan mess.

Resident General Gilbert Grandval, known to be close to General de Gaulle, dismissed several French police officers, expelled the head of Présence Française, and arrested three suspected French counterterrorists linked to the Lemaigre-Dubreuil assassination. He also released Moroccan political prisoners and opened discussions with the nationalists to work out a political solution that would meet the approval of the exiled sultan. De Gaulle was said to have told Grandval that the only way out of the crisis was the reinstallation of Mohammed V on the throne. Initially the resident general opposed the return but gradually he realized that it was inevitable.[22]

Grandval's attempts to overhaul the protectorate administration provoked new hostility among the archcolonialists, who were not prepared to give up their privileges. In a preview of the French colonial insurrection in neighboring Algeria, French mobs in Morocco denounced Grandval at every occasion, physically assaulting him and hurling anti-Semitic epithets at him. The resident general stood up to the insults, but there was little he could do against the new cycle of violence. On Bastille Day, July 14, 1955, a powerful explosion took place at a popular cafe at Mers Sultan Square in Casablanca, killing seven Europeans and injuring many more. The Mers Sultan bomb provided the pretext for renewed activity by the Organization of Anti-Terrorist Defense. Stephen Hughes writes that the French extremists would cruise around Casablanca in black Citroens, firing indiscriminately on Moroccans and terrorizing citizens.[23]

Although the French government still opposed the return of Mohammed V, it had agreed to meet with his representatives and nationalist leaders at the resort of Aix-les-Bains in September 1955. Bouabid, who headed the Istiqlal delegation, told me that he hoped the talks would restore the Sultan to his throne and bring about reconciliation between the French and Moroccans. But once more, a political solution was undermined by extremists on both sides.

On the second anniversary of the sultan's exile a few weeks before the peace talks got under way, riots broke out in several Moroccan cities, and dozens of Moroccans were killed by security forces. This was followed by tribal uprisings at the Middle Atlas town of Oued Zem and the phosphate mines at Khouribga, in which 300 European employees and their families were massacred. In response hundreds, perhaps thousands, of Moroccan tribesmen and their families were killed by the French army and air force.

No one claimed credit for the bloodbath, which seemed aimed at destroying any chances for a negotiated settlement to the Moroccan crisis. An immediate result was the removal of the liberal Resident General Grandval and his replacement by a disciple of General Juin, General Pierre Boyer de La Tour. His mission was to get control over the tribes and the colonialists and persuade the ineffectual Sultan Ben Arafa to abdicate in favor of a throne council.

The French-Moroccan talks continued at Aix-les-Bains but soon bogged down over the composition of the throne council and the fate of Mohammed V. Bouabid told me the French had agreed to restore Morocco as a sovereign state, with freely accepted ties of interdependence.[24] French leaders, however, refused to restore the deposed monarch, because it would mean a loss of face and rebellion by irate colonials.

The political process was again interrupted by violence. On October 1, 1955, the Liberation Army launched its offensive from Spanish Morocco against French posts in the northeastern region of Taza. From Cairo, Allal el Fassi announced that the Moroccan Liberation Army was engaged in a struggle to free Sultan Mohammed V and all of North Africa. The Moroccan and Algerian offensives were now under a joint command. This was the first time the Istiqlal leader assumed responsibility for the clandestine guerrilla movement, providing justification for a new campaign of repression against the Istiqlal party.

As Morocco was once more caught up in a cycle of violence with no end in sight, I flew to New York for the publication of my book. I wanted to get the Moroccan story out before it was too late and the country sank into chaos. My book was hardly in print when everything changed.

The Return of the Exiles

As the North African liberation armies stepped up their pressure on the ground, Paris concluded that to save French Algeria, a settlement must be reached in Morocco as soon as possible. Events surged forward at an incredible pace. French emissaries dispatched to Madagascar won the sultan's approval of a throne council and arranged for his return to France. But French ultras in Morocco categorically rejected this solution and called for armed resistance. Resident General Boyer de La Tour reassured the colonial establishment that there would be no throne council and that Mohammed V would not return to the throne. In reaction to this hard line, the Istiqlal delegates, who had accepted the throne council, now rejected it and demanded the immediate return of the sultan and abrogation of the protectorate treaty.

Ironically, the stalemate was broken by the sultan's erstwhile foe, the Glaoui. On October 25, 1955, the *pasha* of Marrakech issued a statement expressing hope for the prompt restoration of Mohammed V, "who alone is able to unite the people in peace." The next day, the Istiqlal declared that the Aix-les-Bains accords were obsolete and demanded the return of Mohammed V. On October 30, Ben Arafa was persuaded to abdicate, and Sidi Mohammed ben Youssef was flown from Madagascar to Nice.

The French government had planned for the royal exile to remain in the south of France, but the monarch insisted on going directly to Paris, according to his biographer. "As soon as the Sultan stepped upon French soil, he made it quite clear that he did not consider himself a refugee, but a sovereign," Rom Landau says.[25] He describes the Glaoui's moving act of submission in the grand reception room at Mohammed V's French headquarters in the Henri IV Pavilion at St. Germain en Laye:

> Glaoui crawled in on hands and knees, his head bowed to the floor. He kissed Sidi Mohammed's grey robe, then his feet, and prostrated himself four times. "I am a slave at the feet of Your Majesty," whispered the seventy-eight years old "leader of the Berbers," and then expressed the hope that his sovereign might forgive him. Mohammed ben Youssef showed his perennial magnanimity, by forgiving instantly his most implacable enemy of many years. "Do not speak to me any more of the past," he said. "What counts is the future and it is on what you do in the future that you will be judged."[26]

On November 6, the sultan told French foreign minister Antoine Pinay that he was ready to form a Moroccan government, representing different political currents, which would prepare institutional reforms and negotiate new links of interdependence with France. Paris had finally accepted the inevitable.

Ten days later, Mohammed V flew home as a national hero and was given a frenzied welcome by more than a million Moroccans. On November 18, the twenty-eighth anniversary of his accession to the throne, Mohammed V called on the nation "to mobilize all the energies available for the construction of a new Morocco." Addressing a euphoric crowd massed in front of the palace, the monarch declared, "Our first objective is the constitution of a responsible and representative Moroccan government, truly expressive of the people's will." The Moroccan sovereign emphasized that cooperation with France and the West was essential, but these relations were not incompatible with preservation of the spiritual and cultural bonds with other Arab peoples.[27]

Shortly afterward, the sultan formed his government of "national union," naming his old friend M'Barek Bekkai as prime minister. The cabinet was dominated by the Istiqlal but included representatives of the Democratic Party for Independence, independents, and a member of the Jewish community.

On March 2, 1956, France abrogated the Treaty of Fez and recognized

Moroccan independence, while Moroccans agreed to work out conventions on the rights of French citizens and cooperation in fields of common interest. On April 7, Madrid recognized Moroccan sovereignty over the northern zone, with the exception of five small presidios and Spanish Sahara in the south. The international zone of Tangier was reintegrated into the kingdom a few months afterward, but retained its financial privileges for several years.

Touring the United States for the publication of my book, I had missed the triumphal return of the royal family. But when I went back to Morocco a month later, the country was still in the throes of celebration. I had sent a telegram of congratulations to the prince and told him that the *New York Times* and *Time* had hired me as a part-time correspondent but wanted me to report on Algeria, where the struggle for independence was gaining momentum.

Shortly after my arrival in Rabat, Moulay Hassan and a group of old palace friends came to the tiny villa where I was renting a room to invite me to a Christmas Eve/Independence Eve party. I seized the chance to apologize for the misleading title of my book, *The Prince and I* (the publisher's idea). Graciously, Moulay Hassan said what mattered was the contents not the title. Then he urged me not to give up on Morocco.

"Independence is just the beginning of our problems," the prince said. "We've got to start all over and build a nation out of chaos. In forty years, the protectorate succeeded in sapping our national strength and natural resources and left us in a vacuum with only the throne to cling to."[28]

The prince was right about the monumental problems. The kingdom was totally unprepared for self-government, lacking cadres in every domain, and yet the public demanded a new and better life. While the monarchy was an important unifying factor, it was a mistake to believe that the nationalists, who had struggled so long and hard for independence, would be willing to retire and simply cling to the throne.

The Long Shadow of King Hassan II

4

*F*or the Moroccan masses, he was an all-powerful ruler, spiritual guide, and national savior. For his enemies and victims, he was the embodiment of tyranny and oppression. For the world at large, he was a political leader of exceptional abilities, one of the foremost statesmen of his time. What is undisputed is that modern Moroccan history essentially revolves around the controversial figure of King Hassan, who succeeded his revered father, King Mohammed V, in 1961, and ruled as an enlightened despot for thirty-eight years.

Under Hassan II, Morocco gained renown as an oasis of stability in a troubled continent, a moderate pro-Western Muslim country, and a force for peace in the Middle East. Since independence, the country gradually developed a prosperous national elite and a growing middle class. Morocco's progress and calm, however, could not hide enormous social disparities. Nor could it erase *les années de plomb*—the years of lead in the 1970s and 1980s— a time of political trials, torture, disappearances, rebellions, and repression.

I had known Prince Moulay Hassan as an engaging, brilliant, French-educated nationalist who admired the American way of life and was imbued with his mission to modernize the archaic country. But after he donned the ceremonial robes of king and Commander of the Faithful, he seemed transformed into a distant and arrogant autocrat.

Mohammed V and the Séquelles of Colonialism

Mohammed V was known as the liberator of his country and had regained his throne as a powerful unifying force. His moral stature and ability as an arbiter got Morocco through the extremely difficult postcolonial period. He also proved to be a skilled politician, retaining good relations with the former protectors while establishing new ties with the United States and Communist countries and consolidating links with the conservative Arab world and African radicals.

Although he had not received a modern education, Mohammed V was a man of his times and fully aware that independent Morocco could not revert to the feudal autocracy of the precolonial period. After his triumphal return from exile, the monarch declared in his Throne Speech of November 18, 1955, that his first objective would be to establish "a responsible and representative Government," whose primary mission would be "the creation of democratic institutions resulting from free elections and founded on the principle of the separation of powers, with the framework of a constitutional monarchy, granting Moroccans of all faiths the rights of citizenship and the exercise of public and trade union freedoms."[1]

I first met Mohammed V not long after independence. The sultan had changed his title to king as a sign of his determination to transform his country into a modern democracy. Prince Moulay Hassan had promised to introduce me to his father, and the opportunity came on the royal train during an official visit to Marrakech. It's not easy to talk to an idol, but the king had the gift of putting strangers at ease. His regard was direct, his manner gentle, and his handshake cordial and firm. He said that he already knew of me and then, soberly, thanked me for my friendship toward his country "during our difficult time."

It was King Mohammed's simplicity and dignity that impressed me and almost everyone who encountered him. He did not appear to be a feudal lord who delighted in pomp and lavish living. He generally dressed in the plain wool robe, or *djellaba*, that traditional Moroccans of every class wear. The king had received little French schooling and was more at ease speaking in colloquial Arabic with his servants than frequenting intellectual salons. It is difficult to reconcile this modest, retiring, popular monarch with the image depicted in Ignace Dalle's book of an avaricious ruler secretly transferring much of his fortune abroad should he have to go into exile again.[2]

What is certain is that Mohammed V proved to be a master of compromise and reconciliation. As soon as he returned to the throne, he set out to unite the country's divergent political factions and went out of his way to restore good relations with the former colonial powers and their Moroccan collaborators. When people were calling for a settling of accounts, the sovereign pardoned his adversaries. On the eve of independence, Mohammed V appealed to Moroccans for calm, warning that independence does not mean the reign of license and anarchy.

Those were heady, unbridled days—the early months of independence.

It was a time of liberation and participation in the affairs of state. It also meant rivalry among the nationalists. The Istiqlal party, which had led the fight for independence, demanded a dominant say in the new government. The Liberation Army, whose pressure had accelerated the rush to independence, wanted its due. Other factions formed parties and competed for a voice in the new Morocco. At the same time, there was a dangerous vacuum of law and order. Moroccans disdained colonial law and demanded new laws, while public opinion was a law unto itself. The uneducated masses believed that independence meant that the French and Spanish should go, leaving their villas, farms, shops, industries, and jobs to the victors.

Morocco's industries and finances were still largely controlled by European banks, mainly French. French settlers also owned most of the country's 3 million acres of good farmland. Many of the 500,000 French colonials and 100,000 Spanish held the senior jobs in the administration, official services, and military. The overwhelming majority of the 10 million Moroccans was poor and had benefited little from colonialism's economic miracle. Public expectations of the new independent rulers were high, too high. The nationalists' dream had been to eliminate the two Moroccos and bring about equal opportunity for all. But the continued widening of the gap—no longer between colonials and colonized but between the privileged Moroccan elite and the others—created public frustration, at first exploited by the radical Left and more recently by Islamic extremists.

Mohammed V was clearly aware of the imbalance of wealth in his country, but he was no revolutionary. The king resisted pressures from the Left for agrarian reform and the nationalization of productive sectors. There was no takeover of colonial lands until 1973, and by that time most foreign settlers had sold their properties and gone. Instead, King Mohammed called for education and technical training to prepare Moroccans to participate in a modern economy. For the king, agrarian reform meant modernization of traditional agriculture—which had been left virtually untouched under the protectorate. In the fall of 1957, His Majesty mounted a tractor to support the nationalist government's Operation Plow, which aimed to introduce agricultural machinery and improved methods to small farmers. But the program was doomed to failure because of the absence of any real agrarian reform.

The immediate challenge facing King Mohammed was insecurity. Security forces were almost nonexistent in the post-independence period. The population would no longer accept the French police, and a Moroccan police had to be formed. The Liberation Army became a major problem, with guerrilla bands roaming the countryside, living by the rule of violence. In urban centers, resistance groups turned on each other or demanded high administrative posts as their just reward for their role in the fight for independence.

The king moved resolutely to deal with these unruly loyalists. Within a few months, most of the urban resistants were incorporated into the ranks of the new police force, under direct control of the palace. At the same time, the majority of the Liberation Army soldiers were absorbed by the Royal Armed Forces, led by Prince Moulay Hassan. Some irregulars made their way south, with the blessings of the authorities, to join the Saharan Liberation Army, which continued to press Spain to abandon its Saharan territories.

There were still four foreign armies present in independent Morocco. The U.S. forces were the least visible; they kept close to their bases and avoided any incidents with the local population. French troops posted around the country clashed frequently with the budding Moroccan army. And there were battles with Spanish forces stationed along the disputed Saharan frontier. With persistence and diplomatic ability, Mohammed V was able to persuade the United States to close its bases by June 1960, France to pull out its troops by March 1961, and Spain to evacuate most of its territory the following year.

The other foreign force, which Morocco couldn't get rid of easily, was the Algerian Liberation Army. Moroccans at all levels identified and sympathized with the Algerian cause. Independent Morocco served as a key military base for the Algerian guerrillas and a conduit for arms and shelter for some 50,000 Algerian refugees—all under cover because of the constraints imposed by links of interdependence with France.

Prince Moulay Hassan, who was charged with setting up the Royal Armed Forces, spoke to me of Morocco's delicate predicament several months after independence. Morocco, he stressed, had received important aid from France to build the new army and could not send troops off to fight against the French in Algeria. Moroccan negotiators, still working out the terms of interdependence with France—including a substantial loan—could not turn around and give material aid to the Algerian Liberation Front. Nor could Morocco import arms for the Algerians in the view of sizable contingents of French military. "We can support the Algerian nationalists morally and diplomatically, but our first duty is to rebuild Morocco into a strong nation after our long struggle for independence," the prince told me.[3]

Algerian nationalists, aware of Morocco's dilemma, carried out their operations covertly. "All we want from our Moroccan brothers is freedom of movement and logistics," an Algerian Liberation Army chief told me. In fact, an important source of aid for the Algerian fighters came from the Moroccan Liberation Army, which not only provided soldiers but also villas, farms, and automobiles, which had been confiscated from "traitors." The Algerians got some arms from the Moroccan irregulars, but obtained the bulk of their weapons and munitions for high prices through international dealers in the still-open city of Tangier.

It was a *drôle de guerre*. Algerian Liberation Army chiefs could be seen buying copies of Mao Zedong's handbook on guerrilla warfare in fashionable French bookstores in Casablanca and Rabat. French forces in eastern Algeria openly fired across the border into independent Morocco at suspected Algerian targets. (Even an American Quaker family, working on the Moroccan side of the border, had been shot at.) The Moroccans threatened hot pursuit but didn't follow up.

Meanwhile, in the glow of the independence accords, Moroccan, French, and Spanish leaders were pledging eternal friendship and cooperation and dreaming of a "West Mediterranean Union." But the euphoria dissipated as suddenly as it had materialized. An international incident served to puncture the Moroccans' illusions of liberty and remind them that their fate was intricately linked to Algeria's.

In October 1957, a Moroccan airliner flying the Algerian nationalist leader Mohamed ben Bella and four companions from Rabat to Tunis was rerouted to Algiers by the French pilot. King Mohammed denounced this act of air piracy against the Algerians, who had been his official guests, and demanded their immediate release. While the king's cabinet ministers wanted to sever diplomatic relations with France over the incident, Mohammed V characteristically chose to compromise, merely recalling Morocco's ambassador to Paris. The Moroccan public, however, was enraged over the hijacking, seen as an insult to their king and their independence. A group of militants went on a rampage in the prosperous farm area of Meknès, burning a dozen French farms and killing fifty Europeans, mostly French. Mohammed V declared that whatever the reason, street disorders would not be permitted and ordered the rioters to stop. They did.

In those difficult early years of independence, King Mohammed demonstrated wise and effective leadership. There were no revolutionary courts, no mass expropriations, and fewer vendettas than expected after the bitter struggle for freedom. In fact, the king granted pardon to all penitents. I believe that had Mohammed V not died prematurely, the country would have been spared much of the political infighting and violence that characterized his son's rule.

Palace Politics

Moroccan independence hadn't taken place in a vacuum. It followed a historic event in 1955, the first Afro-Asian Conference, remembered simply for its venue, Bandung in Indonesia, where Third World leaders stood up and declared themselves opposed to colonialism and imperialism. This marked the birth of the Non-Aligned Movement, which rejected Cold War alliances and struck out on a path of its own, voting often with the Communist bloc, developing close links with Communist mavericks Cuba, China, and Yugoslavia, but preserving economic and cultural ties with the West.

It wasn't an easy time for Arab monarchies. Jordan's King Abdullah was assassinated in July 1951, to be succeeded by his grandson Hussein, who managed to preserve the throne despite the volatile situation in the Middle East. In Egypt, the heartland of the Arab world, the dissolute King Farouk was overthrown in 1952 by a group of leftwing military officers, who declared a republic. In Tunisia, the nationalist leader Habib Bourguiba won independence for his country a few weeks after Morocco's independence and terminated the monarchy the following year. Iraq suffered a wrenching coup in July 1958, when a group of military revolutionaries overthrew the monarchy and murdered the young King Faisal.

Morocco's King Mohammed, however, had regained his throne at the end of 1955 with enormous political capital. Here was a nationalist martyr, who before exile had worked closely with the independence movement. At the outset of his reign, Mohammed V appeared to be the single unifying figure in this ethnically, socially, and politically diverse country. Conservative leaders El Fassi and Balafrej showed the utmost respect for the monarch, while young leftists like Ben Barka and Bouabid had only words of praise for him. Feudal lords and wealthy merchants supported him fervently. Berbers of the High Atlas Mountains, who resented the dominant urban Arabs, pledged unconditional loyalty to Sidi Mohammed ben Youssef.

Under the independence agreement of March 2, 1956, the king retained all sovereign powers. He named his close friend M'Barek Bekkai to be prime minister and other palace men to the key ministries of defense and interior. The National Police Force was put directly under the king, and his son Prince Hassan was given the delicate mission to establish the Royal Armed Forces.

It was evident, however, that an important sector of the nationalist movement was influenced by modern, Western thinking and would be unwilling to return to the arbitrary rule of the past. The first government was divided among the different political forces, the Istiqlal receiving the most posts because of its dominant role in the struggle for independence. However, in an effort to unify the nation, King Mohammed brought in representatives from the smaller Democratic party and independents.

True to his promise to introduce democratic rule, the king took the first step by setting up the National Consultative Assembly in October 1956. This experimental parliament, with only deliberative powers, was to be a forum for debate on the budget, social and economic questions, and foreign policy. Its seventy-six members were appointed by the king and represented the political parties and independents, labor unions, agricultural associations, professional groups, and religious scholars. Dominated by the Istiqlal and the Labor Federation, the assembly elected Ben Barka as its president and became a loud voice for reform and public grievances.

Ben Barka soon demonstrated his leadership qualities. Using the Istiqlal machinery, he launched various projects to mobilize the general public. His most spectacular success was the Unity Road, inaugurated by King Mohammed in the summer of 1957. Some 10,000 young volunteers worked together to build a forty-mile road through the rugged Rif Mountains, linking the former French and Spanish zones, in just two months. Also with government backing, Ben Barka launched a mass literacy campaign, using party and labor union facilities. When King Mohammed inaugurated Operation Plow, it was Ben Barka who mustered the Istiqlal's grassroots to implement the program. It became apparent to the palace that Ben Barka was a formidable organizer and achiever—virtues uncommon among the Moroccan elite. King Mohammed wisely put to use Ben Barka's talents, but Prince Hassan considered him a dangerous rival.

In the early years of independence, King Mohammed V appreciated Socialist leader Mehdi Ben Barka for his leadership and organizational skills, but Prince Hassan viewed the activist as a dangerous rival. Here, in the late 1950s, King Mohammed, center, wearing a light djellaba and dark glasses, with Ben Barka on his left, dressed in a dark Western suit and fez, with Prince Hassan behind him in his uniform as chief of the Royal Armed Forces. (AFP/Getty Images)

In the wake of independence, Ben Barka and other Istiqlal leaders had demanded "a homogeneous government," another way of saying a one-party state, prevalent in the newly independent countries. The nation faced overwhelming problems in transforming colonial economic and social structures, they argued. Since there was a desperate lack of cadres to tackle these tasks, the country could ill afford the luxury of democratic politics. But King Mohammed insisted that political forces be balanced and kept his trusted friend Si Bekkai as prime minister. He also delegated more powers to his son Prince Hassan, who played an increasingly active role in the affairs of the state.

The Crown Prince's Political Debut

Ben Barka told me privately that King Mohammed had changed during his two years' exile, and the Istiqlal no longer seemed to enjoy his confidence. He attributed this change to the influence of Prince Hassan. "Moulay Hassan is his father's only real weakness," was Ben Barka's laconic comment.[4]

In an effort to restore cordial relations with the prince, Ben Barka got the Consultative Assembly to propose royal succession by primogeniture. (Traditionally Moroccan sovereigns were selected by the *oulema*.) Thus Moulay Hassan received the title of crown prince on July 9, 1957, his twenty-third birthday, a move Ben Barka and his friends would later regret.

The crown prince made no secret of his distrust of Ben Barka. When I saw Moulay Hassan on his return from his first visit to the United States in November 1957, he brought up the subject of Ben Barka:

> Mehdi is too ambitious. He wants to do too many things and won't accomplish anything important. I'm ambitious too, but I'll settle for four or five *grands coups* in a lifetime—like doing something to bring an end to the Algerian war. There is only one man in this kingdom— excluding my father of course—who is my equal, Abderrahim Bouabid. And I assure you I can be just as much of a Socialist as he is.[5]

Moulay Hassan admitted that he would like to reign one day, but stressed that his father was still a young man. "I have plenty of time to learn how to be king," he said confidently, adding that he would learn from others' mistakes. He told me wryly that some Americans had compared him to Egypt's former King Farouk. "Farouk was brought down by vice and debauchery, and that will never happen to me," he vowed.

The atmosphere of mutual suspicion between the crown prince and Ben Barka was symptomatic of a broader rivalry between the palace and the Istiqlal. It might not have had such disastrous consequences had King Mohammed lived longer. While King Mohammed believed that all political forces should be represented in the government, his son worked behind the scenes to undermine the dominance of the Istiqlal.

In a move to reduce the Istiqlal's influence, the crown prince got his friend Ahmed Reda Guedira to set up the Liberal Independents, composed of well-known palace supporters without political affiliation. The group took part in the first two governments but never attracted a substantial following. Later, as minister of the interior and director of King Hassan's cabinet, Guedira created the Front for the Defense of Constitutional Institutions. This organization fared better than the Liberal Independents because it forged an alliance with the Popular Movement, another palace creation.

The Popular Movement first appeared in 1957, under the leadership of two unconditional monarchists, Mahjoubi Aherdan, a Berber tribal chief, and Dr. Abdelkrim Khatib, a former head of the Liberation Army in the Rif. The Popular Movement professed "Islamic socialism" but was essentially based on rural resentment of urban politicians, namely, the Istiqlal. This largely Berber movement is believed to have stirred various tribal uprisings against the Istiqlal-dominated government and was later used to contain the influence of Sheikh Yassine's Islamist movement.

In hindsight, the crown prince could have saved himself the trouble of creating new political parties to counter the Istiqlal. By the time the Istiqlal had come close to majority rule, the party itself was torn by deep divisions. In the spring of 1958, King Mohammed had given in to most of the Istiqlal's demands, naming Ahmed Balafrej as prime minister and foreign minister and Bouabid as minister of finances and economy, but keeping palace men in other key posts.

That summer, the Istiqlal's left wing broke with the party's conservative leadership. First the unions called a wave of strikes, denouncing the Balafrej government for continuing the protectorate's antilabor policies, and the security forces reacted brutally. Later, when some Rif tribesmen rebelled against the central authority, the crown prince personally led the Royal Armed Forces to crush the revolt. At this point, Bouabid resigned, declaring that the government must be given the power to assume its responsibilities, namely, control over the police and army.

His patience sorely tried, Mohammed V appealed to Allal el Fassi to work out a truce among his party's factions and get on with the nation's business. When El Fassi failed, the king called on a gentle but stubborn trade unionist, Abdallah Ibrahim, to head a new government of leftists and independents, with Bouabid again as head of the economy. This event confirmed the split in the Istiqlal, which had dominated Moroccan politics from the early struggle against colonialism.

The division in the Istiqlal was not just a quarrel among personalities but reflected deep differences between the two wings of the party. The majority, led by El Fassi and Balafrej, was essentially conservative in politics and liberal in economics. The dissidents, led by Bouabid and Ben Barka, were democratic Socialists, who believed in social welfare and state control of vital sectors of the economy.

In those days, I saw Bouabid quite often because the official residence of the minister of the economy was across the street from the home of my boss, *New York Times* bureau chief Thomas Brady. An invitation to lunch from Bouabid could very well turn out to be a picnic of bread and sardines "to boost the national industry." Unaffected by ministerial honors, he remained the committed nationalist, totally absorbed in his mission to liberate Morocco from the bonds of underdevelopment. Under the Ibrahim government, Bouabid was given free rein to work out a progressive five-year plan with the help of a group of Moroccan and French experts. This plan provided for genuine social and economic reforms, including agrarian reform, hardly palatable to the palace entourage.

Early in 1959, Ben Barka broke away from the Istiqlal to form the National Union of Popular Forces (later renamed the Socialist Union of Popular Forces), with the support of the Moroccan Labor Federation and other leftists. Ibrahim and Bouabid were openly sympathetic but did not join the new party until they left the government. The Istiqlal expelled Ben Barka and tried to get the king to dismiss him as president of the National Consultative Assembly, but Mohammed V kept Ben Barka in his post.

For the crown prince, the emergence of Ben Barka's party was a potential threat to the monarchy. To counter what he saw as a revolutionary organization, Moulay Hassan took steps to revive the Popular Movement, despite its links to the tribal uprisings. It seemed that the prince was ready to commit the same mistake as the French protectorate in adopting a so-called Berber policy of pitting rural tribesmen against urban political activists. The crown prince had seen in the Rif the genuine hostility of the tribal chiefs to the Istiqlal-dominated government and clearly decided this was the best way to weaken both the Istiqlal and the National Union, the only two forces that challenged the palace's absolute rule.

Plots and Counterplots

In December 1959, the authorities moved directly against the National Union, seizing its Arabic daily, *Al Tahrir*, for daring to write that "the government should be responsible to the people." At the same time, two of the new party's leaders, Mohammed Basri and Abderrahmane Youssoufi, who had been key links to the former Liberation Army, were arrested on vague allegations of plotting against the state.

I had come to know the quiet, self-effacing Youssoufi when he was editor in chief of *Al Tahrir*. Youssoufi came from Tangier and shared the city's international outlook. Of modest origins, he had given Arabic lessons to retired English residents to pay for his law studies. It was difficult to believe that this scholarly gentleman had been in charge of procuring funds and arms for the Moroccan Liberation Army and was the liaison with the Algerian Liberation Army. Youssoufi was generally respected by the Left and conservatives as "a pure nationalist," someone who had remained true to his ideals even after independence. Shortly before he was jailed, I asked him what those ideals were. He thought for a moment before replying: "I believe that no man should have to bow to another man—or woman. This is why we fought against colonialism and it's why we must fight against feudalism."[6]

In February 1960, the palace announced that a plot had been discovered to assassinate the crown prince. A number of National Union activists, friends of Ben Barka, were arrested. The Socialists denied any involvement in the mysterious affair and suggested that it was an attempt to discredit the young party. Several weeks later, the palace released all of the prisoners, implicitly admitting the lack of evidence of a plot.

This and other alleged plots were overshadowed by the tragedy of Agadir. On February 29, 1960, a massive earthquake laid waste to the southern resort, killing 15,000 people. Demonstrating his leadership in a crisis, the crown prince established a military cordon around the devastated region, and with the help of French, American, and other foreign forces, dug out thousands of wounded and flew them to hospitals.

Meanwhile the harassment of Ben Barka continued, although his friends were still nominally in power. Unbeknown to Prime Minister Ibrahim, the police took over the National Consultative Assembly, including the president's office. At this point, Ben Barka went into voluntary exile. Even then, the oppositionist did not cut his bridges with the palace. "Solid democracy can be achieved through a union of the people with the king, if he could only free himself from the pernicious influence of an entourage of inefficient and corrupt adventurers," Ben Barka wrote to me.[7]

One of the main tasks of the Ibrahim government had been to prepare for the country's first local elections. On May 23, 1960, less than a week before the polls, King Mohammed—at the instigation of the crown prince, I learned—dismissed Ibrahim and his cabinet, and took over the post of prime minister himself, naming Prince Moulay Hassan as vice president. The new cabinet was made up mostly of palace loyalists and a few members of the conservative Istiqlal.

Ibrahim and Bouabid promptly joined Ben Barka's National Union, which had declared its opposition to the new royal government. With charges of fraud in the preparation of electoral lists, the National Union boycotted the municipal elections, which were easily won by the old guard Istiqlal.

The break between the palace and the Left was now finalized. For the first time, the National Union and the Moroccan Labor Federation openly accused the monarchy of "absolutism" in their newspapers. Bouabid directly attacked the palace for forsaking its promise to establish democratic rule. The royal government responded by seizing the opposition press and arresting labor union militants.

It was a palace coup d'état, nationalist friends told me. Mohammed V had entered the political fray, but the crown prince was effectively in charge of the government.

King Hassan Takes Over

Barely a month before his death, King Mohammed achieved a foreign policy triumph, with the organization of a meeting of Africa's most radical leaders, including Egyptian president Gamal Abdel Nasser, Guinea's Ahmed Sekou Toure, and Ghana's Kwame Nkrumah. What became known as the Casablanca bloc met in January 1961 to discuss the situation in the Congo, the Algerian war for independence, and the Palestinian question.

Mohammed V had made his mark in foreign policy as a moderate statesman and a man of balance. While Morocco remained heavily dependent on France, and to a lesser extent on Spain, for financial and technical aid, the kingdom established new ties with the United States, China, and the Soviet Union. In the Arab League, the king was known for his pro-Western policies, but he was careful to remain on good terms with Arab and African radicals. In fact, Morocco had sent an important contingent of troops to the Congo (today's Democratic Republic of the Congo) to support the progressive prime minister, Patrice Lumumba, against the Katangese separatist movement. Although the Casablanca conference did not resolve any of the troublesome issues on the African agenda, King Mohammed's stature as an independent leader was enhanced.

On February 26, 1961, King Mohammed died unexpectedly of a heart attack, following a minor nose operation. He was only fifty-one. The loss was tremendous for the million Moroccans who attended the funeral and for the nation as a whole.

In his memoirs, Hassan II recalled telling mourners at his father's funeral: "You walk behind the coffin of one person, but I am burying not only my father but the Crown Prince." He also admitted having "an authoritarian temperament" but insisted that he was not dictatorial: "I simply like things to be done well at the time that they should be done."[8]

After ascending the throne, King Hassan abandoned his worldly ways, at least in public. In keeping with the times, he tried to give himself a democratic image. One of his first acts as king was to produce the 1962 constitution, which guaranteed an elected parliament, a multiparty system, and democratic freedoms, but left real power in the king's hands. Despite opposition charges that the national charter was "absolutist," it was overwhelmingly approved by over 95 percent of the voters in a referendum.

In *The Commander of the Faithful*, John Waterbury describes in detail the king's monopoly of power by placing trusted personnel in key positions: "The administration in a global sense, but particularly the Ministries of Interior and Justice, the army and police, the royal cabinet and the press are the essential instruments of royal control." Specifically, he notes that the royal cabinet had taken on aspects of "a shadow government" to become the body where "most major policy decisions are made."[9]

Pursuing his course of controlled democratization, Hassan II held the first national elections in the spring of 1963. As expected, the royalist coalition of Guedira's liberals and the Popular Movement won the most seats, but the Istiqlal, National Union, and independents constituted a majority.

Several months later, on the eve of local elections, another alleged plot was discovered. This time, officials said that the National Union was planning to assassinate King Hassan in his bed in the royal palace. Ben Barka, out of the country at the time, was named among the leading conspirators. Police raided the National Union's headquarters in Casablanca and arrested the party's leadership and hundreds of militants. In the treason trial the following year, the court handed down eleven death sentences with seven in absentia, including Ben Barka. None of the death sentences was carried out, and the king eventually pardoned most of the other prisoners.

In the wake of this crack-down on the National Union, friends in the American embassy warned me that the palace was unhappy with my reporting and "could make things very difficult for me." Rather than risk expulsion, I decided to move to Portugal in the summer of 1963. Both the *Times* and *Time* were interested in my plan to set up shop as a freelance correspondent in Europe's last empire and its troubled African colonies. From Lisbon, I remained in contact with Moroccan friends, including the exiled Ben Barka, and continued to follow the volatile Moroccan scene.

Apparently in a move to revive national unity, Hassan II focused the country's attention on the unresolved border question with Algeria. Before the 1912 protectorate treaty, France had unilaterally carved out substantial portions of the Moroccan desert, including the oasis of Touat and the region of Colomb-Bechar, attaching them to Algeria. In his memoirs, King Hassan says that shortly after Moroccan independence, the French had proposed border talks. King Mohammed V had responded, "There is no question of my engaging in negotiations under these circumstances. It would be like stabbing in the back the Algerians fighting for independence. We'll settle our affairs afterwards."[10]

After independence in 1962, Algerian president Ben Bella made it clear that he was not prepared to restore any of the hard-fought land to Morocco. But Moroccans still hoped to persuade the Algerians of the justice of their cause. Isolated border skirmishes broke out in September 1963 at the disputed oasis of Hassi el Beida and soon turned into a full-scale war, with tanks, aircraft, and heavy artillery. At the end of October, Hassan II and Ben Bella agreed to a ceasefire, under the good offices of Ethiopian emperor Haile Selassie, head of the Organization of African Unity. Later, an African commission established the border, which followed the frontier traced by France. It was a major victory for Algeria, whose troops had been defeated on the ground by the better-equipped, more-disciplined Moroccans. Worse, Morocco came out of the affair looking like the aggressor, since the Third World had agreed on the "intangibility" of borders inherited from colonialism.

After the unfortunate border conflict, the palace uncovered yet another leftist plot, with alleged Algerian involvement. The main instigator was said to be a former Liberation Army leader known as Sheikh al Arab, who had formed a clandestine group, the Armed Front for the Republic of Morocco. Accused of trying to overthrow the monarchy, the sheikh killed himself when he was caught by the police in a Casablanca hideout. The authorities said that his followers had received training and arms from the Algerians. This time it was serious: eighteen men were executed and another score given long jail sentences.

It seemed that the country was ready to explode. On March 23, 1964, students from Casablanca high schools organized demonstrations against a government decision to expel all students over seventeen "for lack of space." Leftists, unemployed people, and *bidonvilles* dwellers joined the student protest, which rapidly turned into citywide rioting and was crushed by the police. The number of casualties is not known, but independent sources estimated some 50 dead, 200 wounded, and 850 jailed. Twenty-five leftists, convicted as instigators of the riots, were sentenced to ten years in prison. Sympathy protests were held in other cities, and there were unconfirmed reports of a thousand dead and several thousand arrests.

Concerned over this popular protest, Hassan II received opposition leader Bouabid on April 10, 1965, to discuss a political solution to the crisis.

Four days later, the king amnestied the prisoners of the July 1963 plot, including Ben Barka. National Union sources said this amounted to recognition that the plot had been created as a pretext to crack down on the Socialist party.

Behind the guise of a constitutional monarchy, the king had demonstrated that he would wield a big stick at any hint of dissidence. The monarch retained personal control of the security forces, and his word was law. The government was his malleable instrument, with ministers hired and fired at whim. A carefully controlled parliament held lengthy debates but exercised no real power. The Moroccan press knew its boundaries and was slapped down whenever it went astray.

But this was not enough. On June 7, 1965, the king declared a state of emergency, dissolved parliament, and proceeded to rule by decree. Hassan II was at last completely in charge.

L'affaire *Ben Barka*

The Ben Barka story is a dramatic example of King Hassan's efforts to coopt, control, or crush his opposition. It is a murky tale of political intrigue involving French secret services and their underworld agents and the highest Moroccan security officials. It is a scandal that nearly caused a rupture in relations between France and Morocco. And it is still an unsolved mystery because Ben Barka's body has never been found. More important, it has not been determined whether the late king was personally involved in the *affaire*, or if it was an act of excessive zeal by his most trusted aides, or simply an unfortunate accident at the hands of petty thugs.

I have put together the facts of the case from the court testimony, personal contacts and interviews, hundreds of articles, and numerous books, which have continued to appear decades after the event. It must be pointed out that the key players are dead, and most witnesses died in suspect circumstances.

The first time Ben Barka understood his life to be in danger was after an automobile accident in November 1962. He and a colleague had been riding with a chauffeur on the main road between Casablanca and Rabat when a Peugeot forced them off the road at a dangerous curve. Ben Barka was thrown from the car but able to call to farm workers nearby for help. Later, the opposition leader told me that he saw policemen getting out of the Peugeot, and he accused security chief Ahmed Dlimi of instigating the incident.

Ben Barka flew to Germany for medical treatment, then to Switzerland to convalesce. Still wearing a cast on his neck, he came home for the national elections in the spring of 1963 and was elected deputy from a poor quarter in

Moroccan nationalist and opposition leader Mehdi Ben Barka, whose abduction in Paris and probable murder in 1965 would cause an international scandal (author Marvine Howe, then stringer for the New York Times, *in the background). (Socialist Party Archives)*

Rabat. Back in Switzerland in July for a check-up, he received an emissary from the king, asking him to return to Morocco to discuss the formation of a Socialist government. About to leave on a mission to the Middle East, Ben Barka suggested that the monarch speak to the other party leaders. Several weeks later, the police announced the discovery of another plot to murder the king. Mass arrests were made among political and labor union militants. Ben Barka was again sentenced to death in absentia.

The Socialist leader traveled widely in those days, campaigning for the release of his colleagues and representing various African organizations. He was in contact with a broad circle of journalists and would frequently send out bulletins on the situation in Morocco accusing the police of "Gestapo-like tortures" and other crimes. Named executive secretary of the Afro-Asian Solidarity Committee, Ben Barka set up his headquarters in Geneva. Among his tasks was the organization of the first Tri-Continental Conference to be held in Havana in January 1966. Ben Barka's widening influence from Cairo to Beijing was a permanent source of annoyance to King Hassan, who had personally courted Third World leaders.

Ben Barka was well aware that, even abroad, he was under Moroccan surveillance. Generally he took precautions not to publicize his movements, but he was not a man for secrecy. Early in 1964, I received a letter from the ebullient oppositionist telling me that he had been forced "to disappear from circulation" for several weeks, leaving his apartment and going into hiding. He explained that the Moroccan police, with the complicity of the French, had tried to kidnap him in Geneva. Several months later, he wrote that "for security reasons, I'm obliged to move about constantly." In the spring of 1965, Ben Barka wrote again that it was difficult for him to travel to France, Spain, or Portugal "for security reasons."

On April 25, 1965, Prince Moulay Ali, the king's cousin and ambassador to Paris, met with Ben Barka and offered him a royal pardon to return to Morocco. The meeting took place in the Frankfurt home of Ben Barka's brother Abdelkader, a businessman, who told me later: "This time, Mehdi took the king's offer seriously and promised to return as soon as he had finished preparations for the Tri-Continental."

In Morocco, the king met with the National Union leaders and discussed the possibility of a Socialist government and a general amnesty. Then, apparently annoyed at Ben Barka's refusal to return immediately, the monarch declared a state of emergency. Meeting with Bouabid in August, the king said he would resume contacts with the National Union in October. Correspondence I received from Ben Barka that September was cheerful and optimistic. He spoke of "new options," even the possibility of reaching a modus vivendi with the palace.

The last time Ben Barka was seen in public was October 29, 1965. He had been lured to Paris by a French publicist, Philippe Bernier, with what seemed like a serious proposal for a documentary film on decolonization, which would culminate with the Tri-Continental Conference in Havana. Marguerite Duras had agreed to write the script and French movie-maker Georges Franju would direct the film. Bernier and a ne'er-do-well associate, Georges Figon, set an appointment for Ben Barka to meet Franju at noon on October 29, at the popular Brasserie Lipp in the St. Germain des Prés quarter of Paris.

According to French court testimony, a Moroccan intelligence agent, identified only as Chtouki, notified Antoine Lopez, Air France superintendent at Orly Airport, of Ben Barka's planned arrival in Paris. Lopez, a French Secret Services agent, told the court that he had been instructed to have Ben Barka escorted to a private home in the Paris suburbs to meet "a senior Moroccan personality," presumably General Mohammed Oufkir, Morocco's all-powerful interior minister and confidant of the king.

Ben Barka arrived early for the appointment, accompanied by a Moroccan student, Thami el Azemmouri. They were idling in front of a bookstore near the *brasserie* when two French plainclothesmen approached them, saying they had orders to escort Ben Barka to a meeting. When he asked for their identification, they showed him official French police IDs. The Moroccan oppositionist got into a police car parked nearby, without any resistance, but Azemmouri was barred from accompanying him.

Lopez later testified that Ben Barka was driven to a luxurious villa in the suburb of Fontenay belonging to a French gangster, Georges Boucheseiche, and kept under guard by several French thugs. Then Lopez and Boucheseiche went to Orly to call General Oufkir, who was apparently not in his office. There is a record of phone calls from Orly to the Moroccan Ministry of the Interior and national security offices. The next afternoon, General Oufkir flew to Paris, preceded by security chief Major Dlimi. Lopez said he drove Oufkir to the villa at Fontenay.

The most detailed account of what happened in the Fontenay villa was published by the French weekly *L'Express* on January 10, 1966. The eyewitness report, "I Saw Ben Barka Killed," was taken from a tape made by Georges Figon, who said he had followed the police car to Fontenay by taxi. Figon reported that Ben Barka had been comfortably installed on the second floor of the villa. The Moroccan Socialist showed signs of impatience when Boucheseiche announced that "the boss" had been delayed, but Ben Barka did not appear unduly alarmed because he was under French police protection, according to Figon.

Figon recounted that Dlimi arrived the next day and told Ben Barka's captors: "We're going to liquidate him." The thugs argued that was not what had been agreed but Dlimi insisted, and so Boucheseiche and three thugs beat up the prisoner until he was bleeding and unrecognizable, Figon recalled. When Oufkir arrived, he made a number of incisions on Ben Barka's throat and chest with a decorative Moroccan sword, according to Figon's account. He said Ben Barka was then moved in a car with diplomatic license plates to Lopez's villa in Ormoy, where he was taken to the cellar and tied to the boiler, but was "already finished."

Figon then quotes Oufkir as saying he had left Rabat too hastily to bring the money (Chtouki reportedly had offered a hundred million francs—$16 million—for the "recovery" of Ben Barka, and Figon clearly hoped for a share of the reward), but warned it would be "a fatal mistake" to speak of the incident. And so it was. Figon was found dead in a Paris studio barely a week after his revelations to the press. An official investigation ruled it to be suicide.

In June 1967, the French court sentenced Oufkir, Chtouki, and the French thugs to life in prison in absentia. Dlimi and Bernier were acquitted, and Lopez was given eight years in prison. Boucheseiche and his thugs fled to Morocco and disappeared. Three defense lawyers died of heart attacks in 1967. The student Azemmouri, who became a teacher, was said to have hung himself with a bicycle chain in 1972.

President de Gaulle had been outraged over the scandal and that it should occur in France just prior to presidential elections. He accused the Moroccan interior minister of responsibility for Ben Barka's disappearance and sacked his own head of counterespionage. King Hassan's projected state visit to France was canceled, and relations remained strained until De Gaulle left the presidential palace four years later.

Hassan II called De Gaulle's position "intolerable" and stood up for Oufkir until the interior minister was implicated in the 1972 coup. In his memoirs, the king swore that he had nothing to do with the disappearance of Ben Barka and that it was a fait accompli by Oufkir. On the contrary, the king claimed, he had been trying to get the oppositionist to return and work at his side. The monarch stressed that only much later did he understand that Oufkir was opposed to his rapprochement with the Left. Every time the king had tried to initiate a dialogue with the politicians, a new plot would be uncovered. Over the years, widely divergent accounts have appeared on what happened to Ben Barka. Stephen Hughes quotes knowledgeable sources in Paris as saying Ben Barka was either killed or died from injuries "in the presence of Oufkir, Dlimi and Chtouki" and his body was buried on a bank of the Seine.[11] A report, published by *Jeune Afrique* at the end of 2004, alleges that Figon transported a body to a French pilot, who flew it to a private airport in the South of France, where it was transferred to a Moroccan Beech 50.

In his book *Le Secret*, Ahmed Boukhari, a former agent of the Moroccan Secret Services, recounts in gory detail how Ben Barka's body was disposed of in a vat of acid in the headquarters of the secret police in Rabat.[12]

But the truth is: We do not know what became of Ben Barka.

The question comes up time and again: what did Hassan II know of the barbaric acts apparently perpetrated by close associates against his opponents and the families of his opponents, as in the case of Oufkir's wife and children, imprisoned without charges or trial for nearly two decades? The king himself has said he liked to delegate authority to trusted aides, and it is just possible that these aides believed they were accomplishing the monarch's will and were carried away by excessive zeal to please. But then again, it is difficult to believe that Hassan II, the absolute monarch, was kept ignorant by underlings about important affairs of state.

Military Coup Attempts

After crying wolf so many times—new allegations of leftist "plots" in January 1969 and the spring of 1971 were followed by the usual crack-downs—the king was totally unprepared for two serious coup attempts, which nearly succeeded. Both conspiracies emanated from a hitherto unsuspected source, the Royal Armed Forces. From the early days of independence, Prince Hassan had personally supervised the formation of the Royal Armed Forces as a nonpolitical, professional, disciplined institution, loyal only to country and king. He had used them to quell the dissidence in the Rif—even though many soldiers were Berbers—and to break strikes, suppress riots, and defend national border claims. In return, elite members of the officer corps were pampered with honors, privileges, and other emoluments. Disdainful of the political parties, King Hassan saw the army as "the only disciplined, effective branch of government," according to Abun-Nasr, who points out that the armed forces absorbed one-fifth of the state's expenditures.[13]

Thus, the attempted putsch of the summer of 1971 caught almost everyone by surprise. The unlikely coup leader was General Mohamed Medbouh, head of the Royal Military Cabinet, a Berber from the Rif known for his rectitude. It was the discovery of rampant corruption in high official circles that triggered Medbouh's rage, according to knowledgeable Moroccan officials. Medbouh, who had gone to the United States for medical treatment, had been asked by the king to find out why Pan-American Airlines had abandoned plans to build an Intercontinental Hotel in Casablanca. The company explained that it had been put off by requests for substantial "commissions" by Moroccan officials. When Medbouh submitted his report, the king immediately fired four cabinet ministers. This was not enough for Medbouh, according to Hughes, who says the officer felt that the ministers should go before the anticorruption court and be punished.[14]

I have talked to Moroccans present at the Skhirat massacre, and they blame Medbouh's co-conspirator, Colonel M'hamed Ababou, for the failed coup. Commander of the Military Training Academy, Ababou was described as a Nasserite. Later it was said that Medbouh too was influenced by Nasser.

The incident took place during festivities for the king's forty-second birthday at his favorite palace on the Atlantic coast at Skhirat, south of Rabat. It was a gathering of around 800 of the most important people in the kingdom—all male—including cabinet ministers, senior military officers, other members of the establishment, and the diplomatic corps. Some guests were relaxing by the pool, others were milling around the bar, and the golf enthusiasts were engaged on the palace golf course when the firing began. At first it looked like fireworks, one guest recalled. But it soon turned into a deadly free-for-all. For two hours, some 1,200 cadets fired machine guns and other automatic weapons at random, killing nearly 100 guests as well as General Medbouh. The coup leader was shot by cadets, who seemed to be firing at anyone who moved. Some eyewitnesses say the assailants were incensed at the luxury of the scene, the poolside bar stocked with alcoholic drinks, and the banquet tables set with fine silver and crystal, laden with caviar, pâtés, and other imported delicacies. Others say the cadets appeared to be heavily drugged.

King Hassan and his closest aides, among them General Oufkir and Colonel Dlimi, took refuge in an out-of-the-way bathroom. Afterward, the king recounted that a group of soldiers finally opened the bathroom door and forced him out at gunpoint. Suddenly, one cadet froze, apologizing that he had not recognized the monarch in sport shirt and shorts. The king exhorted him and several other cadets to recite with him the opening verse of the Koran. The cadets joined in crying, "Long live the king!"[15] Once free, General Oufkir ordered loyalist troops to go to Rabat, where Ababou and his cadets had seized the radio station and announced to the world that the army had taken control and established a republic. Then the mutineers moved on to army headquarters, where Ababou was killed in a shoot-out. The rebellion was over.

At first, King Hassan blamed the political parties for the bloody massacre, charging that their negative press had portrayed the regime on the brink of collapse. Later however, the king treated the abortive coup as the work of a group of power-hungry officers with no support from the rest of the armed forces. Ten alleged coup leaders were summarily executed; seventy-four members of the military school's staff were given stiff prison sentences; and fifty-eight of those were dispatched to the desert prison of Tazmamart, where half of them died from the harsh conditions. Some 1,000 cadets were acquitted because they were acting on orders. General Oufkir was rewarded with the post of minister of defense.

But the king was very wrong. Barely a year after Skhirat, Hassan II was the target of another coup, this time by young air force officers. On August 16, 1972, the monarch was flying home from a visit to France, when his Royal Air Maroc Boeing 727 was intercepted by six Moroccan F-5 fighter planes over the northern city of Tetouan. The Boeing was riddled by gunfire and landed with one engine and one wheel at the Rabat airport at Salé. Again the sovereign escaped unscathed and went to the VIP lounge, where his cabinet ministers and the Royal Guard were waiting, presumably unaware of what had happened. Shortly afterward, three fighter planes flew low over the capital, while three other fighters strafed the airport, killing eight people and wounding forty. The king managed to escape in an airport employee's car and made his way to the palace at Skhirat.

Hassan II said he had never doubted Oufkir's loyalty until the attack on his plane. "Oufkir, as Minister of Defense, alone could authorize the takeoff of the F5s with ammunition," the king noted in his memoirs. The night of the incident, Oufkir was called to the palace. When he arrived, the king was in his bath. Received by the king's mother, Oufkir said, "Oh, Lady, I swear to you I had nothing to do with all this but you'll see, they're going to blame me for everything." For the monarch, this amounted to a confession.[16]

The morning after the aborted coup, an official announcement said that Oufkir had committed suicide. At first it was widely accepted that Oufkir had put an end to his life out of shame for not preventing the attack. Two days later, however, the minister of the interior told the press that Oufkir was behind the coup attempt. He said that the minister of defense had gone to Skhirat and, when told that the king knew of his responsibility, shot himself three times during a struggle with royal aides.

Oufkir's family, however, refused to believe the suicide story. In her book, *Stolen Lives*, Malika Oufkir tells how she found five bullet marks on her father's body, in the liver, the lungs, the stomach, the back, and the neck. It is not known whether it was fear of this testimony or other possible revelations that led to the imprisonment of Oufkir's widow and six children for nineteen years. Oufkir certainly had much to answer for, but this does not justify the cruel punishment meted out to his family.

Surprisingly, King Hassan gained in popularity from the miscarried coups. The monarch had demonstrated his courage in a crisis and showed he possessed the *baraka*, or divine blessing to escape unscathed. But the king realized that he could not count on the military, and the armed forces underwent a complete reorganization. The sovereign assumed direct control of the military, supervising promotions, movements of officers, and arms stocks. He also appeared increasingly suspicious of politicians.

Eager to make up for their lapses, the security forces showed new zeal in detecting plots. In the spring of 1973, they revealed a conspiracy to trigger a national insurrection, allegedly instigated by National Union radicals abroad, among them Fqih Basri. Several hundred armed insurgents were said to have been arrested after crossing secretly into Morocco from Algeria, and a number of unexploded bombs were found in public sites in Casablanca and Rabat. Bouabid denied any involvement of the National Union, but as usual, the party was shut down and its leaders arrested, only to be acquitted in time. More than eighty people were given death sentences, most of them in absentia, including Fqih Basri. Constant harassment led in 1975 to a new split in the party, with most of the membership following Bouabid to the newly created Socialist Union of Popular Forces.

While the country was still reeling from the fallout of the alleged left-wing uprising, the authorities uncovered yet another plot, this time plans by several extreme leftist organizations to overthrow the monarchy. The most influential of these groups was Ilal Aman (Avant Garde), founded by Abraham Serfaty. Serfaty was accused of leading the subversive movement with the aim of becoming president of a new People's Republic of Morocco.

Stephen Hughes, who covered the trials, notes that the evidence was flimsy, made up mainly of tracts and bulletins full of Maoist and Cuban rhetoric. "The idea of a Jew leading a Muslim state struck many as unreal and tended to make the charges implausible," Hughes points out.[17] The leftists told the court that they favored independence for Western Sahara, and were accused of treason. Serfaty and 43 other militants were sentenced to life in prison, while 129 received jail terms of five to thirty years.

It was the aborted military coups that ushered in *les années de plomb*. The palace saw itself besieged by the Left—and its sympathizers in the armed forces—and responded with systematic and extreme brutality.

Islamist Challenger

King Hassan's religious authority was challenged for the first time in 1974 by Islamist leader Sheikh Abdessalam Yassine in his open letter, "Islam or the Deluge." In this lengthy opus, Yassine contested Hassan's legitimacy as Commander of the Faithful, noting that in Islam, the leader must be chosen by the *oulema*. "God has warned you twice," Yassine wrote, in a reference to the two failed coups, adding, "He saved you but you turned away from him. This letter is the third warning." He urged the king to repent and become "a good Muslim." I obtained a text of the sheikh's letter from the Islamist Association's spokesman, Fathallah Arsalane, in July 1995, when we met at his modest apartment in Rabat.

The sovereign initially viewed the Islamist's warning as an isolated case and dispatched him to an insane asylum without trial for three and a half years. All the while, Yassine's Justice and Charity Movement grew in influence. When the popular sheikh was set free, King Hassan had him barred from preaching in government-supervised mosques, his publications seized, and his followers arrested. Early in 1984, Yassine was tried for his fiery articles and sentenced to two years in prison. On his release, Yassine and his home became a pilgrimage site for thousands of visitors from around the country. His thoughts were spread widely by audiocassettes and videotapes. Finally Hassan had enough and placed his adversary under house arrest at the end of 1989, with no visitors allowed. He remained there until after the monarch's death.

Meanwhile, King Hassan assumed his role of Commander of the Faithful in earnest, apparently to counter the Left and at the same time to undercut Yassine's movement. After the failed coup of 1972, Hassan launched a campaign of religious awareness, which some Islamic experts have said was inspired by Mao Zedong's Cultural Revolution. In the mid-1970s, Islamic

King Hassan II announces on the airwaves the launching of the Green March to stake Morocco's claims to Spanish Sahara in November 1975. (Moroccan Ministry of Communications)

studies were incorporated into the public school system from an early age. At the same time, philosophy courses disappeared from the curricula to be replaced by more advanced Islamic studies. Leading *oulema* and educators were asked to review books used in the Islamic courses to make sure they were religiously correct, that is, presented no challenge to the Commander of the Faithful. But at this point, there was no attempt to screen publications or sermons for *intégrisme*, a kind of religious fundamentalism that rejects all change.

Saharan Crusade

Assailed from right and left and no longer sure of the military's loyalty, King Hassan succeeded in diverting attention from serious domestic problems with his crusade to recover the Spanish Sahara. In a series of brilliant political maneuvers, the king was able to forge national unity with his Green March, persuade Spain to withdraw from the territory, and assume control of Western Sahara.

Aside from phosphates and rich coastal fishing, there was no known wealth in these 102,700 square miles of desert, as large as New York, New Jersey, and Pennsylvania combined. But for many Moroccans there was a Saharan mystique, a consciousness that their great dynasties had come from the desert and that its occupation by Spain in 1884 had marked the beginning of the kingdom's loss of independence.

Seizing the initiative, Hassan II announced his Green (for Islam) March. He called up 350,000 civilian volunteers from all over the kingdom to march unarmed into Western Sahara, demand the departure of the Spanish, and proclaim Moroccan sovereignty over the land. The idea of a Green March in the desert appealed to the international press and won widespread sympathy for the Moroccan cause.

Meanwhile, Spain panicked, fearing that things would get out of control. Agreement was reached on Spain's withdrawal from the Sahara by the end of February 1976. Western Sahara would be divided with two-thirds going to Morocco and one-third to Mauritania. The king had won this round.

But this victory marked the beginning of Morocco's problems in Western Sahara. A small group of Saharan students, who had formed the Popular Front for the Liberation of Saguia el Hamra and Rio de Oro (two Spanish colonies that made up Western Sahara), or POLISARIO, launched their war for independence at the end of 1975. With decisive backing from Algeria, POLISARIO stood up to the larger, better-equipped Moroccan army. Finally in 1988, Morocco accepted a United Nations peace plan for the self-determination of Western Sahara. Peace talks resulted in a truce in 1991 and preparations for a referendum, which has proved to be an interminable process, probably what King Hassan had envisaged all along.

Dams, Schools, and Boatpeople

Morocco was undoubtedly a richer country at the end of King Hassan's long rule, and life has improved for many Moroccans. Life expectancy rose to sixty-eight years from forty-six at independence. At independence, 80 percent of Moroccans lived in the countryside, mostly at subsistence level. With the rural exodus, triggered by successive droughts, urban dwellers outstripped the rural inhabitants by 1994, and the trend was accelerating. The urban population has greater access to social services and modern amenities, but these have been unable to keep pace with the population increase. The social balance sheet of Hassan's long reign was not brilliant; in 1999, the year of his death, the UN Development Program classified Morocco a shameful 126th out of 170 countries in its Index of Human Development.

Yet the cities have changed dramatically with new modern office buildings, apartment blocks, hotels, schools, shopping centers, industrial quarters, and affluent residential suburbs. The countryside too has seen some change, at least the more accessible regions. Roads have multiplied around the country; electricity and water have been introduced to many areas for the first time. Even consumer goods like automobiles, television sets, and cellular phones have proliferated in rural districts.

The French colonial dream of 1 million hectares (2.5 million acres) irrigated by 2000 was in fact realized by King Hassan. Under his aggressive dam-building program, fifty large dams have been constructed since independence. Hassan's irrigation policy has benefited the modern sectors but done little to improve the livelihood of the majority, who live by traditional farming. In his sober 1987 book *Moroccan Mirages*, Will Swearingen notes that the government-financed irrigation development has been geared to the modern export sector and benefited a small land-owning elite, whereas the traditional agriculture of more than 90 percent of the farmers remains "essentially untouched by government policies."[18]

Faced with bankruptcy in the early 1980s over the sharp rise in oil prices, the drop in phosphate earnings, prolonged droughts, and the staggering costs of the military effort in Western Sahara, King Hassan sought help from the International Monetary Fund. The structural adjustments, which included trimming the bloated bureaucracy, the liberalization of state sectors, and the removal of government subsidies on essentials like sugar, improved the country's financial situation but increased the hardships borne by the masses.

New wealth was created under Hassan II, but the gap between the rich and poor has grown even broader. The World Bank reported that in 1999 some 5.3 million Moroccans, or 19 percent of the population, lived below the poverty level of $1 a day, a substantial rise from 3.5 million, or 13 percent, in 1991. While the bourgeoisie and palace circles have flourished, the numbers of illegal emigrants and jobless have soared.

Social development has lagged because of budgetary constraints and priorities. From the outset of his rule, King Hassan emphasized the need to generalize education, and new schools and universities were opened around the country. Despite major efforts, however, the illiteracy rate was a devastating 55 percent (69 percent for women) in 1998, according to the World Bank. Hospitals and clinics, concentrated in cities, were woefully inadequate. Anyone who could afford to do so would go abroad for medical treatment. The majority of the population was not covered by social security and relied on quacks and charlatans in the *souks*. Private associations have stepped in to tackle problems like the proliferation of street children, single mothers, and adult illiteracy, but they cannot compensate for the inadequacies of the government in this domain.

Ironically, there has been a sharp rise in the number of high school and college graduates unable to find jobs, estimated at 217,000 in 1999, according to the National Association of College Graduates. Whereas, just a generation before, there had been a dearth of cadres, new jobs have not kept up with graduates. Students have not been oriented into sectors where there is a demand. Under the International Monetary Fund's adjustment program, privatization has meant layoffs and reduced government hiring.

Making matters worse, the escape valve is gone. Ever since independence, Moroccans have looked to Europe for work, primarily to their former colonizer France. Officially there are said to be 2.5 million Moroccans living abroad, but the number is believed to be much higher. At first, male laborers looked for work in construction, mining, and other industries, then as shopkeepers, and young women sought jobs as domestics. Recently, professionals and *diplomés chomeurs* have been trying to get immigrant visas. In early 1990, Europeans began to require visas for North Africans, and the doors all but closed to legal immigration.

The boatpeople—thousands of clandestine immigrants, who wash up on Spanish shores alive or dead each year—are the most serious indictment of the vacillating economic policies pursued by Hassan's governments under the guidance of the IMF. They are the most dramatic symptom that something was very wrong in Hassan's Morocco with its façade of progressive economic development and stability.

Political Openings

As social and economic problems intensified, King Hassan seemed to mellow. Maybe it would have happened anyway as the sovereign became increasingly conscious of his own mortality. In the spring of 1990, the king formed a Consultative Council for Human Rights and met with a delegation from Amnesty International to respond to complaints about his repressive policies. The new period of relaxation followed the publication in September 1990 of the devastatingly critical book *Notre ami le roi* by Gilles Perrault.

Later, Hassan II shrugged off the criticism, saying all regimes had their faults. However, he did take the negative publicity seriously because preparations were under way for an official visit to the United States in September 1991. He had been warned that he would face tough questions about his human rights record, which had come under increasing criticism in the U.S. State Department's annual human rights report. Also, Nancy Touil, the American wife of a Moroccan Air Force lieutenant, and Christine Daure Serfaty, the French wife of Abraham Serfaty, had been working separately as effective lobbyists in Washington and Paris to liberate their husbands and all political prisoners from the desert fortress at Tazmamart and other jails.

King Hassan took several measures to clean up his regime's image in the spring of 1991. Oufkir's widow and six children were released after nineteen years' arbitrary detention; the twenty-eight survivors of Tazmamart (including M'barek Touil) were freed and the prison shut down; forty leftists were amnestied; and Serfaty was deported to France. In his memoirs, the king disclaimed any knowledge of the horrors of Tazmamart. He said that he thought the Oufkirs were being kept under house arrest "in normal conditions." But he showed no sympathy for Serfaty, insisting that "human rights stop when it has to do with Moroccan Sahara."[19]

King Hassan's moves to ease his regime's policies only increased pressures for democratic reform. The Istiqlal and the Socialist Union boycotted the 1992 referendum for a new constitution on grounds that the monarchy retained its absolute powers. Despite the abstention of the two main parties, the royal charter won more than 99 percent of the vote, confirming the public's suspicions that the elections were deeply flawed. National elections that summer were said to be fairer than usual, but the royalist parties came in first over an alliance of the opposition parties, the Istiqlal and the Socialist Union. Crying foul once more, the opposition rejected overtures by the king to join a government in which he continued to name people to the key posts and to wield arbitrary power. And so the country hobbled along under a government of technocrats, as the critics became more vociferous.

Hassan II went to New York in October 1995, for the fiftieth anniversary of the United Nations. There he fell ill and was taken to the Cornell Medical School Hospital, where the public diagnosis was bronchial pneumonia. However, sources close to the monarch say that he was told he was seriously ill. At any rate, he underwent a profound change, and for the first time admitted privately to have made mistakes.

The mood in Morocco was morose during that fall of 1995. People didn't talk openly about the king's health, but they were worried about where Morocco was headed. Moroccans of the Left and Right were critical of Hassan's autocratic rule, but were even more anxious over the fate of the country without Hassan. One concern on Moroccan minds was the upsurge in the Islamists, who had taken over the universities and were opening new cultural and philanthropic associations around the country. King Hassan had managed to contain Islamic radicals, and there had been no spillover of the ongoing sectarian violence in neighboring Algeria. But people wondered if his successor would exert similar influence. Socialists and conservatives contended that the regime's failure to strengthen democracy had fueled the current Islamic thrust.

My old friend M'hamed Douiri, then a member of parliament for the Istiqlal party, said the growth of the Islamist movement stemmed from economic and social problems: "What is necessary is the urgent reform of state management and the budget to deal with poverty, inequality, and injustice."[20]

Youssoufi, who had taken over the Socialist party after Bouabid's death in 1992, said that a "credible government based on really free elections could counteract any extremist movement." He spoke soberly of the government's failure to come to grips with the major national problems: the widespread corruption, lack of investments, soaring unemployment, anarchy in education, and young people with no present or future.[21]

In the winter of 1995–1996, Hassan II began to prepare for his succession. His primary concern was the future of the monarchy, according to members of his entourage. Thus, he had a new constitution drawn up, one that would assure the transition to a constitutional monarchy acceptable to the political class. To placate the opposition, the new charter stipulated that all members of the House of Representatives (instead of two-thirds, as previously) be elected directly.

Elections in November 1997 were less controlled than previous polls, although there was reportedly a good deal of vote-buying. The Socialists came in first and with their partners held a plurality in the House of Representatives. Accordingly, King Hassan named the Socialist leader Abderrahmane Youssoufi to be prime minister, with the mission to form a government of Alternance, dominated by the opposition for the first time in almost four decades.

In April 1998, Youssoufi presented to parliament his government's program to modernize the administration and the education system, spur economic growth and rural development, and promote human rights, particularly women's rights. The Socialist leader's brave new agenda was enthusiastically welcomed by most Moroccans, who were longing for change. However Youssoufi's Socialist Union lacked a majority and had to make compromises with six other parties in the coalition. Also, the king had retained his prerogatives under the new constitution, including the direct control of five key cabinet posts. Soon the government appeared bogged down in bureaucracy. The independent press lashed out increasingly against official paralysis.

Nevertheless, when King Hassan died of a heart attack on July 23, 1999, the country did not sink into chaos, as many had feared. There were no angry diatribes against the late king for all of the suffering during those long "years of lead," no bloody vendettas against members of the royal entourage known to have plundered state coffers, no people's revolt against an elite that had profited from a system of nepotism, cronyism, incompetence, and petty corruption. Prime Minister Youssoufi's multiparty government was able to ensure a smooth transition and preserve the kingdom's stability. And the nation as a whole rallied around the young, unknown, and untested heir apparent, Mohammed VI, in the hope of change.

Society in Motion

III

Islamic Revival

5

*I*t couldn't happen here, Moroccans boasted confidently, referring to the explosion of radical Islam which had threatened other countries from the Philippines to Afghanistan, from Turkey to Egypt. In fact, Morocco at the dawn of the twenty-first century appeared like a calm oasis in the midst of the turbulence sweeping across the Muslim world.

Somehow, the devastating war in neighboring Algeria between Islamic extremists and the military-dominated regime had failed to spread to Morocco. On the contrary, firmly devout Moroccans subscribe to nonviolence and seem to have heeded the Algerian lesson. Moroccans insist that the sectarian conflagration in that neighboring North African state could not occur in their tranquil kingdom.

Nor have there been the xenophobic campaigns against foreign visitors that crippled tourism in Egypt. Only once, in 1994, did Islamic zealots attack a hotel in Marrakech, killing two Spanish tourists. The authorities identified the two terrorists as French citizens of North African origin and part of a gang smuggling arms into Algeria.

In my experience, average Moroccans are relatively pious but unconcerned by political Islam. They oppose fanaticism and violence in the name of religion and believe that the real Islam is a religion of love and peace and tolerance.

No one can say with any certainty how many Islamists—believers in political Islam—there are in Morocco. However, in the mid-1990s, the Socialist party estimated there were as many as 3 million Islamist militants and sympathizers, out of a population of 28 million, and the movement has grown since then.

Middle East expert John P. Entelis noted in the late 1990s that "given the degree of violence occurring in Algeria and the oppressive political environment being created in Tunisia," it appeared that Moroccan officials, Islamist activists, and independent-minded intellectuals had chosen "a more moderate path that emphasizes public dialogue and discourse rather than confrontation and violence."[1]

The Moroccan monarch, as Commander of the Faithful, was widely considered to be the principal barrier against Islamic radicals in the kingdom. Prayers are said in the king's name throughout the country, and he supervises all religious institutions through his Ministry of Islamic Affairs. The late King Hassan II and now his son King Mohammed VI have always preached an Islam of moderation and dialogue.

Without hesitation, King Mohammed condemned the terrorist attacks against the United States on September 11, 2001, and gave his firm support to the war against all forms of terrorism. In a rare interview with *Paris Match*, the king declared: "Those who committed these acts have no right to call themselves Muslims. Islam is life. Suicide is the negation, the antithesis of Islam."[2]

Later, the monarch stressed: "Terrorism has no justification in the faith and law of Islam, nor in its lofty values based on co-existence, the establishment of peace worldwide, nor in Muslims' traditions and ethics, which are based on beneficence, mutual help and piety."[3]

The principal Islamist organizations, which were increasingly visible on the Moroccan scene, bent over backward to denounce violence and emphasized that they sought to restore an Islamic state and Islamic moral values through peaceful means.

Moroccans would continue to believe that their country was an exception, immune to the fanatical deviations of Islam, until May 16, 2003.

An Islamic Kingdom

Historically, Morocco is an Islamic kingdom, founded in the eighth century by Idriss I, a great-grandson of the Prophet Mohammed. The succeeding Almoravid and Almohad dynasties were Berbers from the Sahara, but they were pious Muslim reformers and their empires were ruled in the name of Islam. The Berber Merinid Dynasty sought legitimacy by building Islamic schools and sanctuaries and promoting *Sufi* orders. The Saadians and the currently ruling Alaouites also claimed to be *chorfa*, or descendants of the Prophet.

The population has generally followed the relatively flexible Malekite school of orthodox Islam. Nevertheless, whenever the central authority was weakened, the people turned to their *zaouias*, or Islamic brotherhoods, which served as cultural, spiritual, and political centers. Historian Abdallah Laroui notes that the *zaouias* dominated North Africa for three centuries, until the end of the nineteenth century and the appearance of *salafism*, the pan-Islamic reform movement inspired by Egyptian Muhammad Abduh.[4]

Nationalist leader Allal el Fassi introduced *salafism* to the movement for independence. Under the *salafi* influence, the nationalists tended to dismiss the *zaouias* as divisive and retrograde because many religious chiefs had co-operated with the French occupiers. El Fassi and other *salafists*, however, recognized the popularity of Sultan Mohammed V, and supported him as the Commander of the Faithful and leader of the *jihad* against French and Spanish occupation to recover Moroccan independence.

The late King Hassan was always careful to reaffirm his devotion to Islamic tradition. Although the monarch's declared aim was to modernize Morocco, there was no question of establishing a secular state on the Turkish model. Despite pressures from the women's movement, Hassan II made no significant reform of the Islamic civil code, and the king assumed the leadership of the Islamic renewal in Morocco. He reactivated Koranic preschools, enforced prayers in secondary schools, favored Islamic studies, and promoted lectures and publications on Islamic themes. He had new mosques built around the country, including the grandiose Hassan II Mosque in Casablanca, and founded Dar al Hadith El Hassania to train scholars in the sayings of the Prophet.

While Hassan II gained credit in the West for his conciliatory policies toward Israel, he was careful to take balancing pro-Islamic measures. After discreetly permitting some 200,000 Moroccan Jews, or two-thirds of the Jewish population, to emigrate (presumably to Europe, but in fact most went on to Israel), King Hassan organized the first Islamic Summit in Rabat in September 1969. Later the Moroccan king assumed the presidency of the Islamic Conference's Jerusalem Committee, a position his son holds today.

Even the historic Green March to reclaim Western Sahara from Spain in November 1975 was presented as a peaceful Islamic crusade; the marchers were armed only with copies of the Koran. With this Islamic façade, the king hoped to win support from the Muslim world for Morocco's claims to the Sahara.

Superbly sure of his Islamic credentials, King Hassan held that radical Islam could not become a threat to Morocco because of its 1,200 years of history and the racial mix of Berbers and Arabs. "Morocco is a country of the golden mean," the king said in his memoirs. "Moroccans are not a people of excess."[5] The king made a distinction between Islamic fundamentalism, with which he had no quarrel, and *intégrisme*—an intransigent adherence to tradition—which could be dangerous.

By the mid-1980s, the palace had realized that Islamic radicals were a potential threat. King Hassan openly encouraged so-called moderate Islamists, that is, those who recognized his authority as Commander of the Faithful, and tightened controls on the others. Under his stern reign, this system seemed to work. Nevertheless, Islamic experts noted an increase in clandestine Islamist groups, nurtured basically by the same causes that have spawned Islamic extremism elsewhere: the failure of left- and right-wing governments to fulfill their promises to strengthen democratic institutions, clean up the administration, improve living standards, and provide greater social justice.

Modern Political Islam

Before 1970, political Islam occupied little space in the Muslim-Arab world, and Morocco was no exception, according to Moroccan scholar Abdellatif Agnouche. Although most constitutions mentioned Islam as the state religion, the governments were imbued with modernizing, secularizing ideas and engaged in the fight against underdevelopment, Agnouche emphasizes. He notes that any mention of religion by traditionalist groups was generally perceived as "a reactionary incantation to defend class interests."[6]

To be sure, an Islamist movement, whose ultimate objective is to come to power, has been waiting in the wings for many years. As in other Muslim countries, Islamism first appeared in Morocco in the 1960s, essentially in opposition to the Socialist nationalism of Gamal Abdel Nasser, and was encouraged by the palace. Morocco turned to Saudi Arabia for help in facing challenges from the Left, influenced by Nasserites and Marxist-Leninists. In return, the Saudis were given free rein to introduce Wahhabism to Morocco, through preachers, publications, audiocassettes, and generous monetary contributions. Although the Moroccan leadership was wary of the influence of Wahhabism, the natural friendship between the two Arab monarchies was reinforced by their common strategic alliance with the United States during the Cold War and Saudi aid in Morocco's Saharan conflict.

Also, the Iranian revolution of 1979 had an enormous impact in this country, although Moroccans are Sunni Muslims, not Shiites as in Iran. Moroccans, who suffered more than two decades of harsh political repression, could easily empathize with the Iranians' revolt against a corrupt monarchy and repressive security forces serving as vassals of the West.

Mohamed Darif, an Islamic expert, notes that as early as 1964, King Hassan II had developed a new religious policy "based on the encouragement of Islamism to counteract the Arab nationalist dimension of Nasserism." To head Dar al Hadith, the school for Islamic theologians, the king called on

Farouk Annaban, a prominent Syrian exponent of the Muslim Brothers, who were arch-opponents of Nasserism. Furthermore, the palace established "an objective alliance" with Chabiba Islamiya, or the Islamic Youth Association, inspired by the Egyptian Muslim Brothers, according to Darif.[7]

The experts agree that the first organized Islamist group in Morocco was the Islamic Youth Association, founded in 1969 by Abdelkrim Moutii, a primary-school inspector and a leader of the National Teachers Union. The square-faced, ebullient Moutii, who was a former militant of Ben Barka's National Union of Popular Forces, broke with the Left, accusing it of Communism and atheism while attacking the Right as bourgeois and reactionary.

The Islamic Youth Association was active among high school and university teachers and students and tolerated by the palace as long as it opposed the foreign ideologies of Marxism and Maoism. The group's overt aims included the moralization of society, including the banning of alcohol and other forms of "depravity" like prostitution, the Arabization of education, and the implementation of Islamic law. The unstated, long-term goals, however, were to undermine the Left, destabilize those national institutions considered "un-Islamic," and come to power.

Little attention was paid to Moutii or his association until it was implicated in the assassination of the prominent National Union leader Omar Benjelloun on December 18, 1975. The assailants were identified as belonging to an extremist Islamic organization, Al Moujahidoune al Maghriba (The Combatants of Maghreb), which was said to have links with Moutii's group.

Fearing arrest, Moutii fled abroad, denying anything to do with the assassination. He accused the Moroccan security services of instigating the killing to discredit the Islamic Youth Association. Faced with prison at home, Moutii chose to direct his movement from Belgium, publishing a militant newspaper, *Al Moujahid*, and seeking foreign support for the Islamic revolution in Morocco. From the security of exile, Moutii used leftist rhetoric to denounce the allegedly corrupt monarchy and to call for an Islamic republic.

Weakened by repression and internal disputes, the Islamic Youth Association eventually split into several groups, and the main activists disassociated themselves from Moutii and his radical pronouncements. Some splinter groups continued to operate in secret under Moutii's directives, but his influence waned. He made headlines again when two dozen heavily armed guerrillas crossed into Morocco from Algeria in July 1985 and were promptly arrested. Several infiltrators claimed to belong to Moutii's movement of armed struggle, which aimed to set up an Islamic state in Morocco. A Casablanca court handed down fourteen death sentences, with nine in absentia, including Moutii. Later, the Islamic revolutionary took refuge in Libya, then disappeared from the front ranks of the Islamist scene, according to French Islamic expert François Burgat.[8]

Moutii, with bushy graying hair and beard and smiling eyes, resurfaced in 2000 with the publication of a book in Arabic entitled *Jurisprudence of Power*. Islamic expert Mohamed Darif writes that Moutii is now critical of the Islamic Youth Association and the Islamist movement in general and calls for a political system based on the *Shoura* (Islamic consultation) "that ends all forms of despotism and guarantees equality of all citizens." Moutii is no longer "the activist who wanted to change the regime by force," according to Darif, "but has been transformed into a theoretician endeavoring to formulate a new vision of political Islam."[9]

After spending time in jail because of Moutii's seditious statements and tracts, the main leadership of the Islamic Youth Association broke away in 1982. The following year, Abdelillah Benkiran, a former physics student, and several other former Islamist Youth militants announced their decision to take part in the democratic process with the formation of the Jemaa al Islamiya, the Islamic Community. But the country was not ready for an Islamic political party. Failing to obtain official recognition, Benkiran and his friends changed the name of their association several times, dropping any reference to Islam. Finally, in 1996, the former Islamic Youth militants regrouped under the label of the Movement for Unification and Reform and were permitted to join a small party headed by Dr. Abdelkrim Khatib, a former resistance leader. Dr. Khatib, an expansive Santa Claus figure now in his eighties, is above all a staunch royalist and hardly anyone's idea of an Islamic militant. This merger became the country's first legally recognized, Islamist-inspired political group, the Justice and Development party.

I have come to know leaders of the two main Islamist organizations: Sheikh Yassine's tolerated Justice and Charity Association and Dr. Khatib's Justice and Development party. Both groups have publicly condemned violence and injustice and call for the respect of human rights. Both castigated the terrorists who attacked the World Trade Center and the Pentagon, declaring that such deeds "are not Islamic." But just as forcefully, the two organizations condemn "American terrorism"—including the bombardment of Afghanistan and attacks on Iraqis—and unconditional support of Israel in the Palestinian conflict.

Sheikh Yassine's association does not recognize the king as the leader of Moroccan Islam and insists that the ruler must be designated by a consensus of the Islamic scholars. The group refuses to take part in elections, arguing that they are "a Western concept" and have been systematically falsified. On the other hand Dr. Khatib's party recognizes the king as Commander of the Faithful and is fully involved in the democratic life of the country.

The so-called moderate members of Dr. Khatib's organization appear at times to be more radical than Sheikh Yassine's followers. It is the Justice and Development party which has led moralizing campaigns against alcohol, rock music, beauty pageants, obscenity in films, and the use of Latin script (instead of Arabic) for Berber instruction.

While the tactics of the two Islamist groups differ substantially, they share the same overall goal, to establish a modern Islamic state. And should they ever get together, they would represent a formidable force.

The Islamist Challenger

Although there had been various coup attempts against former King Hassan, the seventy-five-year-old Sheikh Yassine is the only person to have directly challenged the king's religious authority. Once a member of the Boushichiya religious order (like the current minister of Islamic affairs), Yassine gave up Sufism in the early 1970s in favor of political action. Refusing to participate in what he has denounced as an immoral and secular democracy, Yassine seeks to restore a modern version of the caliphate, or Islamic rule.

In 1974, Yassine, an unknown inspector in the Education Ministry, published his 124-page open letter to King Hassan II, urging the monarch to make "an act of redemption." Yassine denounced the reign of corruption and waste, the absence of democracy and freedom, and called for a return to the caliphate system under which the ruler was chosen by Islamic scholars, not by heredity. The defiant Islamist was dispatched by the king to an insane asylum for what was viewed as an act of blasphemy.

King Hassan did not really take the Islamist movement seriously until the Iranians unseated his old friend the shah in 1979. Obviously there were great differences between Shiite Iranians, who are led by an array of clerics, and the orthodox Sunni Moroccans, who have no clergy. Nevertheless, like Muslim leaders everywhere, the king took a new look at his own Islamic dissidents. The authorities were instructed to take harsh measures against any group that smacked of radical Islam.

Sheikh Yassine again came into royal focus. The religious leader was known to be inspired by the Iranian revolution, according to Islamic expert Darif. He notes that Yassine published a book on Ayatollah Khomeini's thoughts just three months after the overthrow of the shah. "The importance of the Iranian revolution is that it legitimized Islamism," Darif says.[10]

From the beginning, the most active and dedicated Islamists were Sheikh Yassine's disciples, who had grouped together to form a loose association that was continually harassed by the authorities. Yassine was again arrested in

1983 for publishing a critical editorial showing contradictions between the king's words and acts, and this time he was sentenced to two years in prison.

"The regime wasn't used to this kind of language. People didn't dare criticize the king because he is a descendant of the Prophet," said Fathallah Arsalane, a member of the executive committee of Yassine's organization. The balding, thickly bearded Arsalane is often mentioned as a possible successor to the elderly, frail Yassine. During an interview in the fall of 2001, Arsalane spoke to me of Yassine's stormy relationship with King Hassan, emphasizing that the sheikh had always refused to ask for pardon for his words of defiance.[11]

Sheikh Yassine formally established Ad Adl wal Ihsane (Association for Justice and Charity) in 1985, based on the principles of social justice and nonviolence, Arsalane said. The sheikh, who continued to publish his nonconformist views, was put under house arrest in 1989 and remained confined for a decade, until after the death of King Hassan. Arsalane and other followers of the sheikh were harassed and arrested, their publications seized, and their requests to form a political party systematically refused.

In spite of or perhaps because of the repression, Sheikh Yassine's association has become the most influential Islamist organization in the country. It has taken over the high schools and college campuses (sometimes by force), and its militants bring food, health care, and literacy classes to the urban poor. It is also the principal mobilizing force in the kingdom and has brought close to a million people into the streets for popular causes like Palestine liberation and the denial of women's liberation. Although King Mohammed released the sheikh from house arrest, Yassine's movements are still closely controlled.

Mohamed Tozy, a leading scholar on Islam, says Sheikh Yassine can be considered "probably the most important theoretician of Morocco's Islamist movement." He notes that the sheikh published fifteen works between 1973 and 1989, including *Al Minhaj Annabaoui* (The Prophetic Way), which presents an original synthesis of the teachings of Sufism and the politicoreligious thoughts of Hassan Al-Banna, founder of the Muslim Brothers, and Sayed Qutb, whose texts on the conquest of power have served as the basis of revolutionary Islamism.[12]

"Yassine epitomizes the concerns of an Islamic modernist," states the Islamic scholar Emad Eldin Shahin, who emphasizes that the sheikh operates out of "an intense sense of the need for change at the individual and community levels." Like other Islamic thinkers, Yassine has a critical view of the West, rejects secular, Western-inspired development, and considers "an activist Islam as an alternative to the current ideology of the state and the society," according to Shahin.[13]

Sheikh Yassine's personal spokesperson is his daughter Nadia, the wife of a militant Islamist and mother of four girls. When I first telephoned Nadia in the fall of 1995, she seemed nervous about meeting a foreign journalist in a hotel, which would be under surveillance, and insisted we meet near the railroad station. She was at the wheel of her car, accompanied by her husband, Abdallah Chibani, a science teacher who had lost his job and spent two years in prison for belonging to Yassine's movement. They took me to their home, a traditional apartment in a working-class neighborhood of Salé, across the river from the capital. Over mint tea, Nadia talked to me about her father's life and "struggle to return to the sources of Islam." Despite his long confinement, he was always optimistic, and spent most of the time reading and writing, although he enjoyed giving French lessons to his grandchildren.[14]

Enveloped in a royal-blue silk *djellaba* and headscarf, Nadia, in her mid-thirties, had an ethereal, ageless charm. When I asked the militant Islamist if I could take her picture, she said she needed to ask her father for permission. His response was: "No, the people aren't ready for it." She suggested that I photograph her paintings instead, "because there you can see my soul."

After King Mohammed VI acceded to the throne, the seventy-year-old Sheikh Yassine fired off another scathing open letter. This time, he urged the young monarch to restore his father's fortune—which he estimated at between $40 and $50 billion—to the people. The royal coffers, he said, could easily resolve the country's economic crisis. In his thirty-five-page epistle, the sheikh called the king a "novice" and presented statistics demonstrating the country's ills: the poverty, inequalities, unemployment, corruption, and illiteracy.

Rather than punish the unrepentant religious leader, as King Hassan had done, Mohammed VI took the daring step of setting Yassine free. One of my Socialist friends conceded that the sheikh's ideas concerning the royal fortune were valid, although his numbers might be exaggerated, and he only wished that the Left had the courage to make such a proposal.

I was to see Nadia many times afterward. Usually we would meet in front of the penitentiary near her home. Once she showed up in an elegant *djellaba* mounted on a Vespa and laughed when I admitted I'd never ridden one. I couldn't help remarking that in Saudi Arabia, Muslim women weren't even allowed to drive a car. This, she explained, was an example of the Saudis' more restrictive Wahhabi school of Islam.

As time went by, Nadia appeared discouraged despite her father's release and the more open era. She said there had been no real change for Ad Adl wal Ihsane; the sheikh was kept under constant surveillance and his followers harassed. The movement's prayer meetings at the beach and other demonstra-

Nadia Yassine, spokesperson for her father, Islamist leader Sheikh Abdessalam Yassine, denounces the government's plan for women's rights as "a plot against Islam," on July 11, 2001.

tions had been banned, and any defiance was met with repression, "harsher than before." Nadia and her whole family had been arrested and given four-month suspended sentences after a peaceful demonstration for human rights in December 2000.

Nadia's own position had changed, however. She had been discovered by the press. For the first time, her picture appeared, along with interviews in leading French and Spanish newspapers, as well as the independent Moroccan press. Now she readily agreed to being photographed, with only one condition, that her hair be covered, even indoors. Occasionally she accused journalists of misquoting her, like a statement to the Spanish daily *El Mundo*, in April 2002, where she purportedly called for an Islamic republic.

In fact, a photo of her face—framed by a headscarf—graces the cover of her book, *Toutes voiles dehors*, brought out by the progressive Casablanca publisher Le Fennec early in 2003 and openly sold in the main bookstores. The title, she explains, has nothing to do with "a panegyric on the headscarf," but comes from the French expression meaning "full sail ahead." It's a serious work, an accumulation of Nadia Yassine's views as a modern Islamist woman on a variety of subjects from Darwin to Descartes, from globalization to the clash of civilizations. In a preface written after the attacks of September 11, 2001—for whose victims she expresses compassion—she rejects

George W. Bush's ultimatum that those who are not with us are against us. She emphasizes that she is neither for nor against the United States but "for wisdom and balance, two concepts lacking as a basis for U.S. policy."[15]

By and large, Nadia Yassine has skillfully performed her mission: to portray a human, reasonable face of the Islamist movement. When I asked her about the rise of attacks attributed to radical Islamists, she reiterated that her father's movement was against violence. "It is the members of our movement who are the main victims of the Wahhabi extremists," she stressed.[16]

Islamist Moderates

When the Islamist movement emerged as an increasingly significant force in the Muslim world in the early 1980s, King Hassan adopted the same divide-and-rule tactics that he had used so successfully against the political opposition. Casting about for a moderate Islamist group to play against the radicals of Sheikh Yassine, the palace settled on the Jemaa al Islamiya (Islamic Community) as the best challenger.

Abdelillah Benkiran, the former Islamic Youth militant who had split off from Moutii's clandestine organization, recalls that at first Jemaa al Islamiya activists were arrested and tortured, and its newspaper seized and suspended. The persecution ended only when the regime became convinced that the association did not contest the king's spiritual authority and had opted for legal struggle within the system. Dr. Khatib's new Party for Justice and Development (PJD) fared well in the 1997 elections, sending ten deputies to parliament but refused to join Socialist prime minister Youssoufi's coalition cabinet. As the government's popularity waned, the moderate Islamists became more critical.

For the most part, the Islamist party acted as a responsible opposition, attacking the Youssoufi government for its failure to come to grips with national problems. But occasionally PJD militants indulged in verbal excesses that belied the party's mask of moderation. One of the most publicized incidents occurred on a steamy summer day in 2000, when the usually amiable Benkiran launched an indignant diatribe against a woman television photographer for daring to appear in a short-sleeved T-shirt in parliament. Most politicians and the press came to the defense of the photographer.

In July 2002, ignoring my short sleeves, Benkiran welcomed me warmly to his unpretentious home in a middle-class neighborhood of Rabat, shaking my hand energetically. The Islamic activist, with grizzled beard and broad smile, seemed to be trying to dispel any prejudices that an American woman journalist might harbor against Islamists.

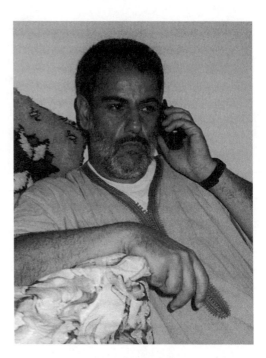

Abdelillah Benkiran, a leader of the moderate Islamist-based Party of Justice and Development, on July 3, 2002, expresses admiration for the ruling Turkish Islamist party of the same name.

"The world is afraid of us, even if they call us moderates . . . and we are moderates," the jovial Benkiran remarked, acknowledging that his party favors the restoration of the *Sharia,* or Islamic law. Benkiran emphasized that the PJD was dedicated to improving society and reforming the state: "We want to restore the moral principles of Islam against permissiveness, depravation, drugs, and corruption."[17]

Questioned about Al Qaeda, Benkiran said categorically: "Islam is not known for killing; it is nonviolent. Bin Laden's interpretation of Islam is false. It is no solution but leads to a circle of violence."

How does the Justice and Development party differ from Morocco's other main Islamist organization, Sheikh Yassine's Justice and Charity Association? I asked. Benkiran's response was simple: "We want to work within the system; the sheikh has problems with the system."

Participating in the national elections in the fall of 2002, the young and openly Islamist Justice and Development party astonished the nation by coming in third, after the Socialist Union and the conservative Istiqlal. Yet the PJD had presented candidates in only half of the districts. Had they run everywhere, the Islamists could have become the first party of the kingdom. In fact many people think they did come in first and were persuaded to graciously turn over a few seats to the two runner-ups, a rumor that Dr. Khatib categorically denied.

That winter, the Movement for Unification and Reform—the dominant Islamist current of the PJD—held a triumphal congress and reelected the fiery Islamic lawyer Ahmed Raissouni as president. A final communiqué stated that since Morocco is an Islamic country, the *Sharia* should be stipulated in the constitution. The movement declared war against "the rampant secularism" of French-educated Moroccans and accused the security services of "returning to the old methods of the *années de plomb*, like torture and kidnappings."[18]

But what attracted considerable attention at the congress was the presence of Fathallah Arsalane, the number two figure in Sheikh Yassine's Ad Adl wal Ihsane. It was the first time that leaders of the two rival Islamist movements had come together publicly, and the prospect of some kind of budding alliance sent shock waves through mainstream political circles.

Early in 2003, the PJD looked confidently to communal elections set for June and predicted it would win the mayorships of the main cities and towns around the country. That was before May 16.

Islamic Democrats

In the wake of the PJD's strong electoral performance in the fall of 2002, Moroccan newspapers began talking about an obscure group called Badil Hadari (Alternative Civilization). As its name implies, Badil proposes an alternative to other Islamic organizations. Its leaders have been called Islamic revisionists, leftist Islamists, and secular Muslims, but prefer the label Islamic Democrats (a counterpart to European Christian Democrats).

The founders of Badil are graduates of the radical Islamic Youth Association, like some PJD militants. Badil's spiritual leader is Brahim Kamal, who began his career in the National Union of Popular Forces before joining Abdelkrim Moutii to set up Chabiba Islamiya in 1969. After the murder of National Union leader Omar Benjelloun, Kamal spent four years in jail and then retired from politics until 1997, when he joined his old friends in Badil.

Badil activists have distinguished themselves from other Islamists on several important issues. The Islamic Democrats did not join the movement against the Socialist-led government's plan to emancipate women, and they have opened a dialogue with other political groups, including leftists, secularists, and Berbers. Finally, they were the only Islamists welcomed by the majority to take part in the march against terrorism after the May 16 suicide bombings.

Badil is an elite group with only a limited mass appeal—barely a hundred members, mostly teachers in the sciences. They transformed their association into a political party in 2000. Badil's views are increasingly sought by journalists and politicians concerned about the growing radicalization of Islamists. I met with representatives of Badil at my hotel in downtown Rabat in the wake of the May 16 Casablanca attacks.[19]

"The difference between us and the other Islamist groups is that we're open to all currents," said Badil's spokesman, Amine Ragala, a forty-four-year-old endocrinology professor at Fez. He told me the group had studied Marxism-Leninism and the Iranian revolution to see if these models could be applied in Morocco. (Their conclusion was that the United States wouldn't "permit" either system on the doorstep of Europe.) "We decided that the Islamist movement must be revised along democratic lines," he emphasized.

During the crisis that pitted Islamists against the Left on university campuses in the 1980s, Badil found its vocation as a bridge between Islamists and the Socialists, according to Ragala. "They were all violent. We began talking about democracy and got them to stop the violence in 1990," the Badil spokesman said, adding that they began publishing a monthly newspaper, *Al Jisr* (The Bridge), in 1992.

Mustapha Moatassim, Badil's secretary general and an alumnus of Chabiba Islamiya, pointed out that his group shares many ideals with the Left: the fight for human rights, social justice, a state of law, and democracy. On the other hand, they share with militant Islamists their piety and solidarity with the resistance movements in Palestine and Iraq. But Moatassim made it clear that Badil has substantial religious differences with other Islamists: "We don't say we have the Truth as they do, and we certainly don't speak in the name of God."

Badil condemned the September 11, 2001, attacks on the United States as "criminal acts" and declared Osama Bin Laden to be "anti-Islam," Ragala stressed. Likewise, the group denounced the American attacks on Afghan villages as "criminal acts."

As for the May 16, 2003, suicide bombings, the Badil spokesmen said it was necessary to determine the sociocultural causes, while differentiating between those who carried out the plot, who came from a marginal, socially excluded sector, and the manipulators. The state had opted for a security response to the violence; Badil agreed but insists that human rights be guaranteed and democratic gains not be sacrificed. "Democracy is the main rampart against terrorism," Ragala insists.

The Muslim Majority

When I first lived in Morocco in the 1950s, there was no Islamist problem. Moroccans were either devout or less devout but they were all Muslims, except for the small Jewish minority. The Islamic leadership had been largely discredited because most religious scholars, like the tribal chieftains, had fallen in line with the dominant protectorate authorities. Many *oulema* had actually supported the French maneuvers against the sultan, which shamed them in the eyes of the nationalists and the public at large.

Even today, it must be emphasized that the overwhelming majority of Moroccans are not Islamists, that is, those who seek political power. Most are practicing Muslims, but they do not belong to either of the mainstream Islamist organizations or to the radical subgroups.

In isolated mountain hamlets, the mosque is still the center of community life, where all important decisions are taken. Even very small villages, which have no other public building, will invariably have a mosque, often built with local contributions.

In Moroccan cities and towns, people appear to be more observant than in the past, but it is generally a tolerant, relaxed form of Islam. More men go to mosques; more women wear headscarves; and there are more Islamic volunteers working with underprivileged groups. Even Socialist activists observe Ramadan, the month-long period of daytime fasting and joyous evening family get-togethers.

On the other hand, there is an increasing tendency for Moroccans, particularly young men, to overlook the Koranic ban on alcohol, at least in the cities. "We're selective about sinning," a successful young businessman remarked over a Scotch at a charity reception. Long lines form outside Casablanca groceries that sell beer, and young people can be seen enjoying a glass of wine in cafes or restaurants, which supposedly serve alcohol to non-Muslims only. In the big cities, there are private, unpublicized dens of iniquity that specialize in beer and hashish and sexual companionship. Some households keep alcohol on hand for foreign guests but most tend not to serve it at family meals.

Over the many years I have lived and traveled in this country, I have never sensed any hostility from Moroccan individuals or even crowds directed toward me as a non-Muslim, even though I have an inescapably American look. Nor have any Moroccan Islamists refused to shake my hand because I am a woman, as often happens in Lebanon. No Moroccan I met justified or even condoned the terrorist attacks of September 11, 2001.

But Washington's policies have taken their toll. A poll in the popular Arabic daily *Al Ahdath Al Maghribia* showed that 75 percent of Moroccans denounced the attacks against the World Trade Center and the Pentagon as "the work of fanatics who blacken the image of Islam." At the same time 72 percent believed that Osama Bin Laden was innocent and that the cause of these attacks was "American policy in favor of Israel." And 97 percent thought the U.S. war in Afghanistan was solely to preserve economic and political interests.[20]

Radical Islamists

To be sure, a number of radical *imams* emerged in the 1990s, taking advantage of the more liberal atmosphere. Their discourse was one of hatred and intransigence, and from time to time they would issue bombastic *fetwas* that were nonbinding. But their violence was verbal, and it was not clear how much influence they exercised. These radical preachers and their followers formed loosely structured groups, poorly organized and not coordinated, according to Mohamed Tozy, professor of political science at Hassan II University in Casablanca and author of the book *Monarchy and Political Islam in Morocco.*[21]

Among the most popular radicals, the outspoken Sheikh Abdelbari Zemzmi, sixty, was a preacher at Casablanca's Ould Hamra Mosque. Known for anti-Semitic pronouncements, Sheikh Zemzmi delivered a virulent attack on August 31, 2001, against "the Left and Jews," calling them "enemies of Islam." In what was seen as reference to the murdered Socialist leader Ben Barka, the sheikh said that anyone who rebelled against the sultan, fled his country, and renounced his religion "deserved to be killed." Zemzmi's *fetwa*, which was reproduced in some Moroccan newspapers, was denounced by human rights organizations.

Another fiery *fetwa* was issued just one week after the terrorist attacks on the World Trade Center and the Pentagon. A group of eighteen *oulema* condemned Morocco's support of the American bombardment of Muslim Afghanistan. The *oulema* also proclaimed the banishment of any Muslim participating in religious rites in a church or synagogue, emphasizing that this was "one of the greatest sins." This was an indirect attack against the prime minister, members of the government, military officers, and other dignitaries, who had attended a religious service in Rabat's cathedral in memory of the victims of September 11. The group of *oulema* even criticized the minister of Islamic affairs for imposing a prayer of "fraternity and peace" in mosques around the country on September 14, as "an infringement on the freedom of *imams*." The *oulema* did express their "emotion" over the attack on the American people but said the American government "should seek the reasons for such hatred and review its international policies."

After some arm-twisting by the Ministry of Islamic Affairs, eight of the *oulema* recanted, declaring that their names had appeared erroneously on the fetwa. A few days later, however, a group of 244 *oulema*, professors, parliamentarians, and preachers expressed their solidarity with the September 18 *fetwa*.

No heads rolled, but the minister of Islamic affairs issued a statement closing the chapter. Declaring that a *fetwa* must be the work of "honorable persons," Minister Abdelkébir Alaoui M'daghri stressed that it should be made in consultation with specialists. It is the Council of Oulema that has the task of drafting *fetwas*, to be submitted to the king, as *Amir al Mouminine* and president of the Higher Council of Oulema. No one outside this procedure is authorized to proclaim a *fetwa*, the minister emphasized.

Even the most radical Islamists have generally refrained from attacking the king and the royal family, because this is forbidden by law. But Islamists have no compunctions about denouncing the government or Muslims they deem to be wayward unbelievers, particularly women.

Women's groups had been warning for some time about the violent language against women that was being used in some mosques, religious books, and audiocassettes. The Democratic League for the Rights of Women reported an increase in threats against women since the national debate over the reform of the Moudawana or Family Code in 2000.

"The Casablanca Book Fair has been flooded by books preaching racism, hatred of women, and anti-Semitism, published in Egypt and selling for one or two *dirhams* [10–20 cents]," said Najat Ikhich, a professor of Arabic who heads the league. She said that *intégristes* had besieged the stands of the women's associations and blocked a speech by Saïd Saâdi, the main author of the government's reforms of the Family Code.[22]

Ikhich recalled that during the league's Caravan for Justice and Equality that summer, the *imam* of a mosque in Marrakech had declared: "There cannot be equality of the sexes because women lack reason and religion. . . . Science has proven that the masculine brain weighs an average 100 grams more than the feminine brain." During Friday prayers, another *imam*, at Kasba Tadla, a market town in the Middle Atlas, accused the women in the caravan of being "unbelievers" and said they should be stoned.

At the end of January 2002, the league held an international conference at Casablanca on "Women and the Discourse of Religious Extremists." At that time, the league warned of the dangers of such violent speech for women and society as a whole and called on the government to control the cassettes and books that preach hatred in the guise of religion.

In the weeks that followed, a number of violent acts were linked to religious extremists. There was the murder of a notary, several aggressions against young girls and boys for walking together in public, the murder of a girl by her father for secretly meeting a boy, and the murder of a policeman for insulting religion. The Moroccan Women's Center of Information and

Observation, a partner of the league, accused the authorities of "ignoring the acts of violence by religious extremists and allowing *fetwas* justifying assassination." In an urgent appeal, the center demanded that the government stop the spread of books and other materials inciting hatred, ban the use of mosques for politics, establish ethical and educational criteria for religious personnel, and review school programs dealing with Islamic education.

But little attention was paid to the women's warnings until May 16, 2003.

The Al Qaeda Connection

Moroccans were stunned in June 2002 by revelations that the security services had broken up an Al Qaeda network in Casablanca and arrested ten persons. The terrorist group was allegedly planning attacks against American and NATO naval vessels in the Strait of Gibraltar, similar to the Al Qaeda attack that crippled the USS *Cole* in the Yemen port of Aden on October 12, 2000. The Casablanca cell was also said to have worked out plans for other terrorist actions, including bomb attacks on cafes at Djemaa el-Fna Square, the popular tourist site in Marrakech, and against a Moroccan bus company.

Although it was emphasized that the leaders of the conspiracy were three Saudi nationals, their accomplices were Moroccan. More disconcerting for the Moroccan public was the fact that these Saudis were said to have integrated themselves into the local society for more than two years, establishing businesses, marrying Moroccan women, and developing multiple contacts.

Even in the wake of the discovery of this Al Qaeda cell, the then minister of Islamic affairs, Abdelkébir Alaoui M'daghri, stressed that the group had been detected by the vigilant secret services. "Moroccans refuse terrorism," the minister insisted and added, "For this reason, Morocco will never become a base for terrorist activities."[23]

In the wake of the publicity given to the Al Qaeda connection, Morocco's main Islamist groups vehemently reiterated their opposition to violence. They emphasized that the suspected terrorists practiced Wahhabism, which is opposed by Morocco's mainstream Muslims of the Malekite rite. Some Islamists suggested that the revelations were aimed to scare the public and dissuade them from voting for the moderate Islamist party in the forthcoming elections.

Ordinary citizens, who had thought that Morocco was immune to this kind of Islamic extremism, were shaken to learn that their country too was vulnerable. When several weeks later, police services announced the discovery of a clandestine network of Salafiya Jihadia Islamic extremists who were implicated in vicious crimes, people began to panic.

In July 2002, a young Islamist preacher, Youssef Fikri, was arrested for trying to steal a taxi in Tangier. This incident led to the discovery of a group of Islamic vigilantes, said to have terrorized communities around the country. Fikri, who goes by the title of *emir*, turned out to be the leader of a religious organization known as Hijra wa Takfir (Excommunication and Retrenchment). The *emir* boasted that Hijra wa Takfir aimed to root out evil and restore order in the decadent Moroccan society. He reportedly admitted to committing six murders, including that of his own uncle because he "reeked of alcohol."

In the wake of Fikri's confession, the judiciary police arrested fifteen militants of Hijra wa Takfir on charges of murder, kidnapping, abduction, and illegal possession of weapons. The group was accused of more than 150 criminal acts in a three-year period; their weapons of choice were knives and swords. The other activists in the group were said to have gone into hiding. The police identified the spiritual leader of the group as a Casablanca herbalist named Ben Daoud, who escaped arrest. He was said to have encouraged the militants to seize money, jewelry, and other valuables from their irreligious victims.

As the horrors attributed to the Fikri gang were reported in great detail, some independent newspapers and political sources suggested that the Al Qaeda and Salafiya Jihadia threats had been blown up by the national secret services to enhance their role and win favor with the United States. It was pointed out that the original tip-off about the Casablanca Al Qaeda cell had come from Moroccan prisoners held in the American camp at Guantanamo Bay.

Khalid Jamai, a maverick columnist, writing in the independent French-language weekly *Le Journal*, summed it all up as "bullshit," using the English term to make his point. He stressed that the operation had been first reported abroad, that no plans had been revealed and no arms seized. Jamai argued that the Al Qaeda sleeper cell was just another exercise in American "disinformation."[24]

Yet international investigations continued to link Moroccan suspects to Al Qaeda. A typical case was that of Mounir Motassadeq, a twenty-eight-year-old Moroccan charged with links to Al Qaeda's Hamburg cell, who had resided in Germany since 1995 and spent three months in Afghanistan in 2000.

It appeared that most of the Moroccans arrested in connection with Al Qaeda were living abroad, mainly in Europe, and had been there for years. This was a certain consolation for those Moroccans who continued to believe in the national myth that local Islamists were nonviolent.

In an article on the "Moroccan Taliban" in August 2002, *Maroc-Hebdo*'s

Abdellatif Mansour noted that a number of Moroccans implicated in Al Qaeda activities were overseas residents, "all indoctrinated and recruited in mosques on the outskirts of European cities." The writer pointed out that the two presumed assassins of Northern Alliance commander Massaoud in Afghanistan were Belgian Moroccans. Zakaria Moussaoui, the first suspect held in the United States on charges of involvement in the September 11 attacks, is a French Moroccan. The 1994 Islamist attack on Spanish tourists in Marrakech was said to be the work of French Moroccans, whose leader belonged to Al Qaeda and received training in Afghanistan.

"The Moroccan exception is still valid," Mansour wrote. "But Morocco is not protected from *intégrisme* without borders."[25] This was another way of saying that terror in the name of Islam was now globalized, and no country was immune.

The Islamist Threat

Meanwhile, the authorities were investigating other radical Islamic groups linked to Salafiya Jihadia. This umbrella organization of small cells of Islamist zealots was set up in the early 1990s by Moroccans returning from the war in Afghanistan, high-level security sources told me, on condition of anonymity. The Casablanca-based movement was said to have 400 members, known as *jihadists*, organized in separate cells around an *emir*, without any central leadership. As a rule, the Salafiya Jihadia militants held prayer sessions and debates in private homes. Their main source of inspiration was said to be Osama Bin Laden, although direct connections have not been proven. One of the better-known local ideologues was said to be the radical preacher Mohamed Fizazi, who favors the strict implementation of the *Sharia* and *jihad*. The *jihadists* contest the religious legitimacy of the monarchy and the validity of the constitution and hold that religious leaders must be chosen by the *oulema* and that the Koran is the supreme law of the nation.

Security sources told me bookstores reportedly linked to Salafiya Jihadia were found selling extremist Islamic literature, audiocassettes, and videos, just as the women's groups had warned. Some of the material was said to have been imported from Saudi Arabia and other Gulf states and reproduced in studios and publishing houses in Casablanca and other cities. Security services admitted they were only beginning to discover the extent of this subversive, clandestine network.

The Moroccan public was appalled by increasing reports of criminal actions by Islamic extremists. The Socialist daily *Libération* lashed out against "the phony theologians" and "fanatics," who have no project to combat poverty and injustice and resort to violence. Ordinary Moroccans questioned anxiously if the country was becoming another Algeria—shorthand for the bloody civil war between Islamic extremists and the military-led regime that has torn the neighboring North African country apart for more than a decade

Dismissing the grim revelations as an aberration, a leader of the main Islamist party, Abdelillah Benkiran, told me reassuringly: "Morocco is not Algeria and never will be. . . . We moderate Islamists are part of the political landscape and form a wall against the radicals."[26]

Could Morocco's moderate Islamists turn violent? I asked Islamic expert Mohamed Tozy. "Yes, it is possible, if they believe they are right and are deprived of that right," Tozy replied.[27]

The Conflicting Worlds of Women

6

One of the main differences between then—pre-independence Morocco—and now is the women. Before, they appeared like silent extras on a male stage, although there were militants behind the veils. Today's women are the most dynamic sector of Moroccan society, pressing to improve the lives of their families, correct social ills, and eliminate lingering inequalities. Maybe they are not present at the highest echelons of the administration, but they predominate in nongovernmental organizations and have climbed to the top in the private sector. And they are determined to break through any remaining artificial barriers.

What is astonishing is that nearly a half century after independence— when women cast off their veils and went out into the world—more and more women are putting on the *hijab*, the veil or tight-fitting headscarf, which has become an Islamist symbol in Muslim societies everywhere.

There seem to be two divergent worlds coexisting side by side: one in which women are struggling to participate fully in the twenty-first century and another where they are clinging to tradition and religion in opposition to what they see as the pitfalls of modern life. Some believe they can have the best of both worlds. They are pious, headscarved women, who have pursued their education, mastered computers, worked beside men, and entered the halls of parliament.

Many of these young women who don the *hijab* today do not know how grim life was for their grandmothers or how hard the struggle has been for their mothers merely to participate in decision making in their families and communities.

Harem Life

On the eve of independence, women were practically invisible. Ghostly shapes in voluminous white *haiks* or plain, dark *djellabas* glided along the city streets. Silent domestics shuffled in and out of salons, bearing huge platters of exquisitely prepared food. Figures bent in two, laden with firewood, trotted along the mountain roads, hardly distinguishable from other beasts of burden. Those few Muslim women who were educated could do little with their instruction, except to pass it on to their children and hope for a better future.

As a woman, I was permitted to penetrate the harem—that secluded world of feminine fantasies. The Moroccan harem was not the Orientalists' vision of curtained chambers, where wives and concubines languished in sensual bliss. It was simply what the Arabic word implies, "a place of security," where the women and children of a household gathered to exchange confidences and to dream, where no males were welcome, except immediate family. It was a small world of great passions, bitter resentments, hatred, ambition, desire, and frustrations.

In the mid-1950s, however, it was already possible to observe a generational change in the harem women. Typically, there was the grandmother, a victim of Islamic tradition and colonial neglect, whose education was primarily in the Koranic principle of female obedience. Wrapped in cotton fabric with tattoos on her forehead and chin—ancient signs of beauty—she was formless from excessive childbearing. Generally sold off in an arranged marriage by age thirteen, she would have a dozen or so children and lose half of them in infancy. By the time she reached twenty-five, she was old. Her husband would often repudiate her for a second wife, and she would go home to her family. Day in and day out, she could be found sitting on the floor, kneading bread or singing Arabic lullabies to a grandchild. She never left the house.

The daughter in her forties would go out to visit female neighbors or relatives, but she always wore a *djellaba* and a veil that covered her face except for the eyes. She had usually been married by fifteen to a cousin or some other suitable mate, chosen by her family. After ten years of marriage, the husband frequently abandoned his wife for a younger woman. Or, if he were well-to-do, he might keep her for the sake of the children and take a second wife. As a rule, the abandoned wife was illiterate, but some did speak a smattering of French in addition to Arabic or Berber because they had worked as servants in French homes. Usually she would spend most of her time in the kitchen preparing meals over a charcoal fire. Her only distractions were the radio that played Egyptian music all day long, a weekly visit to the neighborhood *hammam* (Moorish bath), Friday afternoon strolls in the public gardens, and occasional all-women tea parties. But she would send her sons and youngest daughters to school because *Sidna* (our Lord, meaning the sultan) said girls should get an education too (she couldn't afford to send all of the girls).

The ten- to thirteen-year-old girls seemed to come from another planet. Wearing French skirts and sweaters, they spoke fluent French and Arabic and a smattering of English and were determined to obtain their *baccalauréat* degree. They wanted to work in an office to have economic independence. They would not marry until they were twenty at least, and then it must be to a man of their own choosing.

These young girls were the modest results of forty years of France's "civilizing mission." Official French statistics confirmed that in 1952, only 163,000, or 10 percent, of Moroccans of school age were enrolled in public schools and barely one-quarter of them were girls. Most of these were in primary or vocational schools; there were only two girls at university level. (These figures do not include Moroccan Jewish girls, who were almost all educated in schools of the Alliance Israelite.)

I came to know pioneers of this first generation of Western-educated Moroccan women: bright, aspiring misfits. Having shown that they could compete favorably with their European and male peers, there was no place for them to go. Nice Muslim women did not work outside the home and were discouraged from appearing in public places. For this elite, the only way they could find freedom was to continue their studies abroad and, if possible, marry a foreigner.

Royal Champions

The first champion of women's rights in modern Morocco was Sultan Mohammed V, who had raised his daughters as modern, educated woman and urged his countrymen to follow his example. Bound by their ancient patriarchal society, most Moroccans, however, were reluctant to send their daughters to school, the royal example notwithstanding.

"My father forced me into feminism," the oldest princess, Lalla Aicha, an attractive, fun-loving young woman, told me once before independence. She was fourteen when the sultan ordered her to make her first political speech, demanding rights for Moroccan women. She admitted she didn't know what he was talking about at the time because she had been raised by French *gouvernantes* and wasn't aware that Moroccan women needed help. Later, while working for her *baccalauréat*, the Western-dressed Lalla Aicha frequently spoke at openings of private Arabic schools, calling on families to send their daughters to school. In April 1947, at her father's bidding, Princess Aicha broadcast a speech from Tangier that rocked the nation. She recalled her words in an interview in 1956, and they were hardly incendiary. Urging Moroccans "to root out and reject bad customs and prejudices," she declared: "His Majesty wants the Moroccan woman to be able to cope with her obligations towards her country and her King as well as to perform her duties as wife and mother in the home."

Traditionalists were incensed, not so much by the message as by the act of a Moroccan woman—albeit a princess—speaking in public. A zealous official in Tangier went so far as to arrest some unveiled women to demonstrate that the behavior of a princess was not necessarily acceptable for ordinary citizens. But it was the local French authorities who were most disturbed by the princess's Tangier speech. They promptly labeled her as a radical nationalist, and forbade her from speaking in public. French colonial officials rightly saw that if they encouraged the emancipation of Moroccan women, it would be difficult to turn around and deny the liberation of the society as a whole.

Silenced, Lalla Aicha soon stirred further controversy by acting like her French peers: smoking, driving a car, riding horseback, and going to the beach. In fact one reason given by the French and their feudal allies for the expulsion of the sultan and his family in 1953 was that he had allowed his daughter to wear a bikini on a public beach.

Crown Prince Moulay Hassan followed his father's lead as president of the Moroccan Students Association, which encouraged women to play a more active role. I recall the students' association sponsored an exhibition of Morocco's first publicly recognized woman painter, Meriem Mezian. It was 1952. Challenging Muslim restrictions on reproducing the human form, Mezian presented a handsome parade of Moroccan men—and women without veils. The exhibit was warmly received in Casablanca and Rabat, but there were rumblings that such a display by a woman might anger the religious authorities.

I met the twenty-two-year-old artist, who came from a prominent family of the Spanish zone, in the home of an aunt in Casablanca, where Arabic, French, and Spanish were spoken fluently. Wearing an elegant European suit, Mezian confessed that she did not have any formal art training but had studied the techniques of Spanish and foreign masters at the Prado in Madrid. She planned to return to Spain to initiate art studies. "One day I will come back to live and work in my country, when my country is ready for me," she told me.

The deposing of the sultan and the exile of the royal family to Madagascar in 1953 galvanized the nationalist movement for independence and, with it, Moroccan women's longing for personal liberation. For a time, the two struggles were synonymous. In the name of the exiled sultan, women began taking off their veils in Casablanca and other cities and participated in nationalist gatherings and protest demonstrations. Many women, even those who kept their veils, served as nationalist liaison agents, distributing tracts, collecting funds, or carrying weapons for the resistance. Some men were known to have disguised themselves as veiled women to escape attention. It is ironic how important the veil, that symbol of a retrograde Islam, was to the nationalist movements in North Africa.

Independence and the Women's Struggle

In the joyous aftermath of independence, women thought their fight was over. When I interviewed Princess Aicha after her two years' exile, she appeared more mature and confident of her role as a leader. She pointed out that before 1953, talk of women's rights had been practically taboo. But women had won recognition for their role during the country's struggle for the return of the sultan and national sovereignty. When the nationalist struggle got really tough, North African men discovered the role of women in society. They also saw that independence couldn't be won by only half the nation. "Today there's no problem," the princess assured me:

> Everyone is for the emancipation of women. It's a question of education. But mind you, it's the men who must be educated. They are the despots, the masters in a Moroccan home. Moroccan men must be made to understand the utility of women in society. Thank God a lot of them understand now. What I want is equality, political and social equality. Equality is possible if the women are good sports about it and the men are less mule-headed.[1]

The princess, who was named coordinator of Moroccan charitable institutions by her father, acknowledged that there were still many veiled women. "We won't force them to remove their veils," she stressed. "We'll give them the right to vote and then their veils will fall off automatically."

Of course it didn't happen that way, but at least women had the choice.

The most dramatic change after independence was the rush for education. New schools were opened all over the country. The enrollment of girls in primary and secondary schools more than doubled in two years, from

60,000 at independence to 140,000 in 1958. Even traditional dignitaries, who had denounced the sultan for giving too much freedom to his daughters, were soon encouraging their daughters and granddaughters to pursue their studies.

Independent Morocco, badly in need of cadres, opened the doors of the administration to women, but not at the top levels. Like women in other countries, Moroccans initially turned to jobs as nurses, social services workers, receptionists, and secretaries. The first women to hold political office were Jacqueline Cohen, a Jewish lawyer, named attaché to the prime minister, and Latifa Hassar, a Muslim with a master's degree in Latin and Greek from the Sorbonne, who was named an attaché in the Ministry of Education.

Early on, the Moroccan government drafted legislation to protect women, setting fifteen as a minimum marriage age for girls, banning repudiation, and providing favorable pension terms and maternity leave with full pay. It was a timid start, Moroccan feminists stressed, enviously eyeing Tunisia, which had won independence from France at the same time. Tunisian president Habib Bourguiba, a benevolent dictator, had gone much further, ruling out polygamy, giving women the right to vote, and banning the veil in public schools and government offices. Tunisia's 1957 Personal Status Code explicitly guaranteed women equality in civil rights, abolished polygamy, banned forced marriages, and corrected abuses in the divorce law.

Advocates of women's rights in the political parties held that individual liberation—after national liberation—was inevitable. They were overly optimistic. The Istiqlal party, which had an active feminist organization before independence, apparently lost enthusiasm afterward for women's concerns, such as illiteracy and political participation. There were many other, more pressing problems that concerned the male-dominated party, like national security, economic development, and political power.

"The feminist movement has progressed less than any other national effort since independence," Douglas Ashford wrote in 1961. "Adequate treatment of illiteracy and feminist problems requires a vast social change which the political system has not yet encouraged."[2]

Nevertheless, the impact of independence on Moroccan women's lives was noticeable on city streets, on cafe terraces, and in shops. Young women and girls were suddenly very visible, unveiled with long braids, wearing skirts and sweaters, rushing to school or the workplace, chatting with friends (including males) in snack bars, milling through department stores. The countryside, to be sure, looked much as it had before. Women were still laboring in the fields, gathering firewood, carrying water, and grinding grain, in addition to their tasks of keeping house and having babies. But, at least, they were beginning to send their children to school.

Slow Road to Emancipation

Some four decades later, things have changed for women, but not nearly to the extent that I had expected or that most Moroccan women desired. Since my return, I have talked to scores of women from varied walks of life, and none are happy with the slow progress of women in the society. The tradition of male domination is more deeply rooted than women had believed.

Feminism in Morocco was mainly instigated by the state, political parties, and civil society and generally has not taken the form of a direct struggle against men, according to Fatima Sadiqi, author of *Women, Gender and Language in Morocco*. "In Morocco, feminism is a result of the encounter of the Moroccan indigenous culture/civilization and ways of life with Western culture/civilization and ways of life," she writes, adding that this encounter is often referred to as "modernism."[3]

Sadiqi points out that from the 1980s to the present, two basic trends of Moroccan feminism have coexisted: "Whereas liberal feminism is secular and takes universal human rights to be its major reference," conservative feminism is religious and takes Islamic law to be its major reference.

It is difficult for the modernists, who see the manipulation of religion as the principal obstacle to their emancipation, to understand their Islamic counterparts or conceive of cooperating with them. Nouzha Skalli, a pharmacist by profession, has dedicated her adult life to fighting for women's rights through various women's nongovernmental organizations. Elected a member of parliament in 2002 for the Communist-inspired Party of Progress and Socialism, Skalli articulated the modernists' suspicions and fear of radical Islamists at a seminar in the wake of the May 16, 2003, suicide bombings. The terrorist attacks were "the prolongation of another form of terrorism—the discourse of hatred, racism, discrimination and violence of Islamic extremists," she said. Their main objective was "to terrorize the population, block the project for a modern society, including women's emancipation, and replace it with an Islamist project. . . . in sum, a dictatorial regime in the guise of religion."[4]

It is equally difficult for Islamic feminists to convey their views of Islam as a liberating force. Nadia Yassine can be considered an Islamic feminist, although she might reject the epithet. In her book, *Toutes voiles dehors*, she depicts the Prophet Mohammed as a leader who opened the doors of mosques to women "as a sign that they are equal to men before God." Yassine denounces the succeeding autocratic regimes in Muslim lands as being imbued with "a slave mentality that turned women into ordinary, if beautiful, merchandise for speculation." Blaming politics—not religion—for this degrading situation, she emphasizes, "The liberation of women from the yoke of tradition must be part of the global struggle to eliminate archaic and authoritarian political systems."[5]

The dichotomy in feminist activism in Morocco could be one explanation for the slow progress of women in achieving equal rights, according to Sadiqi. She emphasizes, however, that both the conservatives and the modernists condemn current practices in Morocco as antiwoman.

Most statistics show a sorry picture of the condition of Moroccan women, although one relatively positive development is the sharp decline in the birth rate. In 1960, women had an average of seven children; by 2000, that figure was down to three. The palace, along with the main political parties, launched a national family planning program in 1965 to control the rampant population increase. The slowdown in births has been brought about by the widespread use of contraceptives. But there were also negative factors: the prolonged economic crisis and the scarcity of jobs and housing have significantly delayed marriages and births.

For me, the most appalling fact was that 67 percent of women were illiterate (89 percent in rural areas) compared to 41 percent for men, according to the government's 1999 Plan for the Integration of Women.[6] The literacy rate of children aged seven to twelve was better: 55 percent for girls (only 34 percent in rural areas), compared to 74 percent for boys. The number of women in the workforce was still abysmally low at just over 17 percent (housewives, of course, and rural women working on family farms were not counted), according to official statistics. Of equal concern was the fact that urban working women were hardest hit by unemployment, nearly 30 percent, compared to 17 percent for their male counterparts. Although education was theoretically compulsory for children between seven and thirteen, child labor was still common. Children were employed in the rug making, textile, and leather industries. Very often they were used as domestics without wages, or as child prostitutes.

On the surface, it seems that women are making slow headway toward their goal of equality and have even regressed if one takes into consideration the large numbers of young women who have put on headscarves in recent years. In the fall of 2002, the Moroccan weekly *TelQuel* devoted a cover story to the question: why is the *hijab* gaining ground?[7]

Among the reasons for this return to the veil cited by *TelQuel* is "intellectual harassment"—persistent campaigns for the *hijab* as a religious obligation, through mosques, audiotapes, religious literature, and Arab television networks from the Middle East. Televangelists present "the model Muslim woman" as one who affirms her faith and identity through the *hijab*. Also, the *hijab* is becoming big business. Catalogs, Internet sites, and international franchises offer an array of clothing for the veiled woman. Social studies show that some girls put on headscarves in hopes of getting a husband because it is widely held that a "covered" woman is more likely to be a virgin—and that still counts in Moroccan society. Students are quoted as saying they wear the headscarf as a means of winning "social respect."

In personal conversations with many young Moroccan women, I concluded that they wear the *hijab* for all of these reasons and because they want to, not because of pressures from devout families. As a rule, girls are free to wear the *hijab* or not; one sister may cover, another dress in the most provocative Western fashion. Morocco had apparently come to terms with the headscarf issue. Moroccan women were generally free to wear headscarves in classrooms, public buildings, and the workplace. Mainstream Islamist parties did not force their members and sympathizers to cover during political rallies, although most of them did.

But in the wake of May 16 and other acts of violence by Islamic extremists, positions have begun to harden. The *hijab* is increasingly seen as a symbol for another lifestyle competing with the modern, Western-oriented way. On the one hand, there are reports of certain preachers in urban areas exhorting women to "dress religiously" and zealots in remote towns castigating women for "un-Islamic" appearance. In the opposing camp, some factories and businesses reportedly have barred headscarves from their premises. The Islamist press protests that girls wanting to attend military academies, become flight attendants, or join the police force are not allowed to wear headscarves.

The growing tension over the *hijab* has all the appearances of a storm in a teacup—except that it comes as yet another obstacle to reaching unity between modernist women and their Islamist counterparts. This religious symbol can raise powerful emotions, as seen in the demonstrations in France, protesting a ban on religious dress in public schools. In the "headscarf war" in secular Turkey, the prohibition of headscarves in schools and government buildings has become a major human rights issue.

Success Stories

When given the chance, Moroccan women have demonstrated that they can hold their own with their counterparts anywhere. One area where women have gained prominence is the media. Hinde Taarji, a real professional by any standards, made her name in 1986 at *Kalima*, the first Moroccan magazine to openly discuss taboo subjects like abortion, child prostitution, and sexuality, before it was shut down in 1989. Subsequently Taarji wrote for different political publications and openly denounced the catastrophic education system, the neglected public health service, and the pervasive corruption, not mincing her words. "Before, honor was fundamental," Taarji told me. "Under Hassan II, money became the main value, the measure of success."[8]

After a prolonged tour of the Middle East, Taarji brought out a book, *The Veils of Islam*, in 1990, an objective picture of contemporary Muslim women, followed by a television documentary on the subject. Her 1998 book, *Thirty Days in Algeria*, is a straightforward look at the Algerian civil war, based on interviews with different players in this tragedy. She now writes a controversial column on social and political issues for the weekly *La Vie Economique*.

Bahia Amrani studied political science at Rabat Law School and was "fascinated by politics." She made her way to the top in journalism, working at different political publications and the French service of the BBC. Today she is publisher of a small independent political weekly, the *Reporter*. Amrani doesn't hesitate to investigate official scandals, but she does it without the insolence and sensationalism that characterize the reporting in some of the other independent journals. She admits that she is afraid of Islamists, even the so-called moderates. "They have said they want to impose *Sharia* and that would be the end of my freedom," Amrani said in a conversation in her comfortable Casablanca flat. "I believe they must be integrated into the system. But there must be a more active counterforce to push the democratic agenda."[9] This was a reference to the mainstream political parties, the increasingly active civil society, and the press.

The glossy women's magazine *Women of Morocco* is run largely by women for women and deals with much more than food, fashions, and beauty tips. Publisher Aicha Zaimi Sakhri emphasizes that in a country where nearly 70 percent of the women are illiterate, a woman's magazine must have a strong educational content. And so every issue contains articles to help women adapt to modern life. There is a wide range of subjects: how to obtain small business loans, the activities of volunteer organizations, the need to change civil law, life after divorce, adult children living with parents, how to find a husband, and the nuts and bolts of elections. Sakhri says the magazine is completely independent, but "we don't give space to *intégristes*."[10]

There are also a number of very competent female political reporters. One of the best known, Narjis Rerhaye, has had a politically diverse career, working for a Communist daily at one time and currently reporting for *Le Matin du Sahara*, the voice of the establishment. Critics fault her for volatility but she is a good writer and an excellent interviewer and brightens otherwise stodgy political reporting.

Another young woman, Amina Talhimet, writes on foreign policy for the Socialist party's daily, *Libération*. Her style is clear and strong, and she will call a spade a spade. For example, commenting on the preparations for war in Iraq, she wrote: "The Bush administration wants to impose on the world a war against Iraq. And the world doesn't want this war. . . . The world had unanimously said yes to a war against extremist terror. Today it is almost unanimous in saying NO to total war against Iraq and its people."[11]

Women have invaded other domains formerly reserved for men. Perhaps the best example of a successful woman in a heretofore man's field is Amina Benkhadra, the country's first woman mining engineer, who today heads two important state agencies, the Bureau of Mines and the National Petroleum Office. A bright, hard-working woman, Benkhadra made her way up through the administration by her personal achievements. But even she emphasizes she would have remained at director level if the late King Hassan hadn't shown confidence in her work, naming her secretary of state in charge of mining development in 1997. "There are many women today in medicine, education, industry, business, even in geology and mining," Benkhadra told me in an interview. "Without King Hassan's support and now that of King Mohammed, it would have taken a lot more time."[12]

Today's urban women are busy, not only raising families and attending to household chores but engaged in activities outside the home. They are

Amina Benkhadra, director of the Departments of Mines and Petroleum, on July 18, 2001, expresses hope that offshore oil exploration will yield positive results.

mobile, multitrack women, like their sisters in the United States. Souad Douiri, wife of my old friend and a leader of the Istiqlal party, puts in a full work week running her family's bookstore in Rabat. Malika Jebro, a journalist's wife, has opened a boutique with her daughter, and together they design and market traditional and modern clothes.

Hnya Benchakroun-Brick, wife of an engineer with two young children, started out as an architect and found her vocation as a jewelry designer. Learning the trade by watching traditional craftsmen, Benchakroun-Brick, who comes from a prominent Moroccan family, transforms ancient pieces of silver—generally with Jewish or Berber motifs—into exotic modern jewelry by adding bits and clusters of semiprecious stones. She has opened her tiny shop, AyourBijou (which means Moon Jewelry from the Berber word for moon and the French word for jewelry), in a working-class quarter of Rabat. In early May 2004, Benchakroun-Brick made her international debut with a display of her art at the Paris fair "Riches of the World," and now she is launched.

Her sister Zeinab Benchakroun, a senior financial analyst in an insurance company, is married to a business executive and they have two children. She decided in the spring of 2004 that she could no longer sit back and enjoy her

Hnya Benchakroun-Brick, Moroccan wife, mother, and architect, makes her debut in a new career as jewelry designer, inspired by traditional Berber and Jewish motifs.

family and job, but had to do some kind of social work. She took a year's leave of absence to join the social committee of the Moroccan Confederation of Businesses, which aims to serve as a bridge between business and the new world of neighborhood associations. Benchakroun explains her job was to work with RESAQ, a network of some fifty associations in the greater Casablanca area, to help them market their projects.

Many Islamist women are not shy recluses. They attend coeducational schools and, along with male Islamists, have virtually taken over the student organizations. They have gone into professions like law and medicine and work in nonsegregated shops and offices. Visible in their tight headscarves, showing no hair, they are educated, devout, and hard working.

Hakima Moktari, twenty-seven, is a social services worker at Rabat's Avicennes Hospital and also a member of the leadership of the Women's Section of Sheikh Yassine's Justice and Charity Association. This Islamist heads the hospital's unit of the Women Victims of Violence. At Moktari's insistence, the hospital admits to the emergency ward women who are chased from their domiciles without identity papers and cannot pay for treatment. "The number of victims is increasing daily," she emphasizes. "They come from all milieus, even a judge who was beaten up by her husband."[13]

A prominent member of parliament is Bassima Hakkaoui, the elegantly veiled deputy of the Islamist Party of Justice and Development for Casablanca. Hakkaoui, forty-three, acknowledges that she was an atheist until age twenty. A woman with an inquiring mind, she says she sought truth through her studies in philosophy and social psychology "and found it in Islam." She has worn the *hijab* since she turned twenty-two but sounds at times like a feminist. She is critical of the lack of gender equity in Morocco and says: "Men are true to themselves and don't consider women equal, even those with the same level of studies. Women have more obligations than rights." At the same time, the Islamist deputy insists that the legal base of family relations must be the *Sharia* and not foreign jurisprudence. She claims that the question of guardianship is "a false problem" because nowadays families do not force girls to marry against their will. And she defends polygamy as "a woman's right because men are required to face their responsibilities."[14]

Then there are all those apolitical women who have to work all day just to make ends meet and care for their children and home at night. Khadija is a grade school teacher in Casablanca with two children. Her husband was an alcoholic and treated her "like a slave," but refused to give her a divorce. Now he has disappeared, and she is thankful to have a job. Aicha is a thirty-eight-year-old housemaid who wants to do something better, and so in her spare time she goes to a government-sponsored literacy class. Even in Casablanca's grim shantytowns, many women run small businesses in addition to taking care of their shacks and children. They run modest dress shops, grocery stores, and outlets for the household goods they buy at the flea market.

Entrepreneur Nourredine Ayouch, who operates a vast network of small business loans in the shantytowns, makes it a practice to give loans only to women "because they are hard-working, successful, and always make good on interest payments."[15]

An exciting measure of how far Moroccan women have come was the Global Summit of Women held in Marrakech at the end of June 2003. It wasn't the best organized conference: there weren't enough seats in the main conference hall, and leaders of the Moroccan women's movement were missing because they hadn't been invited. But this forum was important for two basic reasons: because so many bright, dynamic Moroccan women were there from business and civil society and because a record number of more than 600 women from eighty countries—with large contingents from the Arab and Muslim worlds—attended the conference, barely six weeks after the terrible suicide bombings in Casablanca.

Irene Natividad, the impassioned summit director, admitted that there were a hundred cancellations following the terrorist attacks and some sponsors had backed out. "But what kind of message would that be if we had pulled out?" exclaimed Natividad, the Filipino-born former head of the U.S. National Commission on Women at Work. She told me that Morocco had been chosen as the site for the Thirteenth Global Summit of Women, the first such event in the Arab world, because of "the encouraging momentum in the advance of women."[16]

Labeled as "the Women's Davos" by the Casablanca press, the forum's main achievements were women's networking, contacts with delegates from countries like Yemen and Algeria, attending the meeting for the first time, and a delegation from the new Iraq. Korean women talked to Bangladeshis about microcredits, and Egyptians spoke of the newly established International Business Center set up by Arab women's organizations. Some forty women cabinet ministers took part in an informal discussion on economic development for women from Arab states—another first.

Opening the summit, Her Highness Princess Lalla Hasna, the king's sister, read a message from King Mohammed, emphasizing that since his accession to the throne, he had worked relentlessly "to enhance the status of Moroccan women and to preserve the rights which our holy religion granted them, thus putting them on an equal footing with men." The monarch noted that substantial headway has been made in this domain but acknowledged that a large number of women continue to "live on the fringes of society, suffer from exclusion or are denied their rights."[17]

Yasmina Baddou, member of parliament and secretary of state for women and family affairs, represents the young generation of the old Istiqual party.

Yasmina Baddou, the youthful secretary of state for the Moroccan family and social affairs and a summit host, declared that while Moroccan women "still suffer from disparities" with their male counterparts, they now occupy high positions like counselor to His Majesty the king, cabinet minister, and director of government offices in key sectors like tourism, mines, and energy. She also noted that there are now 35 women in the 325-seat parliament. (Baddou herself was elected as an M.P. on the Istiqlal ticket from Casablanca in 2002.) And she stressed that Moroccan women had made significant progress in the economic field, where they are now chief executive officers and managerial cadres in public, semipublic, and private enterprises.[18]

Morocco's new women executives were the stars of the forum, people like Nezha Hayat, who has barely turned forty, a former head of the Casablanca Stock Exchange and current director of investments for a leading private bank; Souad Benbachir, board director of the CFG Group, a Casablanca think tank; Miriem Ben-Salah Chaqroun, managing director of Oulmes Mineral Water; Farida Bennani, director of development and marketing for DHL Morocco; Leila Sbiti, chief of a division in the state Department of Investments; Meriem Kabbaj, director of communication and development for Sochepresse, the main newspaper distributor; and many others.

They are not token women or even pioneers—but success stories that are beginning to be the norm.

Flourishing Civil Society

When I recall the first years of independence and the women's dreams of a new life, it is easy to understand the frustrations of the women's organizations over the slow progress of reforms. But at least now there *are* women's organizations. This is one of the most important transformations that has occurred in Moroccan society in recent years: the explosion of volunteer organizations around the country. And many of these are led by women.

In the old days, there were virtually no women's groups except for the royal charitable associations and the women's sections of the political parties. But since the early 1980s, many more Moroccan women have discovered power in working together. These women tell me that they had lost hope in the masculine society around them, the male-dominated political parties and labor unions, professional associations, and governing institutions. And so they struck off on their own, forming women's associations and cooperatives around the country. Now they are tackling questions of national concern such as illiteracy and workers' rights as well as "women's problems" like violence against women, street children, the promotion of women entrepreneurs, and the development of rural woman.

On recent visits, I have run into a host of volunteer organizations led by women and involving women's issues. These women compare favorably in commitment and advocacy to any I have met anywhere. Aicha Ech-Chenna, for example, heads Feminine Solidarity, a private organization set up in 1985 to defend single mothers. Solidarity, which receives funding from Spanish, German, and other foreign associations, is not a charity organization. It provides training and jobs for the women and preschool for their children. The single mothers, mostly illiterate countrywomen, run two restaurants, four snack stands, and a bakery. There are about thirty women enrolled in Solidarity at a time, and they receive legal and psychological counseling to help them reintegrate into society.[19]

"Actually, we call our women 'abandoned mothers' because Islamists view single mothers as prostitutes and have accused us of protecting prostitution," Ech-Chenna, a forceful former social services worker, told me when I visited the association in Casablanca. "They are victims of rape and often incest, in this society where there's still strict segregation of the sexes. Or they get pregnant and are repudiated by their husbands, with no means of livelihood. If they can't go home, their only solution is to get rid of the baby and become a prostitute—or they can come to us."

"We also help with weddings," Ech-Chenna said proudly, referring to a number of cases where fathers had been persuaded to marry their partners. Yet Solidarity has been denounced as a den of iniquity by some Islamists. In the summer of 2000, several *imams* directly attacked Ech-Chenna in their sermons, accusing her of encouraging prostitution, and one *imam* even threatened her personally. Other women's groups came to her defense and blamed the government for allowing such slander against women in mosques. Subsequently, the minister of Islamic affairs reportedly ousted the *imam* who had threatened Ech-Chenna. That fall, when King Mohammed VI opened his annual Solidarity Campaign for the needy, he personally gave the leader of Feminine Solidarity a special decoration for her social work.

Fattouma Benabdenbi set up the Moroccan Association for the Promotion of Women's Enterprises, known by its French initials ESPOD, in Casablanca in the early 1990s. This sophisticated sociologist, who looks like she stepped out of the pages of *Vogue*, has established partnerships with local business organizations in a dozen cities around the country. She also works with village women to promote traditional products like wood, hand-woven cloth, and argan oil. The argan tree is a miracle plant, which is said to grow only in southwestern Morocco. It seems to cure everything but until recently was appreciated mainly by goats.

"I saw several surveys showing that women in civil service soon run into a glass ceiling and rarely make it to the managerial level, but in the private sector there were no brakes. And so ESPOD was born," Benabdenbi told me, when we met at her office in the state Social Security Hospital at Casablanca. While most women activists were concerned with women's political and social issues, Benabdenbi chose the economy because "when women get money, they'll have empowerment."[20]

ESPOD has promoted a variety of small business projects around the country. For example, village women in the Tangier region have set up a weaving cooperative and hope to go into haute couture. In the farming area of Meknès, a group of women is processing *couscous*, the national staple, which traditionally involves long hours of manual labor. A cooperative has been set up at Essaouira to commercialize argan oil, known to be beneficial against ulcers, acidity, and cholesterol, which is now sold for cooking purposes. The oil has also been found to have valuable properties for the skin, and talks are under way with German, French, and Japanese cosmetics firms.

If there is one person who has had a decisive influence on the new Moroccan woman, it is undoubtedly the independent sociology professor and writer Fatema Mernissi. Author of the 1975 classic *Beyond the Veil*, Mernissi is a pioneer in the struggle against male domination and the patriarchal society in Morocco and the Islamic world. Seizing advantage of the political opening in Morocco in 1991, Mernissi gathered together a brilliant group of young women and men who held workshops, formed associations, and published group books on a wide range of subjects. "Fatema has the wonderful

*Sociologist Fatema Mernissi, a
major figure in the Moroccan
women's movement and leading
advocate for civil society, at home
on July 21, 2001.*

capacity to unite people and excite them with a creative *élan*," commented
Benabdenbi, one of Mernissi's followers.

Mernissi provides a different view of Muslim society. She does not write of
weak, submissive women but of weak, fearful males, intimidated by female
sexuality, a taboo subject even now. She tells us of Aisha Kandisha, a repugnant
female demon in Moroccan folk culture with pendulous breasts and lips, who
is more than ever present in Moroccan daily life. Mernissi explains that fear of
the emasculating female is a legacy of local tradition and seen in many forms
in popular beliefs and practices and in both novels and religious literature.

In the early 1980s, Mernissi and a group of about thirty university professors and students, including several men, joined forces to do something
about the great void in research on women's issues. With help from Leila
Chaouni, a young Casablanca publisher, they produced *Approaches*, a series
of books on women's condition, women and work, women and power,
women divided between work and home, and the female body. This was followed by other series on women in North Africa, women and the law,
women and the media, social security, politics, women and violence in Algeria, and women and Islamists. Mernissi is also deeply involved with the
movement for truth and justice, encouraging former political prisoners to
write down their memoirs and helping to promote their stories.

Now Mernissi devotes much of her enormous energy and passion to the development of civil society, in particular that of the remote corners of the Atlas Mountains. She has organized various workshops to help small private organizations communicate with the modern world and to bring other concerned Moroccans and foreigners to these forgotten villages.

It is strong women like these, working with grassroots associations, who are bringing change to Morocco.

The Political Lag

Despite important advances, the different women's groups complain about the slow pace of the acceptance of women into the political life of the country. In the 1997 national elections, only 2 women were elected to the 325-member Chamber of Representatives and 2 in the 270-seat upper house. In local elections that year, 83 women were elected, out of a total of 24,000 council members. The Socialist-led government had only one woman with the rank of cabinet minister.

Concerned over the absence of women in positions of political responsibility, a group of associations set up the Center for Women's Leadership in 1997 to prepare for future elections. In a memorandum to the prime minister, the center proposed a quota system under which preferably 33 percent of the candidates should be women, and no fewer than 20 percent. Rachida Tahiri, head of the center, said that at first, the main political parties fought the idea of quotas as "antidemocratic," but later they came around. The Socialists and Communists set aside 20 percent of their candidate positions for women and the conservative Istiqlal surprised many people with a 25 percent quota. These quotas still left women in a minority place on the electoral lists, but it was a step forward.

For this reason, the women's movement was dismayed when King Mohammed, who had spoken out for equal opportunity for women, told the French daily *Le Figaro* in September 2001 that he opposed any system of quotas, which he said "automatically doomed women to a minority status." Quota advocates blamed themselves for not explaining the need for affirmative action and vowed to pursue their struggle. By the time of the legislative elections in the fall of 2002, the women's groups had succeeded in imposing quotas even on the Islamist party.

Dr. Abdelkrim Khatib, whose Islamist Justice and Development party had taken the lead in the fight against the government's plan for equal rights for women, insisted that his party favored more women in politics and would put up women candidates in the elections (and it did). And Nadia Yassine, daughter of Sheikh Yassine, told me proudly that there were several women in leadership positions in the Justice and Charity Organization, even in the Central Committee.

Thanks to the quota system, the face of parliament changed dramatically with the elections of 2002, which produced thirty-five women deputies, or a respectable 11 percent of the seats in the lower house. But the women's movement had not come out of the political desert. It was to suffer yet another setback when the new, modern, technocratic Prime Minister Driss Jettou dropped the only woman minister and the Ministry for the Condition of Women, replacing them with a woman as secretary for the family. Furthermore, local elections the following year were disastrous for women, who were unable to convince the parties of the need for quotas this time and won a pitiful .5 percent of the seats.

The Moudawana *War*

But it was the *Moudawana*, the Family Code, which most angered advocates of women's rights and was considered the main obstacle to women's participation in the life of the country. For more than two decades, a bitter debate had taken place between women's groups and Islamic traditionalists over the reform of the legal code for women and the family. Under pressure from the women's movement, King Hassan permitted minor modifications of the *Moudawana* in 1993. These alterations did not even outlaw polygamy but simply required that a woman be informed if her husband planned to take another wife. Men could continue to repudiate their wives at will. A woman could sue for divorce if her husband took a second wife, abandoned her, or abused her, but the procedure was so complicated that many women preferred to pay off their husbands. Women inherited only half as much as male heirs and remained under male guardianship.

Even though the 1993 reforms were superficial, it was "an enormous step because it removed the sacred aura around the code," according to Leila Rhiwi, who heads Printemps de l'Egalité, an organization of twenty-six women's associations, whose sole purpose was to reform the Family Code. Their demands would have been quite reasonable in Western societies: reforms based on the "principle of equality between men and women in the exercise of their rights as well as the fulfillment of their duties and responsibilities."[21]

Since the late 1990s, most Moroccan urban women were at least emotionally involved in the battle of the *Moudawana*. Many women activists had come to the conclusion that while they could make an impact through volunteer organizations, it was necessary to change the discriminatory family law to make any real improvement in women's condition.

Aicha Belarbi, Moroccan ambassador to the European Union and a long-time advocate of women's rights, told me how it all began. In 1997, a group of nongovernmental organizations met with a representative of the World Bank to discuss how to implement the United Nations' Beijing Platform for the equality of women. The World Bank delegate suggested that a national network should prepare a long-term plan for the integration of women into the country's development. The idea was launched. The Moroccan secretary of state for charities, with backing from the World Bank, organized a workshop in February 1998 to draft the main priorities for a national action plan. Taking part in the workshop were representatives of women's associations, human rights groups, and government departments.[22]

When King Hassan named his long-awaited government of *Alternance,* headed by the opposition leader Abderrahmane Youssoufi, the women's movement thought its time had come. The new prime minister declared that women's equality would be one of the four top priorities of his government (the others being education, unemployment, and corruption).

Until this point, no Moroccan government had taken up the women's issue as a whole. There had been piecemeal attempts to tackle problems of women's health or education, but always as part of general social issues. Under the leadership of Saïd Saâdi, secretary of state for social welfare, the Women's Network, assisted by technical experts, put together the first draft of a national plan. Finally, in March 1999, Prime Minister Youssoufi presented to the nation the Plan for the Integration of Women in Development. The 120-page document describes the need for reform in four sectors: education and literacy; health; economic development; and the juridical, political, and institutional status of women.

Members of the women's movement told me that the plan represented "the basic minimum" as far as their demands were concerned. The reforms called for under the Personal Status Code were hardly earth-shaking: raise the marriage age for girls to eighteen from fifteen; eliminate repudiation and provide for divorce at the request of either spouse; abolish polygamy except in extraordinary cases; grant an adult woman the right to conclude a marriage contract without a guardian; and recognize the mother as the legal guardian of her children in the absence of the father.

"It was a document of consensus," said Najia Zirari, an activist in the Democratic Association of Moroccan Women, who took part in the workshops. "We didn't even bring up the delicate issues like the inequality of inheritance laws [stipulated in the Koran] and the problem of single mothers."[23]

Assuming that the matter was settled, the government set up an official commission to convert the plan into legislation.

The first blow against the plan came from within the government itself.

The minister of Islamic affairs, who had been kept closely informed of the work on the plan, publicly rejected any change in the Family Code. Following his example were the *oulema* and leaders of the so-called moderate Islamist party, who usually did the king's bidding. The Islamist opposition accused proponents of the women's plan of heresy. It was a plot by the West, they said, to destroy the Muslim family.

The polemics subsided in July 1999 with the death of King Hassan II. From the outset, Mohammed VI demonstrated his intention to be a modern monarch, which presumably included the emancipation of women. Sounding very much like Mao Zedong, King Mohammed asked in one of his early speeches: "How can we hope to achieve progress and prosperity when women, who constitute half of the society, are deprived of their rights, without taking into consideration that our holy religion considers them equal to men?"[24]

Encouraged by the new king's words, the Women's Network, composed of some 200 volunteer organizations, held a number of public meetings and made statements to the press to explain the merits of the women's plan. They also presented several well-known Islamic authorities who publicly approved of the plan. Professor Abdelhadi Boutaleb, an adviser to the king, noted that Islam was a "message of renewal and reform," and cited verses that demonstrated that Islam advocated the equality of men and women. "It is true that a bird needs its two wings to fly," Boutaleb said, a statement widely reported in the Moroccan press that September 1999.

At long last, the Women's Network believed that the much-awaited modifications of the *Moudawana* would be enacted. But they underestimated the strength and persistence of the enemy.

Islamist Backlash

Tension rose in the fall of 1999, when prominent Islamists formed the National League for the Protection of the Moroccan Family. This ad hoc group called on Islamic experts to draft another plan "to promote and protect the family," in other words, to counter the government's reforms for the *Moudawana*. They were joined by two prominent figures of the prime minister's Socialist party. Also, some leaders of the main conservative Istiqlal party said they could not support the women's plan if it were contradictory to Islamic law. Clearly, the rejectionist camp was spreading.

To try to understand Islamist objections to the reform, I met with Nadia Yassine, who in the past had appeared quite reasonable. Was she opposed to the women's plan and, if so, why? I asked.

"At first glance it is difficult for anyone to reject the plan—without appearing reactionary," Yassine acknowledged, noting that the old Family Code was unjust and should be changed. "But this plan comes in the framework of a strategic global policy. There are undeclared interests behind the plan. It was sponsored by the World Bank in the framework of Beijing. It's part of the effort to break up the nuclear family, part of the Western concern over demographics in Islamic countries."[25]

I objected, pointing out that the women's plan was really the work of Moroccan voluntary organizations and that Beijing had not been dominated by the West. What evidence was there of a global plot against the Muslim family? But rational discussion with Yassine on this subject was impossible.

As voices opposed to the women's plan grew louder, the government retreated in silence and the Women's Network grew impatient. A group of women academics from the faculties of medicine, pharmacy, and dentistry at Casablanca addressed an open letter to the prime minister, urging him to "re-dynamize" the women's plan. Declaring that all Moroccan women had placed their hopes in him when he had proclaimed the integration of women as a priority of his government, they stated their concern over the absence of any mention of the implementation of the new legislation.

In an effort to put the women's plan back on the national agenda, the women's movement, human rights organizations, left-wing political parties, and trade unions organized a mass demonstration on March 8, 2000, International Women's Day. Participants said they had never seen such a huge crowd of women, families, and activists marching through the normally quiet streets of Rabat. Estimates of defenders of the women's plan ran between 500,000 and a million.

The Islamists, however, mobilized an even larger crowd in the streets of Casablanca that day to denounce the women's plan as an assault on Islam and Islamic family values. The demonstration, according to observers, was better organized and more disciplined—like a military show without arms.

The Casablanca march was considered a major victory for the Islamists, not only as a setback for the new *Moudawana* but because it proved their mobilizing capacity.

Royal Intervention

Prime Minister Youssoufi was clearly concerned over the snowballing opposition to the government's initiative and the street power of the Islamists. "We don't want a civil war," he told me in an interview. "We must be cautious and try to resolve the problem with persuasion."[26]

The controversy continued to rage. Some pragmatic leaders of the women's movement suggested that maybe it would be better to accept the parts of the government's plan that had caused no problem (education, health, and economy) and postpone the changes in the Family Code. Others wrote angry columns in the political press, accusing Youssoufi's government of deserting the cause and even killing its own baby.

At the end of July 2000, some three dozen women's and human rights organizations issued a declaration accusing the government of going back on its public commitments and sacrificing the rights of women. Emphasizing that Youssoufi's coalition had raised the highest hopes since independence, the NGOs asked bluntly if the government had the political courage necessary to achieve its objectives.

In private conversations, many women's rights advocates said the king had to intervene. The sovereign had openly supported the cause of women's emancipation when he came to power, and now he must take a stand. After all, he was the country's spiritual ruler. It was up to him to take the final decision on religious matters. But palace sources confided that even the progressive monarch would have to tread carefully where Islam was concerned. Veteran politicians said it would be dangerous for the king to take a position on this issue which has so deeply, so emotionally, divided the country.

A cabinet reshuffle in September 2000 was viewed by the women's movement as a bad sign. Saïd Saâdi, the secretary of state for social welfare and champion of the women's plan, was eliminated—apparently sacrificed to the government's Islamic backers. The prime minister did create a Ministry of Women's Condition—a long-standing demand of the women's movement—and named Nezha Chekrouni, a Socialist, as minister. But the ministry was put under the aegis of the Ministry of Social Affairs, headed by Abbas El Fassi, the leader of the conservative Istiqlal party, which had criticized the women's plan. This move was seen by some women activists as a slap in the face and a sign that the women's plan had been shelved.

Others, like Amina Lemrini, head of the Democratic Association of Moroccan Women, said that the Women's Network must step up the fight for the revision of the *Moudawana*: "The time is now to win our rights when we have a progressive king and prime minister, because who knows what could follow!"[27]

I raised the issue of women in government with Prime Minister Youssoufi. He replied that he would like to name more women to the cabinet, but it was up to the parties of the coalition to submit candidates for ministerial positions. "Unfortunately, the parties—even the Socialists—don't present women," he acknowledged.[28]

Finally, in the spring of 2001, the king received leaders of the women's movement, who had sent him a memorandum urging him to pursue efforts to reform the *Moudawana*. The monarch chose the diplomatic way, naming another commission charged with the revision of the Moudawana. Headed by Driss Dahak, the conservative president of the Supreme Court, the fifteen-member commission was made up of Islamic theologians, magistrates, and academics, with only three women and no representatives of the women's movement.

The women's rights advocates were appalled by the composition of the royal commission, noting that all but two or three members were known to be opposed to reform. But they did not protest out of fear of alienating the king. It was the task of the commission, the king declared, to reconcile the unalterable values of Moroccan identity with the spirit of the times as represented by universal human rights.

Islamists welcomed the royal commission, and in an effort to show the king their conciliatory spirit, they agreed to minor changes in the *Moudawana*, such as a simplification of the divorce procedure. Bassima Hakkaoui, leader of an Islamist NGO, the Organization for the Renewal of the Feminine Conscience, warned that any attempt to abolish polygamy or repudiation would mean the abolition of the *Moudawana*. Defending the concept of polygamy, Hakkaoui explained that this system enables the first wife to keep the family together, while it assures the dignity of the second wife and the responsibility of the husband toward both wives and their children. For Hakkaoui, the current debate over the *Moudawana* represents a conflict between those who respect the *Sharia* and those ideological groups who prefer international conventions even when they contradict Islamic sources.[29]

The Democratic Association of Moroccan Women, the lead group in the Women's Network, decided to work with the king's commission and provided it with texts of the laws it wanted changed. Nouzha Skalli, a founder of the association, insisted that gender equality was part of universal human rights and "in no way contradictory to the precepts of Islam." She pointed out that raising the marriage age to eighteen, doing away with male guardians, abolishing polygamy, and eliminating repudiation "can only strengthen the institution of marriage."[30]

The reformist and Islamist camps informally declared a moratorium on public demonstrations to enable the royal commission to pursue its delicate mission of reconciling these discordant views. The Democratic Association of Moroccan Women, however, kept up its pressure, publishing a study showing that women are victims of discrimination under the penal code, even though Morocco ratified the UN convention against discrimination in 1993. For example, if a husband catches his wife in the act of adultery and kills her, he risks only one to five years in jail. If a married woman flees a violent husband without his authorization, whoever gives her refuge risks up to five years in prison.

As the work of the royal commission dragged on in silence, some members of the women's movement began to express misgivings privately. The government should have taken the women's plan to parliament, where there was a good chance of getting it passed into law. They weren't at all sure that the royal commission would produce any substantial changes in the Family Code or that the king would be able to push through any significant reform.

The royal commission's deadline of the end of 2002 came and went. In early 2003, the king announced the nomination of a new head of the commission, M'Hamed Boucetta, the retired head of the Istiqlal party, a skillful, seventy-eight-year-old lawyer.

Shortly after taking on the task, Boucetta announced confidently that the new text of the *Moudawana* would be "revolutionary and accepted by all the parties."[31] Publicly, the leaders of the women's movement welcomed the change, but privately they expressed concern that this was just another delay in making any changes in the civil code.

Midst the general uncertainty, I recalled what Fatema Mernissi had said six months earlier. The country was moving ahead, she pointed out, more girls were going to school, women were going into every field of work, couples were marrying later, and all political parties were looking for women candidates for the next elections. "The women's plan has already won because they have demonstrated that the *Moudawana* must be reformed on the basis of equal rights," Mernissi stressed.[32]

Nouzha Guessous-Idrissi, a member of the royal commission and a professor of parasitology at Hassan II University, told me in the summer of 2003 that there was still no consensus. There were in fact two irreconcilable positions, which she defined as "a choice between modernity and obsolescence." The commission, she added, was heavily weighted in favor of the *oulema*, about ten to four (one member had died). Her main hope lay in King Mohammed, who had publicly come out for gender equality and an end to injustice. Even if the commission were unable to reach a consensus, Guessous-Idrissi expressed the conviction that the king and the political leadership "will surely choose the way of modernity—particularly after the fanatical explosion of May 16."[33]

She was right. Once again, the *Moudawana* was to be a test of strength between the Islamists and the modernists. But in the wake of the Casablanca suicide bombings, the mainstream Islamists retreated, disassociating themselves from any kind of radicalism. This time, they were in no position to challenge a reform of the *Moudawana*, particularly if it came from the Commander of the Faithful. Seizing the initiative, the king came down firmly in favor of reform, going much further than the women's movement had dared to hope.

Split Identity

7

According to the constitution, Morocco is a sovereign Muslim state whose official language is Arabic, a part of the greater Arab *Maghreb*, and an African state.

In fact, the Moroccan identity is far more complex. Moroccans are a fascinating blend of Islamic, Arab, Berber, European, and some Jewish influences. This Moroccan mix is evident above all in the languages, which have helped to shaped the nation's identity, customs, and arts.

Arabic is the language of government, administration, instruction, religion, and urban life. But about 40 percent of Morocco's 30 million inhabitants still speak a Berber dialect—the language of the original inhabitants—observe Berber customs, and produce Berber art.

The ancient Jewish community has mostly emigrated, but many Muslim families are descendants of Jewish converts to Islam. Jewish synagogues and shrines remain, and Jewish designs can be seen in the art and crafts.

The educated elite tend to send their children to French or Spanish schools in Morocco or abroad for a modern education in the language of their former colonizers. Even much of the middle class prefers French or Spanish journals and books, and they go to Europe for holidays and medical care. When the impoverished lose hope for a better life, they turn to Europe for salvation.

And there is Morocco's increasingly visible Islamic facet. Interpretations of Islam differ widely. Berbers tend to be less austere than Arabs in their attire, customs, and attitudes toward women. Islam has been an important influence in decorative arts, architecture, and music but an inhibiting factor in the development of painting, sculpture, and dance.

This combination of languages and cultures has enriched the Moroccan identity but has also caused strains as the different components assert themselves. If the Moroccans, with their diverse identity, manage to come to terms with themselves, it would be an important precedent for all those who believe that the clash of civilizations is not inevitable.

The Arab Mystique

Things were much simpler in the early 1950s. To be Moroccan in those days was to be Muslim, Arab, and a nationalist, although the small Jewish minority was recognized as citizens. There was however, a linguistic split in education and public life. It was a cleavage between Arabic—the national tongue and the language of religion—and either French or Spanish, the languages of the protectorate powers. There was of course the Berber-speaking population, a largely rural, uneducated people, who didn't count in those days until they learned Arabic or a Western language. The divide was essentially between European-educated modernists and Arab traditionalists and was reflected in the country's literature, other arts, and political thinking. There was also a limited Moroccan elite, who had bridged the two worlds.

The nationalist movement as we have seen included three distinct groups: the Arabists, the Europeanists, and the Berbers. Allal el Fassi, an exponent of the Karaouyine, sought an independent Morocco closely linked to Arab culture and the Middle East. French-educated nationalists like Ahmed Balafrej and Abderrahim Bouabid, who assumed leadership positions in Morocco's first independent government in 1956, looked to France and Europe as primary partners, without negating Arab ties.

The Berbers formed the backbone of the armed struggle against the colonial powers, but did not try to impose their culture at that time lest it be considered a form of separatism. The French colonialists had sought to use the Berber card, pitting Berber chiefs and tribesmen against Arab nationalists in the cities. This tactic was so counterproductive that it stirred the indignation of Muslims everywhere. While a few Berber notables supported the French protectorate and many Berber tribesmen joined the colonial armed forces (for lack of other jobs), many more supported the nationalist movement and were the first to take up arms against the French colonizers.

At the dawn of independence, the Arab mystique dominated Moroccan hearts and minds. Moroccan nationalists, who had been inspired by the Arab reform movement of Muhammad Abduh, took up the cause of pan-Arabism. Having been supported by their Arab brothers in the struggle against colonialism, Moroccans strongly approved of Gamal Abdel Nasser's crusade to liberate the rest of the Arab world, namely, Algeria and Palestine. At that time, the quest for Arab unity appeared to be a realizable goal, in fact the only way to restore Arab pride.

Morocco promptly joined the Cairo-based Arab League. Not until much later did some Berbers express reservations about joining the Arab club. Privately, some Moroccan leaders did not subscribe to the league's militantly anti-Israel policies but they paid lip service to its tenets. Morocco's Arab commitment was repaid in the early 1980s, when most of the Arab League countries supported Moroccan claims to Western Sahara. On the other hand, the majority of the members of the Organization of African Unity sided with Algeria and recognized the Saharan nationalists' government-in-exile, the Saharan Arab Democratic Republic.

Early on, Moroccans—even those of the French or Spanish schools—proclaimed their adherence to the Arabization of the administration and education. It was a natural reaction since they had struggled for so long to free the kingdom from European domination.

But all too soon, the nationalists realized that Arabization was easier said than done. Colonial authorities had condoned the creation of private Arabic schools, but these had provided mainly religious-based studies for the training of Islamic scholars. Public schools that provided modern education were either French or Spanish and were few and far between. According to French estimates at the time of independence, about 10 percent of the children of school age were in schools. (They did not count those in Arabic-language schools.)

Morocco faced a serious dearth of qualified Arabic teachers and books. Reluctantly the country imported Middle Eastern teachers, with some disastrous results. Some Egyptians were said to have been caught spreading Nasser's revolutionary, republican ideals—hardly acceptable in this proud monarchy. Later, teachers imported from Saudi Arabia brought with them the intolerant Wahhabi brand of Islam, which proved to be almost as risky.

Another handicap that still has not been resolved satisfactorily is, which Arabic should be taught? There is the Arabic of the Koran and the great Islamic thinkers, classical Arabic that not many Moroccans speak or understand. And there is Moroccan Arabic, known as *Darija*, the language of the home and the streets, a lively Arabic enriched by Berber, French, and Spanish vocabulary. Some experts say that there is almost as much difference between the two Arabics as there is between present-day and classical Greek.

Moroccan linguist Mohamed Dahbi says that, if they had been pragmatic, the fathers of independence could have standardized and adopted Moroccan Arabic as the national language right after independence: "But nationalism, Pan-Arab ideology and inviolable religiousness did not allow such a choice. Furthermore, the question did not even come up."[1]

*Inside the Karaouyine, the university/mosque in Fez and seat of
Morocco's Arabic culture since the twelfth century, students sit
on straw mats and use slates, but now some are studying
English.*

When the country finally decided to Arabize the language of instruction,
the decision was for classical Arabic, ready or not. King Hassan, who had
originally favored a modern education system based on French or English,
acquiesced to pressures from traditionalists and declared in the fall of 1978
that Arabization was "irreversible," both in public and private schools. By
1980, schools had been Arabized up to the *baccalauréat*. As of 1985, there were
pressures for the Arabization of universities, but many textbooks were still in
French. By 1995, most higher education was Arabized except for mathematics and technical courses.

Ali Ben Bachir Hassani, a counselor to the prime minister and a member
of the commission charged with drafting the National Charter on Education,
recalls the wrangling between the pro-Western and pro-Arabic camps. "The
language problem was so sensitive that the result was forty years of beating
around the bush," Ben Bachir told me. There was serious concern that the
French- and Spanish-educated elites would be "detached" from the Arabic-
schooled masses, he noted. After the views of the political parties, labor
unions, and other groups were heard, Ben Bachir said it was decided that

there would be one national language, Arabic, and that French would be introduced in the third grade and English in the fifth grade. It had also been decided to create three chairs in the *Amazigh* language at Meknès, Tetouan, and Marrakech. He quoted King Hassan as declaring at the time: "He who speaks only one language is an illiterate."[2]

Even today, as pressures mount for reinforcing the teaching of Western languages, the Arabic mystique remains strong. The French-educated former minister of public works and Istiqlal activist M'hamed Douiri said, "If anyone dares [to] touch Arabic, the national language, there will be a revolt."[3]

The Modernists

Nationalist leaders like Ben Barka and Bouabid were fervent believers in mass, bilingual education. Children should be schooled in Arabic but also in a Western language as an opening to the rest of the world, they told me many times. Although Arabic was declared the national language, most educated Moroccans were either French or Spanish speakers. France, eager to maintain its cultural influence in the former protectorate, provided thousands of *coopérants* as teachers, and Spain did likewise, to a lesser extent. Thus bilingual Arabic-European education continued in a piecemeal fashion. For a while, Moroccan public schools hobbled along using Arabic in elementary classes and later switching to French or Spanish, while private schools continued with French or Spanish as the language of instruction.

The Arabic versus European languages debate was not so much a Muslim problem, although in general, the religiously devout tended to favor the Arabic camp. There were exceptions. In his book, *Maroc 1961–1999: L'espérance brisée*, Ignace Dalle recounts that Sheikh Yassine and four other Moroccan education inspectors had firmly opposed Arabization at the time of independence. They said the country wasn't ready for it and urged keeping French in the national programs. Dalle quotes the sheikh as saying later: "As we predicted, this measure [Arabization] has proved to be catastrophic."[4]

Following independence, schools were opened around the country because free education for all had been one of the main goals of the nationalist movement. But facilities, equipment, and personnel were stretched, and the quality of public education, whether in French or Arabic, was generally unsatisfactory. Faced with limited resources, the government decided to pursue the bilingual approach but restricted access to secondary education. This triggered an offensive by traditionalists, who accused the authorities of acting against the Koran and the constitution. It was at this point that former King Hassan came down on the side of the traditionalists.

The decision to Arabize education really did not resolve the language issue, but it did mark a general exodus of European teachers from public schools. For many years afterward, the country pursued a two-track education system, which was widely criticized by students themselves, who said it led nowhere. Any number of young people told me that after their secondary schooling in Arabic, they were totally unprepared for many university courses in the sciences and medicine, which were taught in French.

Even after the royal order to Arabize, it was clear that Moroccans were unwilling to abandon their windows to the West. The most dramatic evidence is the continued popularity of the French and Spanish mission schools, although English is increasingly seen as a passport to jobs. French and Spanish cultural centers are widely seen as an integral part of the cultural life of the country, not as propaganda tools of the former colonial powers.

Moroccan daily life is a multicultural experience to the extent that any visitor who knows French or Spanish can communicate easily and feel quite at home. Most road signs are in Arabic and Latin script. Political parties still find it necessary to put out French newspapers in addition to their Arabic organs. The most popular independent weeklies are in French. Television programs and films are generally shown in the original language with subtitles, and there are daily newscasts in French and Spanish, besides the regular Arabic programs. If an older person speaks only Arabic or Berber, there's likely to be a child around who can interpret in Spanish or French. The Gregorian calendar is in general use although deference is paid to Muslim holidays. The Christian sabbath is observed as the weekly day off from work, but most employers give time off for noontime prayers on the Muslim holy day of Friday.

With the advent of the Internet, English has invaded Moroccans' consciousness. Even French *lycée* graduates now say that the only sure way to get a job these days is to speak English and to know how to communicate on the Internet. Although expensive, American language centers have long waiting lists for admission.

Once the domain of the moneyed elite, foreign languages and cultures are increasingly accessible, thanks to Moroccan overseas residents. Every August, more than 2.5 million Moroccans, working or seeking work in Europe, return home for the holidays, bringing presents, funds, new ideas, and their European patois to enrich Moroccan Arabic.

The Amazigh Revival

As every Moroccan schoolchild learns, the original inhabitants of North Africa were Berbers, and some of the greatest dynasties were Berber. But the country has been progressively Arabized, since the Arabs arrived as conquerors at the end of the seventh century. Under the French protectorate in the first half of the twentieth century, the colonial authorities tried to oppose the Arab-led nationalist movement by favoring the Berbers, but this proved counterproductive.

Independent Morocco did not see fit to count the number of Berbers (it would have been considered unpatriotic to do so), but it was said that nearly half the population speaks one of the three main Berber dialects. Berbers are located mainly in the Rif Mountains in the north, in the Middle and High Atlas mountains, and on the Souss plain in the south—although large numbers have migrated to the cities.

For the newly freed Moroccans in the late 1950s, everything was about national unity. There was no Islamic issue, no Left-Right problem, no Berber question. Any attempt to revive a Berber identity would have been treated as antinationalist and a separatist threat. The Berbers themselves bent over backward to prove that they were good Moroccans and to dispel memories of those tribal leaders who had collaborated with French colonial authorities.

Among educated Moroccans at that time, the common image of Berbers was that of noble warriors with colorful folk dances. It was conventional wisdom that with education and time, they would become full-fledged Arabic-speaking members of the Moroccan community. There was, after all, the example of the Soussis. When these Berbers left their villages on the Souss plain to settle in the cities and towns, they opened grocery shops, learned Arabic, and often intermarried with Arabs until nobody could tell the difference. It was, however, generally up to the Berbers to learn Arabic, not the other way around. Any move to promote Berberism was portrayed as part of an anti-Arab conspiracy to divide the Moroccan nation.

Initially, the Berbers kept silent although it galled them that the Berber language was not officially recognized by independent Morocco. They resented the fact that there were French, Spanish, and Arabic schools but no Berber schools. There wasn't even a standard Berber written language. Berbers wrote in Arabic, French, or Spanish.

In the 1960s and 1970s, Berber groups founded scores of cultural associations around the country for the purpose of preserving the Berber identity or, as they called it, *Amazighte*. The associations' demands were modest; what they wanted was the official recognition of Berber language and culture. Their demonstrations were peaceful, but they were looked on with suspicion by the dominant Arabic-speaking society, as though they presented some kind of threat to the nation.

The Berber revival really dates from 1980, according to Ibrahim Akhiat, who heads one of the first *Amazigh* cultural groups, the Moroccan Association of Research and Cultural Exchanges. After persistent pressure from numerous Berber cultural associations, the parliament passed a law that year for the creation of an Institute of Berber Studies, but there was no follow-up. In fact, when a small group of academics of Berber origin published a cultural magazine in 1982, they were promptly arrested and jailed for a month. One of the leaders, who dared claim that *Tamazight* (Berber) is a language "on a par with Arabic," was sentenced to a year in prison. This was at the height of *les années de plomb*, when human rights were meaningless. In those days too, the authorities were promoting Arabization and Islamization to counter leftist and secular trends.

What is considered the first political act of the Berber movement is the Agadir Charter of August 5, 1991. It was the year King Hassan began to liberalize his regime, but even then the Berbers' demands were cloaked in cultural terms. Six Berber associations produced what is formally known as the Charter on the *Tamazigh* Language and Culture in Morocco. Emphasizing that the 5,000-year-old *Amazigh* culture was in danger of extinction, the group demanded that *Tamazight* be inscribed in the constitution as a national language alongside Arabic. They also revived requests for the long-promised Institute of Berber Studies. This audacious move had no dire consequences, but neither was anything done about the Berber demands.

Akhiat points out that at the time the country was in the throes of the language debate between Francophones and Arabists. There was no question then of publishing in *Tifinagh*, the original Berber alphabet, because "nobody could read it," he told me. In the transition period, they would have to use the Latin alphabet. Meanwhile, he added, his association had been adapting *Tifinagh* to modern requirements, eliminating many dots, and now the language could be computerized.[5]

In 1994, a group of Berber teachers was arrested and given heavy prison terms for merely demanding education in Berber during a May Day parade. Public reaction to the arrests was so strong that King Hassan announced in his Throne Speech shortly afterward that the Berber language would be taught in schools. But again nothing happened, and Berber resentment grew.

When I traveled around Morocco in the spring of 2001, I was astonished to find the country in the midst of a Berber renaissance. Visiting Berber country, I became keenly aware of a new Berber consciousness, including pride in Berber dances and music, Berber handicrafts, Berber cuisine, Berber architecture, and Berber ingenuity. In the cities, Berber poets and musicians were included in artistic events.

Even the government had climbed on the Berber bandwagon and had begun to promote festivals of Berber popular arts—what used to be called folklore. For example, the new *Ahidous* Festival at Ain Leuh in the heart of the Middle Atlas was sponsored by the minister of culture and the local Berber cultural association. Dancers come from all over the region in mid-July to perform this joyous line dance, which appears to be closely related to Greek dances. The aim of the festival is to introduce *Amazigh* art and promote tourism, according to Hammou Ouhali, president of the Ain Leuh commune. Increasingly, *Amazigh* cultural events, including poetry recitals, concerts, and festivals, are taking place around the country.

For the first time in modern history, a head of government, Prime Minister Youssoufi, recognized publicly the *Amazigh* dimension of Moroccan identity shortly after taking office in 1998. This came as a major boost to the Berber cultural movement, which took on more importance under King Mohammed VI.

Equally important, the press is no longer afraid to address issues of *Amazighte*. The independent weeklies like *Le Journal* have reported on Berber efforts to defend their ancient culture. *Le Reporter* wrote of divisions in the *Amazigh* movement over the creation of a political party, while *Maroc-Hebdo International* has warned against "the Berber threat." But even the main progovernment daily, *Le Matin du Sahara*, has published favorable articles on the promotion of the *Amazigh* language and art.

And it has become fashionable to be an Arab-Berber. There have always been Arab-Berber marriages, starting with the royal family, but the most urbane Arabists now like to note that they have a Berber mother or father. Even the minister of culture, Mohammed Achaari, one of the country's leading Arabic poets, told me: "My father is Berber, my mother Arab and I am proud of the two cultures."[6]

Nevertheless, political observers were astonished when a group of Berber intellectuals made public the Berber Manifesto of March 1, 2000, which went beyond cultural demands to accuse their Arab compatriots of "ideological hegemony aimed at ethnocide." The 229 signatories of the manifesto, prominent professors, writers, artists, and industrialists, called for a national debate on the Berber question, official recognition of Berber as a national language, and the rewriting of Berber history. The manifesto contained bitter recriminations against all of the governments since independence, attacking them for the policies of Arabization which, it said, were aimed at killing Berber dialects, the economic marginalization of Berber areas, and falsifying history in favor of the Arabs.

The lead author of the manifesto was not some young firebrand but the highly respected scholar Mohamed Chafik, long-time head of the Royal College. The palace seems to have been involved in the Berber revival from the outset. Under King Hassan, it was part of his divide and rule policy directed against the pro-Arab Istiqlal. King Mohammed VI, whose mother is Berber, has gone out of his way to show sympathy for the Berber cause—as long as it was not political. Early on, the king named as palace spokesman a Berber activist, Hassan Aourid, head of the influential Tarik Ibn Zyad Research Center, which has spurred the publication of Berber authors and translations.

Shortly after the presentation of the Berber Manifesto, the sovereign recognized the Berber movement by establishing a Royal Institute for *Amazigh* Culture. Unlike King Hassan, Mohammed VI followed through, appointing the senior members of the institute and seeing to it that it received funds to begin operations. His nomination of Professor Chafik as dean of the new institute was widely applauded. But if the monarch thought that would be the end of the Berber problem, he was seriously mistaken.

One of the initial tasks of the institute was to standardize the *Amazigh* language and determine which alphabet should be used to transcribe what has been essentially an oral culture. The Linguistic Center, attached to the institute, was charged with deciding whether Berber schoolbooks should be written in Arabic, Latin, or *Tifinagh* characters.

An impassioned debate ensued among Berbers over the alphabet. The question has broad political implications. A majority clearly favored the Latin alphabet as a means of reaching a broader public. The royal institute's Chafik, who hoped for a consensus on the issue, indicated in an interview that he favored Latin letters as "an opening to universal knowledge." He pointed out that most of the modern-day studies on Berber language and history have been done in European languages.[7]

Representatives of some seventy Berber associations met in the central city of Meknès in the fall of 2002 to discuss the alphabet issue. Berber scholar Lahbib Fouad presented to the meeting a study entitled "*Tamazight* between the Devil and the Deep Blue Sea: The Linguists and the Politicians." He argued forcefully for the need to adopt the standard, universal alphanumeric keyboard which is used by the leading languages and is "the basis of all present telecommunications and all technologies of the future."

It was "a civilizational option," according to Berber poet Ahmed Assid, "a choice between Arabic-Muslim letters and modern Latin-based languages." The assembly was unanimous in favor of using the Latin alphabet in teaching *Tamazight* and at the same time developing the ancient *Tifinagh* script.[8]

In opposition to Latin, a small minority held that Arabic script should be adopted in keeping with the national language and the language of Islam. This group won vehement backing from Islamists. The Islamist Party of Justice and Development published various articles in its Arabic-language press, bitterly attacking partisans of the Latin alphabet, accusing them of hatred of Arabs and Arabic. The party's secretary general, Saad Eddine El Othmani, said that if they chose the Latin script, it would mark "a rupture with *Amazigh* historical heritage and civilization and its integration into Western civilization."[9]

Another group, led by Professor Akhiat, rejected any foreign script and insisted that since there is an *Amazigh* alphabet, *Tifinagh*, it should be used and if necessary, updated for the needs of modern times. Akhiat pointed out that *Tifinagh* is an extremely simple script with thirty-three consonants, four vowels, and two semivowels, which has been preserved as a decorative form in Niger, Mali, Egypt, and the Canary Islands, and is used today by the Touaregs of Sudan.

In the end, to nearly everyone's surprise, the royal institute adopted *Tifinagh* over Latin and Arabic as the written language for the new Berber studies program. The decision, announced in early February 2003, was approved by a two-thirds majority of the institute's board and represents a compromise in the fierce Latin-Arabic struggle. It was a victory for the Amazighophiles, represented by Akhiat, who have fought so long for recognition of Berber culture. The Socialist daily *Libération* hailed the rehabilitation of the 3,000-year-old *Tifinagh* script as "a veritable revolution in the cultural life of the country."

I did not fully understand the depth and passion of being Berber until I came to know Meryam Demnati at the Royal Institute for *Amazigh* Studies

Meryam Demnati, forceful advocate of Amazigh *culture, openly favors a secular state.*

during the summer of 2003. She is the daughter of a Moroccan army colonel, graduate of the French Ecole Normale Superieure in sociology, a professor of French literature, and the divorced mother of two young sons in prep school in France.

"At last I can devote myself to my language," Demnati said with obvious satisfaction. She and her team of six pedagogues worked against time to put together the first manuals in *Tifinagh* to be used in 317 Berber primary schools around the country in the fall. A thousand Berber teachers of French and Arabic were taking crash courses in *Tamazight* at nine training centers. "By 2008, the teaching of *Tamazight* will be obligatory in primary schools around the country," she predicted confidently.[10]

When I suggested that with her red hair and green eyes she looked more Irish than Berber, Demnati bristled. "There is no physical Berber type; we can be blonde with white skin from the Rif, brown-haired with olive skin from the Souss, or black from Marrakech, but what counts is our *Amazigh* identity," she stressed.

She recalled how her grandfather used to say: "You must speak Arabic well if you want to succeed in Morocco." Her cousins were ashamed of being Berber and always spoke Arabic in public. Her school friends used to laugh at her when she spoke Berber or Arabic with an accent. "It was racism. I developed a blockage against Arabic. I can understand the language, but to this day I cannot read it," she admits.

"Nobody voted for Arabic in the alphabet controversy because we knew that would mean the death of our culture," Demnati stressed, noting that the partisans of Latin and *Tifinagh* were about equal. She and others favored Latin script essentially as a means of communicating with other Berbers who use Latin, including the Kabyles in Algeria, Guanches in the Canary Islands, Berbers in France, and the World *Amazigh* Congress.

But she said there was strong opposition from the Islamists, who had joined forces with the Istiqlal and the extreme Left against the opponents of Arabic script. There were threatening letters and press statements, which accused the Berbers of Christian and pagan sympathies, trying to divide the nation, and receiving funds from France and the United States.

"By choosing *Tifinagh*, we have consolidated our identity, and neither culture is insulted," Demnati said. But she stressed that they would use modern tools: "We will continue to work in Latin letters, but we have a computer program that transforms the letters into *Tifinagh*."

The Berber revival has met other obstacles. Any attempt to give the cultural movement a political dimension has been promptly quashed (ethnic parties are barred by the constitution). An attempt to celebrate the second anniversary of the Berber Manifesto was banned. The authorities have also outlawed demonstrations of solidarity with the Kabyle protests in neighboring Algeria, apparently fearing a spillover of the Kabyles' nationalist demands.

But despite the authorities' attempts to silence them, the advocates of *Amazighte* have indirectly acquired a political dimension. In communal elections during the fall of 2003, almost all of the political parties found it expedient to use *Amazigh* slogans. What's more, the rural, Berber-based Popular Movement won first place in the elections for the renewal of one-third of the upper house of parliament, defeating its traditional rival, the Istiqlal.

A husband and wife team, Rachid and Amina Raha, activists in the Berber movement since their student days in 1990, put out a monthly newspaper from their modest apartment in Rabat, where they live with their young child. *Le Monde Amazigh* contains news and views from around the Berber world in French, Arabic, and *Tifinagh* and does not hesitate to criticize the authorities.

In the spring of 2004, *Le Monde Amazigh* denounced police brutality against students of Agadir University demonstrating for "*Amazigh* as an official language in North Africa." The newspaper also announced that the Tamaynut, a leading Berber cultural association, and a number of *Amazigh* militants have brought a lawsuit against the Moroccan Ministry of Education for "the falsification of history" in the current ninth-grade history manual. Their main complaint is that thousands of *Amazigh* heroes and numerous battles have been ignored in the account of Morocco's struggle for independence. The official textbook is also criticized for presenting the Arab people, language, and identity as "sacred" and therefore instilling in the *Amazigh* students "an inferiority complex and self-hatred."[11]

Berbers claim that their voices can no longer be silenced. There are numerous *Amazigh* Websites, mostly in French but some in English, and

The masthead of the Berber newspaper The Amazigh World, *with the letters in* Tifinagh *(top),* Arabic *(middle), and* French *(bottom).*

www.Tinghir.org provides an *Amazigh* yellow pages with some 220 Websites and more than fifty categories, from art and cinema to press, sports, history, and businesses. There's a comprehensive listing of *Amazigh*-related news stories in French from Morocco and Algeria, including features on Berber books and proverbs, *Amazigh* law, and the Koran in *Tamazight*. A related site provides information on Berbers in English. Morocco's Berbers now have a place on the international scene at www.mondeberbere.com.

Late in 2004, the World Amazigh Congress, which groups Berber associations from Morocco, Algeria, Tunisia, Libya, and Europe, presented an "alternative" report on Morocco to the UN Committee for Human Rights in Geneva. Its demands include: official recognition of the Amazigh language, an end to discrimination, a return of plundered land, and compensation.[12]

Jewish Memories

Moroccan Jews like to point out that they've been around for 3,000 years. It makes it all the more poignant that this ancient minority, which became an integral part of the Moroccan identity, appears doomed to disappear.

It is not clear when Jews first came to Morocco, but they were believed to have accompanied early Phoenician sailors around 1100 B.C. Historians say that when the Romans arrived in the second century B.C., they found Jewish communities established along the coast and entire Berber tribes converted to Judaism. With the Vandal invasion in the fifth century A.D., some Jews fled inland to the Souss plain, the High Atlas, and as far as the edge of the Sahara. The Arabs, who conquered the country in the eighth century, granted the Jews the status of *dhimmi*, or "protected persons." But they suffered persecution, forced conversions, and massacres under some Muslim rulers, particularly the Almohad zealots in the twelfth century, and again sought refuge in the mountains and the desert, where the central authority exerted little control. When Jews were expelled from Europe—mainly Andalusia or southern Spain—in the fourteenth and fifteenth centuries, many came to Morocco and reinforced the dwindling Jewish communities. By 1912, when the French and Spanish established their protectorates over Morocco, there were Jewish communities in all of the main cities and towns and in some 200 villages in the High Atlas and the pre-Sahara.

Demonstrating the art of adaptability, Jews spoke Moroccan Arabic in cities and towns and Berber in the countryside, and often French or Spanish, while retaining Hebrew, the language of their religion. They played important roles in the society as craftspeople, traders, businesspeople, bankers, and professionals. In urban areas, they lived as tightly knit communities in designated neighborhoods called *mellahs*, under royal protection, but were generally treated as second-class citizens. They are said to have enjoyed much greater freedom, if fewer conveniences, in the Berber villages of the hinterland.

Jews and Muslims lived together in much closer contact in the rural regions than in the cities, according to Daniel J. Schroeter, author of numerous works on Jews in Morocco. "The Jews were integrated into the cultural fabric of rural Morocco, they had common customs with their Muslim neighbors: in dress, food, the worship of saints, even women saints, as well as style of life," Schroeter writes. He notes that in the Berber villages, Jewish traveling salesmen (by mule or donkey) often acted as "agents of modernization," bringing new products to the local *souks*, while Jewish women introduced "modern technology" like the Singer sewing machine.[13]

The mass exodus of Jews occurred at the end of the protectorates and during the first years of independence, although the Moroccan monarch had firmly defended the Jewish citizens against discriminatory rulings by the French Vichy regime and against any local acts of anti-Semitism. Jews had risen to senior positions of responsibility in the new administration, as cabinet ministers and royal counselors, had become executives in big private enterprises, and were leaders of the left-wing opposition. But with the departure of the colonial protectors, the mood of uncertainty after independence, and the instigation of Zionist organizations, the Jews left. The community which had numbered more than 300,000 at independence in 1956 had dwindled to fewer than 4,000 by 2004, according to community sources. The terrorist attacks of May 16, 2003, on a Jewish social center, restaurant, and cemetery were a terrible blow to the remnants of the Jewish community in Morocco.

But Jewish memories have been preserved. Efforts have been made to maintain the synagogues, like the splendid Beth El Temple in Casablanca, completely refurbished in 1997. And there are the cemeteries and saints' tombs, many kept up with help from local Muslims. The saints' tombs are remarkable examples of shared identity, particularly in the regions of Fez, Marrakech, and Casablanca, and have become popular sites for Muslim and Jewish pilgrimages, even groups coming from Israel.

American anthropologist Lawrence Rosen recounts in his book *The Culture of Islam* that several of these shared saints were quietly transferred to Israel in the 1980s, among them Esther Messaoudi, a seventh-century Jewish holy woman from the central town of Sefrou, who came to be revered by Muslims as Lalla Sitti Messaouda. Most likely, Jewish émigrés appeared in the 1980s with documents proving that Lalla Sitti Messaouda was Jewish and were allowed to reclaim her remains, Rosen writes. But Muslims of Sefrou were unhappy about their loss and are concerned that "the Jews may be seeking to repatriate yet another saint."[14]

Aware that much of their patrimony has deteriorated, been dispersed or stolen, the Jewish community of Casablanca has established what is probably the first Jewish museum in an Arab country. Museum director and university professor Simon Lévy and his Muslim curator, Zhor Rehili, have managed to put together a priceless collection of Judeo-Moroccan memories: religious objects, rare books, artwork, traditional clothing, old photographs, jewelry, and furniture from around the country. The Moroccan Jewish Museum of Casablanca, located in the Oasis suburb, opened at the end of the 1990s, has become a center for cultural activities, and has attracted Jews and other visitors from around the world. It stands as an important monument to the Judeo-Moroccan heritage.

Multiculturalism

Multiculturalism has been encouraged in the schools for a long time. The country paid lip service to Arabization, but functioned essentially in French. Finally, since 2000, Morocco has begun to implement a major reform of the educational system, more than a decade in the making. The National Charter on Education reaffirms Arabic as the language of instruction but provides for a choice of foreign languages early on, not just French but Spanish and English. For the first time the Berber language is being taught in more than 300 pilot schools and will be progressively introduced in elementary schools throughout the country as teachers and manuals become available.

Mohammed Guessous, a member of the national charter commission, sees no reason that Moroccans can't have two national languages and learn one or more foreign languages at an early age. "In the era of globalization, we must take advantage of our multicultural identity," says Guessous, a professor of sociology at Mohammed V University in Rabat.[15]

"Morocco has jumped from the age of tradition and religion to the modern, global times, based on science and technology; it's not easy," Guessous remarked in an interview. Under the current reform, Arabic and foreign languages have been reinforced, as have the sciences and computer science. The aim is to provide a broader foundation since the best students change careers two or three times.

Ironically, an example of multicultural identity is the Saharans, who evolved from a fusion of Arabs, Berbers, and Africans and are found all over southern Morocco, Western Sahara, southern Algeria, and Mauritania. The

Sahraouis, as they are known, have distinct physical features, their own dress and ways, and they speak an ancient dialect of Arabic called Hassania.

Originally the Arabic-speaking Bedouins came from Yemen, settled in southern Morocco in the thirteenth century, and intermarried with Berbers to form a group of tribes called the Beni Hassan. Later, these pastoral nomads were forced by Moroccan rulers to move southward into what is today Western Sahara, where they intermarried with black Africans. They continued to speak Hassania Arabic, which contains some Berber words and some Spanish, the language of the former colonizer. They are Muslims but tend to be relaxed in their observances, and Saharan women have more freedom than their sisters to the north.

The Sahraouis have been engaged in a struggle for independence for the past three decades, which I describe in detail later. Morocco has offered them autonomy, but must show that it means it if the country hopes to make peace with its rebellious southerners and retain this multicultural dimension.

Multilingual Literature

Morocco's primary art form is literature and that is why language is so important. Currently, Moroccan literature is thriving in both French and Arabic, and a Berber revival is under way. Many Moroccan authors, educated in French schools, have chosen to express themselves in French. Also, for a long time, what some had to say could not be published in Morocco. Several authors told me they felt freer in French and could write about subjects like sex, still not easily accepted by the broad Arabic-reading public.

Abdelhak Serhane, who grew up in the Middle Atlas and obtained a Ph.D. in France, rebelled against Moroccan society through his novels, poems, and essays written in French. He is currently a professor of French at Lafayette University in Louisiana, but returns to Morocco regularly to renew ties. Fatema Mernissi, the sociologist, writes in French, and her books have been translated into languages around the world. But at home, several of her works have been denounced by Islamic theologians, and her 1992 book, *Le Harem politique, le Prophète et les femmes,* was banned. Ahmed Marzouki wrote about his appalling experiences in the desert prison in *Tazmamart: Cellule 10* in French, to test the waters. It became an instant bestseller and then was translated into Arabic. Moroccan expatriate Tahar Ben Jelloun, winner of France's prestigious Prix Goncourt, is perhaps more famous in France than at home. A fifty-nine-year-old psychotherapist, Ben Jelloun won the 2003 International IMPAC Dublin Literary Award for the English translation of his novel *This Blinding Absence of Light*, which is a scathing denunciation of the atrocities carried out in King Hassan's jails. Edmond Amran El Maleh, eighty-seven, a popular Moroccan-Jewish novelist, writes in French and divides his time between France and Morocco. His reminiscences constitute a warm and personal record of Jewish life in Morocco before the exodus.

Hassan Najmi, who heads the Moroccan Writers' Union and is a poet himself, says the current literary production is astonishing. The number of book titles has multiplied from a few dozen in the 1980s to about 400 each year at present. He emphasized that the majority of books coming out nowadays are written in Arabic and are not very well known abroad, because of the lack of good translations.[16]

Until now, Berber authors have expressed their social protest in French or Arabic. The works of Mohammed Kheir-Eddine, who wrote in French, have become bestsellers in the wake of his recent death. Paul Bowles introduced several Moroccan writers to the English-reading world, the best known being Mohammed Choukri, a street boy from Tangier. Choukri made Moroccan history with his shocking autobiographical tale, *For Bread Alone*. He likes to recall how he translated his book directly from the Arabic into Spanish for Bowles, who then translated it into English.

The Berber poet Ahmed Assid no longer writes in Arabic but prefers to express himself in his native *Tamazight*. His father was a grocer from a village in the anti-Atlas, who migrated with his family to Kenitra. Assid recalls growing up tongue-tied because he spoke *Tamazight* at home with his mother, while he had to learn classical Arabic in Koranic school, French in public school, and Moroccan Arabic on the streets. Although his mother and grandfather were respected poets back in the village, his father wanted him to go into business. He mastered Arabic but continued to write poems secretly in *Tamazight*. Then, coming out of the linguistic closet, Assid formed his own musical organization, the Mamora Group, which performed Berber music and poetry at Berber weddings and other events. Now a professor of philosophy at Mohammed V University, Assid is a member of the board of the Royal Institute for Berber Studies.[17]

What is remarkable is that this country, which is nearly 50 percent illiterate, which lived under tight censorship for decades, and which has been engaged in the process of Arabization since 1978 should continue to produce so many first-rate works in French as well as Arabic.

The Multiple Roots of Music

Other arts are divided along the same lines as literature, with traditional Arabic and Berber arts flourishing and a new thrust in Western modes of expression.

Moroccan music shows multiple roots, from haunting Sephardi strains to mystical Sufi chants. Andalusian orchestras, which can cast a spell with their hypnotic refrains born in fourteenth-century Muslim Spain, are much in demand for special events and a mainstay on television. The *Gnaoua* drummers, whose African slave music was discovered by the Western rock world in the 1960s, now have their own annual festival at Essaouira. Heard increasingly at festivals and on television is the *malhoun*, a cross between popular and classical Arab music many centuries old, usually involving poetic repartee and percussion instruments.

Touria Hadraoui, an activist for women's rights, has set out to preserve Morocco's musical patrimony. In the early 1990s, she became a pioneer in the masculine world of *malhoun*, bringing out several cassettes, and recently, she has produced an album of Andalusian music. Popular young singer Amina Alaoui, who lives in France, has made a name for herself in Europe with her Andalusian songs. She has also done research into Morocco's musical origins and brought out recordings that represent a synthesis of Arab modular music, Byzantine tones, and Berber rhythms.

Modern popular Arab music was actually born in Egypt in the nineteenth century. Moroccan musicologist Ahmed Aydoun recounts how Egyptian singers then conquered Morocco and the rest of the Arab world in the 1930s through records, radio, and movies. He discloses that King Mohammed V commissioned an Egyptian musician to teach Moroccans the modal scale and Arab rhythms. Moroccan orchestras imitated not only Egyptian songs but also the musicians' Arabic dialect and dress.

Modern Moroccan music dates from the post-independence euphoria, according to Aydoun, who notes that there were two trends in structure and language: classical Arabic and the Moroccan dialect. Only with the death of the great Egyptian singers like Oum Kalthoum and Abdelwahab were Moroccans free to develop their own style. Aydoun asserts that Morocco's musical problem today is the relationship between tradition and modernity. Because the Moroccan public was so enthralled with Egyptian singers and their style, Moroccan composers have been hesitant to break out into new forms. "An excessive emphasis on safeguarding tradition can paralyze innovative work and curb creativity," Aydoun concludes. "Morocco cannot be considered a museum."[18]

The Moroccan public has always been open to other genres of music. A popular form of modern music is the *rai*, which comes from Algeria and has been adapted by local singers. Western rock, jazz, and pop bands come regularly to Morocco on tour or are brought in by foreign cultural missions. They have been received with unbridled enthusiasm and emulated by budding local groups. One of the best known cultural events is the Festival of Sacred Music at Fez, an annual presentation of music from religions around the world and a platform for local Sufi singers.

As the Islamists have become more vocal, they have waged press campaigns against the foreign influences in music as "anti-Islam." Most of the press reacted angrily to these attacks, accusing the Islamists of fanaticism, but the attacks continued.

The episodes were troubling. It seemed that some Islamists were determined to amputate an important cosmopolitan part of the Moroccan identity that is reaching out to modernity.

An Islamic-European Synthesis

The golden age of Moroccan art and architecture lasted from the eleventh to the fifteenth centuries, which is known as the Hispano-Moorish period. This synthesis of Arab, Berber, and European forms and techniques was born in Muslim Spain and exported to Morocco, where it has indelibly marked the kingdom's architecture and decorative arts. Many of the artists were Andalusians from Spain: Muslims, Jews, and Christians commissioned by the sultans to work on monuments in Morocco.

Most of the great urban monuments—the grand mosques with tiled courtyards, ribbed domes, mosaic columns, and ornate Islamic inscriptions; the *medersas* (religious schools) with tiled walls and elaborately painted ceilings; the walled palaces with intricately carved cedar doors, stucco walls, marble fountains, and lush gardens; and the grand arched gateways—are built in the Hispano-Moorish tradition.

Today's architecture is still dominated by the Hispano-Moorish style—simplicity of exterior with extravagant interior decoration. In his work *Islamic Monuments in Morocco*, Richard Parker declares that from the fifteenth century to the present, Moroccan architecture has gone through a period of "stasis," although some attractive structures have been built. "There has been no innovation but merely a repetition of earlier techniques and motifs, with occasional minor changes by individual craftsmen, who have handed the trades down by a system of apprenticeship," he writes, adding that young Moroccans are more interested in "central heating and Swedish modern furniture."[19]

An exception, which should not be forgotten, is the Portuguese influence seen in fortresses and other buildings along the Atlantic coast. In the summer of 2004, UNESCO added the sixteenth-century Portuguese settlement of Mazagan at Al Jadida south of Casablanca to the list of World Heritage sites. Mazagan was cited as "an outstanding example of the interchange of influences between European and Moroccan cultures, well reflected in architecture, technology and town planning." Of special note were the ramparts and bastions of Renaissance military design and the cistern and Church of the Assumption built in Portuguese late Gothic style.[20]

In fact, both the French and Spanish protectorates developed a neo-Moroccan genre in public buildings, which uses simplified Hispano-Moorish elements like arches, columns, and tiles in a tasteful fashion. But the Moroccans seem to prefer concrete and glass for their new administrative buildings.

Rural monumental architecture has also changed little through the ages. The *kasbahs*, or fortresses, and the *ksour*, or walled villages, are generally of Berber design, less sophisticated than the Andalusian style but powerful and functional. Generally made of stone in the mountains and adobe on the pre-Saharan plains, they can have crenellated walls and towers, which are sometimes decorated with geometric patterns. Usually the adobe structures were left to crumble in the desert, but Hollywood has discovered that the *ksour* make magnificent stage sets, and so there has been a major rehabilitation effort in recent years.

Where Moroccan art has evolved is in painting, which was traditionally inhibited by Koranic strictures against reproducing the human form. There is a limited Paris school, painters who grew up under the protectorate and managed to perfect their art in Paris. Among these, Karim Bennani from Fez is not afraid to portray ordinary faces and figures like shepherds. Ahmed Cherkaoui is known for his ingenuity and the astonishing variation of his colors and graphics.

Many painters have skipped the figurative phase and plunged directly into abstraction. The late Mohamed Kacimi's abstractions seem inspired by Jackson Pollock, but he often played with Islamic arabesques and floral motifs. Farid Belkahia's experiments with different forms and materials take him to that undefined world between painting and sculpture, a mystic world which resonates with ancient signs and symbols.

If there is an original Moroccan school of painting, it is probably the Group of *Naifs* of Essaouira. In fact, they are not simply *naifs*, nor are they primitive, tribal, or traditional artists. Critics have found it difficult to define this community of self-taught painters and sculptors, who come from families of day laborers, farm workers, fishermen, and artisans. Michel Thévoz, Swiss art critic and curator of the Musée de l'Art Brut of Lausanne, insists that their work cannot be classified as rough art, which is the rejection of any cultural heritage. He notes that most of these artists see themselves as tools or toys of supernatural forces and are influenced by the religious currents around them, including Sufism, animism, African rituals, and above all trance and magic. Thévoz also emphasizes the importance of Essaouira as a creative environment, a port city, a crossroads of civilizations, a complex, living memory. "Arabs, Berbers, Jews, Blacks [descendants of slaves] coexist in relative harmony, without counting the hippie movement, which perhaps gave the decisive push," he said in an interview with the Moroccan weekly *Maroc-Hebdo*.[21]

The main center for modern art in Morocco is Tetouan, the capital of what used to be Spanish Morocco. The Spanish established a School of Fine Arts as early as 1945, which led to the creation of what is known as the Tetouan school, with well-known exponents such as painter-sculptor Abdelkrim Ouazzani.

But Tetouan has its limitations. "Here in Morocco, an artist can't work on the form of a woman because it is considered anti-Islamic," said Karima Faouzia, at a showing of her brash abstracts in acrylic and collages in the gallery of the Ministry of Culture in Rabat. A student at what is now called the National Institute of Beaux Arts in Tetouan, Faouzia says that a six-month scholarship in Paris has changed her outlook. For the first time she was able to paint the naked body of a woman.[22]

On the other hand, artist Latifa Tijani says she has never been inhibited in her work by Islam or Islamists. An adviser to the minister of culture since 1990, Tijani is a pioneer among Moroccan women painters and took part in the First Salon of Women Painters organized by the Pan-African Women's Congress in Rabat in 1971. She also penetrated the predominantly male world, participating in the First Arab Biennale of Plastic Arts in Baghdad in 1974. While she studied art in France, Austria, and Portugal, her work resonates with her Moroccan-Muslim identity. Her installations are large and strong, almost like architecture, mostly bright acrylic compositions with evocative titles: *The Tent, Sheherazade Speaks, The Rainbow of Fatima Az-zahra, The Gate of Holiness*.[23]

On International Women's Day on March 8, 2003, Tijani and seven other non-Islamist women were honored by the Party of Justice and Development (PJD). "They know I'm involved in the Beijing women's movement, but I also believe in dialogue," she remarked. When the Casablanca suicide bombings occurred several weeks later, Tijani was one of 500 Moroccan artists who contributed to *Prints of Hope*, white handprints on red panels, in a solemn commitment to work for peace and tolerance.

People like Tijani show that dialogue is still possible in this divided society.

Islamic Morality

While Islamic taboos have had a certain effect on the plastic arts, the ban on the human form has without question stunted the development of dance in Morocco. Moroccans have innate rhythm and graceful movements, but their dances have been long relegated to the domain of folklore because of the Muslim attitude toward the body. Participants in traditional folk dances are fully clothed in their holiday best and may sway but are forbidden any unseemly contortions.

I recall when Katherine Dunham discovered Morocco in the early 1950s, she was so excited over the colors and sounds and movements of the traditional dances that she incorporated some elements into her own program. Yet when a Moroccan tried to form a modern dance corps, he was mercilessly put down by the authorities.

Lahcen Zinoun is a Berber dancer and choreographer, who became a star with the Royal Belgian Ballet because his own country wasn't ready for him. When he finally came home, he opened a modern dance school in Casablanca, in hopes of forming a ballet troupe. Parents sent their girls to the school, but the only boys were his two sons and nephew. "It is considered shameful for boys to dance," he told me.[24]

In the past few years, Zinoun has almost single-handedly created his own contemporary dance festival, bringing European groups to Casablanca in hopes of developing among the population a taste for modern dance. But the public has been reticent and the government reluctant to sponsor such a controversial art form. In an interview, a frustrated Zinoun said that he has gone into movie making because "maybe the public can enjoy on the screen what it cannot accept on stage."

At last Zinoun was given official recognition in 2003, when he was named director of the Marrakech Festival of Popular Arts. Although this is not the dance troupe of his dreams, it is an exciting beginning. At least he can choreograph the traditional dances and train the dancers—which does not happen in the usual folklore performances. Dean Chafik of the *Amazigh* Institute has also given the artist a challenging mission: to research and record the country's rich and varied history of traditional music and dance. After that, he confides, he hopes to create a Berber opera.

However, he will have to contend with the Islamists.

Almost imperceptibly, Islamists have become increasingly aggressive in seeking to impose their morality on the rest of society. At first it seemed that the so-called moderate Islamists of the PJD were merely trying to enhance their religious credentials in their rivalry with Yassine's Islamist movement. But increasingly, bearded bullies have appeared in public places, such as the

Casablanca Book Fair, and openly threatened people they consider to be "un-Islamic," like authors of books they consider blasphemous, women campaigning for equal rights, or Berbers writing in Latin script rather than with the alphabet of the Koran.

Since the end of King Hassan's authoritarian rule, moderate Islamists have increasingly assumed the role of moral guardians, striking out against people who transgress against their particular interpretation of Islam. Among the first targets of their wrath was the Miss Rabat Beauty Contest in 1999, which they considered a product of Western immorality. Islamists called on the public to occupy the hall where the beauty contest was to be held, and it took 400 police agents to enable the show to go on. But the state television station didn't dare to broadcast the ceremony.

Undaunted, the Islamists renewed their assault against the Miss Morocco 2002 Contest, which was renamed the Gazelle of the Atlas Contest to appear less Western. Impresario Anas Yazuli, called "Morocco's Salman Rushdie" by the Islamist press, said that, in spite of the threats, 14,000 Moroccans had vied for the 30 places in the contest, or just as many as in France. The contest was scheduled right after national elections and Yazuli expressed the view that the virulent campaign against the Miss Gazelle contest was more about winning votes than ideology.

The Islamist deputy who led the campaign against the beauty contests was Abdelillah Benkiran, who had denounced a television camerawoman for wearing a T-shirt while covering a parliamentary debate. Another victim was a woman poet, accused by the PJD of blasphemy.

By 2001, the Islamists' moralizing campaign had gathered force. They called for a cleansing of Moroccan cultural life of what they viewed as anti-Islamic influences. In one action, they led a boycott of the Pokemon characters as part of "degenerate Western culture," quite ignoring their Japanese origins. They also accused the organizers of the Festival of the *Al Aïta* at Safi of "depravity." The *aïta* is traditional music of the Atlantic plains and combines a religious invocation with rhythmic body movements, which can turn into a sensuous hip, shoulders, and belly dance although the dancers are fully clothed.

After their electoral success in the fall of 2002, the Islamist party struck out again, this time against one of the most popular young Moroccan filmmakers, Nabil Ayouch. His film *Une Minute de Silence*, which had not been shown in Morocco, was denounced as encouraging pornography and homosexuality. PJD members of parliament demanded that the film be permanently banned, any public financing reimbursed, and legal action taken against the officials responsible. Railing against the film, the Islamist daily *Attajdid* emphasized: "Obscenity is obscenity whether it walks in the streets, on the beaches, in out of the way places or on the television and cinema screens, and it is rejected by Islamic law."[25]

Even more serious was the Islamist attack against foreign cultural missions, which play such a vital role in preserving Morocco's multicultural diversity. France, Germany, and Spain all operate cultural institutes, which organize film festivals, concerts, and lectures and serve as windows to Europe. Early in 2003, the PJD demanded that the government exercise strict control over the foreign cultural centers "so they are no longer free to spread immoral values."[26] The press reaction was so vehement that Islamist leader Mustapha Ramid hastened to explain that his party did not seek the closure of the foreign institutes but the inclusion of Islamic principles in their programs.

"What Do the Islamists Want?" Chafik Laabi asked in the sober Casablanca weekly *La Vie Economique*: "We must conclude that Islamists, of all tendencies, in the name of their interpretation of Islam seek to impose on us their way of life, their mentality, their way of dressing, their ideas and their convictions."[27]

The Socialist party has taken the lead in the counteroffensive to the Islamists' morality war. Habib Malki, minister of national education and youth, defended the principle of cultural diversity and insisted that Morocco owes a great deal to the foreign centers, particularly in science and culture. A Socialist daily *Libération* columnist, M'Hamed Hamrouch, pointed out that in the beginning Islamist activists occupied the universities, taking advantage of the winds of freedom to establish themselves on the public scene. Now they have attacked Moroccan cinema and foreign cultural centers, he wrote in January 2003, suggesting that the next target would probably be the theater or music or plastic arts. In an urgent appeal, he called on men and women of culture to be more vigilant than ever against the ambitions of "obscurantists."

The usually unflappable Abdelmounaim Dilami, publisher of the daily *L'Economiste*, wrote in an editorial, "The Islamists have launched an assault to control Morocco." He noted that in some high schools, girls are sanctioned for failing to wear headscarves, and in poor neighborhoods Islamists have imposed their law by force. Emphasizing that Morocco's newborn democracy is threatened, Dilami said: "If the leaders are incapable of protecting Moroccan society, incapable of imposing respect for its institutions and laws, then they should withdraw and make way for those who are determined to react firmly."[28]

It was the trial of fourteen young hard-rock enthusiasts, accused of "Satan worship," that shocked progressive circles. Early in 2003, when the country was grappling with the revelations of secret Islamist cults, the Casablanca police arrested a group of rock musicians and the owner of the cafe where they performed, accusing them of "assault against the Muslim faith." Black T-shirts, posters, CDs, and rock instruments were seized as "proof" against the young people, who came from respectable bourgeois families and had no prior arrests. A Casablanca court went so far as to convict the rock group on the charge of "offense to good morals" and handed out sentences of one month to one year in prison.

After severe editorials and emotional demonstrations by the rock musicians' parents and fans, they were released. Although the case had a happy ending, it demonstrated how a rigid form of Islamic "morality" has begun to penetrate Moroccan society and can be used to manipulate the security services and even the courts.

Under cover of the compliant Party for Justice and Democracy, hard-core Islamists periodically renew their attacks on Western influences. The PJD's ideologue, Ahmed Raissouni, shook up progressive circles during the summer of 2004 with a diatribe against the music festivals as "sites of debauch and homosexuality." *Aujourd'hui le Maroc*, a progovernment daily, accused the PJD of seeking to outlaw music, festivals, and other tourist and cultural activities—in fact, "any opening to the rest of the world."[29]

Islam has been a powerful unifying factor in Morocco since the Arab conquest in the eighth century. Islamic influences permeate the language, arts, and daily life. But it has generally been an open, flexible version of Islam that has tolerated the diversity of the Moroccan identity. It would be a sad loss for Morocco if a group of radical Islamists succeeded in its goal to reduce the nation to its Arab-Islamic identity and, in the name of religion, obliterated the rich cultural legacies of Berbers, Europeans, and Jews, which also form Moroccan society today.

Grappling with Mirages

8

*L*ooming from the barren plain between Casablanca and the Mohammed V Airport is a huge ungainly structure that looks like a headless robot. This is Technopark, Morocco's Silicon Valley and symbol of the kingdom's aspirations to become a regional platform for new information technologies.

Casablanca has come a long way from the seedy French colonial port of the 1940s made famous by the legendary film that took its name. Today, Casablanca is one of Africa's major metropolises, with some 5 million inhabitants. The new heart of the city is the financial quarter, with its flashy modern stock exchange, imposing banks, skyscrapers, and incredible traffic jams.

Along the *corniche*, fashionable restaurants and nightclubs flourish—despite the nominal Islamic ban on alcohol—and in outlying residential neighborhoods, grandiose villas abound. Besides Technopark, various other industrial zones, modern apartment blocks, and public housing have sprung up on the periphery. "Another California," the colonials used to say. In fact, there is a fashionable residential suburb called California.

Yet anyone digging below the surface of Casablanca could well wonder if the modern, prosperous-looking city is not mostly mirage. Infiltrating any empty space are the *bidonvilles*, the tin-drum and cardboard shantytowns that have accompanied the rural migration to the city. With those migrants looking for jobs and a better life have come street children, beggars, drug dealers, and other criminals.

Nowhere in this kingdom of contrasts is the gap between the haves and have-nots so flagrant. Casablanca has periodically erupted in violent rioting and could do so again. All of the ingredients for an explosion are here: a large

197

Casablanca's modern stock exchange is dominated by the giant corporation Omnium Nord Africain and its subsidiaries, whose main shareholder is the royal family.

mass of people deprived of the basic needs of modern life, a rampant consumer society, spiraling unemployment, militant labor unions, a dynamic press, and a breeding ground for Islamic extremists.

Taking Up the Challenge

As governor of Casablanca, Driss Benhima was a man in a hurry to get things done. (His secretary sometimes scheduled as many as five appointments for the same hour—like some dentists—and Benhima would briskly move from one waiting room to the other without wasting time on the usual formalities.) Critics said the governor didn't always think things through. For example, once he ordered the streets to be cleared of street vendors without establishing where they could go. But at least he began to tackle the city's proliferating problems. A mining engineer and former minister of transportation, Benhima was a member of the team of technocrats named by King Mohammed to give impetus to his plans for regional development.

Supremely self-confident, the governor, in his late forties, spoke enthusiastically of Casablanca as "Morocco's gateway" for industries, telecommunications, services, and tourism. As a first step, a regional investment center has been set up to help guide potential investors and limit risks, Benhima said in an interview in his office at City Hall, a handsome neo-Moorish building from the 1920s.[1]

He talked at length of his program to decongest the *medina*, the original Arab quarter in the heart of this former French colonial showpiece. The governor was keen to develop Casablanca's tourist potential and had plans to clean up the port and move the fish market to a new site north of the city. Work was already under way on the construction of a marina to handle cruise ships and on the restoration of the ancient sea wall.

Casablanca's main challenges, according to the governor, are like those of other big cities: environmental pollution, traffic congestion, inadequate mass transit, waste management, and traffickers of various kinds.

"Paradoxically, all those illicit activities and the loss of civic responsibility are linked to security," Benhima said. People have been allowed to operate outside the law with the complicity of the local authorities, he noted. They feared an outbreak of social unrest and so let the informal sector grow as an escape valve.

In fact, public safety is relatively good, Benhima stressed. He acknowledged that the security services had traced the presence of several hundred "Afghans," Moroccan Islamists who had been trained in guerrilla camps in Afghanistan. "But they prey on members of their own movement, not on others," he said, adding that the authorities had the security situation under control.

Taking up the perennial question of the *bidonvilles*—there are said to be 350,000 people living in these slums in Casablanca alone—Benhima displayed his pragmatic nature. "It's useless to move the migrants out of [the] *bidonvilles* and put them in high rises; they won't stay," he argued. "They want to be near work opportunities. It's better to improve the *bidonvilles*, give people running water, electricity, streets, and let them stay where they are."

The governor said that a major challenge was the communes, each with its own budget and priorities: "It's like governing twenty-five cities at the same time." Despite many problems, he concluded, Casablanca is a prosperous and dynamic city. "The poorest inhabitants are richer and live better here than they do in the High Atlas," he stressed.

In the fall of 2002, Benhima had laid the groundwork for a project to absorb 60,000 rural migrants a year. His plans included the urbanization of 7,500 acres of land to be set aside for public housing; models of small, low-cost houses; and credit opportunities for workers in the informal sector, which they never had before.

Then, out of the blue, as is so often the case in this kingdom, Benhima was named to head the Northern Development Agency, a government body that aims to promote the underdeveloped provinces of former Spanish Morocco. No reason was given for the transfer but the word in Casablanca was that he had stepped on some powerful toes. His replacement was M'hamed Dryef, a career official from the Ministry of the Interior with a security background. With hindsight, it looks as though the authorities were getting ready for May 16, although of course they couldn't have predicted the events of that day. Unfortunately, once Dryef was in place, many of Benhima's innovative projects for Casablanca were shelved.

Tarnished Miracles

Benhima was right, of course. Casablanca is a wealthy city, crisscrossed by fault lines of extreme poverty and despair, which give it an unreal quality.

The Twin Towers, for example, stand partially empty, like modest stepsons of the New York original, never having realized their potential. Here are the main offices of Méditel, an international consortium for mobile telecommunications, Morocco's newest, most dynamic growth sector. In a country where much of the rural population is still deprived of roads and electricity, the rapid spread of mobile phones is quite extraordinary, but it makes sense.

Anyone familiar with the long delays to obtain a fixed phone line, the erratic service, and the high cost of communications under Maroc Telecom, the former state monopoly, can understand the popularity of the new, accessible, and reasonably priced mobile phones.

It came to be known as the "Moroccan miracle"—the fastest-growing mobile telecommunications system in the world at the turn of the twenty-first century. This feat was largely the work of the National Telecommunication Regulatory Agency, known by its French initials ANRT, set up in 1997 to oversee the privatization of the sclerotic state-owned telecommunications monopoly. ANRT's general director, Mostafa Terrab, an MIT graduate, built up the regulating body from scratch. King Hassan had announced at that time that the reform of the telecommunications sector was imperative because of the demands of the growing globalization of the world economy and the rapid evolution of technology.

In 1999, the independent regulatory agency engineered one of the most favorable deals ever for a second GSM (Global System for Mobile Communications) license in a country of this size. Previously, Maroc Telecom had held a monopoly over fixed and mobile services. Méditel, a Spanish-Portuguese-Moroccan group, paid the Moroccan state $1.1 billion for the second mobile telecommunications license. It was considered a model international tender: transparent, fair, and professional. Besides providing the government with urgently needed revenue, Méditel forced Maroc Telecom to improve services and reduce prices. Prior to liberalization, the telephone density—number of fixed and mobile lines per 100 inhabitants—was only 6.5 percent whereas in one year's time after the arrival of Méditel, the density had more than doubled to 15.2 percent (with 10.4 percent in mobile phones).

"Cell phones have transformed life in this country," Saad Bendidi, the youthful Moroccan president of Méditel, told me in an interview. "Until a couple of years ago, you'd have to call the grocer to give a message to the plumber; now the plumber is linked to the GSM. Villagers, who still have to walk long distances to get water, can talk to each other by cell phones."[2]

At first, cell phones were playthings of the wealthy and cost between $600 and $1,000 even at Derb Ghallef, the popular flea market. But by 1999, with prepaid cards and competition from Méditel, almost anyone could afford a cell phone. There is now a mass market for mobile phones in Morocco, according to Bendidi. Méditel can cover every town of more than 5,000 people or 83 percent of the population. The company claimed to have 3 million mobile phone subscribers by mid-2004 and had plans to expand operations to other African countries. Simultaneously, Maroc Telecom saw a new surge in its cell phone market, reaching 6 million subscribers.

At the end of 2000, Morocco sold off 35 percent of the shares of Maroc

Telecom to the French conglomerate Vivendi-Universal for the handsome sum of $2.2 billion. It was the largest single investment ever made by a foreign company in Morocco and an important vote of confidence in the country. Soon there were rumors that the troubled Vivendi might pull out of Morocco. But late in 2004, the company announced the purchase of another 16 percent of Maroc Telecom shares to become the majority shareholder. The state company had now gone private.

Licenses were accorded to five international companies for satellite services, and leasing agreements were made with a number of Internet access providers. And there were plans to sell a third GSM license. But this economic success story may have been rooted in sand.

One problem was that the funds generated by the privatization of telecommunications did not go to develop the sector as originally planned, but rather to cover gaps in the regular budget. The brilliant chief regulator Mostafa Terrab publicly criticized the government for its handling of this revenue. In an interview published in June 2001, Terrab warned that if the country continued to treat telecommunications as a means for the state to meet its payroll obligations, it would soon make a mockery of the primary objective of opening that sector to private competition, which was to turn Morocco into a hub for regional telecommunications services.[3]

In the spring of 2002, Terrab quietly resigned over the government's intrusiveness in the agency's affairs and accepted the post of lead regulatory specialist in global information and communication technologies with the World Bank in Washington. With his departure, the Moroccan telecommunications bubble has deflated somewhat. Another serious blow to the country's ambitions in telecommunications came with the announcement at the end of 2002 that of twelve pretenders, there was no serious bidder for a license to establish a second fixed telephone service. Blaming "the financial crisis" in the sector worldwide, the minister of commerce, industry, and telecommunications, Rachid Talbi Alami, indicated that Morocco would renew the tender at a later date. It came as no surprise that Moroccan plans to expand its outreach in telecommunications beyond its borders have been put on hold.

Morocco's first showcase for new technologies in information and telecommunications, Technopark, is a futuristic building with a past. Originally constructed as headquarters for the National Customs Department, it remained closed for four years before being opened in the fall of 2001 as Morocco's home to high-tech companies. Technopark is a semipublic management company, with 37 percent of the shares held by the state and the rest by the main Moroccan banks.

By most accounts, the glow had already worn off Technopark within a year's time. A good part of the company's capital of about $4.6 million had gone into renovating and upgrading the building. Some 110 small and medium businesses had moved into Technopark, including 52 startup firms, but only one big company, Maroc Telecom's main server, Menara. At first it seemed that Technopark was going through the usual growing pains—problems with electricity and air conditioning and the lack of service facilities like a restaurant, newsstand, and bank—and that these matters would be resolved in time. But there were also grievances about the high cost of the rents, and a number of the startups were threatened with expulsion. More serious were complaints of difficulties accessing the Internet. Frequent connection breaks were aggravated by the arrival of Menara, which overloaded the lines. These kinds of glitches were inexcusable in a center for new information technologies.

Perhaps because of the inherent problems of Technopark, the government announced in the fall of 2002 plans to build the entirely new Technopole, devoted to telecommunication and information technologies, to be located at Bouznika Valley, midway between Casablanca and Rabat. The Hassan II Development Fund was to invest nearly $9 million to get the ambitious project off the ground. With Hewlett Packard and a Chinese firm, Huawei, as partners, Technopole's plans included a training school for information technologies, a science and industry nucleus, a research and development center in telecommunications, and an Internet lab with various work stations. The need for such a training facility was highlighted by officials who pointed out that presently only 1,500 cadres in telecommunications were trained each year whereas the country needed at least 5,000.

There was also talk at the beginning of 2003 of a second technopark in Casablanca—the third in the country—and feasibility studies were carried out. However, the semiofficial daily *Le Matin du Sahara* pointed out three major handicaps, which continued to plague the first Technopark: the high rents, the exorbitant costs of telephone and Internet access, and the lack of trained personnel.

Perhaps because of the competition, Technopark had made advances by its third year of operations and was adjusting to reality. A Website (www .casablanca-technopark.ma) was created to enable the fledgling information and communication businesses to expose their products and develop contacts with similar companies in the Mediterranean region. In June 2004, Abderrafie Hanouf, director general of the management firm, announced a 90 percent occupation rate with 130 businesses located at the site and said that the World Bank had provided $250,000 to help finance new companies. But he acknowledged that the board had lowered rents considerably, and there were difficulties in financing the startup businesses.

One basic problem is that the Internet market is relatively limited. A study released by Maroc Telecom in the summer of 2004 reported nearly 2 million Internet users in Morocco, but these were mainly cybercafes and workplaces. The primary handicap was said to be the high cost of access. This has had a serious effect on the number of Internet service providers, which has plunged from 100 to a dozen. At year's end, however, the government announced that the number of Internet subscribers had reached 3 million—thanks to cost-cutting and the introduction of the Asymmetric Digital Subscriber Line (ASDL).

Morocco entered the Internet age in 1995, and for a while it seemed the country had gone cybercrazy, despite the high levels of illiteracy and poverty. There was an explosion in cybercafes to a total of 2,500 in June 2002, or double the number of two years before. Because of the costs involved, Internet access was still a luxury—only 5 percent of urban homes and one-third of the businesses on the social security register boasted a computer at the time. But the industry remains hopeful and expects the number of users to reach 10 million by 2010, with official investments planned for the new technologies sector and more competitive prices.

While the loosening of the state monopoly in telecommunications has begun to have a beneficial effect for consumers, most of the private wealth is still concentrated in the hands of a few. Moroccan entrepreneurs proudly point to the young Casablanca Stock Exchange, an exciting, modern glass structure that exudes prosperity, as a force for modernity. In fact, so few companies are traded on the exchange—about fifty-five in all—that it is like an exclusive club, with almost no foreign investment. The market is dominated by ONA (Omnium Nord Africain), Morocco's largest conglomerate, which controls more than 100 enterprises from mining to agribusiness. The CEO is named by the king and the royal family is known to be the largest shareholder with 35 percent of the shares. Its rival is the family-owned Benjelloun Group, dominant in banking and insurance and the Moroccan partner in the Méditel consortium.

At the end of 2003, Casablanca's banking and business sectors were stunned by the news of the merger of the country's main corporate bank, the Commercial Bank of Morocco (BCM), linked to ONA, with a major retail bank, Wafabank, to form a world-class giant. The new union would be the largest banking enterprise in North Africa, under the aegis of Omnium Nord Africain. The mega banking group would enable Morocco to operate with greater efficiency in an increasingly global market, banking sources stressed.

But the independent press warned of the risks of this concentration of financial power in the hands of ONA, that is, the palace, which would be immune to regulatory bodies. "The mixture of business and religion with the function of the monarchy saps the legitimacy of the regime at the base," *Le Journal*'s Aboubakr Jamai cautioned.[4]

Behind the façade of modern skyscrapers, the rush for new technologies, the privatizations and consolidation of megaholdings lie fundamental flaws. The rules of the game have yet to be clearly defined; a sound legal and regulatory system must be established and the laws enforced.

American Dreams

You'll find it on the edge of the *medina*, down a dingy alley past a neighborhood mosque with one side facing Casablanca port. There it is, as real as life, Rick's Cafe. Over the years, countless visitors have combed the streets of Casablanca looking for that seductive place of romance and adventure, only to be told that it was the figment of Hollywood's imagination.

Fittingly, it is an American woman, Kathy Kriger, who fell in love with Morocco and left her foreign service job to create that Casablanca icon. With aid from American decorator Bill Willis, known for his inspired works in Marrakech, Kriger set out to recreate the spirit of Casablanca that was captured on film in the 1940s.

The project was easier conceived than done. Rick's Cafe opened in the spring of 2004, a year late, because of a vast array of bureaucratic difficulties that were only resolved through powerful intervention, although everyone was in favor of the idea and thought it would be a boon to tourism in Morocco's economic capital. But that is her story. She will undoubtedly write of the Byzantine process she had to go through to set up a business in a country supposedly eager for investments in tourism.

On an individual level, Kriger's experience illustrates the obstacles that foreign investors—particularly Americans—face in Morocco. While the king and his government have repeatedly claimed their determination to open and modernize the economy, and probably mean it, the system remains dominated by ancient practices of influence, cronyism, and favors. The French and other Europeans have had generations of experience in coping with the local customs and have created an economic and financial network interlaced with the main Moroccan powers. But only a few big American companies have managed to establish themselves in Morocco with the view of using this strategic, modernizing country as a regional hub. Microsoft is a believer in Morocco's vocation as a center for new information technologies and has established its regional headquarters in Casablanca. The director general of Microsoft's North African operations, Karim Bernoussi, is a French-trained telecommunications engineer. He told the press that the information giant chose Morocco as the hub of its operations because of the strong potential development, the existence of competent human resources on the local market, and its geographic location. Microsoft has established a close working partnership with the Moroccan government to develop information and communications in the different ministries and to train their technical personnel.

Announcing the results of Microsoft's free summer program for retraining college graduates, Bernoussi said that the job placement rate was 100 percent for the first two years in 2000 and 2001. However, only 70 percent of the 100 graduates in 2002 had found jobs. He declared that as of 2003, Microsoft would concentrate on Morocco's school system, noting that only 2,000 schools out of a total of 15,000 offer computer technology. He also spoke of a new program to train handicapped persons as operators in call centers.

Several other American companies have set up regional operations in Casablanca. Coca Cola is a pioneer, present since 1947, prior to independence. Khalil Nouara, a Coca Cola executive, said the company chose Morocco as the hub for its Northwest African operations for several reasons: the political stability, young population, economic stability, and security. He said that more than 70,000 jobs are associated with the production and distribution of the soft drink and other products like Orangina and mineral water.[5]

But, basically, American companies are underrepresented in this burgeoning economic capital. Several U.S. ambassadors have gone to bat for Morocco, trying to coax and wheedle American investors to try their luck in this friendly Muslim country, which all agree has tremendous potential. But results so far have been negligible.

The head of the American Chamber of Commerce, Eric Stoclet, director general of Citibank for North Africa, told me in an interview that overall foreign direct investments were "stagnant" aside from the telecommunications sector. Citing a survey by the chamber, he said that foreign investors are ambivalent about doing business in Morocco. "They were generally positive about the current investment climate and think the king has good intentions and seems to be placing capable people in key jobs," he said.[6]

"But the respondents were negative on day-to-day business dealings, namely, the inefficient, unfair judicial system, open to corruption, [and] a school system not adapted to the needs of the modern business world," Stoclet pointed out. Other problems cited were related to the work environment, the need to improve productivity, and the need to revise the labor laws, specifically difficulties in the firing process. American investors, he added, refer to an additional problem, the fact that Morocco is basically Eurocentric, and the playing field is not level in some cases.

American and Moroccan businesspeople expressed hope that the new free trade association between Rabat and Washington would enhance relations between the two countries, but many hurdles remain along the way.

Since 1995, the government has taken a number of measures to improve the investment climate, passing a new investment code that favors foreign investors and allows them to participate in the privatization program. Foreign investors can trade on the Casablanca Stock Exchange and repatriate original capital that is registered with the foreign exchange office. Foreign employees may repatriate all of their salaries. The Moroccan *dirham* is a convertible currency for all current transactions. There were commitments to set up the *guichet unique*—the one-stop counter—to reduce the paperwork usually connected with investments. But, as always in Morocco, policy does not necessarily mean implementation, at least not immediately.

Barely installed on his throne, King Mohammed VI showed that he was keenly aware of the country's economic strengths and shortcomings. He frequently stated that his principal concern was urban unemployment, at 23 percent in 1999. One of his first acts was to set up a Royal Commission on Investment to improve the country's competitiveness and reduce the impediments to foreign and national investments.

But private investments stagnated and privatizations crawled along at a much slower rate than expected. At the beginning of 2002, the king wrote a firm letter to Prime Minister Youssoufi announcing his intention to eliminate all administrative obstacles to investments and put an end to the proliferation and complication of legal and administrative mechanisms, which he said were responsible for the miscarriage of many foreign and national projects. The monarch emphasized that the governors would be given the authority to deal with investments under his new program for decentralization and regionalization. This was a clear move to circumvent the central government and would have been applauded if it had increased efficiency and attracted new investments. But the governors seemed hardly prepared to assume their additional obligations.

Two years later, there was still talk in business circles of the need to simplify investment procedures, modernize the banking sector, and bring greater transparency to the system—if Morocco were to benefit from the new free trade agreement with the United States.

Agrarian Myths

The single most important reason given for the sluggish economy is the succession of droughts that have plagued the country off and on for the past two decades—if not longer. Nearly half of Morocco's population still lives from agriculture and therefore the health of the economy is closely linked to the erratic rainfall. King Hassan's answer to the problem was irrigation. The trouble is that with the decrease in annual precipitation, the reservoirs behind the dams are rarely full. Furthermore, barely 10 percent of the farmers benefit from irrigation on the Atlantic coastal plains of the Gharb and Souss, which produce mainly export crops like citrus fruits, early vegetables, and sugar cane. The majority of rural inhabitants live in nonirrigated mountainous areas where they grow grains and raise sheep and other animals.

In his authoritative book on Morocco's endemic agricultural crisis, *Moroccan Mirages*, Will Swearingen wrote in 1987:

> Government-financed irrigation development has essentially followed the vision of the 1938 colonial plan. Irrigation water has benefited the landowning elite. . . .
>
> In short, in terms of all three of its objectives—to raise rural standards of living, earn foreign currency, and provide for the nation's food needs—the irrigation policy has clearly failed. Indeed, it has seemingly been counterproductive. . . .
>
> Land concentration during and since the protectorate period has been perhaps the major cause of the gulf between rich and poor in Morocco.[7]

The farm situation has not changed much in the past two decades, except that more rural migrants have flocked to the cities.

"It's paradoxical that the country's growth still depends on the weather," commented Najib Akesbi, a well-known economist and professor at the Institute of Agronomy and Veterinary Studies in Rabat. He noted in an interview that 2003 was a good year for rain, which was expected to produce a 4.5 percent growth rate, but even so, that is considerably below the 7–8 percent needed to begin to absorb the large numbers of unemployed.[8]

King Hassan's farm policy was to develop modern mechanized centers of development with intensified production which would then "carry along the rest of the farms to modernity," Akesbi said. He pointed out that most of the modern land holdings, starting with the European colonial farms, had been acquired by army officers, government officials, and wealthy merchants. "Thus the state nourished this elite social class through its investments, credit policies, and marketing system," remarked the outspoken academic.

Akesbi stressed that the government invests a "disproportionate" 64 percent of the budget in agriculture, which produces only 8 percent of its income. Although fruits and vegetables from irrigated lands are exported, he said, the country is "dangerously dependent" on food imports, including much of its wheat and corn, half of its sugar needs, 90 percent of its cooking oil, plus legumes, butter, cheese, powdered milk, and meat for the military.

Besides the vagaries of the climate, the economist stressed, the main structural problems of land ownership have not been resolved: the divisions of small holdings that cannot be modernized, the collective tribal lands without title, and religious foundation lands that are rented but can be seized by the state at any time.

Several days earlier, I had heard Akesbi speak at a symposium on the "Economic Causes for the Casablanca Attacks." While emphasizing that there were multiple reasons behind the May 16 suicide bombings, he said that the situation was "the product of forty years of erroneous economic policy—the failure to distribute the country's wealth equitably, the absence of dynamism and inability to enlarge the market." He was particularly critical of the Socialist-led government of *Alternance*, which, he said, in four years "had achieved nothing" and had not even begun to resolve the major problems: the feeble growth, fragile structures, unemployment, antiquated practices, policy of privileges, and above all, the poverty.

"Open your eyes. Never have there been so many beggars and *bidonvilles*, and the poverty is growing," Akesbi said, pointing out that in 1998, 19 percent of the population lived below the poverty line of $1 a day, and by 2003, it was 25 percent. "If the government had succeeded in implementing its project of social and economic reform, the *pateras* [boatpeople] would have stopped struggling to escape to Europe, but now not only the *pateras* continue to flee and drown in the strait, but we have suicide bombers in the heart of Casablanca."9

Oil Fantasy

Unlike its neighbor Algeria, which is also plagued by shrinking rainfall and spreading desertification, Morocco cannot fall back on substantial oil and natural gas reserves, at least not for the time being. Although Morocco shares with Algeria vast stretches of the Sahara and a similar geological structure, deposits of hydrocarbons have not been found in commercial quantities in the kingdom.

There was a much-publicized discovery of oil at Talsinnt in eastern Morocco during the summer of 2000. As I wrote earlier, for a few euphoric days, Moroccans believed that all their problems were solved and that the kingdom would at last join its Arab brothers in the Organization of Petroleum Exporting Countries (OPEC). King Mohammed VI personally announced the happy find of "abundant and high quality oil" during his Throne Speech on

August 20, 2000. The minister of energy went further to declare that the Texas-based firm Lone Star Energy had reported that Morocco possessed up to 12 billion barrels of oil reserves in the area. It was just the tonic the country needed after yet another devastating drought, and the stock market soared.

Sober voices soon prevailed. Amina Benkhadra, the new director general of mines, told the nation that it was not possible to make such optimistic forecasts based on the results of only one well at Talsinnt. Several months later in an interview, the discreet Benkhadra told me that Lone Star was still in the picture but its offshore prospects seemed much more promising than those at Talsinnt.

A lesson had been learned. As the French say: one should not confuse dreams with reality.

Precarious Riches

Some wise souls say it is lucky that Morocco doesn't have oil in sizable quantities because it has had to develop other resources. The kingdom does possess diverse ore reserves, including copper, iron, barite, and anthracite. And it has the largest supply of phosphate in the world; the only trouble is that phosphate prices seem to be in a habitual slump. Nevertheless, the export of phosphates and its derivatives, like fertilizers and phosphoric acid, amounted to nearly 20 percent of the country's exports and bring to the state coffers about $1.5 billion a year.

Fishing has become an increasingly important resource as Iberian fish have headed south in recent years. The problem is that Morocco's fishing fleet is generally antiquated and inefficient and is no match for European and Japanese competitors. In an attempt to attract joint ventures and enforce periodical fishing bans, Morocco failed to renew its fisheries agreement with the European Union in 2000. As a result, all sides have lost, except the fish.

In the 1990s, the textile industry became Morocco's main exporter, after agriculture, and the number one employer, accounting for some 200,000 jobs. Many of Europe's best-known clothing manufacturers—both luxury and low-cost firms—subcontract to Moroccan companies. But in the past few years, Moroccan wages and other production costs have risen substantially, which have been followed by a loss of jobs, more than 22,000 gone in 2000 alone, according to Hassan Chami, head of the Moroccan Businessmen's Confederation. The government has refused to devalue the national currency, the *dirham*, and so foreign clothing firms have been moving to Eastern Europe.

Tourism, however, brings in the most foreign exchange—an estimated $2 billion in 2000. But Morocco, with about 3 million tourists in 2000, lagged woefully behind smaller, less diverse, but better organized Tunisia, which welcomed more than 5 million visitors.

Ironically, in the summer of 2001, King Mohammed declared that tourism would be given top priority with the declared aim of attracting 10 million visitors by 2010. Then, the terrorist attacks of September 11 happened. There was a substantial drop in visitors, tourist receipts, and investments in the following months. By 2002, there were signs of improvement. The Casablanca attacks of May 16, 2003, appeared to be the coup de grace to Morocco's tourism ambitions. However tourists are a hardy race and have returned—though perhaps not in the numbers hoped for or proclaimed. The Tourism Department announced a record 5.5 million visitors for 2004, but that includes 2.7 million Moroccans living overseas.

The Privileged Few

"In Morocco, there doesn't exist a real economic elite in the true sense of the term," according to Hassan M. Alaoui, the young publisher of the respected business monthly *Economie et Entreprises*. In a bold editorial entitled *Une Génération de Rentiers*, Alaoui blames the paralysis of the economy on the elite corps of businessmen who live on unearned income from official favors, such as transportation permits and quarry and fishing licenses. Excluding the large private groups whose investments are known, the publisher emphasizes that there is a group of businessmen who are hanging onto their old privileges. They have refused to go along with the economic reforms initiated under King Hassan that aimed to create responsible investors, he said. His conclusion: all of these persons living on unearned income must be reintegrated into the economy.[10]

The experts have said it many times: the fundamental economic problem in this country is slow and erratic growth, which means that job creation has not kept pace with the population increase. The statistics are devastating and show that Morocco's economic problems are getting worse. Only an average of 200,000 new jobs are created each year, while 300,000 people enter the job market for the first time. King Mohammed VI has emphasized on various occasions that the country's main problem is the ever-increasing disparity between rich and poor.

Yet affluence is increasingly visible. *Economie et Entreprises* published a special report on "The Luxury Business Boom" in its year-end issue for 2002. The big names of fashion in men's and women's clothing and fine jewelry have come to Casablanca and to a lesser extent Rabat, Agadir, and Marrakech. Until recently Morocco's privileged set would have to go to Paris, London, or Dubai to satisfy their tastes for international luxury goods. The American jeweler Tiffany & Company opened a franchise in downtown Casablanca at the end of 2001, followed by the Italian firm Bulgari. Mansfield has established a branch selling its high-end men's shoes in the Twin Towers, and other shops offering men's luxury apparel include Venezia Espace, 303, and Boss. In electronics, Nokia and Siemens are battling it out for the last word in fantasy cell phones; Hewlett Packard and Toshiba exhibit their latest PCs. Not to mention several slick magazines on home decorations and furnishings that flaunt gilt bathroom fixtures and brocade curtains, crystal chandeliers, silk bedding, and silver tableware.[11]

The clients are there—discreetly entrenched behind high walls in their palatial residences in Casablanca's exclusive Ain Diab quarter and other wealthy suburbs. It is considered unseemly in this traditional society to display luxury, although there are some transgressors among the new rich and Gulf Arab transients.

Challenging the walled society, the young rich—the sons and daughters of privilege—parade up and down the *corniche* in their high-powered BMWs, Mercedes, and Porsches. They delight in whiling away the day over leisurely lunches in expensive seaside restaurants. Throwing caution to the winds in this newly galvanized Islamic society, they can be seen nightly doing what is called *la tournée des grands ducs*—the rounds of the piano bars, pubs, discos, and *tapas* bars which have sprung up in the past few years. Legally, these establishments are supposed to serve alcohol only to non-Muslims—but there are places and people that are beyond the law. Prices are usually prohibitive in these clubs, according to *L'Economiste*, which noted that in a hot spot like Vanity, it is customary to buy whiskey by the bottle at $120 to $250, the monthly wage of the average worker.

The Needy Majority

A stone's throw from princely mansions and villas along the *corniche*, migrants have set up their shacks with tin roofs, and television dishes. Some of them raise chickens or goats, which feed off the rich neighbors' garbage.

A number of squatters have even taken over an abandoned insane asylum near the lighthouse. "It's chillingly damp, but it's a room with a roof," says a woman, who would not give her name. She is Muslim but confessed she drinks beer to get the courage to go out on the streets and beg so she and her son have something to eat.

In one of the largest *bidonvilles* in the suburb of Ain Sebaa, Ftna, thirty-eight, and her seven children live in one room. They have piled stones on the tin roof to keep the wind from blowing it away. She is one of the lucky people who have qualified for a small business loan. Several days a week, she'll rent a seat in a *petit* taxi to take her to the bus that goes to Derb Ghallef—Casablanca's vast flea market. There she buys cheap clothing to take home and resell to her neighbors at a minuscule profit. These are neighborhoods where the Islamists are actively finding recruits.

The city's most destitute inhabitants can be found in the port area. They are the street children, who have flocked here from remote rural areas, sometimes with their families, in search of the Casablanca dream. Some of them manage to hide away in container trucks bound for Europe; many get caught by customs but some escape to another life. Most of them live from begging or petty thefts and wind up sniffing glue.

In the summer of 2003, the country was ashamed to learn that no progress had been achieved in the field of human development, which includes health, education, and living standards. Morocco, with all of its wealth and progress, still stood among the least-developed countries, ranking 126th out of a total of 175 countries on the UN Development Program scale, below the other North African countries of Algeria, Tunisia, and Egypt.

Rural Life: Hardship and Hope

The only way to understand the rural exodus to the cities and how the migrants put up with the privations of urban life is to know where they come from. Bouchra Hassoune, a quiet young woman with a master's degree in economic sciences, who works for an insurance company in Marrakech, works with villages in the High Atlas.

Concerned about the precarious situation of rural women, Hassoune set up the Ifarkhane Tizi Association in 1999. With a modest grant of $5,000 from a private organization in Luxembourg, the Tizi Association studied the needs of mountain villages in the province of Tahanaout, south of Marrakech, and is doing something about them. Hassoune urged me to visit the area and volunteered to accompany me in the fall of 2001.

Tizi N'Choug, with 546 inhabitants, is typical of these mountain villages that live from subsistence farming and breeding, barely covering basic necessities. Nowadays, the men, young and old, and even some women are forced to leave home and find work in the cities. The situation of women—particularly widows, divorcees, and the elderly—is dramatic, according to the Tizi Association's survey. None of the girls goes to school, and 98 percent of the women are illiterate and ignorant in matters of health and hygiene. All women give birth at home, and one out of two faces serious problems in delivery. Twenty percent of the women have had eye infections, 15 percent ear infections, and 20 percent other diseases. In addition to household chores, the women work in the fields alongside the men. To earn additional income, most women and girls weave rugs and blankets, but they have no way to market their goods except for the nearest souk down the mountain.[12]

Located high on the Yagourt Plateau above the Valley of Ourika, only fifty-six kilometers south of Marrakech, Tizi N'Choug appears like a North African paradise. The stark magenta mountains with deep ravines, high ridges, and patches of green are pristine and beautiful from a distance. Not much of a mountain climber, I was quite unprepared for the three-hour vertical climb straight up the rocky cliffs on an invisible path that even donkeys fear to tread. (Donkeys take a much longer, winding track to bring butane gas and other luxuries up to the villages.) The natives, of course, scramble up the boulders in a couple of hours, but it's not an easy commute. The rocks are sharp and slippery; there are no trees to cling to; and the sun is bruising. I paused several times to admire the spectacular landscape, the ancient layered mountains, dotted with cacti and scrub bushes, the occasional stone and adobe hamlets with tall, square minarets and tiny, terraced gardens, clinging to the slopes. But in reality, it was to catch my breath and wonder how people could live so completely cut off from modern life.

Originally I had planned to stay several days with a family at Tizi and visit four villages in the area with a Tizi Association monitor, Rachida Khabata. What we had not expected was to arrive in the middle of a war on that warm fall day of 2001. Most of the women of Tizi were nervously standing guard on a ridge that overlooks the steep rocky approaches to the village. Children huddled close to their mothers' long flowered skirts. The men were all engaged in somber discussion on the shady patio of the village mosque. Normal life had stopped.

Tizi was at war with neighboring Anamer. It was a clash over water rights, the same kind of conflict that has stirred people's passions in the remote passes of the High Atlas Mountains for centuries. But the villagers were very aware of belonging to today's global context. "It will be worse than Bosnia," a Tizi elder remarked, trying to persuade me of the gravity of the situation. "Another Afghanistan," emphasized a younger man.

Long-standing tensions had reached a crisis the day before our arrival, when two columns of men and women from Anamer marched on Tizi, forming a threatening cordon on the slope outside the village. Meanwhile, a third group had moved surreptitiously to the spring above and laid pipes, redirecting the water flow from Tizi to Anamer. Enraged by what they saw as

*The Association of Tizi N'Choug has brought the most precious
development to this lost hamlet in the High Atlas: water,
channeled to two public fountains. The water nearly led to war
at the time of my visit in the fall of 2001.*

a brazen act of piracy, the men of Tizi had seized their picks and scythes—
their only weapons—and advanced on the Anamer forces. Violence was nar-
rowly averted that day by the women, who persuaded the men to wait and
take their case to the authorities. But the atmosphere remained strained, and
everybody in Tizi seemed obsessed with the water dispute.

On the outskirts of Tizi, the new stone women's center, built by the Tizi
Association, was empty because of the "war." The center boasts a Turkish toilet—the only one around—and wiring for electricity because Tizi is on the
government's program to be electrified one day. This is where the functional
literacy classes are normally held four days a week for a score of women students. A monitor also gives talks on diet, health, and hygiene like brushing
teeth and using a toilet. But Hassoune acknowledged that the Tizi women are
"resistant" to such notions and insist that the soil is too rocky to dig holes for
toilets. She believes it will take another generation to change entrenched
habits.[13]

Hassoune introduced me to Rachid Mindilli, the wiry, energetic young
man who runs the Tizi Association's experimental farm, producing miracle
plants like quinoa from the Andes, unknown in the High Atlas. Triumphantly,
he brought out a much-fondled piece of paper, painstakingly inscribed in
Arabic. This, he said, was the 300-year-old deed to the spring, which showed

irrefutably that the contested spring belongs to Tizi. Mindilli is a house painter and is studying English and French because he hopes one day to become a guide to the region. He lives with his wife and baby in one of the more comfortable houses, with solar energy, television, and a butane gas stove, but no sign of a toilet and no way to heat the house on the freezing winter nights, except the wood stove in the kitchen.

"People in Tizi are eager to improve their lives," Mindilli said, pointing out that of the eighty households in Tizi, a score have battery television sets, four have cell phones, three have solar energy, and nearly everyone has a portable radio, thanks to relatives working in the cities.[14]

The home where I stayed does not have such luxuries. The Aït Ezzaouyt family lives in a large stone house next to the new public fountain. The main living quarters are located on the second floor and are furnished only with the traditional wall-sofas and rugs. In the kitchen, a wood-burning stove is used for cooking and a butane gas burner for tea. The livestock—a cow and her calf, nine chickens, and eight rabbits—reside on the ground floor, which also serves as a "bathroom." Or one can go out of doors and try to find a secluded spot. There is also a public "toilet house" in the center of the village.

Brahim Aït Ezzaouyt is an amiable man who farms a small vegetable plot down the hill. He can usually be found sitting on his terrace, weaving rope from palmetto grass to sell at the souk. But during the emergency, Si Brahim spent the day with the other men at the mosque, discussing strategy. The first thing they did was to use their cell phones to call for reinforcements—the village boys who work in nearby cities. They also decided to send a representative to the governor at Marrakech to plead their case.

Si Brahim's wife, Amina, mother of eight, now an ardent student in Khabata's literacy class, suggested that the theft of the water might be an act of revenge by the people of Anamer. A fortnight earlier, the two villages had played a hotly contested soccer match. Tizi had won and held a victory *ahouach*. Knowing the emotions raised by soccer in Morocco (and elsewhere), I found Amina's explanation quite plausible, at least for the timing of Anamer's assault.

Dressed in a white embroidered tunic, pink shirt, yellow sweater, white leggings, and a brightly colored headscarf with golden earrings and silver necklace, Amina spoke proudly of her children. Two daughters are married, one is working in an office at Marrakech, one son is a mechanic in Marrakech, and another is a builder at Laayoune in Western Sahara. There are still two daughters, aged thirty and fourteen, and a son, thirteen, living at home. The boy completed elementary school at Tizi but refuses to go to the secondary school at a nearby village and would rather stay home and play soccer. Amina didn't send her daughters to school because they are helpful at home, "and I didn't understand the importance of education." Now she is taking the literacy course because she wants to write numbers and to read letters from her children. While she prepared lunch, the younger daughter took the cow to pasture and the older one cleaned the house.[15]

Over a tasty vegetable *tajine*, Amina talked to me about life in Tizi. She spoke in Berber and Khabata provided a French translation. Amina has never been to a hospital but a midwife helped her give birth at home. There is a dispensary on the outskirts of a neighboring village, where a nurse comes twice a week, but there's no doctor and not much medicine. When a child comes down with fever, Amina soothes it with the fruit of a prickly pear cactus. The people of Tizi are pretty healthy; one man has lived to be 130 years old. There is no dentist in the area (I had noticed that many of the villagers' good looks are marred by missing or decaying teeth), and so when anyone in the family gets a bad toothache, her husband will pull the tooth. People don't use toothbrushes but clean their teeth with a special stick, known as a *swik*.

As Amina described her daily routine, there was no hint of complaint. She generally rises at 5 A.M. to milk the cow and prepare breakfast for the family. Then she gathers grass for the animals, and three or four times a week, she looks for wood for the stove. The new fountain has helped a lot, eliminating frequent trips to the spring. Usually she bakes the bread and prepares the meals, while a daughter will wash up. Her husband grows potatoes, onions, and other vegetables, and so they are almost self-sufficient. They buy meat, tomatoes, sugar, and coffee at the *souk* down the mountain. Once a week, she goes to the village *hammam* to wash and meet friends. Her only other distractions are local soccer games and the *ahouach* dances during the religious feasts and celebrations. But when electricity comes to Tizi, her sons have promised to get her a television set. The postman leaves the mail in a cafe at the bottom of the mountain, where it will wait for anyone who is making the climb to Tizi.

At the end of the afternoon, the Aït Ezzaouyts' son Abd Essadek arrived from Marrakech and said he would stay a few days to see the crisis through. Sportily dressed, the worldly young man in his early twenties, who spoke fluent French, was still closely attached to his mountain roots. He declared that when he got married it would have to be a girl from Tizi. An experienced mechanic, he was currently looking for a job. Even in Marrakech it wasn't easy because so many rural people had migrated to the city during the recent drought. He knew many jobless young men who out of desperation had tried to get to Europe via the Canary Islands. Abd Essadek was confident he would find work at Marrakech, but if not he preferred to join his brother in Laayoune rather than risk the adventure of illegal immigration.

Over breakfast of *café au lait* with warm fresh milk, corn soup, and homemade bread with olive oil and newly churned butter, I asked Amina about the picture of King Mohammed VI on her wall. "We love him," she told me enthusiastically. "He loves the poor people."

Khabata decided to suspend activities at the women's center for the next few days, until the atmosphere cleared. There was no use in our going to Anamer either. In fact, Khabata doubted she would ever be able to give classes there again. The people of Tizi had made it clear she would not be welcome in their village if she went over to the enemy. The journey down the mountain was easier, although Khabata slipped on a boulder and nearly fell. We made the descent in only two hours.

When I spoke to Hassoune in Marrakech a month later, she notified me that there was still no settlement to the water conflict. The authorities had tried to persuade Tizi's residents to share the waters, arguing that if they went to court, the procedure would take years and meanwhile Anamer would keep all the water. But during the *Eid*—the celebrations ending the month-long Ramadan fast—the Tizi men quietly ripped up the pipes used to divert the water and carted them away. When the Anameris discovered this counter-coup, they seized their knives and other makeshift weapons to avenge their honor, but once more, calmer voices prevailed, and the elders decided to let the authorities handle the matter.

In the last news that I received from the front, the Tizi-Anamer feud still simmered. Despite renewed tension, Khabata has resumed literacy classes in Tizi, and another monitor has been named to hold classes in Anamer. The Tizi Association has begun professional training of women in all four villages on the plateau, teaching them how to knit, crochet, sew, and embroider, to encourage them to go to the literacy classes.

It was clear that the only way to bring the isolated villages of the Yagourt Plateau and other mountainous regions into the twenty-first century is the construction of some kind of road, even a dirt track. According to Hassoune, there is a study showing that the donkey path could be improved so that four-wheel-drive vehicles could take necessary goods and services to these isolated populations. All that is needed is money, but that is more than the Tizi Association can dream of.

The story of the Yagourt Plateau is the explosion of another myth, that of *bled as siba*—those "ungovernable" mountain lands. It appears that governments haven't really tried to govern them. Central authorities have looked at the statistics, the population, production, and accessibility and concluded that bringing these areas under "control" wasn't worth the cost. But they did not factor in the heavy toll of rural migration. Now there is an opportunity to recover the mountains—through the local development associations that are cropping up in the most inaccessible places with help from migrant or emigrant sons and daughters. They need assistance, however, from the central government. It is clear that whatever investment is needed to better conditions for the rural population, it would be less than the cost to the cities and towns of new waves of jobless, desperate migrants.

Timid Takeoff

A world away from Tizi N'Choug and Casablanca's *bidonvilles*, in Rabat, Fatallah Oualalou cautiously asserted: "Our reform policies are beginning to take off, but we need to sustain our growth rate." Economic czar under the Youssoufi government, the fiscally conservative Socialist Oualalou has been retained by Prime Minister Driss Jettou as minister of finances.[16]

In a brief overview of the economy, Oualalou told me that progress had been made on the government's top priorities, starting with public housing. Under the program to build 100,000 low-cost lodgings a year to replace the shantytowns, the authorities had adopted a new approach, providing land at a low price, releasing the builders from taxes, and offering state-guaranteed credit to low-income families.

On the second priority of economic renewal, a number of contracts have been signed with Moroccan and foreign private enterprises in tourism and textiles, providing government incentives and guarantees and matching grants from the European Union, he said.

Advances have also been made on what the minister called the "policy of proximity": work on rural roads, electrification, potable water, antidrought measures, and public transportation to bring concrete improvements to people's lives. At the same time, the deficit has been held down to 3 percent of the gross national product (GNP), and prices have been kept stable, he said.

Unemployment remains a problem, at 20 percent in cities and 11 percent nationally, Oualalou conceded. To resolve this, Morocco needs a continuation of the 2002–2003 growth rate, estimated at 5.5 percent. He identified the growth sectors as tourism, telecommunications, electric and electronic components, and fishing.

The growth rate has been erratic due largely to agriculture, according to the minister. He stressed that 2002–2003 was a good farm year, whereas growth had been only 1 percent for 1999–2000 because of the drought. More serious is the fact that the industrial sector accounted for only 17 percent of the GNP in 2003, or down from 1993.

In conclusion, the minister acknowledged that the Moroccan economy faces a serious handicap: the failure to achieve an economic union of the five North African countries that make up the *Maghreb*. Since independence,

Moroccans have lived with the dream of *Maghreb*, where all their problems would be resolved. But as relations with Algeria have deteriorated over borders and Rabat's claims to Western Sahara, the North African union has appeared increasingly like a mirage.

Now the pragmatic minister of finances emphasized: "In this era of globalization, Morocco cannot achieve permanent progress without *Maghreb* . . . and we are working for it." He was not talking about just a free trade zone with neighboring countries but a settlement to the corrosive problem of Western Sahara. For more than a quarter of a century, Morocco has been in a virtual state of war with Algeria, which supports the nationalist POLISARIO front's struggle for the independence of Western Sahara.

In fact, the Western Sahara has been a serious impediment to Morocco's foreign relations, a source of instability, and a major drain on manpower and finances, with 20 percent of the budget absorbed by the military and most development funds going to the contested desert territory, which needed everything. Until this problem is resolved, the kingdom's ambitious plans for social and economic reform and the development of new technologies will remain largely a mirage.

Royal Democracy

IV

Zigzags on the Road to Democracy

9

*T*hirty million Moroccans are living in a vast waiting room, but they're getting sick of waiting for something that never happens," Ahmed Sanoussi summed up the current political situation. Then as an afterthought, he said: "Some people say the country has entered a new era, but how can you have a new car with old parts?"[1]

Moroccan governments come and go and policies change, but Sanoussi, who is better known by his stage name, Bziz, is still around with his perceptive, irreverent barbs that spare no one. And for the past fifteen years or so, he has been the victim of official censorship, even police violence and death threats.

Despite the official ban, Bziz's sober, bespectacled face is probably more familiar to Moroccans than that of the prime minister because of his frequent performances before student groups, private associations, and Moroccan communities abroad. Although his lines change, the primary target of Bziz's political satires and sketches has always been The Power—the omnipotent *Makhzen*, or royal establishment, the excesses of the security services, and corruption in the administration.

Shortly after King Mohammed came to power in 1999, it was reported that among his liberalizing gestures, he had lifted the ban on the forty-six-year-old comedian, who is considered Morocco's Jay Leno—without a microphone.

But Bziz assured me in the summer of 2003 that he was still barred from performing on government television and radio stations and in the main auditoriums, and at times even his university appearances have been canceled. Asked what he had done to deserve the continued restrictions under the new liberalized regime, Bziz suggested with a guilty grin that perhaps the monarch, who loves water sports, was annoyed with his epithet "Sa Majetski," which has become a household phrase.

Commenting on the 2002 national elections under King Mohammed, which had been hailed by the official press as "the first free and transparent elections in Moroccan history," Bziz quipped: "Yes, indeed, these are the first elections to be falsified in a transparent and honest fashion."

Bziz's persistent voice is a sharp reminder that a panoply of democratic institutions does not mean democracy and that the new democratic freedoms in Morocco have limits.

Behind the Democratic Façade

Since independence in 1956, Morocco has taken pride in its image as a stable, moderate Muslim country moving toward democracy. Moroccans enjoy a multiparty political system, a vocal opposition, combative labor unions, national and local elections, and a diversified political press. But in reality, it is an Islamic-based authoritarian monarchy, endowed with a pervasive security system and a democratic superstructure.

When Morocco shed its colonial masters, it had a monarch with full sovereign powers and one dominant political party, the Istiqlal, made up of the nationalist forces that had led the struggle for independence. Wary of one-party rule, which had led to the demise of other Arab monarchies, like Egypt and Tunisia, King Mohammed V, grandfather of the present ruler, named unconditional royalists to the prime minister's office and several key ministries, while giving the Istiqlal a majority of the posts in the first national governments.

As we have seen, the nationalist party split of its own volition in early 1959, with the conservatives under Allal el Fassi keeping the name Istiqlal, and the left wing of the party led by Mehdi Ben Barka breaking off to become the National Union of Popular Forces.

Crown Prince Hassan, who became king after his father's unexpected death in February 1961, viewed Arab Socialism, as personified by Egyptian revolutionary Gamal Abdel Nasser and its Moroccan exponent, Ben Barka, as the main threat to his regime. A skilled politician, King Hassan fashioned a closely controlled pluralistic system that had many attributes of democracy, but was aimed at containing if not eliminating the Left. It was a highly sophisticated game plan, which involved the creation of royalist political groupings to vie with the old nationalist parties and reliance on a dedicated security force to discover, prevent, and repress potential plots against the monarchy.

The centerpiece of this structure was the 1962 constitution, drafted essentially by Ahmed Reda Guedira, an astute lawyer and close friend of the king. The new charter proclaimed Morocco to be "a constitutional, democratic and social monarchy." It consecrated the monarch's position as Commander of the Faithful and gave him unlimited powers as "guarantor of the continuity of the state" and "protector of the rights and liberties of citizens, social groups and collectivities."

In his critical analysis of the Moroccan power structure, *Master and Disciple*, Moroccan anthropologist Abdellah Hammoudi notes that some observers argued that the king derived his prestige from his religious descent and the oath of allegiance. But Hammoudi emphasizes that there were three other factors "crucial" to preserving the political system: "an apparatus of coercion devoted to the monarch; a multifaceted struggle against the urban political forces that grew out of the struggle for independence (basically a petty and middle bourgeoisie supporting the ideal of reform and progress); and an alliance with the rural notables."[2]

During his thirty-eight-year reign, King Hassan actively encouraged the development of competing parties in the name of democracy, but in reality, out of a divide-and-rule concept. Even before independence, then Prince Hassan spurred his loyal aide Guedira and a group of intellectuals working in the royal court to set up a party called the Liberal Independents. Guedira, a slight, urbane lawyer, was named minister of state in the first government. Shortly after independence, Prince Hassan openly favored the formation of the rural-based Popular Movement, headed by two dedicated royalists. Mahjoubi Aherdane, a former officer in the French army, was *caid* of Oulmes, a notable from the Middle Atlas, and seemed more interested in art than politics. Dr. Abdelkrim Khatib, a jovial, heavy-set medical doctor, had been a leader of the Moroccan Liberation Army in the Rif Mountains and would later be entrusted to head the first legal Islamist party.

When Prince Hassan became king, he named his able ally Guedira to be the head of two important ministries, interior and agriculture, as well as director general of the royal cabinet. But Guedira's main task was to create a political organization that would defeat the two nationalist parties, the Istiqlal and the National Union, in the 1963 legislative elections. Guedira formed the Front for the Defense of Constitutional Institutions (the French initials are FDIC), which grouped his own Liberal Independents, the Popular Movement, and friends and relatives of the king, and it duly won the elections.

Later the monarch's trusted minister of the interior, Driss Basri, was charged with setting up several "administrative parties," designed to prevent any group from becoming a serious challenge to the regime. Some were concocted from a few palace stalwarts; others were palace-inspired splinters of already constituted parties. Most of the palace-made parties failed to catch on with the Moroccan public, but a few acquired lives of their own, like the Popular Movement with its rural Berber constituency and the centrist National Rally of Independents, headed by King Hassan's brother-in-law Ahmed Osman.

At the same time, the palace's security apparatus, on the watch for any form of dissidence, periodically uncovered alleged plots against the monarchy. As a result, there were waves of arrests, disappearances, and show trials from the mid-1960s to the early 1990s. This severe repression was directed first of all against Ben Barka's National Union of Popular Forces and to a lesser extent against the more compliant Istiqlal. Although there was no evidence that these parties were prepared to act against the regime, they denounced its abuses through any means available. For their defiance, their organizations were disrupted, leadership depleted, and press muzzled. The best known victim of the palace's witch hunt was the Socialist leader Ben Barka (whose story I recounted earlier), kidnapped in Paris in 1965 by the Moroccan secret service and never seen again.

The small Moroccan Communist party, which generally assumed positions akin to those of the Socialist Union, also suffered from the official repression. Banned in 1960 because of ties to the Soviet Union, the Communist party was revived in 1968 under its present name, the Party of Progress and Socialism, and joined the mainstream political opposition and later took part in the government of *Alternance.*

It was members of the far-left fringe, loosely described as Maoist or Marxist-Leninist, who talked about overthrowing the monarchy and provided the pretext for the regime's periodical crack-downs. They were activists like Abraham Serfaty, who broke with the Communists to form the radical leftist Illal Amam (Forward) in 1970. Two years later, Serfaty was sent to prison, but his disciples formed other far-left groups, and he became a symbol of resistance to a totalitarian regime.

I had first met Serfaty after Morocco's independence in the late 1950s, when he was working with Abderrahim Bouabid, then minister of the national economy. Tall and lanky, Serfaty had Mediterranean charm and passion. He was one of a small group of Jewish left-wing idealists who had fought in the Moroccan nationalist movement against French colonialism, and he continued to struggle against injustice under the independent regime.

The Serfaty story is the stuff of a political novel. Born in Casablanca in 1926 of a well-to-do, progressive merchant family, Serfaty joined the Moroccan Communist Youth at age eighteen and graduated from the prestigious Ecole des Mines in Paris in 1949. The brilliant young mining engineer soon resigned from his senior post in the French colonial administration to join

Abraham Serfaty, leftist leader who spent much of his life in prison and exile for advocating self-determination for Western Sahara, was brought back by King Mohammed and named adviser to the Department of Mines.

the Moroccan nationalist labor union movement. Jailed several times by the French for his activism, Serfaty and his family were deported to France in 1953 and only permitted to return to Morocco after independence.

Reintegrated in the new Morocco, Serfaty was named technical director of the Moroccan State Phosphate Company and taught courses at the Mohammedia School of Engineering. He continued his advocacy for workers' rights and again found himself in and out of jail. Leaving the Communist party over its Middle Eastern policies—he favored more rights for the Palestinians—Serfaty and the militant poet Abdelatif Laabi formed the Marxist organization Ilal Amam, which openly advocated the establishment of a democratic republic to replace the absolute monarchy. Briefly arrested and tortured in January 1972, Serfaty went underground several months later when the police cracked down on Ilal Amam and several other leftist groups accused of plotting against the monarchy. In September 1973, Serfaty and twenty-four other leftists were sentenced to life in prison in absentia, and nineteen others also received harsh jail terms, although the evidence consisted of little more than revolutionary tracts and articles.

Serfaty and two other Ilal Amam activists hid out for nearly two years in an apartment under the protection of a progressive French high school teacher, Christine Daure. Inevitably she and Serfaty fell in love, and inevitably too, the three fugitives were caught. Serfaty and his friends were taken to the infamous Derb Moulay Cherif police station in Casablanca, where he was held for fifteen months and "underwent torture in atrocious circumstances," according to Christine Daure-Serfaty, as she is now known.[3]

A second trial of 139 leftists, plus 39 in absentia, took place in January 1977, this time with Serfaty present. The charge was again plotting to overthrow the monarchy and again there was still no real evidence besides revolutionary statements against the regime. Serfaty seized this opportunity to denounce the government for waging a colonial war against the people of Western Sahara and concluded with "Long live the Moroccan revolution!"

For his outburst, Serfaty was to remain seventeen years in prison, while most of the other leftists were set free or pardoned over time. Daure, who had been expelled a few months after Serfaty's arrest, campaigned relentlessly in France for the Moroccan prisoners. She also won the sympathy of Danielle Mitterrand, the wife of the French president, who intervened personally with King Hassan to allow Serfaty to marry Daure. The wedding took place on November 18, 1986, at the central prison of Kenitra. But Serfaty was not released until September 1991, when he was abruptly deported to France on the grounds that he was not Moroccan but a Brazilian citizen (his parents had lived for a time in Brazil).

The two unsuccessful coup attempts against King Hassan in the early 1970s were not the work of the Socialist Union nor the leftists but of disgruntled military officers opposed to the autocratic corrupt regime.

Now the king had something to worry about and became more security conscious than ever and increasingly dependent on his new strong man, Interior Minister Driss Basri. Finding himself under siege from the Left and the Right, King Hassan embarked on his Saharan crusade in 1975—a brilliant stroke at the time. He succeeded in rallying Morocco's political forces (except the leftists like Serfaty) behind the national campaign to recover Western Sahara from Spain and gave his restless armed forces a noble cause to defend. Naturally, with the state of emergency because of the Sahara, any relaxation of the regime was put on hold.

Splintered Labor

Like the major political parties, the labor movement also suffered from official repression and fragmentation. While the palace is known to have played a role in the break-up of the power of labor, the main responsibility belongs to the rivalry of the political parties.

The Moroccan Federation of Labor (its French initials are UMT), the oldest national labor organization, was a key player in the struggle for independence and closely allied to the Istiqlal party. This explains the symbiosis between the labor movement and the main political parties. As new parties were formed, it seemed that every party had to have its labor federation.

It was the UMT that first distanced itself from its political mentors. Even today it is probably the most independent labor organization, although badly weakened by the splintering of the unions and clashes with the security forces. Mahjoub ben Seddik is the towering figure of the Moroccan labor movement, the founder of the UMT in 1955, and still its secretary general. I first met the charismatic railroad employee before independence, when he was being wooed by the International Confederation of Free Trade Unions. Mahjoub, as he is known, was a left-wing nationalist, trained in the Moroccan branch of the French Communist Confédération Générale du Travail. Essentially pragmatic and wily, Mahjoub came to the conclusion that the fledgling Moroccan unions would have more autonomy as part of the anti-Communist ICFTU.

Although Mahjoub remained a member of the Istiqlal's leadership after independence, the UMT generally took independent positions, frequently conflicting with the predominantly Istiqlal government. "More than any other group in Morocco, the UMT succeeded in gaining legal and social benefits for its members," Ashford writes, emphasizing that the contribution of the union to the development of the new country was "considerable."[4]

In May 1958, Mahjoub pulled out of the Istiqlal's Political Bureau and aligned the UMT with Ben Barka's progressive wing of the party. Soon groups of pro-Istiqlal school teachers and phosphate miners began to split away from the UMT to form autonomous unions. By 1960, the Istiqlal had set up its own labor federation, the General Union of Moroccan Workers (UGTM), which remains allied to the party today.

For several years, the UMT supported Ben Barka's National Union in its opposition to King Hassan's repressive regime. But once again Mahjoub asserted his independence, accusing his Socialist partners of sacrificing the interests of the workers. The National Union's Bouabid privately suggested that Mahjoub was cooperating with the palace. At any event, relations remained strained between the UMT and its political ally, now called the Socialist Union. In 1978, the Socialists set up a new labor organization outside the UMT, the Democratic Confederation of Labor (CDT).

The CDT soon became the country's largest confederation, with its power base mainly in the public sector and semipublic enterprises. But the erratic leadership of Noubir Amaoui irritated his Socialist partners. He would call general strikes at the drop of a hat, whether they had a chance of success or not. When the Socialists assumed the leadership of the government of *Alternance*, Amaoui badgered Youssoufi into giving workers a substantial wage increase that the government could ill afford. Finally, deciding it would be best for the CDT to sever relations with the Socialist Union, Amaoui staged a noisy protest at the party's congress. Soon, however, a number of Amaoui's unions declared their autonomy, which led to the creation of yet another pro-Socialist confederation.

Four labor federations should be enough in a country of 30 million inhabitants with 20 percent of the labor force unemployed. But no, the Communists, the Popular Movement, and the Islamists have set up their own labor organizations, all highly political and more responsive to the needs of their parties than of the workers.

"Today unions have become obsolete," the outspoken Khalid Jamai wrote in *Le Journal* in the summer of 2000, a few months before the rupture between the Socialist Union and the CDT. Calling relations between unions and political parties "incestuous," Jamai stressed: "But now that Morocco is determined to establish a real democracy—at least we hope so—it is in everyone's interest and in the interest of democracy and the economic and social future of the country that this relationship between the unions and the political parties be reconsidered not to say done away with."[5]

It had become clear that the fragmentation of the labor union movement was of little benefit to the workers and only served to reinforce the division of the democratic forces.

Alternance: *Government without Power*

Ironically after so many years of struggle in the political wilderness, the two old nationalist parties, the Istiqlal and the Socialist Union, saw their credibility with the nation seriously damaged by their participation in the government of *Alternance*. It was King Hassan, not the political parties, who had devised the concept of *Alternance*, or alternation of government. Under the king's plan, the opposition would be brought in to head a coalition of the main political parties and independent royalists. It was yet another brilliant royal maneuver. If the government of *Alternance* succeeded, the king could claim credit; if it failed, the opposition parties would be discredited.

According to sources close to the monarch, he had decided as early as 1993 that the socioeconomic crisis was such that he could no longer govern with only his friends and fictitious parties. He would have to come to terms with the opposition—if he wanted to save the throne. However, the king still did not trust the nationalist parties and insisted on keeping his devoted minister of the interior, Driss Basri, and four other "ministers of sovereignty" under his direct control.

At first, both the Istiqlal and the Socialist Union had said no to *Alternance* under those conditions. When elections were again falsified in 1993, Abderrahmane Youssoufi, head of the Socialist Union, slammed the doors and went into exile in France. Two years later, with the obvious deterioration of the king's health and a worsening of the domestic situation, Youssoufi agreed to return, support a constitutional referendum, and take part in new elections. Although the monarch retained all of his powers under the 1996 constitution, he accepted the opposition's demand that the Chamber of Deputies be elected by universal suffrage. He also created an upper house of parliament, a kind of senate, which would be indirectly elected by business groups, labor, and local councils, and have the power to censure the government. Thus the king was able to retain control over the legislature.

Legislative elections in 1997 to prepare for *Alternance* caused upheavals across the political scene. After official promises that the vote would be free and fair, it was widely reported that the elections were rigged, this time in favor of the Socialist Union, which came in first with 57 seats out of a total of 325. King Hassan had clearly decided that Youssoufi's party would lead the next government. The big loser was the Istiqlal, coming in sixth with 32 seats—after having won the local elections a few months earlier.

"The result was a rupture between the Istiqlal and the palace," says Nizar Baraka, an economist and a leader of the Istiqlal's younger generation. Baraka stressed that the defeat had been good for the party because in 1998, it went through "a democratization," bringing in new members and more young people. In a rare gesture in Moroccan politics, party leader M'hamed Boucetta resigned over the electoral defeat, while contesting the results. He was replaced by Abbas el Fassi, the politically ambitious nephew of the party's founder. Although there was a strong movement in the Istiqlal opposed to going into a government still dominated by the king's strong man, Interior Minister Driss Basri, the party leadership decided in the end to go along with the *Alternance* project.[6]

On the Right, under the benevolent eyes of Interior Minister Basri, Dr. Khatib's Party of Justice and Development (PJD) served as a tame opposition. At the same time, the new Democratic and Social Movement, led by Mahmoud Archane, an ill-famed former police commissioner and old friend of Driss Basri, "won" thirty-two seats in the Chamber of Deputies.

Other shake-ups took place on the Left. A Communist leader, Thami El Khyari, quit the party with some close associates to form the leftist Front for

Democratic Forces. Encouraged by Interior Minister Basri, several militants deserted the leftist Organization of Democratic and Popular Action (OADP) to form the new Social Democrat party. Subsequently, the OADP dissolved itself to become the Unified Socialist Group along with three minor left-wing parties, but the new coalition was unwilling to join the mainstream Socialist Union.

Even in the winning Socialist camp, there were protests of electoral fraud. Mohammed el Yazghi, deputy party leader, accused the authorities of depriving the Socialists of forty seats through "manipulation and intervention." On the other hand, Mohammed Hafid, head of the Socialist Union's youth organization, announced that he had been falsely elected to parliament and abandoned his seat.

The portly seventy-four-year-old opposition leader, Youssoufi, now balding with thick, dark eyebrows, took office in early 1998 as head of the government of *Alternance*. It was a seven-party coalition, including the Socialist Union, the Istiqlal, the Communists, and the main administrative parties, with initial support from the moderate Islamists of the PJD.

Some of Youssoufi's political friends had warned him against assuming the responsibility of government without the power. Under the new constitution, all executive and economic powers were still concentrated in the hands of the king. Prominent Socialists suggested privately that it would be a grave error to participate in a government without constitutional changes to assure the separation of powers.

But King Hassan had appealed to Youssoufi's nationalistic fiber in asking him to head the government of *Alternance*. The king, according to palace sources, was aware that he was fatally ill and asked the Socialist leader to assure a smooth transition for his successor, Crown Prince Mohammed. The monarch is said to have been concerned that after so many years of strict rule, the country was in danger of drifting into chaos and ultimately under the sway of Islamist zealots.

When Youssoufi accepted the post of prime minister, he had a clear idea of what was wrong with the country and what had to be done. Presenting his ambitious program of democratic and social reforms to the nation, Youssoufi spoke fervently of his determination to bring about a more prosperous and just society, the establishment of a state of law, the development of modern education, an end to rural exclusion, and a transition to real democracy. These were exciting ideas for people who had been constrained under decades of authoritarian rule.

Initially, Youssoufi enjoyed the broad support of the political class, who respected him for his long-held and uncompromising positions in the democratic opposition. And he inspired widespread hope among the masses, who saw him as "Mr. Clean," an idealist resolved to bring about social change.

When I interviewed Youssoufi a year after he had become prime minister, he seemed chastened and no longer spoke of changing his world. Government by consensus was not easy, he admitted. It meant of course a minimum of parliamentary opposition (only the small Islamist party remained outside the coalition) but also a minimal chance of passing government-initiated reforms.

Youssoufi told me then that his agenda was to "lay the groundwork" for broad reforms and to organize democratic elections. "Structural and constitutional reforms are needed that can only be carried out by a credible government with executive autonomy and a credible parliament based on free elections," he explained.[7]

It was his way of saying that his program required a strong and cohesive government—and time. Youssoufi had neither. He had to work with representatives of six other political parties, whose interests often conflicted. The Socialist leader, however, was not a man to bang heads together but believed in the art of persuasion. This meant it took much time to get even minor things done.

When King Hassan died on July 23, 1999, the nation went into mourning, and leaders from around the world gathered at his funeral to pay homage to the autocratic statesman. Crown Prince Mohammed, thirty-five, acceded to the throne and declared his confidence in Prime Minister Youssoufi and the government of *Alternance*.

For the first six months of his reign, the young king stirred things up by his liberal pronouncements on social issues and his decisive acts, bringing back political exiles; getting rid of unpopular elements in his father's entourage; and freeing Islamist leader Sheikh Yassine. But the new king made no move to enhance the government's limited powers or to delegate authority to the elected officials.

Moroccans, who had waited nearly a half century for change in their lives, were impatient. In contrast to the excitement brought by the king's words and deeds, Youssoufi's cautious and deliberate approach gave the impression of governmental paralysis. When the coalition failed to produce concrete solutions to the country's main problems by the end of 1999, the increasingly vocal civil society—political associations, human rights groups, unemployed college graduates—launched severe attacks against Youssoufi and his cabinet, holding sit-ins and protest demonstrations.

"The basic problem is that Youssoufi made too many promises and didn't have the means to carry them out," said one of his political associates, who asked not to be identified. He admitted that the Socialist-led government had

made no improvement in social services or the job market, and the schools, hospitals, and social security were "a scandal."

The self-assured prime minister tried to ignore the criticism, which, with greater freedoms, attained levels of vituperation unequaled in the most open societies. Publicly, Youssoufi did not react to the attacks but continued to preach national reconciliation. His mild manner was seen by critics as weakness and only gave rise to new barrages of insults.

At the end of November 2000, *Le Journal*, the pit bull of the Moroccan press, published a 1974 letter from Socialist maverick Fqih Basri implicating Youssoufi and the Socialist leadership in the 1972 failed military coup against King Hassan, allegedly instigated by General Oufkir. Two other newspapers also published the story. The prime minister said nothing but shut down the three offending weeklies. Later Youssoufi told me indignantly that he had never had dealings with Oufkir, the man suspected of killing his close political friend, Ben Barka. He said the intent of the letter was to disrupt the Socialists' good relations with the palace, but the king had reiterated his confidence in him as prime minister.

The closing of the newspapers, even briefly, turned out to be a major error because it threw into question the main achievement of the government of *Alternance*—the improvement in public liberties. The newspaper ban was a blot on the honor of Youssoufi's government, which was difficult to live down. Encouraged by victory, the independent press renewed its assault on the government with new vigor.

What distressed Youssoufi more than the virulent opposition of some local weeklies, he told me, was the systematically negative reporting on Morocco by leading French and Spanish newspapers, with which he had kept close contact during his many years as a spokesperson for the Moroccan opposition. "Papers like *Le Monde, Le Monde Diplomatique*, and *El Pais* should support our efforts, but are constantly attacking the government of Alternance," Youssoufi complained in the summer of 2001. He could not fathom why these left-leaning European papers had seemingly turned against Morocco. I suggested that perhaps hopes in the new king and his government had been too high, at home and abroad.[8]

On the second anniversary of King Mohammed's reign, *Le Monde*'s Moroccan experts, Stephen Smith and Jean-Pierre Tuquoi, published a devastating critique of the Moroccan regime, saying: "The big leap forward, the rejuvenation of power in its daily exercise, has not happened." The writers charged that after dismissing his father's minister of the interior and bringing home several political exiles, the young king "has relaxed and enjoyed himself" while the seventy-seven-year-old Socialist prime minister "has turned out to be an element of obstruction rather than an advantage for the emergence of a new Morocco."[9]

When I asked the prime minister in the summer of 2001 about his government's achievements, he cited bills to "moralize" public life (against corruption), draft laws to reform the prisons and the justice system, administrative reforms, education reforms, and a law for compensation to former political prisoners. He also spoke of concrete measures to expand industrial zones and extend electricity and water to remote rural areas, which had passed unnoticed. He acknowledged that he had "a problem with communication."[10]

For the most part, public opinion was unaware of the government's positive actions and tired of reforms that were never implemented. The impression that many ordinary Moroccans had of the government of *Alternance* was that of a distant, aging prime minister, glued to his dossiers, surrounded by squabbling ministers with no real powers.

Worse, when Islamists and other traditionalists erupted over the government's progressive Plan for the Integration of Women, Youssoufi had preferred to shelve the plan rather than risk confrontation. This backsliding stirred sharp attacks from what had been his main constituency, the women, who accused the prime minister not only of indecisiveness but cowardice before the Islamist-led opposition.

There was another problem that the prime minister would not talk about: the increasing visibility of the king's shadow government. As the cabinet appeared bogged down by bureaucracy and bickering, the king's advisers and hand-picked governors were everywhere, launching programs, taking political decisions, and inaugurating works to be carried out by the government. The king's counselor André Azoulay was involved in a broad range of cultural and economic projects, from the Marrakech Film Festival to the establishment of a call center in Tangier. Another royal adviser, the super-efficient Zoulikha Nasri, head of the Mohammed V Foundation, was active in numerous social and women's projects like literacy and training programs and social centers for children and the elderly, as well as the annual National Solidarity Campaign. The king himself seemed to be always in motion, traveling to the different regions with a large retinue, sometimes called "the mobile capital," launching new social and economic projects, without involving the government in the decision-making. The royal activity was important in that it gave the country a feeling of momentum, but it served to further discredit a seemingly static government.

In July 2001, Socialist economist Larabi Jaidi, president of the Abderrahim Bouabid Foundation, publicly raised the problem of "a parallel power" in the royal cabinet.

In fact from the outset, King Mohammed had taken most major decisions on his own—like the dismissal of the former interior minister—without consulting with his prime minister. The monarch's decree expanding the economic powers of the governors was a clear infringement on the government's prerogatives. This kind of autocratic behavior had been the norm under King Hassan, but was not expected under his son in the new era.

The *Alternance* experience was seriously hurting the popularity of the coalition partners, especially Youssoufi and his Socialist Union. This became clear during the party's stormy national congress in April 2001. Youssoufi managed to preserve his position as secretary general and keep his party together, but its forces were diminished by the defection of the labor and youth leadership and other disgruntled individuals.

Mohammed Hafid, the popular leader of the Socialist youth, walked out of the congress with his friends and set up a new leftist association called Fidelity and Democracy. The volatile head of the Socialists' Labor Confederation, Noubir Amaoui, withdrew with his followers to form a new political party, the Socialist Nationalist Congress. The old resistance leader Fqih Basri, who had backed the Islamist movement against the government's plan for women's rights, also quit, but failed to take any significant following with him.

Socialist journalist Abdelatif Jebro claimed that the party congress had brought about "a clarification," that only a few troublesome members had been weeded out, and that the base had remained loyal. In fact, there was no mass exodus from the party and no open schism, but elections the following year showed that the Socialists had been badly hurt by their four-year stint in "power."[11]

To some observers, all this party activity gave the impression of a vibrant political life on the eve of national elections. Yet, everywhere there was widespread disaffection with politics and politicians. For the general public, the Socialist Union and the other parties in the government of *Alternance* had failed to keep their promises. It mattered little that the government had drafted the legal bases for future reforms or that the prime minister's hands were tied in many key domains. There was a new generation of Moroccans born after independence who were fed up with old-style politics, demanding real change, and unsatisfied with the tortuous progress to democracy.

The New Opposition

The principal adversary of the government of *Alternance* was not the Islamist opposition in parliament but the independent press, which had benefited largely from the liberalization of the regime under Youssoufi. As the main political parties had a stake in the governing coalition, their criticism was muted. The main independent newspapers enthusiastically assumed the role of the lead opposition to the government.

Since independence, Moroccans have had access to a diverse political press, although newspapers were very limited in what they could say under former King Hassan. It was often necessary to read between the lines to understand the message. The main political parties published news organs in Arabic and in French, which served for many years as the voice of the opposition. Editors knew the boundaries and usually respected them rather than face seizure or suspension. There was no discussion of delicate subjects like the monarchy, the Sahara, or the military, and it was necessary to tread carefully in dealing with the administration.

During the *années de plomb*, three publications shook up the press scene, introducing a high degree of professionalism and a certain independence, rare in the Arab world. *Lamalif,* a monthly magazine that dealt critically with economic, social, and cultural issues, first appeared in 1966. Published by Mohammed Loghlam and his French wife, Jacqueline, who goes by the pen name of Zakia Daoud, *Lamalif* became the most popular journal in intellectual circles. It was finally forced to shut down after twenty years because of official restrictions. From Paris, Daoud continues to write incisive columns about North Africa in the French and Moroccan press, and she is coauthor of an authoritative biography of Ben Barka.

Another ground-breaking magazine, *Kalima,* came out in 1986 and braved social (not political) taboos like prostitution, single mothers, and drugs. It was a huge success but had to close down in 1989 because of numerous seizures.

Aware of the limitations on the Moroccan press, Jean-Louis Servan-Schreiber of the French publishing family converted a stodgy Casablanca economic weekly, *La Vie Economique,* into a modern general-interest newspaper in the 1980s, highlighting economic news.

This was the beginning of transformations in the press, which gathered steam with King Hassan's move to open up his regime in the early 1990s and exploded under King Mohammed. Although half of the population is illiterate, the press does count and every paper is read, reread, discussed, and passed on. Now that it is relatively free, the independent press has become a formidable force.

The leader of this new aggressive press is the French-language weekly *Le Journal,* which appeared in late 1997, shortly before Youssoufi became prime minister with his program to enhance public liberties. *Le Journal* was founded by Aboubakr Jamai, twenty-nine, an ambitious Oxford-trained economist, and a group of young, irreverent journalists. The eminence grise is the publisher's father, Khalid Jamai, former editor in chief of the Istiqlal's daily *L'Opinion* and author of a weekly column in *Le Journal* that knows no boundaries.

Aboubakr Jamai, who looks more like a sober academic than a hard-hitting newspaperman, insists he has no political axes to grind, that he is "just after a good story, news that the other Moroccan publications don't dare to print." In the process, he has frontally challenged virtually every taboo. *Le Journal* has published interviews with Mohamed Abdelaziz, leader of the Saharan independence movement; Malika Oufkir, author of *Stolen Lives*, her harrowing tale of King Hassan's desert prisons; Lieutenant Mohamed Adib, jailed for denouncing corruption in the military; and Islamic fundamentalists who admire Osama Bin Laden. Jamai has leveled charges of corruption against high government officials, published the names of alleged torturers still in office, and denounced the security services for their campaign against the king's outspoken cousin, Prince Moulay Hicham.[12]

With their daring coverage, *Le Journal* and its Arabic counterpart, *Al Sahifa*, have become the country's leading weeklies, with circulations of 27,000 and 36,000, respectively. After being shut down briefly in December 2001, Jamai's weeklies reappeared with no sign of remorse or compliance. On the contrary, Jamai vigorously resumed his attacks on the government of *Alternance*, and circulation went up.

Le Journal's investigative reports are generally well documented, but the newspaper has displayed hostility toward members of the government in terms that would be considered libelous elsewhere. The main contribution of *Le Journal* has been to open the way for a rash of new periodicals in French and Arabic, which are competing for readership with brazen headlines and provocative articles.

For his investigative work and courage to confront taboos, Jamai was one of four journalists to receive an International Freedom of the Press Award from the Committee to Protect Journalists in the fall of 2003. In a ceremony in New York, the Moroccan publisher announced that he would share his prize with his colleague Ali Lmrabet, who was serving a three-year prison term for cartoons considered "insulting to the king."

Ali Lmrabet became the press's first martyr in Morocco's transition to democracy. A former journalist with Jamai's team, Lmrabet founded in March 2000 *Démain*, an insolent newsmagazine, which rivaled *Le Journal* in disclosing scandals in high places. Like *Le Journal*, *Demain* was closed at the end of 2001 and reopened as *Demain Magazine*. Known as the Moroccan equivalent of the French satiric political journal *Le Canard Enchainé*, *Demain* was so popular that Lmrabet launched an Arabic version, *Doumane*, in the fall of 2002. A cartoon depicting bags of money taken to the palace, published during the parliamentary budget debate, brought down the full wrath of the authorities on the unrepentant Lmrabet.

On May 21, 2003—while the nation was still in shock over the Casablanca terrorist attacks—Lmrabet was expeditiously tried and convicted of "insult to the king and injury to the territorial integrity," and sentenced to four years in prison, which was reduced to three years on appeal. In protest against the action, Lmrabet went on a hunger strike to demand justice. His plight won international sympathy and the solidarity of most of the Moroccan press. As time passed, Lmrabet's doctors, family, and friends expressed concern for his life. It was only through the personal intervention of Prince Moulay Hicham that the journalist was persuaded to abandon his hunger strike on the fiftieth day.

Later, in an interview at his office/villa in Rabat, Moulay Hicham told me that he had persuaded Lmrabet that "he must live and fight for his beliefs." The prince offered to help get his articles published, and Lmrabet's views from behind prison bars have since appeared in *Le Journal* and French newspapers such as *Le Monde* and *Le Courier International*.[13]

Other journalists were jailed under the new antiterror legislation in the wake of the Casablanca attacks. Mustapha Alaoui, publisher of the popular Arabic weekly *Al Ousboue*, went to prison for printing a letter from an unknown group called Assaiqa, which claimed responsibility for the Casablanca attacks. Three journalists in the eastern city of Oujda were arrested in mid-June for publishing articles on *jihad*.

The National Union of the Moroccan Press denounced the arrests and declared: "The spread of arrests has terrorized the press corps and constitutes an unprecedented campaign against the press in the name of the fight against terrorism."[14]

Despite occasional clamp-downs, the independent press has pursued its mission with relatively few inhibitions. The brash French-language weekly magazine *TelQuel* deals with provocative subjects like the increased use of the veil, the decline of the political parties, and the absolute powers of the king, but it is not systematically opposed to the establishment as is *Le Journal*. *TelQuel*'s publisher, Ahmed R. Benchemsi, lean and hungry-looking at thirty, joined Jamai's *Le Journal* after King Hassan's death in July 1999. But six months later, Benchemsi left because of the paper's political activism. "I didn't want to be a martyr, just a newspaperman," he recalls. He became a correspondent for the popular Paris-based weekly *Jeune Afrique*, where he gained professional experience, and in May 2001 opened *TelQuel*, which by 2004 was vying for popularity with *Le Journal* among Morocco's French-speaking elite.[15]

Another pioneer of this more open era, Mohamed Brini and a group of Socialist dissidents created an independent Arabic-language newspaper in 1999, *Al Ahdath al Maghribia*. Strongly critical of Youssoufi's government, *Al Ahdath* became the largest selling daily, with a circulation of 120,000. The success of this newspaper is said to be due in part to the letters to the editor, which often discuss sexual relationships—another taboo until now.

Probably the most influential Arabic daily is *Attajdid*, the organ of the Movement of Unity and Reform, the Islamist base of the Party of Justice and Development. It opened its pages to different Islamist currents, including some of the most radical preachers, like Hassan Kettani, convicted as an ideologue after the May 16 attacks and now serving a twenty-year jail sentence. *Attajdid* has since tempered its criticism of the regime but regularly campaigns for the "moralization" of society.

The best all-around French-language daily is the independent *L'Economiste*, which covers political and economic news in a responsible manner but is quick to criticize official abuses. Editor in chief Nadia Salah has denounced acts of violence and anti-Semitism by Islamic radicals but defends the rights of the Islamic suspects to proper legal defense. Two French-language weeklies—*Maroc-Hebdo International* and *La Vie Economique*—are informative and sometimes critical of the authorities but are not part of the opposition.

This new vigorous press has played a vital role as a watchdog over official misdeeds and failures since 1998, when King Hassan initiated the idea of *Alternance*. With both left- and right-wing parties in the ruling coalition, the only parliamentary opposition comes from the moderate Islamist party, the PJD. At the risk of appearing to be aligned with the Islamists at times, the nonpartisan press has deprived the religious party of the monopoly of opposition. And despite official backsliding and abuses, the perseverance of these independent, critical voices represents an assurance that the kingdom is still engaged in the transition to democracy.

Free Elections: Too Many Candidates and Not Enough Voters

National elections in the fall of 2002 were supposed to be "historic," the first "free and transparent polls" since Moroccan independence in 1956, according to the political establishment. The politicians promised that a new legitimate government and parliament would bring the changes for which Moroccans yearned.

Nevertheless, the electoral climate was glum. There was none of the euphoria that had greeted Youssoufi's government of *Alternance* in 1998 or the

*Morocco's parliament, with members dressed in ceremonial
white-hooded djellabas, at the opening in September 2002 of the
new legislature after the country's first transparent elections.*

accession of King Mohammed the following year. The general public now
appeared turned off by their institutions—the unfulfilled promises of governments, the bickering of political parties, the rivalries of trade unions, a
semiparalyzed justice system, systematically negative newspapers, and an impotent parliament tarnished by fraudulent elections in the past.

Over and over again, Moroccans said they no longer believed in elections
or Western democracy. Many of those who planned to go to the polls said
they would vote for the Islamists because they "are pure" and "haven't been
corrupted by the system."

Most political analysts who have scrutinized the electoral process in Morocco agree that the national elections in the fall of 2002 were probably the
most free and fair in the country's history. Another indisputable fact was
that, for the first time, a significant number of women ran in races for the
legislature and won, thanks to an affirmative action program.

What the election also showed was the alarming degree of decomposi-
tion of the political scene. The plethora of political parties taking part in the
elections not only led to confusion and disinterest of the electorate but also

to the impossibility of any workable majority in the new parliament. There were thirty-six parties vying for their place in the sun, although only twenty-six actually presented candidates.

Both King Mohammed VI and Prime Minister Youssoufi had proclaimed that the legislative elections would be a turning point, a new beginning for Moroccan democracy. The king had named the widely respected technocrat Driss Jettou as minister of the interior and charged him with preparing the elections and guaranteeing their integrity.

Early on, Youssoufi had announced his refusal to resume the post of prime minister, should his party win. He was clearly aware of the erosion suffered by his Socialist Union over four years in government. He told me prior to the elections that he thought it would be good for the party and the country if the Socialists returned to a position of opposition to the government.[16]

The large number of parties competing at the polls—too many for the average voter to understand the different options—did not mean broad participation. Several important sectors boycotted the polls: the leading Islamist group led by Sheikh Yassine, the new Berber movement, and some far left-wing parties, all of which contended that democratic elections could not be held under an autocratic constitution.

After so many years of electoral fraud, the general public exhibited little interest in the proceedings. Some of the main parties had to cancel rallies for lack of a crowd. Conversations with many ordinary Moroccans around the country showed an enormous disaffection from politics and politicians.

Nevertheless, the campaigning took place in a relatively open atmosphere, with free poster space and time on the state television and radio stations for all of the parties. National observers and the international press were able to monitor the voting, although they were not permitted to witness the actual counting of the ballots.

I visited several polls in the Rabat area, where the voting went smoothly, but the turnout was poor to mediocre. Nationwide, there was almost no violence—just a few fist fights among zealous militants. Irregularities were reported at 50 polling stations (out of a total of 37,517), such as the disappearance of ballots at several polls and attempts by some local authorities and candidates to buy votes. Unlike past elections, these cases were publicly denounced and sanctioned immediately.

The only serious incident occurred on election night after the polling stations were closed and while the country waited for results. Journalists and politicians were assembled at 11 P.M. at the Ministry of the Interior, where an information room had been outfitted with some fifty computers to provide results as they came in. But there were no results that evening, only mint tea, soft drinks, almond and honey cookies, and rumors galore. At about 1 A.M., the impatient crowd was told that there had been "a computer breakdown."

Press and political observers alike jumped to the conclusion that the authorities were concocting the election results, as in the old days. According to persistent rumors that night, the main government party, the Socialist Union, had come out the big loser, while the Islamists and the conservative Istiqlal were said to be the winners, along with a record rate of abstention.

Early the next morning, Interior Minister Driss Jettou showed up to confirm a very low turnout and an unexpected rise in the Islamist vote. Officials said that results would be presented later in the day, but nothing was forthcoming. After an unexplained delay of forty-eight hours, Jettou announced the final results.

"The great victor was Moroccan democracy," the interior minister said proudly, stressing that the elections had been "clean and above suspicion" with only "minor infractions." Apologizing for the long delay in proclaiming the results, Jettou attributed the problem to the new system of voting by list and the separate ballots for the women's list.

If the results of the September 29, 2002, elections were doctored, it is hard to say with what intent, as the outcome was hardly pleasing to anyone, except the Islamist opposition and women. Even though the Islamists put up candidates in barely half of the contests, the PJD came in third, tripling its score in the previous legislative elections. As for the women, they saw their tally soar from two seats in the last parliament to thirty-five, thanks to a hard-fought-for quota system. This meant that Morocco now led the Arab world in the number of women representatives, followed by Syria with twenty-five and Tunisia with sixteen.

The elections, however, produced no clear majority. The frontrunners were five political parties, each winning nearly the same number of seats. The incumbent Socialist Union won by an edge but suffered substantial losses to command only 50 seats—down from 57 in 1997—in the 325-seat Chamber of Deputies. Its main rival, the conservative Istiqlal, made significant gains, with 48 deputies compared to 32 in the last election. Contrary to most predictions, the hard-core electorate remained loyal to the two main parties, which in or out of power had dominated Moroccan politics for more than four decades. The moderate Islamists won 42 seats, beating out the pro-palace National Rally of Independents for third place. Finally, two branches of the rural Popular Movement together totaled 47 seats. The other so-called administrative parties did poorly. Various new parties, including several liberal groups, ex-Socialist Amaoui's new labor party, and the Unified Left made a miserable showing. There were of course some charges of foul play, but the real cause for the low scores was public disinterest.

The big disappointment was the high rate of abstention—only a 52 percent turnout, compounded by an exceptionally high 15 percent of invalid ballots. This was especially disconcerting to the authorities and the political parties, which had campaigned tirelessly to persuade the voters that, this time, elections would be different.

"You can't eliminate forty years of falsification overnight," commented Kamal Labib, a member of the new Unified Left and head of the election observers. He stressed that the government had made "an enormous effort" to get people registered and to ensure a fair campaign. There was less fraud than in the past, he said, but some faulty registration lists were used, and some local authorities still exerted pressure.[17]

In the absence of a governing majority, the parties proceeded to do what they do in parliamentary democracies: vie for the post of prime minister and maneuver to form political alliances. Apparently dismayed by the politicking, King Mohammed VI stepped into the fray. Quite ignoring the verdict of the polls, the monarch named his interior minister, Driss Jettou, a private entrepreneur, as the new prime minister, to replace the retiring Youssoufi.

The initial reaction in political circles was one of shock. Jettou was an outsider with no political base. Naturally, the leading Socialists, who had expected to be called on to form the next government, were the unhappiest. Emphasizing that the elections confirmed public support for the outgoing coalition government, the Socialist Union's political bureau declared that "democratic progress" required that the election results be taken into consideration in forming the next government.

Many politicians saw this royal intervention as a setback for Morocco's fledgling democracy and a lack of confidence in the political parties, but were reluctant to criticize the monarch's decision. It was Mustapha Ramid, an Islamist leader, who said openly what others murmured privately, that the royal choice of prime minister "marks a step backward."

The independent press was remarkably subdued over the event. *Le Journal* criticized the nomination of Jettou for not respecting "the logic of democracy" but described it as a vote of no-confidence in the outgoing government. "The king has officially taken charge of economic matters," Aboubakr Jamai wrote, noting that the monarch had reacted to the failure of an economic take-off under the government of *Alternance*.

Abdelmounaim Dilami, publisher of *L'Economiste*, said that Jettou's nomination meant that the king had decided "to take things in hand," because of the interparty conflicts. "The main problem facing Morocco is how to reconcile democracy and efficiency," Dilami wrote in an editorial on October 10, 2002.

Business and financial circles, however, enthusiastically welcomed the king's move as an opportunity to bring new momentum to economic development. Hassan Chami, head of the Moroccan Businessmen's Association, called the selection of Jettou "a judicious" choice and expressed confidence that he would meet the economic challenges facing the country.

The king did not bother to explain his choice of prime minister, and his aides stressed that he had acted within his constitutional prerogatives. But many political observers wondered: why bother to have elections if the prime minister does not come from the winning party?

The Grocer's Son

By chance, I had obtained an interview with Interior Minister Jettou on the eve of his nomination as prime minister. We talked mostly about the repercussions of the elections and the surge of the Islamists.

Driss Jettou, fifty-nine, with a receding hairline and broad open features, is a businessman through and through, sure of his management skills and

Driss Jettou, minister of the interior, who organized the landmark 2002 national elections, in an interview on October 8, 2002, the day before being named prime minister.

ability to win consensus. While he looks as though he grew up on Madison Avenue, Jettou is proud of his Soussi origins (Berber from the Souss plain) and his start in trade at age ten behind the counter of his father's grocery at El Jadida, south of Casablanca. Graduating in sciences from the Mohammed V University of Rabat at twenty-one, Jettou went to work for the Bata shoe company, which sent him to England for additional schooling. On his return, he founded Au Derby, which became the leading Moroccan shoe company. Jettou's success in the leather and textile industries caught the attention of the palace, and he became an adviser to the late King Hassan. In 1993, Jettou was named minister of industry, commerce, and crafts and later minister of the economy, finances, and industry. After the formation of Youssoufi's government in 1998, the grocer's son returned to the private sector, until he was recruited by King Mohammed as an economic adviser and then minister of the interior.

"I've always avoided party politics, and people know it," Jettou said, explaining that he had organized the elections like preparing for a soccer match. "I have a working method and know where I'm going," he stressed. "I choose a solid team, try to keep the flame burning, and coach them to win."[18]

Jettou said that his task had been simple because the king had given him a clear mandate. "His Majesty didn't say he wanted a certain majority but rather, 'I want to know the real political map.' It didn't matter who rose or who fell." He categorically denied any manipulation of votes and said he could show me the official reports from all of the polling stations with the numbered ballots. Besides, the results couldn't be hidden because all of the parties had kept track of the count.

The interior minister was upbeat about the newly elected Chamber of Deputies, which he said reflected the present balance of power, without any dominating force. Pointing out that there had been a renewal of two-thirds of the chamber, he noted that the new deputies were younger, better educated, and for the first time, 11 percent of them were women.

He emphasized the importance of the emergence of the PJD on the same level as the other four main groups. "I do not consider the PJD a danger, but it is a reality that must be dealt with," Jettou asserted. To contain the Islamist movement, he said, the government must attack the real problems that led to the PJD's favorable election score: the increase in poverty, unemployment, bidonvilles, and other social ills.

Another factor behind the PJD's success was the international situation, the minister said: "The party has taken on an Islamic identity by showing solidarity with the Palestinians, Afghanistan, and Iraq." Jettou pointed out that the Islamists had also benefited from their role as the only opposition party in the last parliament. He added that he wouldn't mind seeing the Islamists in a government coalition.

I asked the interior minister about persistent reports of the discovery of radical Islamist groups with possible links to Al Qaeda. He responded soberly:

> We've uncovered no other Al Qaeda cells aside from the Saudi cell apprehended last year. What we've found in some slums are small groups who practice banditry under an Islamist cover. We believe there are hundreds of these radicals trying to recruit young people in Casablanca, Kenitra, Fez, and other cities. They are real bandits, and are responsible for six deaths that we know of in the past five years. No links have been established between them and the Algerian militant Islamists or Al Qaeda. But we're vigilant.

What would be his priorities, should he be called on to assume the office of prime minister? I asked. (Official sources had told me that Jettou might be drafted if there were no clear majority, but he said later he had no previous knowledge of his appointment.) The interior minister responded without hesitation:

> We must update our economy to prepare ourselves as a partner of the European Union and the United States. Our infrastructure must be modernized and our human resources valorized.
>
> Morocco has trumps and we must exploit them: natural wealth— fishing, rich mines, good climate and sun, and ideal geography.
>
> It is necessary to improve our social policy to catch up with the developed countries. The state must put more resources into education and housing. To build modern Morocco, we need more private, national, and foreign investments. Our economy doesn't create 200,000 jobs a year, and we need at least 260,000.

In conclusion, Jettou emphasized:

> Morocco is capable of making the leap from underdevelopment to development. We're on the edge. But we don't have a great deal of means. With a push from our friends, we could put our feet on the other side of the development bar in four or five years. If we don't get help, it will take much longer. The late King Hassan chose the United States and Europe as partners. King Mohammed has reaffirmed his father's choice and is determined to build a real democracy. Nothing will stop him. He proved it with these elections. He has a vision of an open, modern Morocco, a good partner of the United States and Europe, in the Islamic world.

The following day, the king called an extraordinary meeting of Youssoufi's government at the royal palace in Marrakech. Afterward, the Moroccan Press Agency announced that King Mohammed VI had named Driss Jettou as prime minister; the terse three-line statement caught the country completely by surprise. Although the monarch had the constitutional right to choose an outsider—not a party leader—to head the government, his act verged on the heretical, in terms of parliamentary democracy. The reasons given for the nomination were the fragmentation of the political parties and the lack of a workable parliamentary majority.

After lengthy negotiations with the main political groups, Prime Minister Jettou announced the composition of his new coalition government a month later. To general astonishment, it looked very much like the outgoing Youssoufi government, without Youssoufi. The six main parties were proportionately represented in the coalition with a total of thirty-eight ministers, five more than the cumbersome Youssoufi cabinet. The Islamist PJD, reinforced by the elections, remained in the opposition.

There were some new and younger faces in the cabinet. The astute economist Adil Douiri, son of the Istiqlal activist M'hamed Douiri, was named minister of tourism. Mohamed El Gahs, the aggressive director of the Socialist daily *Libération*, became secretary of state for youth. There were also three women at the secretary of state level, compared to one woman minister in the previous government. An important change was the replacement of the old minister of Islamic affairs, Abdelkébir Alaoui M'daghri, who had favored the Islamists on women's rights and other issues, by a modern, respected Sufi scholar, Ahmed Toufiq. More than half of the former cabinet, however, stayed on, even the much-criticized minister of foreign affairs, Mohamed Benaissa, and the controversial Istiqlal leader Abbas El Fassi as minister without portfolio.

Jettou's program followed the concise guidelines set down by King Mohammed in a speech to the new Chamber of Deputies with focus on productive employment, economic development, educational reform with emphasis on professional training, and decent housing. The prime minister did mention the fight against corruption and the need for a free press "that respects the laws." There were no promises of miracles, but it was a concrete plan of action aimed to provide the disillusioned public with hope for a better life.

The basic trouble was that Jettou and his government and their parties were working under a very short deadline to produce results. A veritable marathon of five different elections was scheduled for the summer and fall of 2003: municipal councils, provincial assemblies, professional chambers, a third of the senate, and representatives of the sixteen regions.

The pundits were at a loss to predict the outcome of the upcoming local elections. There were two basic unknowns. Under public pressure, the king had lowered the voting age to eighteen from twenty, which meant a million and a half new voters—and nobody could guess what they would do. The other question involved the Islamists and whether their electoral success in 2002 had been a protest vote against the government of *Alternance* or represented an Islamic renewal like elsewhere in the Arab world. It was also unclear whether the Islamist vote would be affected by the public hostility to the war in Iraq and the government's support of the United States in its war against terrorism.

The Party of Justice and Development settled in comfortably as leader of the parliamentary opposition and began at once to prepare for the elections. The PJD hoped to win support from other Islamist groups, namely Sheikh Yassine's movement, to improve its score in the cities, where it had already made inroads into the Socialists' constituency. Early in 2003, *Le Journal* reported that the PJD made no secret of its ambitions to win the main cities in the forthcoming communal voting and to sweep the next national elections, in 2007, with "an Islamist tidal wave."

The Casablanca suicide bombings of May 16, 2003, would change everything.

The New Society

10

*T*he explosion of civil society, following three decades of ironclad rule, has given the kingdom an atmosphere of freedom rarely found in the Arab world. Moroccan human rights groups openly organize emotional gatherings for missing prisoners, angry pilgrimages to desert prisons, grim vigils at torture centers, and mass demonstrations for victims of police brutality. Sometimes the authorities have tried to silence these voices of protest, but they have continued stronger than ever.

Strong-willed women have formed associations for the defense of single mothers and abused wives, street children and child laborers. Private organizations provide small business loans to shantytown dwellers. Civic groups take potable water, books, and new ideas to remote mountain villages. They are all part of a movement that is tackling their problems directly and setting the country's sociopolitical agenda.

This new society was born as a result of the failure of the state—the palace and a succession of governments and the *Makhzen*—to provide individual security, jobs, schools, and other social structures to keep up with the soaring population and its aspirations. Thousands of fledgling nongovernmental organizations (NGOs) have appeared around the country, dedicated to a broad range of interests, from such nebulous goals as truth and justice, to the problems of battered women and unemployed college graduates, rural illiteracy and poverty.

There were some 30,000 associations in the main cities in 2001 (estimated to be 32,300 by 2004), including cultural, charitable, professional, and religious groups, as well as organizations for the defense of human rights, consumers, the environment, and development, according to a study published by the Socialist daily *Libération.* The report emphasized that the modern concept of NGOs has been easily accepted by Moroccan society because this country has an ancient tradition of welfare associations, based on Islamic law and Berber customs. Modern associations were introduced under the French Protectorate, but only foreigners were authorized to found them. After independence, a royal charter proclaimed the right to association, guaranteed by the constitution, but the government was basically mistrustful of volunteer organizations, and there followed a long period of restrictions. The country has enjoyed a renaissance of the NGO movement since the mid-1980s, substantially aided by international NGOs, the report said.[1]

At first, the late King Hassan looked with some misgiving at the latest breed of activists, particularly the human rights groups. Here was another potential opposition movement to deal with, one that had grown up outside the classic democratic institutions—the political parties, the labor unions, women's associations, and youth groups. These new organizations appeared relatively free of personality cults and ideology. A number of associations were offshoots of political parties, and some retained close links with their nurturing parents, but most went on to have lives of their own. If there was any common denominator, it was the important presence of women in the movements.

After a time, however, King Hassan seemed to grow comfortable with the burgeoning civil movement (although not with the aggressive human rights associations) and came to regard it as a possible counterweight to the political parties. For his successor, King Mohammed, here was a means to circumvent a lethargic bureaucracy and establish a direct link to the population at large. He has encouraged a variety of NGOs directly through funding from the royal foundations.

Initially, the political parties tended to be suspicious of the independent associations and viewed them as possible rivals or tools of the palace. But there has been a growing recognition by politicians that they can work with NGOs, particularly in social and economic development.

This civil awakening has now moved beyond the cities and taken root in different regions, including some of the most remote and least developed communities in the High Atlas. While most associations claim independence, many cooperate with and receive funds from municipal administrations, the central government, and the palace, and some have attracted international support.

Whether by chance or design, the new volunteer movement has appeared as a rival to militant Islam. As elsewhere in the Arab world, Morocco's Islamist activists have been spawned by the failure of the nationalists to fulfill their economic and social promises in the wake of independence. The Islamist opposition, which came out of the mosques, had moved on by the early 1980s to challenge the Left in the universities. At the same time, Islamist social organizations spread out to the underprivileged society at large, offering free schoolbooks and medicine, food packages for Muslim holidays, financial help for funerals, and assistance to victims of fires and other disasters. For a long time, Islamic associations held a virtual monopoly over charitable works at the grassroots level. Now, a vigorous modern civil society is competing with religious groups in many domains, from health care and literacy courses to women's rights. Only rarely do the two worlds get together.

Out of Darkness, Defiance

Morocco in the 1970s and 1980s had been slowly dying. There was virtually no freedom of criticism or initiative under King Hassan's despotic rule. The press and politicians were closely controlled. The economy stagnated while a power elite, with close ties to the palace, got ever richer. In this atmosphere of suppressed discontent, security had become a primary concern for the palace and the *Makhzen*. Thousands of people—no one knows how many—were arrested and tortured, suffered long years in prison, died, or disappeared, in the name of state security.

Several human rights organizations, born in those dark times, were closely linked to opposition parties in their common struggle for a democratization of the authoritarian regime. Later, however, the main political parties were either repressed or coopted by the palace, leaving the volunteer human rights groups to carry the flame.

The Moroccan Association for Human Rights, known by its initials in French, AMDH, and founded in 1979, waged tireless campaigns at home and abroad for justice and freedom. Led by unassuming, hard-working activists, the AMDH has been in the vanguard of the struggle to free political prisoners, promote women's rights, denounce aggression against students and unionists, and defend the freedom of the press. Although restrictions were eased in the last years of King Hassan's reign, the association has pursued its crusade against all forms of oppression. While AMDH militants are generally on the Left, they increasingly find themselves defending the rights of Islamists—the latest target of the administration.

It was the AMDH that organized the moving pilgrimage of hundreds of former political prisoners to the desert fortress of Tazmamart in the fall of 2000. "We wanted to remind public opinion that the prison still exists and so do its secrets," said Mustapha Chafii, a spokesperson for the group. He said the association demands not only the establishment of a Truth Commission but an end to the immunity enjoyed by those officials involved in past human rights abuses, many of whom continue to hold positions of influence.[2]

The AMDH's demonstrations have often been banned, its publications seized, its leaders jailed. It was even closed down for several years, but it has always rebounded. And other organizations have joined forces to take up the cause. The Moroccan Organization for Human Rights (OMDH), a more flexible group formed in 1988, has regularly denounced arbitrary arrests, deaths in detention, and violations of the freedoms of movement, assembly, and the press.

Citing the OMDH's detailed reports of abuses, foreign institutions like Amnesty International, Human Rights Watch, and the U.S. State Department repeatedly urged King Hassan to ease the authoritarian system. As a result of these pressures, the king took a number of measures to liberalize his regime in the early 1990s, freeing hundreds of political prisoners and establishing the position of minister of human rights. In 1994, the sovereign solemnly declared that "the page has been turned" on the matter of political prisoners.

Welcoming the monarch's gestures, Moroccan human rights groups, however, refused to turn the page. The arbitrary system had not changed, they argued. There were still hundreds of missing persons; the security forces continued to engage in torture and other forms of violence; restrictions remained on the freedoms of the press, assembly, and movement; and the courts were still subject to widespread corruption and official influence.

The OMDH openly took up the cause of the Islamist leader Abdessalam Yassine, when he was still under house arrest. In a direct challenge to the king, Abdelaziz Bennani, former head of the organization, told me in the summer of 1995: "We believe Yassine should be set free and his Justice and Charity Association officially recognized." He pointed out that Yassine's group had said no to violence.[3]

These human rights groups reported that the situation improved considerably after Abderrahmane Youssoufi, long-time oppositionist and human rights lawyer, was named prime minister in early 1998. On the death of King Hassan on July 23, 1999, the new monarch, Mohammed VI, pledged in his first Throne Speech "to establish the rule of law and safeguard human rights." He encouraged the return of political exiles, declared a broad amnesty, fired his father's all-powerful minister of the interior, and promised indemnities for missing persons and victims of arbitrary detention.

Whenever the momentum for democratic freedoms has flagged, the human rights organizations have been swift to denounce any return to the repressive measures of the past.

"We have condemned the May 16, 2003, attacks as terrorist and criminal acts against innocent civilians," said Mohamed El Boukeli, a member of the AMDH's executive board. But at the same time, the group has warned the authorities against using these incidents as a pretext to destroy the fragile gains made in human rights. Specifically, the association has denounced the death in custody of one of the main Islamist suspects, emphasizing that there is a strong presumption of death after torture. "We want the criminals arrested but according to democratic norms," El Boukeli stressed.[4]

Perhaps the association that best reflects the changes taking place is the Casablanca branch of Transparency International. For years, corruption at all levels had become an accepted practice in Morocco, from petty bribes to big-time graft. In his book *The Culture of Islam*, American anthropologist Lawrence Rosen points out that kickbacks, nepotism, and political corruption were considered a natural part of everyday life.[5]

Transparency Morocco is a private organization dedicated to fighting corruption in the administration and society at large. Even more astonishing, a leader of the controversial association is Sion Assidon, a Jewish-Moroccan human rights activist, who spent more than twelve years in prison on charges of belonging to a Marxist-Leninist group seeking to overthrow the regime.

It wasn't easy to establish Transparency in Morocco, the scholarly, mild-mannered Assidon admits. For two years, the association was not officially recognized and so could not hold public meetings. Only when the Youssoufi government came to power in 1998 on a platform to moralize public life did Transparency become legal, "even fashionable."[6]

Then, Assidon was invited to speak at anticorruption conferences and workshops around the country. Transparency signed an accord with the Ministry of Education to take the anticorruption campaign into public school civic classes, and drew up programs for the Ministry of Health, the Customs Bureau, and other concerned agencies. The NGO has published a devastating book in French and Arabic, *La Corruption au Quotidien*, on the prevalence of corruption in Moroccan daily life—especially in schools, public health services, public administration, the courts, the construction sector, prisons, and the media.

Transparency has even challenged the sacrosanct armed forces. It publicly took up the case of Mustapha Adib, the young air force captain, who was tried and convicted in February 2000 by a military court for speaking out against corruption in the armed forces. Transparency International gave Captain Adib an Integrity Award for courage, and Amnesty International named him a "prisoner of conscience," but the Moroccan officer served two and a half years in prison and was expelled from the air force.

Probably the main achievement of Transparency has been to create an atmosphere where corruption in high places is no longer acceptable to the general public, which now demands that senior officials no longer enjoy immunity. This has opened the way for the press and parliament to investigate scandals in some of the most powerful public institutions, like the Real Estate and Hotel Loan Association, the National Agriculture Savings and Loan Bank, and the Social Security Savings Bank. Although the courts have been slow to follow through, the first convictions of senior officials in the Agriculture Bank were announced in June 2002, and some received up to fourteen years in jail.

Praising the parliamentary commissions for their inquiries, Transparency's General Assembly criticized the government for failing to correct the wrongs and carry out the reforms needed to put an end to such practices. But the battle has been engaged.

Truth and Justice

The popular poet Salah el Ouadie is a human rights activist who believes it is important to denounce those responsible for past repression to avoid such abuses in the future. A founder of the Moroccan Organization for Human Rights, El Ouadie left the group in 1997 because he thought it was not sufficiently aggressive. The following year, El Ouadie, who has thick dark hair and eyebrows and a sunny disposition, published *Letters to My Torturer*, a calm and straightforward description of the tortures he suffered during his ten years as a political prisoner. The slender volume was an immediate bestseller with three editions in Arabic and two in French.

El Ouadie and leaders of the main human rights organizations had applauded King Mohammed for his decision to indemnify victims of state abuse as an official recognition of past crimes. But this was not enough. The human rights activists demanded public hearings on past violations, the accountability of those persons responsible, and an end to immunity for past offenders.

"We must have a Truth Commission to know what people have suffered and who is responsible," said El Ouadie, explaining why he and other former political prisoners and relatives set up the Forum for Truth and Justice in the fall of 1999.[7]

"How can we make a state of law if we don't say who is responsible for violations of the law?" said Driss Benzekri, another founder of the forum, who had spent seventeen years in prison for advocating self-determination for the Saharans. Benzekri estimated that some 50,000 people, including entire families, have suffered directly or indirectly from state repression.[8]

The main aim of the forum is to create a national Truth Commission, similar to the South African body set up to expose the crimes of the apartheid era. For many months, forum leaders met privately with representatives of the king to discuss their proposal for a public debate on national reconciliation. Benzekri told me that the king agreed "in principle" to the idea, but details on the scope and powers of the Truth Commission had to be worked out.

By the summer of 2002, forum sources acknowledged they were making little headway toward their goal, but both sides appeared reluctant to break off the contacts. The palace was said to be prepared to let sensitive dossiers be opened, as long as certain lines were not crossed. Some forum activists, like Benzekri and El Ouadie, recognized that the palace was the sole authority in a position to open the gates to the recent past and that compromises would have to be reached. Others insisted that there could be no reconciliation without truth first.

Moroccans in general are deeply divided on the idea of a truth and justice tribunal. I have talked to scores of officials, businesspeople, professionals, and human rights activists who argue that the truth about past abuses by the state must be revealed to avoid any repetition in the future. On the other hand, many political figures, civil servants, and ordinary citizens insist that a public exposé of the past repression could threaten the stability of the country and even the monarchy.

Ironically, the most articulate defender of the royal policy "to turn the page" on past wrongdoings was Prime Minister Abderrahmane Youssoufi, who had spent much of his life denouncing official misdeeds. Declaring himself in favor of "national reconciliation," Youssoufi warned that opening dossiers on past abuses could lead to "the destabilization of the regime" because many of the persons responsible still hold posts in the system. For the present, the Socialist leader stressed, it would be better to follow the example of the Spanish Left, which had suffered severely under Franco but chose "to turn the page" and accept the restoration of the monarchy.[9]

I was curious to know the opinion of Abraham Serfaty, who had become an icon of the human rights movement and a symbol of resistance to authoritarianism. He received me in a sprawling white seaside villa at Mohammedia, north of Casablanca, the residence which had been put at his disposal by old friends. After spending seventeen years in prison and seven years in exile, Serfaty had been accorded his full pension.

Now wheelchair-bound from a degenerative muscular disease aggravated by long periods of severe torture, Serfaty was remarkably cheerful. He spoke hopefully of the efforts to set up a Truth Commission, emphasizing that "a public accounting" was essential. "It is important to disclose the whole truth

Khadija Rouissi, head of the Association of Families of Missing Persons and a leader of the Forum for Truth and Justice, at a memorial ceremony organized by the main human rights organizations for her mother, who died in 2003 still fighting to know what became of her son Abdelhaq and other missing persons.

without restrictions, before the country can get on with its normal life," he declared.[10]

Khadija Rouissi, a vivacious and dedicated leader of the Truth and Justice Forum, said that the volunteer group has raised questions about some 600 missing persons in its talks with the authorities. A long-time militant in the Committee for the Families of the Disappeared, Rouissi told me that the relatives of missing persons had not asked the state for money but simply wanted to know what happened to their loved ones.[11]

Rouissi, forty, has devoted much of her life to the search for her brother Abdelhak Rouissi, a young bank clerk and union activist, who disappeared on October 4, 1964. Over the years, the Rouissi family has heard rumors and vague reports that Abdelhak was alive, that he had been seen in different prisons or living in exile, but nothing concrete. "If he's still alive, he must be set free. If he's dead, his body must be returned to the family and the persons responsible brought to justice," said Rouissi.

The Families of the Disappeared have kept their cause alive by holding regular memorial services. I attended one of these meetings in the Rouissi home in Casablanca for the thirty-seventh anniversary of Abdelhak's disappearance. The long, candlelit room, decorated only with photographs of missing persons on the walls, was overcrowded. Some families still spoke with hope of finding relatives who had disappeared during the 1970s and 1980s.

For me, the most troubling aspect of the memorial service was that it wasn't just ancient history. There were recent cases like that of Hamed Drissi, a student from Rabat, missing since February 1997. Leaders of the main human rights organizations paid homage to the Rouissi family for their long struggle and pledged to keep the dossiers of the disappeared open until the problem is resolved. "All democratic forces give top priority to the question of missing persons," said Mouhcine Ayouche, a Casablanca businessman and leftist militant. "Justice must be given to the victims, and those responsible must be brought to justice."[12]

Rouissi won national recognition at the end of 2002, when she threatened to go on an unlimited hunger strike on behalf of three unknown Islamists, who had reportedly been kidnapped by the police and disappeared. The day before Rouissi was to begin her strike, two of the prisoners, who had been held in secret detention for two and five months, were released. The third, jailed for more than three months without charges, was brought before a court. Rouissi was named Woman of the Year by the independent newspaper *Le Journal* for demonstrating that the secret police are still active in "the new era."

Several hundred human rights activists and representatives of left-wing parties gathered together at the Touria Sekkat Cultural Complex in Casablanca on September 13, 2003, to pay a final homage to Fatima Skalli, Khadija Rouissi's mother, who died without learning the fate of the son who had disappeared nearly four decades ago. It was also an occasion for friends and relatives of missing persons to pledge to pursue relentlessly Fatima Skalli's personal quest for truth and justice.

One of the leading advocates for truth and justice is sociologist Fatema Mernissi, who has encouraged former prisoners of conscience to tell their stories. "No state can control its secrets; it will all come out in time," Mernissi predicted.[13]

Women's Causes

Many other human rights issues were relegated by activists to fall under the domain of women's concerns. Among these, the problems of street children, teenage prostitution, single mothers, domestic violence, and HIV/AIDS were taboo in this Muslim society until not long ago.

Women have risen to the challenge and set up numerous organizations —sometimes with the help of men—to tackle these largely neglected social problems. Some women admit privately that they turned to nongovernmental organizations because of the lack of interest of the male-dominated political parties in so-called women's issues.

King Hassan encouraged these women-led organizations, which were not considered threatening. Mohammed VI has gone further to provide significant financial support to numerous associations involved with social issues. The king's sisters frequently appear at fundraising events, giving a major boost to any cause they favor. As president of the National Watch Group for Children's Rights, Princess Meryem launched a human rights campaign in 2000 to alert the public to the problem of child maids—a subject rarely mentioned before then.

Najat Mjid, who looks like she'd be more at home in a fashion salon, knows Casablanca's street life better than most people. Mjid has turned the plight of Morocco's street children into a national concern. With a small group of academics, Mjid created the organization Bayti (which means "my house" in Arabic) in 1995, to rehabilitate minors who have given up on society for the freedom of the streets. A pediatrician in her early forties, Mjid says that in the early 1990s people didn't talk about street children because they weren't supposed to exist in Muslim society. Yet, the situation has worsened over the past decade because of the rural exodus and rise in poverty.

"Children come to Casablanca from all over because they hope to stow away on a boat or hide under the wheels of trucks and buses going to Europe," Mjid said, "and the police system [doesn't] know what to do with them." In an interview, Mjid explained to me how she got involved in this unpopular cause:[14]

> I wanted to do volunteer work and was looking for a mission in the early 1990s. I had noticed the kids on the streets in Casablanca sniffing glue. They washed windshields, polished shoes, sold Kleenex or flowers to earn money for the glue. I followed them to their "homes" in the parks, at the port, near the railroad station, outside the Hyatt Hotel. They live in undescribable filth and lack of sanitation. But for them the freedom of the streets is better than the poverty of the *bidonvilles*.

Bayti offers street children a structured program of sports, artistic activities, functional literacy workshops, and basic hygiene care. The organization works with about forty children at a time. They are required to stop sniffing glue at least temporarily. If they show motivation, they are provided with job training and jobs by Bayti's partners. Meanwhile, social workers try to contact the children's families with the aim of eventual reintegration.

Mjid admits that the return rate to families is low—25 to 30 percent after a five-year period. Nevertheless, Bayti is viewed as a model in the field and receives support from various European foundations, the Hassan II Foundation, and partners in the private sector around the country. At the end of 2000, the French government presented Mjid with its Human Rights Award for her commitment to Moroccan children. "Bayti's main accomplishment," Mjid told me, "is that we lifted the taboo on street children, when the authorities denied their existence."

Another private organization led by a courageous woman has begun to break through the taboos that surround a worsening national problem, AIDS. Hakima Himmich, president of the Association for the Fight against AIDS (known as ALCS from its French initials), has been struggling almost single-handedly to raise public awareness over the danger of AIDS for years, when most Moroccans said there was no problem.

Although Morocco's AIDS problem is certainly not so widespread as in other African countries, it is spreading. The Ministry of Health announced in June 2004 a total of 1,389 declared cases of AIDS since the first case was identified in 1986. But the number of HIV-infected people at the end of 2003 was estimated to be between 13,000 and 16,000.[15] And new AIDS statistics show that the kingdom is headed toward catastrophe, according to Himmich. She referred to a 2004 UNAIDS study revealing that in Morocco, 2.3 percent of prostitutes, 1 percent of the prison population, and one out of every thousand pregnant women are HIV-positive.

"We must react rapidly and efficiently," said Himmich, who expressed particular concern over the situation of prostitutes. The ALCS has been working with this segment of society for years, and today prostitutes are generally aware of the need for protection but they haven't been able to force their clients to change their habits.

There is some encouraging news in this domain, however. In June 2004, the Moroccan Ministry of Health launched an AIDS awareness campaign, aimed to lift the veil of shame and disinformation over this plague. The six-month drive included television and radio announcements—even in Berber dialects—posters, and free HIV testing.

Himmich, whose organization cooperated closely with the official initiative, reported positive results. In the first month of the campaign, the

AIDS Center, run by ALCS, received 1,515 calls (mostly from men aged fifteen to twenty-five) requesting general information, while previously the number of calls ran between 180 and 220 a month. "If we had better logistics, we could have received more calls," Himmich said, adding that this was a good way to reach the clients of prostitutes.

It was the first such campaign ever in this country, where Islamist politicians still claim that the use of condoms is an incitement to debauchery. And it is a case in which a nongovernmental group has laid the groundwork for government action in a delicate field.

L'Heure Joyeuse, another nonprofit private association, runs a day center for street children, but also provides care for infants with malnutrition, kindergarten classes, adult literacy courses, and vocational training for young women. This multipurpose social center is run by the dynamic Leila Benhima Cherif, sister of the former governor of Casablanca and wife of a prominent businessman, to whom all doors are open. L'Heure Joyeuse operates with a staff of twenty-five and many volunteers and receives support from the Hassan II Foundation, various government agencies, embassies, European donors, and local businesses.[16]

L'Heure Joyeuse was founded as a soup kitchen under the protectorate by a French parish priest in 1951, on the present site near the main Casablanca railroad station. In keeping with its charitable tradition, the association offers *couscous* every Friday (the Muslim sabbath) to street children, along with the possibility of a shower and change of clothing. During the holy month of Ramadan, thousands of meals are distributed daily. In 1998, L'Heure Joyeuse went to the countryside, distributing 50,000 schoolbags to rural children in twenty-eight provinces. It was then decided to launch a program to help one hundred remote villages to build their own schools. The first two schools have been built in the Ouarzazate and Zagora regions with support from the Belgian embassy and in cooperation with local village associations.

"We never send a baby away," Cherif told me. She said that since 1973, L'Heure Joyeuse has cared for between 150 and 200 malnourished babies a week, some weighing barely two pounds at ten weeks old. They are kept until they weigh eighteen pounds and then receive follow-up visits every six months. Volunteer pediatricians and aides also give medical care and hospitalization when needed. L'Heure Joyeuse provides classes, lunch, and medical check-ups for about a hundred preschool children. At the time of my visit in the summer of 2002, about a hundred single mothers, orphans, and other needy young women were being given vocational training and help in finding jobs in textile plants and workshops. And twenty-four street children over age fifteen were receiving literacy classes and professional training as electricians, plumbers, shoemakers, and house painters.

I met Cherif a year later at the International Women's Summit at Marrakech, after the Casablanca terrorist attacks. She spoke to me about a program she was working on with the Lions Club and some businesses to give vocational training to 250 young people. "If we don't find jobs for our youth and turn them into consumers, we'll have more kamikazes," she said glumly.[17]

Meriem Othmani set up the National Institution of Solidarity with Women in Distress in 1999, after serving twenty years as head of L'Heure Joyeuse. Owner of a flourishing office supplies business, Othmani is married to a surgeon, has a grown daughter, and spends much of her time on volunteer work. INSAF, as the not-for-profit organization is known by its French initials, has already acquired a national reputation as a champion of single mothers and their babies.

"The main aim of INSAF is to prevent infanticide and child abandonment," Othmani said soberly. She shared with me her repertoire of horror stories about single mothers. There was the pregnant girl beaten to death by her brother not long ago, the young maid who tried to commit suicide after becoming pregnant by her employer's son and losing her job, the new mother who wanted to throw away her baby because her pregnant cousin had been killed by her father.[18]

"Our society has not learned to cope with single mothers, who feel their only choice is to get rid of their babies and take up prostitution," Othmani said angrily. In its first two years, INSAF has begun to correct this situation. It has provided counseling and legal assistance to 500 single mothers, temporary food and lodgings for 210 of them, jobs for 105, and helped 72 to return to their families.

INSAF's original aims have expanded as one problem leads to another. The association is now working to improve conditions for 300 inmates and their children in Casablanca's women's prison and introducing vocational training. INSAF has also taken up the cause of child labor, getting government agencies and businesses to distribute leaflets with the message: "School is a right of all children."

In her drive to get children into school, Othmani has clashed with UNICEF. "Can you imagine, they just tell employers to provide school time for under-age workers! That's no way to end child labor," the outspoken leader of INSAF charged. In New York, UNICEF sources later confirmed this policy but stressed that at least the children would get some education.

I am full of admiration for women like Meriem Othmani, who are out there fighting for unpopular causes. This is the new civil society, people who are making Morocco advance, with or without aid from the palace or the government.

Economic Empowerment

Some nongovernmental organizations have moved beyond social concerns to get involved in development issues on the theory that the best way to help people get ahead is to give them the means to do it on their own. Several groups have been inspired by Muhammad Yunus and his Grameen micro-credit model, which has proved so successful in bringing grassroots entre-preneurship to Bangladesh.

One of Morocco's first microfinance agencies is the Zakoura Foundation, founded by Noureddine Ayouch in 1995. Ayouch, who heads an advertising firm, told me that Zakoura makes it a practice to give loans only to women "because they are hard-working, successful, and can always be trusted to re-imburse credit on time." He said that by the end of 2002, Zakoura had pro-vided more than 200,000 small loans, for a total of about $30 million, with a reimbursement rate of 99.7 percent. Most of his clients are housewives from the *bidonvilles*, working together in small units, covering each other for their interest payments. They develop small enterprises generally reselling clothing and other goods that they buy in the flea market. King Mohammed

Group of microcredit entrepreneurs from a bidonville *at Mohammedia, a resort north of Casablanca. With a starting loan of $100 at 12 percent interest, they buy clothing at Casablanca's huge flea market and operate small retail businesses in Mohammedia.*

has taken a personal interest in this microcredit program and given it a grant of $10 million through the Hassan II Foundation.[19]

Early on, Zakoura developed an education program, making use of its small loan network. Since 1997, the foundation has opened 220 schools, providing three years of education to 11,500 children between eight and sixteen years old who were unable to go to regular school. Since 1999, it has provided classes in functional literacy to a total of 40,000 adults.

But Ayouch has bigger ideas. For several years, he has been trying to sell the government his six-year plan for mass education: 15 million people in 15,000 villages for just $1 billion. The authorities, who acknowledge major defects in the state's education system and especially the widespread illiteracy in rural areas, admire Ayouch's plan but say they simply don't have that kind of money for education.

Nevertheless, thanks to a $2 million grant from the Mohammed V Foundation, Zakoura launched a new program in 2002 for the integrated development of *douars*, or rural hamlets. Under this program, Zakoura is taking charge of the development of sixty *douars* for a three-year period. Community centers comprising a classroom, library, and workshop have been built in all of the *douars*. Schooling (including civic and cultural activities) is offered to 3,000 children, professional training for 3,000 young people, literacy courses for 5,400 adults, and business training for 9,000 recipients of microcredits.

Another group working with microbusinesses is Al Amana, set up in 1997. By the end of 2003, Al Amana had provided credits to 100,000 clients for about $25 million and established a network of 128 sites located in 74 cities and towns around the country from Tetouan in the north to Taroudant in the south—all linked by the Internet. Like Zakoura, Al Amana gives what are called "solidarity loans" to groups of four or five small entrepreneurs, who act as guarantors for one another.

By 2005, the International Year of Microcredit, Morocco boasted 12 microfinance associations, which had granted a total of 2 million loans worth about $500 million to around 450,000 beneficiaries—75 percent of them women. At present the main effect of these small enterprises is to improve the lives of individuals or families. If expanded, however, these groups could become the bases for mutual benefit societies and a powerful tool for the improvement of their communities.

Village Stirrings

Increasingly, volunteer groups are moving into the countryside and setting up local development associations to help bridge the gap between rural and urban life and make up for the insufficiencies or negligences of the state.

Leila Tazi, a pediatrician and former professor in the Department of Medicine in Casablanca, recalls that when she set up the Moroccan Association for Research and Action in Health and Hygiene (the French acronym is AMRASH) in 1988, "the rural world didn't exist—except for tax purposes." The Moroccan state and international agencies like the World Health Organization, driven by principles of feasibility and profitability, concentrated development projects in the cities. Even professionals like nurses wouldn't go to the scattered rural population, and most teachers with rural posts hated the life and were not involved in the community. "There were in effect two Moroccos, and so I chose the High Atlas where access was most difficult and the problems enormous," Tazi explains.[20]

Thus, Tazi began her "small revolution" in a cluster of isolated villages without schools, electricity, or clean water, high above the Imlil Valley, thirty miles southwest of Marrakech. Concentrating on three villages with a total population of 1,000, AMRASH has engineered numerous self-help projects. The volunteers have built community centers with classrooms, workshops, libraries, video clubs, guest rooms, and toilets; introduced solar power; and improved the water supply, including treatment and drainage.

Reviewing their accomplishments, Tazi said nearly 100 percent of the children are in schools in the three villages. Amrash has opened literacy classes and income-generating programs for women and young people in sewing, knitting, and embroidery. Aguersioual was the first village to get all of its boys and girls into school, to provide running water and toilets in all of its homes, and to create the first mixed men's and women's development association in the countryside. "Now Aguersioual is sending out technical assistance to the other AMRASH villages," Tazi said proudly, "and representatives from fifty-four other villages have come to Aguersioual to see how they can change their lives too."

AMRASH has received international recognition in the form of a modest grant from UNESCO and help in training from the Groupe Français de l'Education Nouvelle and the Social Work and Research Center of Tilonia, India. But most of its programs are supported by Moroccan government agencies like the Ministry of Education and the Office of Professional Training and other volunteer groups like L'Heure Joyeuse.

Sociologist Fatema Mernissi has publicized the changes coming to the High Atlas Mountains with her book on the enterprising Ghojdama tribe, *Les Aït Débrouille*. She visited the tribal seat at Aït Iktel, high in the mountains northeast of Marrakech, in 1996 and saw firsthand the small miracles taking place. She says that one reason for the success of the self-help movement in the most ignored zones like the High Atlas is the civic spirit of their educated sons, who return to their villages to share their experiences and to help the people dream new dreams. Mernissi writes that she has never seen peasants so confident in their own ability to change reality as in this small village among the clouds.

During a book signing in Rabat in the summer of 2001, Mernissi introduced me to the unassuming anthropologist Ali Amahan, a leader of the movement to transform life in the High Atlas. Amahan told me how his village of Aït Iktel, located in a hollow of the High Atlas peaks, has been catapulted into the twenty-first century in just five years. The local *djemaa*, or village council, with the help of volunteer groups, has built access roads and brought water and electricity to the village. The Aït Iktel Association, made up of émigrés and villagers, has encouraged local people to send the girls to school (the boys have attended school for a number of years) and to learn French and Arabic, using their native Berber as the language of instruction. Now the villagers have a new source of income: the Aït Iktel Association has built a workshop where the women weave their bright-colored tribal rugs and then sell them through the Internet. And there are ambitious plans for the future: the development of ecological tourism, the extension of an irrigation canal, cattle-raising projects.[21]

Mernissi also introduced me to the Hassoune sisters of Marrakech, who are involved with civic groups working in the countryside. I described in an earlier chapter my visit to the lost hamlet of Tizi N'Choug with Bouchra Hassoune. Her sister Jamila Hassoune is an outgoing young woman who runs the family bookstore and is bringing books and city people to villages in the High Atlas. Since 1996, she has organized mini book fairs in the larger villages and goes regularly to rural schools to distribute books and hold discussions with students.

"Young people in the villages are eager to get books—and are willing to pay ten *dirham* [$1] for a paperback," Hassoune told me. They are practicing Muslims but tolerant and open to other ideas, she said. What they want is educational books on human rights, nature, animals, the United States, and Europe. They also dream of meeting "educated" city people.[22]

In 1999, with support from Mernissi, Hassoune organized the first *caravane civique*, taking urban doctors, lawyers, writers, and artists to interact with the village students she had come to know. Now, every spring and fall, she runs the increasingly popular caravans as forums for community action "to break down barriers between rich and poor, artists and professionals in Morocco."

For me, this is one of the most exciting aspects of the New Morocco: that the lost villages of the High Atlas are no longer alone. Their sons and now daughters, who escaped to find better lives in the cities or abroad, are sending checks to help out their families. But also some of them, like Ali Amahan, have created local development associations. And these groups are getting together to share their experiences and ideas for solving their problems. These associations are not a substitute for government, but they can be a powerful lobby for change.

Political Voices

Growing disaffection with the political parties has led to the creation of associations that seek new political alternatives. At the end of 1995, Socialist dissident Abdelali Benamour founded an association called Alternatives, intended to be a kind of political club, "a space for political debate and reflection." Benamour sees the role of Alternatives not as a passive think tank but rather as "a motor to put pressure on the political parties" through conferences and publications. Initially, he had proposed that the group serve the Youssoufi administration as a conduit for ideas, but the prime minister reacted negatively, accusing the association of aiming to become another left-wing political party.[23]

"The problem is that the parties are afraid of NGOs; they see us as competitors, when they should use our assistance," Benamour said. In an interview, he was critical of the main political parties, contending that they have failed to resolve the country's problems and should be disbanded. He favored a reorganization of the political parties into two large groups representing the Left and the Right.

Another advocacy group critical of the political parties is Maroc 2020. Its leader, Ali Belhaj, a well-known educator, told me that his association aimed to develop a national debate on the main issues, including education, economic, and social questions and also the definition of power and the concept of authority.

"A revolution has taken place in Morocco. Before, individuals had no role in society, but now citizens are conscious of their responsibilities and are speaking out," Belhaj declared. Emphasizing that what was needed now was "a project for the future of the country," he said that King Mohammed has demonstrated that he wants social change, but Youssoufi's government failed to produce results.[24]

Belhaj did form his own liberal party, but it fared poorly in the 2002 elections. The Belhaj experience demonstrated that while political think tanks provide a valuable overview of government policy in Morocco, what is not needed is yet another political party.

The Abderrahim Bouabid Foundation at Salé, named for the popular Socialist leader who died in 1992, has become an important center for democratic debate. The foundation, headed by Bouabid's son Ali, was created in 1994, after King Hassan began to relax the regime, and has not hesitated to tackle the most delicate issues, such as official corruption. Crown Prince Mohammed made his first speech during a debate on democratic transition at the foundation. "We thought then that something had really changed and Hassan II was ready to work with the Left," Bouabid recalls.[25]

In an interview, Bouabid spoke calmly about the controversial question of a national Truth Commission. "Memory is at the heart of the problem. How far can we go without endangering the country?" he asked. "We must find a middle way, somewhere between those who seek political trials and those who want to close the book before we've read it."

Among the most vociferous—and potentially explosive—political groups is the National Association of Unemployed Graduates. And their frustration is understandable. There was a total of 400,000 high school and college graduates who could not find work by 2002, according to the association. Job prospects were abysmal with 37.6 percent of those in the fifteen to twenty-four age bracket unemployed in urban areas, compared to 21.5 percent for all ages.

At first, the Unemployed Graduates held protest demonstrations in front of parliament, but later sit-ins were banned and police repression was brutal. The Moroccan Labor Federation gave them a meeting place; the Liberal party let them camp out in one of its offices; and the Moroccan Human Rights Association and ATTAC, the international movement against globalization, have helped to publicize their cause. But basically the Unemployed Graduates are relatively isolated and have roused little public sympathy because they are viewed as a privileged minority.

Hassan Belguerda, twenty-nine, president of the Rabat section of the Association of Unemployed Graduates, obtained a master's degree in Arabic language and literature from the University at Fez in 1997 and dreamed of becoming a university professor. But he wasn't able to find a job in the administration or in the private sector. He lives with his sister in Salé and spends his time discussing politics with unemployed friends and lobbying state and local administrations for jobs for the association's members.

"We are willing to accept any kind of work," Belguerda stressed, pointing out that many graduates have taken jobs as office messengers or gardeners. He says it is the girls who have the most difficulty because boys can always sell something in the street. "When we complain, the authorities advise us to go back to school—study information technology, management, mathematics, science, engineering. But even people with higher studies are having trouble getting hired."[26]

The danger posed by this elite group is that it keeps getting larger and more militant, as the school population swells, and neither the public nor the private sector has produced enough new jobs to absorb the newcomers.

The most effective political associations are those that promote the interests of women and Berbers. In earlier chapters, I have discussed these two sectors, which have engendered forces for the meaningful reform of the society. The approximately 150 Berber cultural associations have become part of a significant politicocultural movement. Plagued by internal divisions, they are however united in the demand for official recognition of Morocco's *Amazigh* identity, which is Muslim but generally opposed to political Islam.

The main women's organizations grew out of political parties but have acquired considerable autonomy in their struggle for equity in this male-dominated society. Like the Berbers, the mainstream women's associations share a common hostility toward Islamists, who have tried to block changes in the subordinate status of women.

Two Worlds Apart

When I first returned to Morocco in 1995, I was impressed with the dynamism of the new civil society, but soon found that it tended to be divided between "modernists" and Islamists, with very little interaction. The chasm was most noticeable in the women's groups, which had almost nothing to do with each other.

For instance, there were no Islamists present at a seminar of some sixty NGOs sponsored by the UN Population Fund in the fall of 1995. I learned that the UN agencies, which work closely with many nongovernmental organizations, exclude Islamist groups affiliated with the Association for Justice and Charity, because it is not officially recognized. Leaders of several women's associations attending the meeting told me they would not work with Islamists because of the Islamist violence against women in Algeria. They openly admitted that they were afraid of the Islamist ideology, which they considered to be "antiwoman."[27]

Nadira Barkallil, a leader of the influential Democratic Association of Moroccan Women, called Islamists "a dangerous force because they are clandestine, not structured, and repressed." Rabea Naciri, head of a feminist association working with Algerian women, said Islamists were excluded because they "instrumentalized religion."

"We are almost at war with the *intégristes* because women have been their first victims," said Najat Ikhich, secretary general of the Democratic League for the Rights of Women, which has supported the Algerian and Afghani women in their struggle against Islamic zealots. There was no question of co-operation with the Islamists, "who are threatening our choice of democracy and modernity," she stressed.

For their part, Islamist charitable associations that help out in hospitals and provide assistance to destitute families in shantytowns as a rule do not cooperate with non-Islamist organizations engaged in similar activities. On university campuses, Islamists have taken over the National Students Union and tend to exclude others from leadership.

Nadia Yassine complained about prejudice against Islamists in some professions and in women's associations. But her main grievance was with the government, which has yet to recognize Sheikh Yassine's Justice and Charity Association although it is generally considered to be the most important Islamist movement in the country. She also resents the fact that the authorities won't let students meet for prayers on campus and bar attempts by the association to hold prayer meetings on the beach.

Bassima Hakkaoui, one of the first Islamist women to be elected to parliament, said that she had been barred from participating in a meeting of the Democratic Association of Moroccan Women: "I told them, if you are democratic, I have the right to speak . . . but it didn't help."[28]

The climate of mutual suspicion increased with the political advances made by the Islamist Party of Justice and Development, and has turned to hostility since the increase in violence by Islamic extremists.

Leila Chaouni, head of Le Fennec, a Casablanca publishing company, is one of the rare progressive women who is reaching out to the Islamic community. "Moroccans have a lot to learn from the horrors in Algeria," Chaouni told me. Morocco—like Algeria—is faced with "a rupture" between the French-educated elites and the Arabized masses, she said. Le Fennec is trying to bridge the gap with publications in French and Arabic on subjects like women in Islam, which are intended to dispel common myths.[29]

Le Fennec published, in 2003, Nadia Yassine's book, *Toutes voiles dehors*, in which she discusses such controversial topics as American imperialism, globalization, disinformation, and secularism from her own Islamist view.

Yassine told me that some mainstream women's NGOs were quietly recruiting veiled women to work in the field, in the *bidonvilles* and villages. "They have found that people trust women who have worked with our organizations," the Islamist militant smiled.[30]

There are other signs that the confidence gap between the modernist and Islamist sectors of Moroccan society can be bridged. The secular-inspired Moroccan Association of Human Rights, which was created essentially by the Left to defend left-wing victims of state repression under former King Hassan, has taken the lead in the defense of the rights of Islamic radicals during the crack-down on suspected Islamic terrorists. AMDH activists and members of Yassine's movement have campaigned together for human rights and have been indiscriminately beaten and arrested by the police.

The spontaneous growth of civil associations is one of the most significant developments in Morocco in recent years. Their influence, however, has been diminished by their lack of cohesion as well as by the distrust between the modernists and the Islamic traditionalists. Separately, these nongovernmental organizations are just so many drops in the bucket, but together they add up to a new public consciousness and could have a major impact on the course of events.

Saharan Imbroglio

11

Any visitor to Western Sahara might well wonder how this desolate place of mostly sand, rocks, and scraggly shrubs, which even camels have fled, could raise such great passions. The vast, sparsely populated territory, stretching from southern Morocco to Mauritania, has no discernible wealth aside from phosphate mines and a 660-mile coastline with rich fishing waters and possible offshore oil. Yet, for most Moroccans, from the king to ordinary citizens, the preservation of national sovereignty over this disputed desert has become a sacred obligation.

King Hassan launched the crusade with his Green March in 1975 and recovered Morocco's "southern provinces" from Spanish rule the following year. Ever since, Morocco has been engaged in a costly struggle with Saharan nationalists backed by Algeria, first on the battlefield, then in international capitals and the halls of the United Nations. The Sahara conflict has drained Moroccan resources from urgently needed economic and social development, poisoned Rabat's relations with its neighbors, and held hostage its foreign policy.

The bitter legacy of the Sahara conflict constitutes a major challenge for King Mohammed VI, as he attempts to construct a new, more liberal, and modern Morocco. Initially it was believed that the young monarch, who came to the throne with a more open and pragmatic view of authority than King Hassan, would bring a new vision to the intractable question of Western Sahara. But King Mohammed appears locked into his father's Saharan policy in defense of Morocco's "historical and religious rights" over Western Sahara. On his first visit to Laayoune, the rapidly growing capital of Western Sahara, in the spring of 2002, the monarch firmly reasserted Morocco's claims to the territory.

"Morocco shall not relinquish an inch of its Sahara territory, which is inalienable and indivisible," the king declared. In an implicit warning to the Saharan nationalists and their Algerian allies, he stressed: "We are convinced of our full sovereignty over every inch of this land which stands protected by our Royal Armed Forces, the members of the Gendarmerie Royale, the Auxiliary Forces, and the National Security Forces."[1]

Distant Connections

Historically, Western Sahara was a land of passage for nomadic herding people and caravans moving to and from central Africa. As such, there have always been contacts between the Moroccan kingdom and the mobile tribes of the Sahara. During times of great droughts, the Sahraouis would push out of the desert northward in search of pastures for their camels. And sometimes they stayed.

Moroccan claims to Western Sahara go back to the eleventh-century Almoravids, the Berber dynasty that came out of the Saharan oases to conquer all of Morocco and much of Spain, in the name of a fundamentalist form of Islam. (Some Sahraouis suggest that this is an argument for Saharan claims to Morocco and even Spain.)

There are however many documents—maps, treaties, oaths of allegiance, and official nominations—that substantiate Morocco's contention that it exercised nominal authority in the Sahara at different periods. Some of the sultans were more Saharan-oriented than others. In the sixteenth century, Moulay Ahmed el Mansour sent expeditions deep into the Sahara to profit from the lucrative trade in gold, slaves, and salt.

In his classic work, *Tribes of the Sahara*, Lloyd Cabot Briggs devotes a chapter to the Moors—the pastoral nomadic population of Western Sahara. He writes that the modern Moors are physically and culturally products of the mixture between Arab invaders and nomadic Berber tribes living in what is now Western Sahara. Briggs describes the Moors as generally thin, with yellowish brown skin and dark curly hair, and of proud, independent, warlike nature. They share a common history from the eleventh century and the same Arabic dialect known as Hassania—from the Beni Hassan tribe of the Draa Valley in southern Morocco. Briggs notes that Moroccan sultans exercised varying degrees of control over Western Sahara through military governors and local princes until the end of the eighteenth century, when Saharan trade routes shifted eastward and European colonial powers began to penetrate the area.[2]

Spain gained its first official foothold in Western Sahara with the 1860

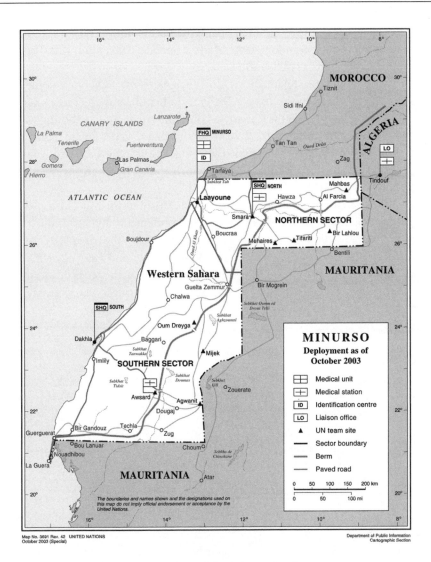

Western Sahara, showing the positions of the UN peacekeeping forces and the berm that follows the whole length of the disputed territory. (MINURSO deployment as of October 2003, no. 3691 Rev. 42, UN Cartographic Section)

Treaty of Peace and Friendship of Tetuán, according to Spanish historian Tomás García Figueras. Morocco was obliged to concede "in perpetuity" the territory of Santa Cruz de Mar Pequena, a coastal fortress, which the Spaniards had occupied during the conquest of the Canary Islands in 1476 and lost in 1524. Spanish colonization of Western Sahara dates from 1884, when local tribal leaders granted Spaniards permission to set up trading posts along the coast. In June 1890, Madrid signed a convention with Paris delimiting the borders of Spanish Sahara.[3]

For a long time, Spain didn't do much with the Saharan colonies. Madrid's first concern was to keep the French, British, and other foreigners out of the area opposite the Canaries. "Until the late 1940s . . . nothing was known about the mineral wealth of Western Sahara," according to Saharan authority Tony Hodges. "It remained a prestige colony of no economic value or strategic value of any kind to Spain, which correspondingly invested almost nothing in it."[4]

While economic growth soared in French Morocco, Spanish Sahara was still essentially a military outpost, with a few settlements and one industry, fishing. Saharan life continued much as it always had—the tribes always on the move, fleeing droughts, searching for new pastures, and carrying on their traditional trade in animals. To preserve the status quo, the Spanish administrators consolidated friendly relations with the tribal chiefs, who were given broad autonomy to manage their own affairs.

Greater Morocco

It was the Moroccan nationalist leader and pan-Arab scholar Allal el Fassi who first laid claim to Western Sahara in the euphoria of Morocco's independence. In fact, El Fassi's map of Greater Morocco, published by the Istiqlal party in 1956, included not only Spanish Sahara, but a substantial swath of the Algerian Sahara, all of Mauritania, and a corner of Mali, with the southern border reaching the Senegal River.

I remember in the beginning many Moroccans didn't take El Fassi's map seriously. But within a year, the political parties and the palace had embraced the new nationalist cause. In 1962, Morocco formally presented to the United Nations its claims to Ifni—a tiny Spanish-occupied enclave on the coast of southern Morocco—Spanish Sahara, and Mauritania, a vast French desert territory more than twice the size of France.

The Moroccan dossier included scores of royal decrees and other official documents, naming governors, judges, and military chiefs, demonstrating that Moroccan sultans had exercised authority over the Saharan territories until the establishment of the protectorates. One of the sultan's representatives, Sheikh Ma El Ainin had led the resistance to foreign incursions at the end of the nineteenth century, and his descendants are among the elite in Western Sahara today. There were also many *beias* by Saharan tribal leaders to Moroccan sultans over the centuries. Numerous international treaties recognized Moroccan control over Western Sahara, prior to Spanish occupation, and various Moroccan conventions with Spain, the United States, and Great Britain guaranteed the protection of their citizens in the area.

Initially Morocco appeared as a liberator of territories still colonized by Spain and France. In the first years of Moroccan independence, thousands of Sahraouis fled Spanish Sahara to settle in the "liberated" part of the kingdom. At the same time, numerous Saharan dignitaries arrived in Rabat to present their allegiance to the sultan, among them a former Mauritanian deputy in the French National Assembly and the *emir* of Trarza from southern Mauritania. Some Sahraouis were given senior positions in the Moroccan administration, such as director of Radio Maroc and delegate to the United Nations. Many Saharan tribesmen joined the Moroccan Liberation Army to finish the struggle for the liberation of Western Sahara, Algeria, and Mauritania. For a while, the Moroccan government gave discreet support to these irredentist forces.

Soon the Moroccan authorities found themselves in the impossible position of trying to consolidate the country's independence with help from the former colonial rulers and struggling to recover territories from those same powers. Pressed by France and Spain to disband the Moroccan Liberation Army, Prince Moulay Hassan succeeded in incorporating most of the northern contingents—between 6,000 and 9,000 men—into the newly formed Royal Armed Forces. Some 3,000 irregulars, mostly from the Middle Atlas, joined the southern command of the Moroccan Liberation Army, known as the Saharan Liberation Army and made up of tribesmen from Ifni and Western Sahara. The guerrilla movement came under the supervision of the local branches of the Istiqlal party—although this was not acknowledged publicly.

Only El Fassi, the combative leader of the Istiqlal party who had no official responsibilities, openly assumed a connection with the Saharan Liberation Army. During a tour of southern Morocco in early 1957, El Fassi declared: "Citizens, the battle of the Sahara has begun. The Istiqlal proclaims the debut of this battle and invites the people confident of their strength to engage themselves there. . . . The most important aid to offer Algeria is to open another front against colonialism in the Sahara."[5]

As in northern Morocco, the Saharan Liberation Army deliberately avoided contact with Spanish colonial troops, directing attacks against the French army in southern Algeria and northern Mauritania, thus taking advantage of the freedom of movement in Spanish Sahara. At first, Spain had hoped to forestall nationalist activity in its Saharan provinces and turned a blind eye to the Saharan guerrillas. But when the liberation army directed a major assault against Ifni's border posts, causing many casualties, Madrid sent air and sea reinforcements from the Canary Islands to defend its Moroccan enclave.

Refurbishing his nationalist credentials, Prince Moulay Hassan dispatched the Royal Armed Forces to the scene to defend the Aït Bamrane—the main Berber tribe of Ifni—from attacks by Spanish colonial forces. Encouraged by this official support, the Saharan Liberation Army became more daring and attacked Spanish positions near Laayoune and as far south as Villa Cisneros (today's Dakhla).

This new guerrilla offensive alarmed Madrid, which finally agreed to French proposals for a joint military operation against the Saharan insurgents. In February 1958, French and Spanish forces, backed by aircraft, moved swiftly across Western Sahara, reoccupying posts that had been seized by the guerrillas. The French-Spanish operation marked the defeat of the Saharan Liberation Army. This time, the Royal Moroccan Armed Forces made no attempt to intervene on behalf of the guerrillas.

A few days after the rout of the Saharan Liberation Army, King Mohammed V addressed a gathering of Sahraouis at the oasis of M'hamid, saying: "We solemnly proclaim that we will pursue our action for the return of our Sahara in the framework of the respect of our historical rights and in conformity with the will of its inhabitants."[6] It was a solemn pledge by the king to reclaim the rest of Greater Morocco, presumably through diplomatic means. And as long as the disputed territories remained under French and Spanish domination, Morocco found international support for its cause.

Barely a month later, Rabat and Madrid announced an agreement on the return to Morocco of Tarfaya, a sliver of mostly worthless desert sandwiched between southern Morocco and Spanish Sahara. This was said to be the reward for the dissolution of the Saharan Liberation Army. In the wake of this defeat, many Saharan guerrillas joined the royal army, and more than 40,000 Sahraouis fled to southern Morocco, according to official Moroccan sources.

France, however, granted Mauritania self-government within the French community in September 1958 and independence two years later. Morocco tried to bar Mauritania's admission to the United Nations but incurred strong hostility from other African countries, which saw this as Moroccan neocolonialism.

The loss of Mauritania was a major blow to Rabat's dreams of a Greater Morocco.

The Diplomatic Route

Morocco finally persuaded the United Nations to take up the question of Spanish Sahara. On December 16, 1965, the UN General Assembly adopted its first resolution urging Spain "to take all necessary measures for the liberation of the Territories of Ifni and Spanish Sahara from colonial domination." In follow-up resolutions, however, the general assembly asked Spain to hold consultations with Morocco and Mauritania on the procedures for a referendum to enable the people of Western Sahara "to exercise freely [their] right to self-determination" and "the right to independence." Later, the Organization of African Unity took a similar position.

King Hassan could see the writing on the wall and discreetly backed away from the Istiqlal's emotional campaign for Greater Morocco. Signaling a shift in tactics, King Hassan met with Spain's Generalissimo Francisco Franco at the Madrid airport on July 6, 1963, in their first summit since Moroccan independence, seven years before. The results of the meeting were not made public, but relations warmed considerably. Morocco no longer pressed for the decolonization of Spain's ancient Mediterranean enclaves, Ceuta and Melilla, and discouraged any efforts to revive the Saharan Liberation Army. In what seems to have been a trade-off, Spain returned Ifni to Morocco in June 1969.

At the same time, King Hassan moved to mend fences with other neighbors. In January 1969, Algerian president Houari Boumedienne made a state visit to Morocco, and agreement was reached on a joint commission to resolve border disputes.

Later that year, Hassan II invited Mauritanian president Mokhtar Ould Daddah to an Islamic summit in Rabat. The two had not been on speaking terms since late 1957, when Rabat had presented to the United Nations its claims to Mauritania and had tried to block its admission to the international body. That same year, apparently in retaliation, Ould Daddah, deputy prime minister of the then self-governing French territory, made his own appeal to "our Saharan brother tribes" of Spanish Sahara to join his planned Greater Mauritania. The king's belated invitation to the man whom Moroccans called "a French puppet" was an implicit renunciation of Moroccan claims to the country and laid the groundwork for the establishment of diplomatic relations.

At the Organization of African Unity summit in Rabat in June 1972, the goal of King Hassan's reconciliation drive and plans for Western Sahara became clear. There was no official communiqué on the subject, but statements by the Algerian and Mauritanian leaders indicated an understanding whereby once Spain left Western Sahara, the territory would be split between Morocco and Mauritania, with the tacit approval of Algeria.

Spain, however, had other ideas. In the late 1960s, Madrid had begun to develop its desert province, making substantial investments in infrastructure, mining, and fishing, which attracted Spanish workers and fishermen as well as Saharan nomads. To preserve its growing interests and undercut pressures for decolonization, Madrid embarked on a new policy of local self-government in 1967, setting up a *djemaa*, or assembly of tribal elders, known for their loyalty to Spain. In September 1973, General Franco announced that Spain was prepared to grant Western Sahara "internal autonomy."

King Hassan, who had believed in the success of his private diplomacy with Franco, was furious to learn of Spain's plans for a self-determination referendum in Western Sahara in early 1975. On July 5, 1974, Hassan II publicly warned Madrid against "any unilateral action on Saharan territory." Several days later, he declared that Morocco would oppose "by any means" the creation of "a puppet state" in the Sahara.[7]

The Moroccan king had survived two unsuccessful military coups in the early 1970s and faced growing public dissatisfaction over his authoritarian rule. In a classic move to divert attention from domestic problems, the embattled monarch seized the Spanish plan for a referendum as the pretext to launch his drive for the recovery of Western Sahara. First, he galvanized the dispirited armed forces with the idea of a Saharan mission, dispatching restless units to the south. Then he mobilized all of the political parties behind the national cause, except for several small leftist groups, which supported the Saharan nationalists. There had not been such a display of national unity since independence nearly two decades earlier.

Next, to gain time, the king persuaded the UN General Assembly to turn over the Saharan problem to the International Court of Justice at the Hague. A United Nations fact-finding mission sent to the area in May 1975 resulted in a new setback for Morocco. The delegation reported finding Saharan nationalist demonstrations everywhere and "an overwhelming consensus" in favor of independence.

On October 16, 1975, the International Court of Justice published its conclusion that there was no proof of "any tie of territorial sovereignty" with either Morocco or Mauritanian that would affect the decolonization of Western Sahara. Ignoring this finding, King Hassan chose to emphasize another part of the court's judgment, confirming that there had been "legal ties of allegiance" between the sultan and some tribes of Western Sahara at the time of Spanish colonization.[8]

That same day, the king broadcast his appeal for a Green March, calling for volunteers from all over the country to march into Western Sahara "to re-

*Some 350,000 elated volunteers take part in the 1975 Green
March to reclaim Spanish-occupied Western Sahara for
Morocco. (Moroccan Ministry of Communications)*

unite with our brothers." Armed only with Korans, some 350,000 marchers
moved joyously into Western Sahara on November 6. There was no confrontation because, forewarned, Madrid had removed its forces from the
border area.

At Algeria's demand, the UN Security Council condemned the march
and urged Moroccan marchers to draw back from the Spanish territory.
Spain also denounced the Moroccan move publicly, but a Spanish emissary
privately advised King Hassan that Madrid was ready to negotiate its withdrawal from Western Sahara. Three days later, the king ordered the marchers
to return to their base because they had "achieved the desired objective."

Under the Madrid Accords of November 14, 1975, Spain agreed to pull its
forces out of Western Sahara by the end of February 1976. A temporary administration was to be established over the territory with the participation
of Morocco, Mauritania, and the Saharan Assembly. The details of the accords were not made public but included recognition by Morocco and Mauritania of Spanish fishing and mining rights in the area.

Immediately after the Green March, a Moroccan force of some 40,000 troops discreetly occupied northern Western Sahara, while Mauritania took over the southern part of the territory. Thousands of Sahraouis, fearing Moroccan reprisals, fled the territory and took refuge in the nationalists' camps in southern Algeria.

King Hassan declared a few days later that the dossier of Western Sahara was closed—but he was very wrong. Rabat had indeed recovered the territory from Spain through a combination of diplomacy and theatrics. But the king had failed to recognize the new nationalist consciousness among the Sahraouis, and he misjudged Algeria's support of the Saharan nationalists.

The Saharan Nationalist Movement

The father of the Saharan nationalist movement was a young journalist by the name of Bassir Mohammed Ould Haj Brahim Ould Lebser, who was arrested by Spanish security forces on the night of June 18, 1970, at Laayoune and has never been heard from since. Familiarly known by his pseudonym, Bassiri, he is credited with declaring "Sahara for the Sahraouis" as early as 1968 and established the first nationalist party, the Movimiento de Vanguardia para la Liberación del Sahara, the following year, according to the authoritative Spanish journalist Tomás Bárbulo.[9]

A member of the important Saharan Reguibi tribe, Bassiri was born at Tan Tan in Spanish Southern Morocco (Tarfaya) in 1942 and taken in 1957, along with many other children, by the Saharan Liberation Army to Morocco for schooling. Completing high school studies in Casablanca with a Moroccan government scholarship, Bassiri made his way to the Middle East, where he attended the universities of Cairo and Damascus and became influenced by pan-Arabism.

Bassiri, who had a trim mustache and short, thick, dark hair and eyebrows, returned to Morocco in 1967 with a degree in journalism and created a Saharan nationalist journal called *Al Chihab*, or the *Torch*. Hodges says Bassiri left the following year for Smara, an important interior town in the northern Spanish Sahara, where he worked as a Koranic teacher and formed his clandestine movement.[10]

By June 1970, Bassiri's movement had decided to come out of hiding and organized a mass rally to present its demands for social reforms and decolonization to the Spanish authorities. Bassiri had opposed the demonstration as too risky and was not even present when a crowd of some 1,500 Saharan nationalists gathered on the morning of June 17 at Zemla Square on the outskirts of Laayoune to submit their petition to the Spanish governor general.

That afternoon, one of the governor's aides returned with an imposing squad of territorial police. There were several arrests and the angry crowd attacked the police, who reportedly fired into the air. It is not known how many people died that day, but Rabat protested against the slaughter of ten people. In the following days, hundreds of Sahraouis were arrested, including Bassiri.

In the wake of the "Zemla massacres," a small group of Saharan students at Rabat's Mohammed V University formed the nucleus of a new Saharan Liberation Front in 1970. The leader of these Sahraouis was Mustapha Sayed El Ouali, the son of a Saharan nomad, who was studying law on a Moroccan government scholarship. It is said that about a thousand Sahraoui students had been admitted to Moroccan schools after the 1958 dismemberment of the Saharan Liberation Army. El Ouali and his friends contacted the Moroccan political parties about reviving the Saharan liberation struggle and received words of sympathy but little else.

Discouraged by the lack of response from Moroccans, El Ouali's group went to the iron-mining town of Zouerate in northern Mauritania, where some Sahraouis had settled after the 1958 war. There, near the Western Saharan border, in May 1973, they established the headquarters of the Popular Front for the Liberation of Saguia el Hamra and Rio de Oro—the two provinces that made up Spanish Sahara—to be known as the POLISARIO front.

POLISARIO had tried to get help from Algeria, but the Algerians were reluctant to jeopardize their relations with Morocco and Spain for the unknown Saharan group. In the fall of 1974, Algerian president Houari Boumedienne told an Arab League summit that he supported the Morocco-Mauritania plans to liberate the territory from Spanish occupation.

Only Libya's Colonel Qadhafi, who at that time was ready to support any liberation movement, provided POLISARIO with diplomatic backing and arms in the early days of its struggle for independence. And only a limited amount of that aid got through because of Algerian obstruction.

The 1975 Madrid Accords changed everything. Algeria refused to recognize Spain's agreement on the partition of Western Sahara between Morocco and Mauritania and called it "an act of aggression." It was at this point that Algeria began to provide substantial logistic and political backing to POLISARIO.

With Algerian support, POLISARIO declared war on the Moroccan and Mauritanian forces that had begun to replace Spanish troops in the area at the end of 1975. Early on, POLISARIO seized the initiative in its Land Rover guerrilla war, attacking Moroccan and Mauritanian military positions across the desert territory, but was unable to hold any ground. Nevertheless, on February 27, 1976, from the oasis of Bir Lahlou in northern Spanish Sahara, POLISARIO unilaterally proclaimed the formation of the independent Saharan Arab Democratic Republic. Several days later, Algiers recognized the new Saharan state, provoking an immediate rupture in diplomatic relations with both Morocco and Mauritania.

Initially POLISARIO's guerrillas directed most of their attacks against Mauritania—the weaker occupying power. President Ould Daddah's small army had difficulty defending its primary resource, the iron mines operated by a French-led consortium at Zouerate, and the railway from the mines to the sea. Fired by success, POLISARIO became more daring. In early June 1976, El Ouali personally led a column of Land Rovers with several hundred men across the desert to attack the Mauritanian capital of Nouakchott on the Atlantic. A small band of guerrillas reached the outskirts of the capital and bombarded the city center, the presidential palace, and the embassy quarter, causing little damage but widespread shock. As they were withdrawing, El Ouali was killed in a shoot-out with the Mauritanians, when his group attacked the water depots. The death of the guerrilla leader was a serious blow to POLISARIO, but the daring raids continued.

When I reported on the Saharan conflict in 1977 for the *New York Times*, POLISARIO seemed to be gaining the upper hand. Moroccan forces occupied the towns and settlements, while the guerrillas had free run of the desert. Rabat's larger, better-equipped army was unused to the fierce desert conditions of extreme daytime heat and freezing nights, and suffered heavy losses.

Both the Moroccans and POLISARIO had underestimated each other's determination to attain their goals. In Morocco, virtually everyone from the Socialists, Communists, and Istiqlal conservatives to ordinary citizens was solidly behind the king in what they believed was a just cause. The only declared opponents to the Saharan war were leftists, who were either in jail, in hiding, or afraid to speak out. The Socialist leader Abderrahim Bouabid told me at the time that Algeria aimed to create "a puppet state" in Western Sahara and was getting away with it because of the lingering prestige of the Algerian revolution. In what now appears to be a prophetic statement, he said that while Morocco had recovered its Saharan territories, the problem would not be resolved "until the Moroccan regime developed credible democratic institutions."[11]

The POLISARIO front, on the other hand, came across as an authentic nationalist movement, but it was totally dependent on Algeria for material and political support. With a group of other foreign journalists—mostly Spanish and East Europeans—I visited POLISARIO's headquarters at Rabouni, near the dusty, bleak city of Tindouf in southern Algeria, for ceremonies marking the first anniversary of the declaration of the Saharan republic.

POLISARIO's secretary general, Mohamed Abdelaziz, a lanky figure in battle dress, welcomed visiting dignitaries from North Korea, Vietnam, Libya, the Spanish and French Communist parties, and various NGOs. Denying charges that POLISARIO was "a creation" of Spain, Mauritania, Libya, or Algeria, Abdelaziz attacked "the aggressive regime of decadent Morocco and its lackey Mauritania." Before a crowd of cheering Sahraouis, he declared: "We have faith in our cause . . . faith in our people who are African, Arab, Islamic, and nationalists."[12]

A military parade followed, with some thirty Land Rovers and as many trucks, two antiaircraft batteries, guerrillas armed with Kalashnikovs, and veiled women making victory signs and waving the Saharan flag—black, white, and green stripes, with red star, crescent, and triangle.

After the ceremony, Bachir Mustapha, El Ouali's younger brother and a member of POLISARIO's Council of Revolution, wearing a Saharan robe over his European shirt, answered the journalists' questions.

The POLISARIO spokesman said that the total population of Western Sahara is 750,000, including 200,000 people inside the territory, 150,000 refugees at Tindouf, and the rest divided between Mauritania and Morocco. The organization's political orientation is nationalist—not a foreign import—and based on the traditional *djemaas* that existed before colonialism, Mustapha said, refuting press reports that the movement was a Communist front. He stressed that POLISARIO's program calls for the just and equitable distribution of wealth and added: "If that is socialism, then we are socialist."

Outlining the movement's strategy, Mustapha said the aim was to defeat enemy forces by striking at economic infrastructures, for example, land communications in Mauritania and traffic in southern Morocco. He claimed that 60 percent of POLISARIO's materiel and arms was seized from the enemy; the rest comes from friends like Algeria, which provides unlimited aid.

The nationalist leader declared that there would be no reconciliation with Morocco or Mauritania without recognition of the sovereignty of the Saharan Arab Democratic Republic and its territorial integrity.[13]

We toured several refugee camps, which I am told have not changed a great deal since. The tents were inhabited mostly by women and children; the men were said to be with guerrilla units or to have died in combat. Red Cross sources said there were twenty-two camps in the region with a total of 105,000 refugees from Western Sahara. Living conditions were extremely difficult—no electricity; scant water brought in by trucks; a serious lack of medicines; minimal supplies of sugar, tea, flour, rice, *couscous*, and macaroni; very little milk or meat; and no fruit. A nurse told me that Sahraouis had lost more babies to malnutrition than the number of births in 1976.

But the organization of camp life was impressive, with women guards, nurses, and monitors in charge of food rations, literacy, political education, and making rugs and blankets. The morale of the refugees seemed good, but they did not hide their anger. Over and over again, we heard denunciations of "the betrayal by our Moroccan and Mauritanian brothers," whom they accused of entering Western Sahara on the pretext of ousting the Spanish and then staying on to exploit Saharan resources.

A few foreign journalists remained after the official celebrations to visit the fluid front inside Western Sahara. Riding in a convoy of four Land Rovers, we saw how the guerrillas were able to cross the entire territory by avoiding the towns and encounters with Moroccan troops. We traveled by night and slept by day under acacia trees—the only protection the desert offered against the Moroccan Air Force. Our food consisted of sugary tea, cookies, sand-baked bread, *gofio* (a porridge of corn flour, rye, and milk), and birds shot en route.

In four days, we covered more than 800 miles of trackless desert. We skirted the town of Mahbes in the northeast corner of Western Sahara and stopped at Tifariti, a former Spanish garrison and now a ghost town near the Mauritanian border. At one of the POLISARIO's well-camouflaged military bases in the region of Smara, we saw a nurse working in a clinic in an earthen dugout. We also met four families who were traveling on foot from Dakhla in the south to join the camps at Tindouf and a convoy of eighteen Land Rovers heading south. Finally, on the outskirts of Laayoune, we could see the Atlantic Ocean in the distance.

On our return to Tindouf, Mohamed Salem Ouled Salek, the twenty-eight-year-old minister of information, who had studied international law in Madrid and Paris, told me that POLISARIO controlled 55–60 percent of the territory. "Moroccans occupy only three cities: Laayoune, Smara, and Boujdour. We're next to all their posts and towns and can attack at will," he boasted confidently.[14]

A few months after my tour of POLISARIO's camps, the guerrillas succeeded in shutting down Mauritania's Zouerate iron mines, where several hundred French technicians were working. Mauritanian leader Ould Daddah recognized that his army was no match for the Saharan guerrillas and called on his old enemy, King Hassan, for reinforcements. The Moroccan monarch was only too glad to comply. But the guerrillas intensified their raids, and so Mauritania turned to France for additional help. Abandoning their neutrality, the French sent combat aircraft to bombard POLISARIO's forces. Although the guerrillas suffered heavy losses, they continued to target Mauritania's mining sector, wreaking havoc with the country's economy.

Distressed over the high costs of the war and the ineffectual government, Mauritania's armed forces overthrew Ould Daddah in a bloodless coup in

July 1978. A year later, the military-backed Mauritanian regime signed a truce with POLISARIO, withdrawing its claims to Western Sahara and agreeing to turn over its part of the territory to the nationalist movement.

But that didn't happen. Morocco seized this opportunity to dispatch more troops to the disputed territory and simply annexed it as the province of Oued ed Dahab (Rio de Oro).

With Mauritania out of the game, POLISARIO expanded the Moroccan front, ambushing military convoys, kidnapping Saharan civilians, raiding towns in Morocco proper, and attacking foreign fishing boats off the coast of Western Sahara. It seemed that POLISARIO might actually drive the Moroccan forces out of the Sahara.

It was the Great Wall of the Sahara that turned a disastrous military situation in Morocco's favor. It's not clear who first thought of building a wall in the desert, but the United States was certainly involved. Hodges reports that as early as May 1979, the U.S. State Department had approved plans by a subsidiary of Northrop Corporation to sell Morocco a $200 million electronic "integrated intrusion detection system," which was eventually installed on the Saharan defensive wall.[15]

In the spring of 1981, the first section of the earthworks was completed around the nerve centers of Western Sahara: the capital of Laayoune, the ancient caravan post of Smara, and the Bou Craa phosphate mines. The wall, or berm in military parlance, consists of six-foot-high banks of sand and rubble, with electronic sensors and radar along the top, which is lined with barbed wire and minefields; observation posts and artillery are placed at different points. This early-warning system was costly but effective and drove the guerrillas south to areas not protected by the wall. By 1987, an extension of the wall ran for some 900 miles along the Algerian and Mauritanian borders around a greater part of the territory.

The military situation has changed many times since my visit, but the hard life in the camps remains virtually the same. I cannot forget the words of Bachir Mustapha: "There have been many revolutions in the world. . . . Our specific characteristic is that only a certain number of plants can live in our territory. In very difficult conditions, only the tough can endure. Our people have survived a natural selection; the hardness of the country has formed the Sahraouis."[16]

Internationalization of the Saharan Conflict

Morocco was losing the diplomatic battle for Western Sahara by the early 1980s. Fifty countries (there were eventually more than seventy), mostly from

Africa and the Non-Aligned Movement, had recognized the Saharan Arab Democratic Republic. The big powers, including the United States, Europe, China, and the Soviet Union, assumed a neutral stance, refusing to recognize either the Saharan republic or Moroccan sovereignty over Western Sahara. But privately, Morocco's closest friends, Washington and Paris, which have important interests in Algeria, pressed Rabat to show flexibility in response to the demands for self-determination of the Sahraouis.

Although King Hassan had gained the upper hand militarily, it had come at an enormous price in manpower and expenditures. Morocco increased the size of its armed forces almost threefold to 140,000 in 1982 from 55,000 in 1974. Military expenditures were said to amount to about 40 percent of the national budget. Although Saudi Arabia provided generous grants (said to be around $1 billion a year), Morocco was forced to borrow heavily to cover military costs, the sharp rise in oil prices, and the fall in phosphate revenues. In the spring of 1981, the International Monetary Fund forced Morocco to raise its prices on subsidized items like sugar, flour, cooking oil, and milk. Angry riots at Casablanca were harshly put down, and the situation turned explosive.

In a dramatic about-face, King Hassan told the Organization of African Unity summit at Nairobi in June 1981 that Morocco accepted the principle of an internationally supervised ceasefire and referendum in Western Sahara. The king's gesture came too late to stave off recognition of the Saharan republic as the OAU's fifty-first member. Morocco promptly walked out of the African club—taking with it nineteen other members. It was the most serious crisis ever faced by the African group. Finally, when it was clear that Algeria and its friends would prevail, Morocco pulled out of OAU in November 1984, and has not returned.

That same year, the ever-resourceful King Hassan surprised everyone by announcing a Treaty of Union with Libya. In his memoirs, the king explained that the goal of this unnatural alliance was to halt the flow of arms and other aid from Libya to POLISARIO. The maneuver worked until July 1986, when King Hassan publicly received Israeli prime minister Shimon Peres. Libya and Syria branded the Moroccan king as a traitor, and he responded by severing his union with Qadhafi.

By the mid-1980s, it was widely recognized that neither side could achieve a military victory in the Sahara. There was concern in Western capitals that Morocco's conflict with POLISARIO could turn into an all-out war between Morocco and Algeria, jeopardizing the stability of the Moroccan monarchy and aggravating the troubled situation in Algeria. It was also feared that if Algeria decreased its aid to POLISARIO, Libya and eastern bloc countries might fill the gap, dangerously enlarging the conflict.

Thus, there was urgency to get the belligerent parties to the negotiating table. In 1985, the UN Secretary General Javier Perez de Cuellar began the arduous process of working out a ceasefire in Western Sahara. Over the next few years, the secretary general held meetings with POLISARIO, Morocco, Algeria, Mauritania, and Saharan tribal leaders. Finally, a ceasefire was agreed to on September 6, 1991, and it has miraculously held all these years.

That same year, the UN Mission for the Referendum in the Western Sahara, known as MINURSO from its French initials, was established by a UN Security Council resolution to monitor the ceasefire and set the conditions for a "free and fair referendum." In this poll, originally scheduled to take place in February 1992, the people of the territory were to choose between independence and integration with Morocco. It was MINURSO's task to draw up lists of eligible voters. No one had any idea that such a straightforward task in such a sparsely populated territory would present such monumental problems.

The main difficulty was to determine who should take part in the referendum. Complicating factors were the nomadic habits of the Sahraouis, the tribal structure of the society, mass migrations over the years, and the loose administration of the former Spanish rulers. POLISARIO held that the referendum lists should be based on the 1974 Spanish census, which showed a population of 74,000 in Spanish Sahara. Morocco contended that many thousands of Sahraouis had fled or migrated from the territory or simply not been counted. The identification of an electoral corps ground to a halt at the end of 1995, after POLISARIO objected to the inclusion of tribes which had settled in Morocco.

In March 1997, the UN secretary general, Kofi Annan, appointed former U.S. secretary of state James A. Baker III as his personal envoy to revive the Western Saharan Settlement Plan. Baker managed to bring the two sides together for talks, and they agreed to pursue the identification process. By late 1999, registration was complete. MINURSO had accepted 86,000 eligible voters, leaving 131,000 appeals unsettled.

Faced with this stalemate, Baker was instructed to contact the concerned parties to determine if they could agree on any other political solution to the Western Sahara question. But UN sources said privately that the basic problem was that Morocco would not abandon its sovereignty over the disputed territory, and POLISARIO would not accept less than independence.

Meanwhile, the Saharan issue acquired a new international dimension: oil. Since the discovery of substantial quantities of oil in Mauritania's offshore zone in May 2001, there has been new international interest in the waters off Western Sahara. In a move aimed to consolidate its sovereignty over the disputed territory, Morocco granted permits in the fall of 2001 to two major international firms to explore for oil off Western Sahara: the French company TotalFinaElf and the American Kerr-McGee Corporation. They have been followed by a London-based firm, Wessex Exploration.

Contesting the legality of Rabat's agreements, POLISARIO urged the UN Security Council to cancel the offshore contracts, declaring that there should be no exploitation of oil reserves "until the final status of Western Sahara was resolved." While the security council did not take a stand on the matter, the UN legal counsel issued an advisory opinion in February 2002 stating that the exploration contracts were not illegal per se. The memo warned, however, that foreign firms would be in violation of international law if they actually produced and sold oil in disregard of the interests and wishes of the inhabitants of the non-self-governing territory.

Not to be outdone, POLISARIO awarded its own contract to an Anglo-Australian company, Fusion Oil and Gas, for exploration in the same offshore area. Two small British companies, Premier Oil and Sterling Energy, have also signed contracts with the Saharan nationalists. As long as all of these companies confined their activities to exploration, there was apparently no problem. But should anybody actually find oil, the complicated situation would become impossible.

It was King Mohammed who pronounced the death sentence for the UN resolutions calling for a self-determination referendum on Western Sahara. Marking the twenty-seventh anniversary of the Green March on November 6, 2002, the monarch unilaterally proclaimed the proposal of a Saharan referendum "null and void and inapplicable" and stressed that a political solution must be found to "the artificial conflict."[17]

On the Front Line

From the air, the desert at Oum Dreyga looks more like an endless glacier with occasional piles of rocks and mounds. As the United Nations' Antonov cargo plane landed and the door opened, we were almost smothered by a rush of heat. We were lucky, it was only in the mid-40s Centigrade (105-plus Fahrenheit); the day before, it had reached 55 Centigrade (131 Fahrenheit) with a stinging sandstorm to boot, according to the MINURSO personnel who came to greet us. General Claude Buze, military commander of MINURSO, was making a tour of several of the team sites along the berm, and I had been authorized to go along.

We headed immediately for the post's Canadian Arctic tent, with welcome air conditioning, water, toilets, and other amenities like television, computers, and easy telephone access to Europe. Eleven military observers were stationed at the MINURSO team site at Oum Dreyga, one of nine team sites on the Moroccan side of the border. Their task was to check on any troop movements or changes in artillery at the strong points of the Royal Moroccan Army.

A Moroccan stronghold, located barely a mile from the UN site, did not appear threatening. Several soldiers were tinkering on decrepit military trucks; a gardener was tending to the precious patch of artichokes, cucumbers, grapes, and mint; and a few goats were milling about the well. On the outskirts of the base, a grocer from Agadir who had set up shop said that most of his goods came from the Moroccan resort city.

There are 700 Moroccan army strong points like this along the Great Wall, each manned by about 100 soldiers, with machine guns and mortars but nothing heavier, according to MINURSO sources. Moroccan reinforcements are stationed at least thirty kilometers west of the wall. Any change in the military deployment requires permission from MINURSO.

Similarly, a MINURSO liaison at Tindouf controls movements at fifteen POLISARIO observation posts along the Algerian border. Their reinforcements of tanks and armored personnel carriers are twenty-five kilometers away.

General Buze told me that his teams have reported no violations of the five-kilometer no-man's-land between the Moroccan and POLISARIO positions. The observers make two inspections daily by car or helicopter along the ceasefire line. Occasionally, he said, Bedouin traders try to cross the berm and get caught by the mines.

The next team site we visited was at Aousard, in the southeast, where there is a Moroccan garrison and a ghost village. Scrawled on a mountain in the distance are the Arabic words for "God Country King." Before the 1991 truce, POLISARIO guerrillas harassed the inhabitants of Aousard so much that the Ouled Delim tribal leaders moved all of the civilians to the safety of Dakhla, and they have not returned. Some Bedouins have occupied a few houses, but most remain empty. In the old part of town, a mosque, school, and supermarket appeared to be abandoned. The eeriest aspect of the desolate Aousard was the cluster of new bright-colored houses—also vacant—being built by the administration to welcome returnees from Tindouf, who might never return.

"Worse than the heat and the sand is the awful isolation," a member of the UN team remarked.

Back at MINURSO headquarters in Laayoune, the UN secretary general's special representative, William L. Swing, said with some satisfaction: "There has never been a major incident, never a shot fired across the ceasefire line." But Ambassador Swing was less sanguine about the prospects of a political solution, noting that Morocco and the POLISARIO were still very far apart, "each with nonnegotiable positions."[18]

Fait Accompli

While discussions over the fate of Western Sahara dragged on in the United Nations, Morocco has been quietly building a fait accompli on the ground. This was my overriding impression after a week's visit to the remote territory during the summer of 2002. King Hassan had pledged to modernize "our Sahara" and raise it to the level of the most developed regions of the kingdom, and King Mohammed was pursuing his father's mission. At a tremendous national sacrifice, Rabat has brought water, electricity, roads, schools, hospitals, housing, and jobs to what is now called "the southern provinces." An

Laayoune is no longer a dusty Spanish garrison town but the capital of Morocco's "southern provinces" with a majestic mosque, convention hall, and palm-lined central esplanade. (Moroccan Ministry of Communications)

unintended result of this development, however, has been a heightened consciousness of a Saharan identity.

I was pleasantly surprised at my freedom of movement in Western Sahara. Less than a year earlier, journalists had been obliged to obtain prior authorization, and their activities were closely controlled. Yet I was able to wander at will through the *bidonvilles*, attend a left-wing political rally, tour UN posts along the front lines, and talk to Sahraouis of every opinion: pro-Moroccans, pro-POLISARIO nationalists, and those who have been disillusioned by unkept promises on both sides.

The most striking change is that Western Sahara is no longer the isolated no-person's-land left by the Spanish when they pulled out at the end of 1975. King Hassan opened a modern international airport on the outskirts of Laayoune in March 1985, with a capacity to handle 200,000 passengers annually, and airports at Dakhla and Smara have been rebuilt. The Saharan highway system now has a network of 3,400 kilometers (compared to only 70 kilometers in 1975) of hard-surface roads, linking Guelmim in Morocco proper to Lagouira on the Mauritanian border to inland oases like Mahbes and Smara. A new port has been built at Laayoune to handle phosphate and fish exports and other commercial traffic. Smaller fishing ports have been constructed at Tarfaya and Boujdour, and installations at Dakhla have been expanded.

As a result of the new urbanization, the old nomadic lifestyle has almost died out. Sahraouis have settled in towns and cities so their children can go to school. Successive droughts, the guerrilla war, and the defense wall with its minefields have greatly reduced the camel herds. I didn't see a single camel throughout my visit, although I visited several oases, where camels were said to graze. Several well-to-do Sahraouis told me that they still keep camels and goats in the desert for weekend family excursions.

Although the population of Western Sahara is the subject of international debate, it has unquestionably increased substantially since the Spanish census of 1974 (74,000). According to official data, the two provinces had a total of around 350,000 inhabitants in 2000, which is probably an undercount. The city of Laayoune alone was estimated at more than 220,000 residents in 2002.

Thousands of Saharan migrants have returned from southern Morocco and Mauritania to take part in the long-delayed UN referendum on independence. Furthermore, there has been an important migration to the territory by "northerners" attracted by jobs and other incentives. Sahraouis do not hide their resentment over official Moroccan "inducements" to attract settlers to the Sahara, although they also benefit from tax exemptions, the 25 percent salary increase for civil service jobs, cheap gasoline (half price), and subsidized foodstuffs. Wherever I went in Laayoune, in government offices, private businesses, and shops, I found a one-to-two ratio, one Sahraoui for two employees from "northern Morocco"—places like Marrakech, Agadir, Erfoud, and Ouarzarzate.

Laayoune has been transformed from a sandy Spanish garrison town into the sprawling capital of the Western Sahara. Overlooking the Saguia el Hamra River, the Old Town is a reminder of the Spanish era with its domed houses originally built for Spanish military and their families, offices, shops, Quonset huts, and Catholic church. Sahraouis used to live on the plateau above the colonial town—tribal dignitaries in luxurious walled villas and the others in poorly equipped housing and *bidonvilles*.

Moroccan offices and lodgings are now located in the Old Town, and the UN personnel use the church. An entirely new city has been built on the plateau around the *Mechouar* (royal parade ground) and the grand Moulay Abdelaziz Mosque. Here are a majestic new convention hall and a sports complex seating 40,000 people, a handicrafts center, two hospitals, numerous schools, and extensive housing developments. On the edge of town, thousands of attractive new villas are empty, waiting for "returnees"—Sahraouis from the POLISARIO camps at Tindouf.

"There was virtually no development here under the Spanish," Governor Abdelatif Guerraoui told me in an interview. Only the port and the administration buildings were electrified in 1975, but now the province has been linked to the national grid. The Spanish used to supply the colony with drinking water from the Canary Islands; now all needs have been met by more wells and desalinization. When the Spanish pulled out, there were only 600 students in schools, and at present there are 56,000.[19]

"Fathers were nomads with camels; their sons will be fishermen with ultramodern boats, and daughters will have jobs in fish canning and frozen fish industries," Guerraoui asserted. He outlined the government's plans, already under way, to expand Laayoune's port, build a new industrial zone, and create six new fishing villages linked to tourism, "which will change the lifestyle of Sahraouis."

The governor acknowledged an unemployment problem, with returning Sahraouis and the influx of northerners. Although 13,000 jobs had been created in the past two years—more than the national average—he estimated the number of unemployed to be about 20,000.

Another unsolved problem is Wahada—the vast, unsightly *bidonville* on the edge of the capital, which mushroomed after the government called on Sahraouis to return in 1991 for the UN-sponsored referendum. At first, the potential voters lived in tents; then, when the registration process dragged on, many put up cinderblock homes in the *bidonville* and are still there.

The United Nations had specified that Sahraouis must register for the referendum at Laayoune, according to Governor Hamid Chabbar, the Moroccan coordinator with MINURSO (Laayoune has two governors). And so the Sahraouis came back by bus and truck, and everybody thought it would take about six months.

"But registration proved to be an extremely complex procedure in a community based on oral tradition and devoid of the usual identity documentation," said Governor Chabbar, a specialist in international law, emphasizing that there had been many irregularities in the identification process.[20]

In the interim, Moroccan authorities were left with thousands of potential voters on their hands and have been running an expensive mini–welfare state in the Sahara, providing them with their basic needs.

Alaouate Edaha, thirty-two, is a Sahraoui who works for the municipality of Tan Tan. He came back to Laayoune in 1991 to register to vote and was accepted on the UN list. Edaha lives at Wahada with his parents, mother-in-law, brother, and five sisters in a large cinderblock hovel with five rooms—but it is extremely hot, and they must share a communal toilet. Edaha has asked to be transferred to Laayoune, but meanwhile, he has to make the four-hour commute to his job in Tan Tan each week and then return for weekends with his family in Wahada. But he doesn't complain. The government provides free water, electricity, and basic food—meat, vegetables, sugar, flour, cooking oil, tea, and milk.[21]

The Moroccan government also offered incentives to "repatriated persons"—Sahraouis who had joined POLISARIO as young nationalists or were kidnapped and forcibly taken to Tindouf and became disillusioned. More than 5,000 have since returned to Morocco and been provided housing. Various organizations help returnees to adjust and screen them for possible POLISARIO agents.

In a sparsely furnished office in the Old Town, I met leaders of the Saharan Tribune for Unity and Fraternity, who facilitate the reintegration of returnees. The assistant treasurer of the association, Zouin Rabiaa, fifty, a portly woman with a loose headscarf, told me her story:

> I was born in Laayoune, and went to Dakhla in 1970 as a newly-wed and there joined the revolution against the Spanish. In December 1975, we were told the Moroccans were going to take over and kill us, and so I joined POLISARIO, with my three children and some friends. . . . my husband stayed behind in Dakhla. They took us in a truck to a camp near Tindouf, where they confiscated all our identity papers and told us we had to fight Morocco and get our independence. They organized us into committees and made us manu-

facture bricks. It was hell—the heat, cold, flies, fleas. My baby died of diarrhea. They sent my daughter to Libya and my son to Cuba, without my consent. I was obliged to marry again and had two more children. . . .

In 1982, there were rumors that Moroccan agents had been detected in the camp. There was a wave of arrests, and I was among the victims. I was kept in an old French military jail for a whole year in a state of suffering and distress. . . . Five years later, I took part in a popular revolt against the POLISARIO and was sent to prison again, where I went through unbearable torture and was threatened with death. Finally, in 1992, I was so afraid of POLISARIO, I escaped and walked across the border to Figuig, where I told the Moroccan police my story. They took me to Rabat, and since then they have given me a house and a new life.[22]

Ahmed Kher is leader of the Association of Parents of Sahraoui Victims of Repression in the Camps of Tindouf. He told me he had joined POLISARIO as a student in 1975, "with a clear idea of freedom." But he soon became disillusioned and says that POLISARIO was more interested in "getting free land not human rights." Shortly after his arrival at Tindouf, Kher was arrested as a traitor, held in POLISARIO prisons for eleven years, and subjected to every kind of torture. He managed to escape via Mauritania in 1995 and settled in Spain with his family. Now, he works for a travel agency that brings tourists from the Canary Islands to Western Sahara.[23]

"Morocco has changed completely since 1990 and gone through a kind of *perestroika*," Kher said. He predicted that if there were a referendum with all Sahraouis taking part, the majority would vote for broad autonomy and self-government. But, he emphasized, Sahraouis must be given positions of responsibility in their native territory and this isn't happening yet. For example, his brother Hamma Baida was elected president of the Laayoune region a year and a half ago but has no power.

Even in the newly relaxed atmosphere, POLISARIO sympathizers are wary about speaking out. There are about 200 hard-core POLISARIO partisans in the area, according to Sahraouis who asked not to be named.

The reason for caution was clear. A few weeks before my visit, the local branch of the Truth and Justice Forum published a report on "The Human Rights Situation in Western Sahara." The accusations against the Moroccan authorities seemed to come from a POLISARIO handbook: alleged acts of genocide, mass graves, Sahraouis thrown from helicopters. The forum leadership in Rabat denounced the report and closed down the Laayoune branch.

The Moroccan press published excerpts from the incendiary report, and the foreign press picked up the story. It was another propaganda victory for POLISARIO.

Not intimidated, several members of the main human rights organizations and the left-wing party, the Organization of Democracy and Popular Action, came to the hotel to talk to me about "the Saharan dossier." Things had changed since Mohammed VI came to the throne, they told me. In fact, they wouldn't have been able to meet me in public a year before. There seem to be new rules. No mass arrests were made after the forum's report. Even the pro-POLISARIO militants of the forum were not jailed and were allowed to go abroad.

The trouble is that any social demands and protest demonstrations are still treated by the local authorities as political incidents, according to the human rights advocates. Under former Interior Minister Driss Basri, strikes and sit-ins were brutally repressed and activists jailed and tortured. Journalists who reported social problems were denounced as working for POLISARIO.

My contacts recalled the demonstrations that had taken place in Laayoune in September 1999 and the following month in Smara, shortly after King Mohammed came to the throne. These were the same kind of protests taking place elsewhere in Morocco—students demanding more financial aid, unemployed college graduates demanding jobs, workers demanding promised raises and benefits, former victims of arbitrary imprisonment demanding compensation. But the local police had reacted violently, beating up the demonstrators, making widespread detentions, and accusing activists of links with POLISARIO. In the wake of the heavy-handed police action, several senior government and police officials were dismissed or transferred. And it was said that the incidents provided the pretext for the removal of Interior Minister Basri.

Since then, the police repression has abated, the sources said, but the atmosphere of intimidation remains, and dissidents are still accused of being "POLISARIO spies." The main improvement has come with the growing influence of the national human rights organizations. Now, when security services show excessive zeal, these organizations investigate the cases and report them to foreign groups like Amnesty International. Thanks to such pressures, a number of prisoners have been freed or acquitted.

In my conversations with many Saharan businesspeople and professionals, however, the main grievance was not about a lack of human rights but rather the invasion of northerners. By this, they meant non-Saharan Moroccans, who have come into the territory, taking jobs and monopolizing the positions of responsibility. The Sahraouis acknowledge that people from

Western Sahara have been named to high positions—state attorney, ambassadors, and governors—but elsewhere, not at home. Local architects and engineers resent the fact that most of the building contracts go to northerners.

I was surprised at the degree to which the local people are attached to their Saharan identity. On any occasion, they would insist that Sahraouis are different from northerners. It was not a political statement but rather a social, cultural, and even economic position.

Many Saharan women said they would not marry a northerner if they could help it. Alia Erguibi, the efficient manager of the Saraline Hotel and daughter of the owner, told me, "I can only marry a Sahraoui, someone with the same traditions. The northerners are too European; they don't share our customs of the extended family, our dress, our food."[24]

"We don't have a problem of women's rights like they do in the north," said Daoudi el Batoul, twenty-seven, who works with AFAK, a Moroccan volunteer organization involved in civic projects and development. "Saharan women don't marry northerners. There's no problem with polygamy here, and men don't beat their wives. Saharan girls can say who they will marry and have a maximum of four children—it used to be eleven. If a girl marries and wants to continue her studies, her mother takes care of the children."[25]

Mohamed Laghdef, a Saharan journalist, likes to say he was born under a tree 150 kilometers southeast of Laayoune. He argues that POLISARIO is not a nationalist movement like the Basques and points to the fact that there have been no attacks or internal resistance in Western Sahara since 1976. A correspondent for *Agence France Presse*, Laghdef holds all of the main players responsible for the current impasse. The Algerians are to blame for stirring nationalist ideas in the minds of El Ouali and his friends, whose original aim had been to liberate the Sahara from Spain. POLISARIO gave Sahraouis false hopes of oil and other wealth, if they got rid of the Moroccans. The Spanish give Sahraouis political asylum, particularly in the Canaries and Catalonia. Also at fault are the Moroccan authorities, who under former Interior Minister Driss Basri, arrested entire families and intellectuals on suspicion of being pro-POLISARIO and refused to engage in a dialogue with Sahraouis. Finally, he criticized the Left and Moroccan political parties in general for neglecting to establish a viable presence in the territory.[26]

"It would not be difficult to resolve the problem with real autonomy within a framework of Moroccan sovereignty," Laghdef said. "There's a current among the exiles who believe that independence is not in the cards and that between two hegemonies, they prefer a democratic Morocco to the military regime in Algeria. What young people want is material security and hope of economic progress and democracy."

Like young people in the rest of Morocco.

A positive sign was the nomination of the independent-minded Laghdef as director of the new Saharan television station, which began broadcasting from Laayoune in November 2004.

The Saharan problem has in fact become part of the broader challenge facing King Mohammed. The question is, has he the courage and determination to pursue the path that he set out in his first Throne Speech and often reiterated since: the construction of a modern, decentralized, democratic state with guarantees for the safeguarding of human rights and freedoms and the preservation of security and stability for all?

Friends, Neighbors, and Others

12

*T*he current American courtship of Morocco can be said to date from that troubled spring of 2002, when President George W. Bush warmly welcomed King Mohammed VI to the White House as a leader of his axis of good Arab states.

Expressing gratitude to Morocco as "a great friend" of the United States, the president declared that he appreciated the king's leadership in the region and "your steadfast support" in the war on terror. And in recognition of this friendship, Bush announced that his administration would work toward a free trade agreement with Morocco that would be beneficial to both nations.[1]

Declaring that he was "honored" by the president's words, King Mohammed said he was prepared to accelerate "our cooperation, our collaboration in all fields" and would work closely to bring about the free trade agreement.

"We are also determined to go ahead with you in fighting terrorism," the monarch pledged, adding that terrorism was a matter of as much concern to Morocco as the United States and "all democratic people in the world."

This meeting marked a new chapter in Morocco's foreign relations, which had been essentially Eurocentric and geared mainly to its former protectors, France and Spain. There followed flattering statements from Washington exalting the strategic relationship with Morocco and a parade of high-level American officials visiting the kingdom to consolidate the friendly relations.

But this budding liaison was not without its risks, as it coincided with the American offensives in Afghanistan and Iraq, increased American-backed Israeli attacks against Palestinians, and the general rise of anti-Americanism in Morocco and other Arab states.

Like other pro-Western Muslim countries—Jordan, Tunisia, and Turkey come to mind—Morocco has walked a perilously fine line between official solidarity with the United States in its war on terrorism and the natural sympathies of the broad public for fellow Muslims, who are seen as unjust victims of American policies.

The Casablanca suicide bombings of May 16, 2003, however, raised serious questions. Were the attacks meant to be a condemnation of Morocco's pro-Western and specifically pro-American policies and conciliatory role in the Arab-Israeli peace process? Or was this a new phase of a radical Islamic moralization campaign? Or another sign of the explosive social atmosphere due to the growing gap between rich and poor?

It was probably all three.

Of Two Worlds

Morocco is the westernmost country of the Muslim world. Its name in Arabic, *Al Maghreb Al Aqsa*, means "The Land Farthest to the West." Although Morocco was exploited by French and Spanish colonialism for more than four decades, the kingdom has looked unambiguously to the West—first to Europe and to a lesser extent to the United States—as its principal economic partner and road to modern progress.

After independence, Rabat joined the Non-Aligned Movement, and for the first few years tried to maintain good relations with the rival camps in the Cold War. In the 1960s, however, King Hassan openly embraced the West, largely because of the Soviet support for Morocco's main rival, Socialist Algeria. Morocco reinforced relations with the West when it became clear that the Soviet Union and its Socialist allies were providing arms to the independence movement in Western Sahara, which is claimed by Morocco.

It must be stressed that Morocco is not another Turkey—that resolutely secular state with a predominantly Muslim population, which has consummated the divorce between mosque and state. Moroccans are by and large devout Muslims, and even convinced leftists steer away from the label of secularism, which is popularly equated with apostasy. Nor has there appeared a Moroccan Ataturk to wrench the country from its Arab traditions and language.

Until lately, the Moroccan establishment saw no contradiction between unabashedly pro-Western political and economic policies and an Islamic identity and solidarity with Muslim causes. Only once since independence did Moroccans face the lacerating choice between East and West—during the process of educational reform. Arabic, the language of nationalism and religion, won hands down over French, the language of the former colonial power. But it has taken a generation to Arabize the system, and even today, those who can afford it tend to send their children to French, Spanish, or even American schools.

When the American president told the people of the world that they must choose sides after September 11, either support the United States in its moral crusade against terrorism or be considered partisans of some shadowy axis of evil and suffer the consequences, Morocco balked.

Morocco had been one of the first Muslim countries to sign up for the war on terror. For their cooperation, Moroccan intelligence agents were invited to take part in the interrogation of terror suspects imprisoned at Guantanamo. As a result, Moroccans tracked down a suspected Al Qaeda cell in Casablanca accused of plotting terrorist attacks on NATO ships in the Strait of Gibraltar. Moroccan security services also uncovered a clandestine network of cells said to be part of a nebulous Islamic extremist movement called Salafiya Jihadia (Combatants for Purity), which was said to be linked to Al Qaeda, and widespread arrests followed.

But Rabat drew the line on the war in Iraq. Official reaction was low-key but firm. There would be no Moroccan forces for the American-led coalition. (King Hassan had provided a contingent of peace keepers to help defend Saudi Arabia in the first Gulf War.) King Mohammed declared that any settlement of the Iraqi crisis "must respect international legality . . . and guarantee the unity and territorial integrity of the Iraqi people."[2] Prime Minister Jettou's government issued a statement expressing "great disappointment" over the use of force in Iraq, adding that Morocco "stands beside our Iraqi brothers in this difficult trial."[3]

It was former Prime Minister Youssoufi, freed from the constraints of office, who voiced Moroccan opposition to the war in Iraq, "whose consequences are incalculable." Addressing a meeting of the Socialist International at Toledo in May 2003, the Moroccan Socialist leader declared: "From Madrid to Rabat, from Athens to Ankara, from Barcelona to Cairo, from Marseilles to Rome, the peoples of the Euro-Mediterranean in an unprecedented near-unanimity have said no to this illegal, illegitimate, and unjust war."[4]

Moroccans took to the streets to denounce "American imperialism" against Iraq. The Moroccan press widely condemned the "American aggression" and praised the French stand against the war. At the demand of all of the political parties, the king postponed local elections from June until September 2003, on the pretext that the country was too emotionally involved in the Iraqi crisis. In reality, the ruling coalition was concerned that there would be a massive vote for the Islamist opposition out of reaction to the war in

Iraq. (The Islamists did eventually make a good showing despite severe restrictions.)

Following in his father's footsteps, King Mohammed has tried to pursue a multidimensional foreign policy, in support of the United States in the war on terror, aligned with France against unilateral interventions in the Middle East, and allied with Muslim countries in support of Iraqi and Palestinian rights. But pressures are building up from all sides for Morocco to take a clear stand.

"If the day comes that we have to choose between our interests with the West and our Islamic sentiments, I don't know where Morocco would come down," a Moroccan diplomat, who used to consider himself pro-American, told me.

The Americans Are Coming

It was common knowledge that Morocco belonged to the French sphere of interest and, to a lesser extent, that of Spain. Whenever Moroccan-American relations did come up, both sides liked to recall that the kingdom of Morocco was the first nation in the world to recognize the United States in 1777 and that the Treaty of Peace and Friendship, signed in 1786, is the oldest unbroken pact of this kind. But bilateral relations had stagnated since except for military aid, and people were loath to talk much about that.

Since independence in 1956, Morocco has turned to its former colonial masters for financial aid, investments, trade, and Western culture. Only briefly, when Moroccan opposition leader Ben Barka disappeared in Paris in 1965, did the close friendship between Rabat and Paris come near to rupture. President de Gaulle was so irate with the Moroccan authorities that he suspended all financial aid, which was not restored until he left office in 1970. During his estrangement from Paris, King Hassan approached Washington for aid, but what he received could not compensate for the loss of French assistance.

Later, when a French reporter asked King Hassan if he had ever considered that the United States could replace France (as Morocco's privileged partner), the king responded categorically, "never," citing reasons of history, environment, and mentality. He went on to say:

> Not for a single instant, even during the protectorate, did we envisage the possibility that Washington could take the place of Paris. The United States is another world; there are oceans to cross; while for centuries, there's been a history of neighborly relations between Africa and Europe, between Morocco and France.

No, frankly, it never crossed my mind because it would have been utopian. Although I think that the French always viewed with favor the American military presence in the region. In fact, the only time when America might have played a role in Moroccan affairs was during the last years of the protectorate. It could have tried to exercise a conciliatory action or curb the influence of the residence. But in those days, America was solely absorbed by NATO and NATO was based at Marnes-la-Coquette.[5]

During the Cold War, the United States considered Morocco to be a strategic ally and continued to provide military aid. But Washington was cautious about consolidating relations with Hassan's regime, which was widely criticized for corrupt and repressive policies by Moroccan political opinion and sectors of the military as well as international human rights organizations. The U.S. ambassador, Richard B. Parker, who served in both Algiers and Rabat, wrote that the CIA had reported in 1979 that the Alaouite monarchy's days were numbered because of its inability to deal with basic social problems.[6]

In the early 1980s, when Morocco appeared on the verge of losing Western Sahara to POLISARIO, the nationalist movement, Washington came through with significant military aid—tanks, armored cars, and aircraft—supposedly not for use in the Sahara. In return, Secretary of State Alexander Haig won an agreement for transit facilities on Moroccan airbases for an American rapid deployment force.

In true Cold War fashion, the Reagan administration gave pro-Western King Hassan a public commitment of support on the Sahara and military aid to counter the Soviet arms received by POLISARIO via Algiers and Tripoli. There was considerable opposition to this pro-Morocco policy in the U.S. Congress and business circles, where Algeria, with its oil and gas, was recognized as an important economic partner. By 1988, when it became clear that the war was not winnable, Washington, like Paris, exerted new pressure on King Hassan to renew relations with Algiers and agree to the UN peace plan.

Aside from its strategic partnership with Rabat, Washington has tended to defer to Paris and the European Union on Moroccan affairs. Total Moroccan-U.S. trade was valued at less than 750 million euros in 2001, whereas Moroccan trade with the European Union exceeded 12 billion euros. Major American corporations are present in Morocco, but have seemed unwilling to take on French predominance. Some American businesspeople complain that they constantly face bias on the part of Moroccan authorities and courts in favor of European rivals. The American embassy acknowledged that even in areas of special concern, like the war on drugs, it was the French and the Spanish who were Morocco's main partners.

With the end of the Cold War, the American government became more critical of Morocco's human rights record. King Hassan responded by relaxing his authoritarian rule in 1991, on the eve of an official visit to Washington.

In the wake of Hassan's liberalization, Washington took another look at Morocco as part of an emerging united North Africa with more than 100 million inhabitants. Signaling interest in a more active role in what was once mainly French territory, the Clinton administration launched the Eizenstat plan in June 1998 to expand U.S. trade and investment in the area. This initiative, named for the U.S. deputy secretary of the treasury, Stuart Eizenstat, was a utopian concept based on the idea of one large North African market with open borders, free trade, common goals, and a Western orientation. The American ambassador to Rabat, Edward M. Gabriel, campaigned tirelessly for the Eizenstat plan, which he described as "a dynamic, multilateral and integrated private-sector partnership, based on a foundation of strengthening economic ties between the United States and the Maghreb region."[7]

The "Maghreb" was a reference to the four countries of formerly French northwestern Africa: Morocco, Algeria, Tunisia, and Mauritania, as well as former Spanish Sahara. North Africans usually include a fifth partner in the Maghreb, Libya.

In view of the continuing enmity between Rabat and Algiers over Morocco's claims to Western Sahara and Algeria's support of the Saharan independence movement, however, it soon became clear to Washington that the formation of a united Maghreb was not feasible without a solution to the Saharan problem.

Thus the United States maintained its low-key profile in the area. The USAID program for Morocco for 1999–2005 was relatively modest, focusing on economic growth, water management, health care, and basic education for girls in rural provinces. James Bednar, head of the program, said that in view of shrinking budgets, the aid program was concentrated on pilot projects in five provinces, introducing new techniques to be replicated elsewhere. Innovations include the drip irrigation system, gender-sensitive training for teachers, home improvement loans, and a streamlined registration process for small and medium businesses.[8]

Other American organizations have been successful in the region, perhaps because they are discreet and small. The Peace Corps, which first came to Morocco in 1963, has about 130 volunteers working outside the main centers. The National Democratic Institute, funded by USAID and the Middle East Democracy Fund, organized programs on voter education and worked with observers in the country's "first free and fair elections" in 2002. Most Moroccans are unaware that the International Human Rights Law Group, which works with a score of NGOs around the country to train local cadres, is a Washington-based nongovernmental, nonprofit organization.

After that meeting with King Mohammed in the Oval Office in the spring of 2002, President Bush launched his new high-profile strategy for United States–Morocco relations, which is based on a free trade agreement like similar accords with Mexico, Canada, Israel, and Jordan. The Moroccan government welcomed Washington's initiative as an important step toward opening new trade, investment, and tourism prospects and disregarded the negative aspects of the lopsided accord.

What Moroccans didn't say publicly was that—as farfetched as it may seem—one of the main reasons behind Morocco's acquiescence to the free trade association was the Saharan problem. Officials privately expressed the hope that with a strengthening of ties between the two countries, the United States would be persuaded to back Moroccan sovereignty over Western Sahara. The United States has a decisive voice in the UN Security Council, which is responsible for finding a solution to the Saharan problem. And the UN envoy to Western Sahara, former secretary of state James Baker, charged with drafting a peace plan, was known to have the confidence of the Bush administration.

The free trade zone talks, held alternately in Washington and Rabat, were highly publicized and stirred considerable controversy. Moroccan critics urged that agriculture be excluded from the talks, noting the risks of being engaged to one agricultural giant (the European Union) and flirting with another. Moroccan newspapers reported the "apprehensions" of different sectors of the economy, like agriculture, textiles, and the fledgling generic pharmaceutical industry. Some Moroccans criticized the secrecy of the negotiations. Others questioned the timing of the United States–Moroccan accord—coinciding as it did with the war on Iraq.

Then, like a jealous husband who catches his wife stealing off for a lovers' tryst, Paris stepped into the fray to remind Moroccans that they already belonged to the European zone. On several occasions, the French minister of foreign trade, François Loos, stressed that any free trade arrangement with the United States would be incompatible with Morocco's European commitments.

In defense of the trade talks with Washington, Moroccan authorities pointed out that they would be complementary to the association accord with the European Union, which they stressed had not made much progress in six years. "What we're hoping to get out of the free trade agreement is more American investments in industries and services," Finance Minister

Fathallah Oualalou told me. He noted that currently 70 percent of Morocco's trade was with Europe and only 4 percent with the United States.[9]

The free trade agreement, however, would prove to be not just another economic accord but the first installment of a highly political project and an integral part of the Bush administration's strategy for a new, friendly Middle East. Some Moroccan political observers were leery about the rapprochement with the United States at a time when it was vilified throughout the Muslim world.

That the free trade association got off the ground at such an emotional time was in part due to President Bush's trusted and persistent ambassador to Rabat, Margaret Tutwiler. At the end of 2002, Ambassador Tutwiler was asked by Moroccan journalists if such trade agreements were a "political gift" for countries that collaborate with the United States. Responding with an emphatic no, Tutwiler noted that Morocco had signed free trade accords with the European Union. Then, confirming the political nature of the new trade agreement, the ambassador stressed that "other countries in the region were not happy" with President Bush's choice of Morocco as the first American partner in Africa.

"After the events of September 11, Morocco demonstrated that it is a country of tolerance which rejects violence and denounces terrorism," Tutwiler declared. "If there was a choice between a nation that has denounced terrorism and another that has done nothing, I think we have made our choice." This, apparently, was a reference to Algeria.[10]

But for Morocco, the choice was a dangerous gamble in an increasingly polarized world.

The French Connection

France and Morocco are closer today than they were in the days of the protectorate. France is Morocco's first trading partner, principal foreign investor, and main tourist market by far. French is the kingdom's first foreign language. There are twenty-nine French government schools and four private establishments, with a total of 18,000 students—the most important network of French schools in a foreign country. French cultural institutes in the principal Moroccan cities provide an important window on Western culture. French newspapers, magazines, and television are the main outlet to the rest of the world—although the Arab TV channels, Al Jazeera and Al Arabiya, have become increasingly important news sources since the American offensives in Afghanistan and Iraq. At the same time, France is the primary destination for Moroccan students, workers, and illegal immigrants. Some

600,000 Moroccans reside in France legally, and it is not known how many live there illegally in precarious circumstances. A stable community of between 25,000 and 30,000 French citizens have made Morocco their home.

This is no ordinary partnership. Although a half century has passed since Moroccan independence, the Moroccan elite still tend to express themselves in French. A significant number of Moroccan authors are more comfortable writing in French. Morocco's best-known writers abroad come from the French school, and their works have become Moroccan classics. Among these are Driss Chraibi's novel on the generational crisis, *Le Passé simple* (1954); Mohammed Khair-Eddine's 1967 novel, *Agadir*; Abdelhak Serhane's *Messaouda*, a 1983 novel of life in a Berber village; and Fatema Mernissi's *Le Harem politique* (1987), long banned in Morocco.

Beside a cultural elite, the leaders of business and industry, the professions, technology, and the administration are generally exponents of French schools. Pierre Vermeren writes that in 2001 half of the 30,000 Moroccans studying abroad were in schools in France (others were in Canada, Spain, and the United States). This has led to a serious brain drain, according to Vermeren, who notes that since the 1990s, about 45 percent of Moroccans graduating from French engineering schools either stay there or go on to North America "where they are often more welcome and better paid." Even worse, he notes, Morocco faces "a veritable hemorrhage" of its French-speaking cadres—doctors, engineers, information experts—who are graduates of the best Moroccan schools but who cannot find suitable jobs at home.[11]

French residents and visitors still feel very much at home in Morocco. Even those who don't speak Arabic can generally get along because the everyday working language in cities is French—Spanish in the north—or often a mix of French and Arabic. Most street and business signs are written in both languages. Popular French institutions like cafes, patisseries, and news kiosks abound. French boutiques, specialty stores, and supermarket chains have begun to make inroads in the cities. In their homes, Moroccans invariably serve French and Moroccan dishes, accompanied by French and Moroccan bread.

Not to be underestimated is the influence of French-Moroccan marriages. The phenomenon is not the subject of public discussion, but occurs with increasing frequency. French women tend to marry Moroccan men rather than the opposite, and usually mixed marriages take place among the educated elite. To mention a few of the more prominent Franco-Moroccan couples: former Prime Minister Youssoufi and his wife, Hélène; Berber leader Mahjoubi Aherdan and his wife, Meriem; *L'Economiste* publisher Abdelmounaim Dilami and his wife, who uses the pen name of Nadia Salah.

Admittedly, the two countries have been through difficult times. But decolonization has been kinder and gentler than in most places. Morocco took over a quarter of a century to Arabize the education system and, even then, some university courses were still given in French. Thousands of French teachers left, but would have been welcome to stay on in the Moroccan system had they so chosen.

While agrarian reform had been a goal of the independence movement, Morocco did not nationalize European (mostly French) lands until 1973. By that time, Europeans had sold more than 1 million acres to wealthy Moroccans, out of a total of 2.5 million acres originally owned by Europeans. The remainder included forest land and some 300,000 acres of farms, whose owners were paid compensation. The Moroccanization of foreign industry and commerce took place in the same year and also occurred without great shocks. The legislation stipulated that at least 51 percent of an enterprise must be under Moroccan control, but it was soon clear that this discouraged foreign investors, and the ruling was eventually rescinded.

This idyllic partnership has been marred to a certain extent by restrictions of the European Union. The promulgation of the 1990 Schengen Treaty virtually closed European borders to unwanted immigrants. Previously, Europe had served as a safety valve, an easy, accessible destination for North Africans seeking jobs or greater freedom. Since Schengen, only seasonal laborers and students from well-to-do families, businesspeople, professionals, and other members of the elite are welcome.

Aware of the negative impact of Schengen on its southern neighbors, the European Union organized a Euro-Mediterranean conference at Barcelona in November 1995. Representatives of the EU met with counterparts from twelve countries stretching from Turkey to Morocco to create a "Euro-Mediterranean partnership." Their vision encompassed not only economic and financial accords, but also closer cooperation in the realms of security and social and cultural matters. Under this agreement, Rabat signed a bilateral accord of association with the EU, the first step toward the establishment of a Mediterranean Free Trade Zone.

Progress toward the construction of this new Mediterranean community has been sluggish. Reviewing the meager results of the Barcelona accord, former Prime Minister Youssoufi declared that the process had produced many failed expectations. Youssoufi, a vice president of the Socialist International, told the group at its meeting in Toledo in May 2003 that the main disappointment was "the absence of real political will" by the members of the EU to integrate the southern and eastern flanks of the Mediterranean into European growth and prosperity. Other frustrations he noted were the omission of agriculture (where the southern countries are competitive) from the free trade agreement, obstructions to freedom of movement in the area, and the modesty and slowness of European aid. He also noted that the failure of Europe to advance the Middle East peace process has progressively poisoned Euro-Mediterranean relations, and this has been aggravated by the Iraqi crisis. The Socialist leader stressed however that there was "no alternative" to the Barcelona process. He made no mention of the U.S. free trade agreement.[12]

On the official level, relations between France and Morocco could hardly be better. Rabat has received firm support from both Socialist and conservative governments in Paris on its key foreign policy concern, Western Sahara. The only shadow in this domain has been the open support shown to POLISARIO by Danielle Mitterrand, wife of the former French president. Successive French governments have stressed that she speaks as a private citizen. By the fall of 2003, even Mitterand's Fondation France Libertés criticized the Saharan nationalists for their abusive treatment of Moroccan prisoners and suspended its aid.

French-Moroccan friendship was cemented at the end of 2002, with the inauguration of the Mohammed V Square on the Left Bank of the Seine, near the Paris Mosque and the Notre Dame Cathedral. It was a stirring homage to the father of Moroccan independence, the monarch France had dethroned and sent into exile. Thanking the mayor of Paris for this honor to his grandfather, King Mohammed VI declared that this square would be for generations to come the reference and symbol of the "ever stronger and permanent relations" between the two countries.[13]

Bilateral relations peaked with the three-day state visit of French president Jacques Chirac to Morocco in the fall of 2003. Chirac, who was accompanied by six cabinet ministers, was enthusiastically welcomed with showers of rose petals, a cannon salute, and effusive words of praise from Moroccan officials and the press as a friend, partner, and ally. In return, the French president hailed the vision of King Mohammed VI who is "resolutely engaged on the path of economic development, social justice, and democracy." Chirac promised to be Morocco's chief advocate in the European Union and, even more important, to support Morocco's latest bid to stage the World Soccer Cup in 2010. He didn't go so far as to call Western Sahara Morocco's "southern provinces" as he had done in 2001, but he did say that France favored "a realistic and lasting political solution, respectful of Moroccan sovereignty and the aspirations of the people."[14]

Morocco's main concern is that one day France should bow to Algerian pressures for the self-determination of Western Sahara. Algeria is a major source of natural gas for France and lucrative contracts for French firms. Up to the present, French governments of the Left and the Right have generally abstained on UN resolutions on the Sahara, indirectly supporting Moroccan sovereignty over the territory.

Behind the warm official ceremonies and rhetoric, however, lies a permanent tension between the two countries, due to books and articles constantly being published in France that are critical of the Moroccan regime. While publications in other countries denounce King Hassan's repressive rule and the signs of a return to such abuses, Moroccans don't read these commentaries or don't care. But Moroccans demonstrate a visceral reaction to each and every negative remark from Paris as an act of betrayal.

There is an emotional link between the French and Moroccan elite, stemming from their common education and recent past. For this reason, the French press regularly pays more attention to Moroccan affairs than does the Arab or American press. By the same token, Moroccans care more about what is said in *Le Monde*, *L'Express*, and *Nouvel Observateur* than in *Al Ahram* or the *New York Times*. There are more French specialists on Morocco who will not bow to taboos and more French journalists who seem to relish disclosing Moroccan warts or skeletons. There are also more Moroccans who publish in Paris because they have something to say to the French public or because they fear dire consequences if they publish at home.

Gilles Perrault's *Notre ami le roi*, a devastating critique of King Hassan's authoritarian rule, nearly caused a rupture in relations between Rabat and Paris in 1990. Numerous books on Ben Barka published in France have kept the case alive. The voluminous 1999 work *Oufkir: Un destin Marocain* by *Le Monde* correspondent Stephen Smith recounts the saga of betrayal by King Hassan's closest aide and gives new details on the king's repressive regime. In 2001, *Le dernier roi*, by another *Le Monde* correspondent, Jean-Pierre Tuquoi, presents King Hassan as a medieval despot and his successor as a weak, capricious, insecure leader with good intentions but dependent on his security apparatus. A delegation of irate Moroccan personalities went to Paris to complain about this fierce attack to leaders of the French press, which only drew more attention to Tuquoi and his book. Ignace Dalle, a former bureau chief for *Agence France Presse*, has written a well-documented work, *Les Trois Rois*, which is very critical of all three Moroccan kings: Mohammed V, Hassan II, and Mohammed VI.

Not to be discounted is the large Moroccan community in France, by and large peaceful and hard-working. Since the early 1990s, terrorist actions have been attributed to Algerian extremists of the Armed Islamic Group, like the hijacking of an Airbus in 1994 and deadly explosions in the Paris metro of 1995. But there was no trouble from Moroccan radicals in France.

Since September 11, however, an increasing number of overseas Moroccans have emerged as suspects in Al Qaeda operations, and French authorities are on the alert. It has become clear that no matter how close France's relations are with its southern neighbor, no matter how forcefully Paris opposes American policies in the Middle East, there is no guarantee against actions by Islamic extremists.

Strains with Spain

In contrast to the excellent rapport with France, Morocco's political relations with its other former colonial power, Spain, have been a succession of ups and downs and mostly downs. Madrid has turned a deaf ear to Morocco's repeated requests for the return of the five Spanish enclaves on the Mediterranean coast. Tension between the two kingdoms has been aggravated by disputes over fishing rights in Moroccan waters, illegal immigration, hashish traffic into Spain from Morocco, and Spain's active support of Saharan nationalists.

Yet Spanish-Moroccan cultural and economic contacts have prospered. Although the Spanish community has been reduced to about 12,000, Madrid has a strong educational presence in Morocco: ten Spanish *colegios* serving a total of 4,200 students through high school, with long waiting lists. In addition, five Cervantes centers provide Spanish-language courses to more than 8,500 adults. Spain provides an average of 12 million euros in economic aid yearly, mainly for the development of the northern provinces, and is Morocco's second trading partner, but way behind France.

At Moroccan independence in 1956, it could have been expected that Spain would become a privileged partner. After all, the two countries had shared thirteen centuries of history, culminating in the advanced Hispano-Moorish culture of Muslim Spain. In modern times, Madrid had refused to recognize the French overthrow of Sultan Mohammed V and allowed Moroccan nationalists to operate from the Spanish zone. Above all, on a human level, Moroccan relationships were generally warmer with Spanish colonials than with the French, perhaps because there were fewer Spanish settlers and the Spanish zone was much poorer. Furthermore, having relinquished the bulk of its overseas possessions, Spain cultivated good relations with the Arab world.

The basic problem between the two neighbors is a clash of nationalisms. Madrid had difficulties in abandoning its last colonial outposts, particularly when the English retained their foothold on Spanish soil at Gibraltar. To retrieve its southern territories from Spain, Morocco employed persistence, political wiles, and secret diplomacy, but still hasn't regained the Mediterranean presidios.

Madrid still contends that Ceuta and Melilla are an "integral part of Spanish territory" and have never appeared on the United Nations' list of non-self-governing territories (unlike Gibraltar). Furthermore, Spanish officials note that Morocco cannot claim sovereign rights to the enclaves because it has recognized Spanish sovereignty over the two cities "either explicitly or implicitly" in a number of international agreements, going back to the 1767 Treaty of Peace and Commerce and including the Joint Declaration of April 7, 1956, ending the Spanish protectorate.[15]

On the other hand, Western Sahara continues to be an important bone of contention between the two countries and has seriously affected their political relations. Unhappy about King Hassan's de facto annexation of Western Sahara in 1975, the Spanish authorities and public have not hidden their support for POLISARIO nationalists. Sahraouis easily find political asylum and help in Spain. Spanish NGOs work with POLISARIO refugees in Algeria. The Spanish press is generally sympathetic to POLISARIO's struggle for independence. Madrid has steadfastly backed the UN settlement plan, which calls for the self-determination of the Sahraouis, a position shared by POLISARIO and Algeria.

Explaining Spanish sympathies for the Saharan nationalists, a senior Spanish official, who requested anonymity, said in the fall of 2003 that Spain feels "a moral debt" toward the Sahraouis. He stressed that Madrid had offered self-determination to the people of Spanish Sahara and should have remained there to supervise the decolonization process. The Spanish official called the Baker peace plan "a splendid opportunity to solve the Saharan issue peacefully and democratically."

It seemed that a new chapter had been opened in the intense relations between the two neighbors when King Mohammed VI was invited by Spanish king Juan Carlos to make a state visit to Madrid in September 2000. The Spanish government hailed the visit as contributing a new dynamism and spirit of cooperation to bilateral relations. Likewise, the semiofficial Moroccan press praised "the atmosphere of understanding and cooperation" between the two monarchs.

But the honeymoon was short-lived. A few months later, to protect its fishing industry, Morocco refused to renew the fishing rights of the European Union, a move which primarily affected the large Spanish fishing fleet. Predictably, there was a rise in tension, and any incident set off a new tit-for-tat crisis. Madrid criticized Moroccan authorities for not doing enough to halt the flow of illegal immigrants into Spain; the Moroccan king retorted that the fault was that of "Spanish mafias." Rabat recalled its ambassador from Madrid in October 2001 over the ongoing disputes and plans for a European Conference in Support of the Sahraoui People in Seville.

Against this backdrop of mounting irritations, the Parsley War broke out in mid-July 2002, catching the world by surprise. Most people had never heard of Parsley Island—Perejil in Spanish, or Leila, as the rocky outcrop is called in Morocco. There is virtually nothing to fight over on the thirty-five-acre islet, inhabited by a few goats and scarcely 200 yards off Morocco's Mediterranean coast. Hostilities broke out when most of Morocco was absorbed in week-long festivities for King Mohammed's wedding. At first it seemed like a poor joke as the country watched the events on national television. Then things took a serious turn, and Moroccans braced themselves for national mobilization against a Spanish invasion.

The story as told in the two capitals differs widely. In Rabat, it was reported that on July 11, a dozen Moroccan gendarmes were dispatched to Parsley to set up an observation post against smugglers, illegal immigrants, and possible terrorists in the strategic waters of the western Mediterranean. When I questioned Moroccan authorities about the timing of this action, they told me privately that several Spanish warships had been patrolling the coast near Melilla, and Morocco had to do something to show the flag.

Official Spanish sources, however, assert that a small group of Moroccan military, presumably without the knowledge of the government but with the approval of the king, had decided to test Spain's resolve over the contested enclaves. Madrid called the Moroccan move "a flagrant aggression" and a prelude to a possible attack against the Spanish enclaves of Ceuta and Melilla. Thus the Spanish navy, army, and air force were dispatched to reconquer the island. The Spanish expeditionary forces successfully tore down the Moroccan flag and raised their own over Parsley and captured the remaining six Moroccan gendarmes (the others had fled).

The Parsley *affaire* looked as though it might spill over with untold consequences. Moroccans held angry protests against the Spanish occupation of Leila and demanded their departure from Ceuta and Melilla. Madrid sent reinforcements to Perejil and its other enclaves. Spain's allies, NATO and the European Union, offered verbal support, and Morocco's allies, the Arab League and the Organization of the Islamic Conference, provided moral backing. But neither side seemed eager for war over the disputed pile of rocks.

Finally, after numerous telephone calls, U.S. secretary of state Colin Powell got the belligerents to stand down. The Spanish troops evacuated Parsley, taking their flag, and Morocco agreed that nobody would occupy the rocky point. The two sides also restored their respective ambassadors and began talking about the whole range of bilateral concerns from drug trafficking and fishing rights to Western Sahara. The world press, which had gotten a wry laugh out of the eight-day Parsley crisis, expressed relief that it was over without casualties. From Paris, *Libération* wrote that at a time when Islamists are threatening holy war against the West, it would be disastrous if a mutual blindness dragged the most moderate Arab country into an absurd conflict with the European country historically most closely associated with the Muslim world.

If the Parsley crisis added up to anything, it was a reminder of the abscesses that continue to jeopardize Spanish-Moroccan relations: Spain's five Mediterranean enclaves, including the ports of Ceuta and Melilla, and the Moroccan-occupied territory of Western Sahara. And it showed the depth of passion between the two neighbors, which seem ready to explode over the slightest provocation.

Eastern Horizons

Anyone looking at the map of Morocco might understandably conclude that this is an Atlantic and Mediterranean country and a long way from the Middle East. A glance at Moroccan trade statistics would confirm such an assumption. France is the kingdom's first partner by far, followed by Spain, the United Kingdom, and Italy, with the United States lagging behind and Russia, the Arabs, and sub-Saharan Africans barely in the race.

As we have seen, King Hassan subscribed to the principle of nonalignment, retaining good relations with the Soviet Union—a major client for Moroccan phosphates—but there was no doubt that his sympathies lay with the West. This became clear in the mini East-West conflict in Western Sahara, which pitted Moroccan forces, armed by the United States and France, against POLISARIO nationalists, backed by Socialist Algeria with arms from the former Soviet Union, Eastern Europe, and China.

In the post–Cold War era, the old alliances have waged a diplomatic struggle over the Sahara. King Mohammed has tried to win friends in the East, particularly Russia. Amid global tensions over American policy in Iraq, the king visited Moscow in October 2002 to launch "a new Russian-Moroccan partnership." Although Vladimir Putin made no public promises on the Sahara, the Moroccan monarch demonstrated that he was prepared to compete with Algeria in the former Communist countries.

It is sometimes said that Morocco is an island, surrounded by the Atlantic and the Mediterranean and isolated from the rest of the continent by a hostile Algeria on the east and the disputed territory of Western Sahara to the south. This is true to a certain extent. The long-enduring Saharan conflict has effectively curtailed the caravan trade with central Africa and hurt Morocco's relations with many of its African neighbors. Morocco has boycotted the Organization of African Unity since 1982, when it admitted the Saharan republic as a member. But in recent years, Morocco has opened its schools to African students, initiated joint ventures in telecommunications with Senegal and Mali, and converted the debts of some of its poorer African clients. Also, thousands of sub-Saharan Africans have managed to cross the desert to reach Morocco's Mediterranean coast, the prime starting point for boatpeople trying to enter Europe. In fact, there has been such a flood of illegal Africans that Rabat has begun to send large numbers of them home.

Morocco's northern route to Algeria, which used to be the main passage for Muslim pilgrims going to Mecca, has been blocked for long periods, first because of the Algerian war for independence, then the Morocco-Algerian border disputes, and since 1992, the Islamic extremist insurgency in Algeria.

In the wake of Moroccan independence in 1956, there was much talk of Maghreb, a union of the four countries of North Africa: Morocco, Algeria, Tunisia, and Libya (Mauritania was not yet included as Morocco had claims to the French territory). Intra-Maghreb relations, however, have been strained since the brief but bloody border war between Morocco and Algeria in 1963, and any serious progress toward union has been blocked by the Saharan question.

The tension between *les frères ennemis*—the enemy brothers—was aggravated by Algeria's open support of POLISARIO nationalists' claims to Western Sahara. In fact, it looked as if the two neighbors would go to war again early in 1976, when Moroccan forces surprised a large unit of Algerian troops at the oasis of Amgala, 155 miles west of the Algerian border. Some 200 Algerians were killed, and 100 were taken prisoner. Algeria claimed that its forces were delivering food and medicine to Saharan refugees, but Moroccans pointed out that they were heavily armed. From that time on, Algeria let POLISARIO guerrillas do their own fighting. Nevertheless, each side periodically accuses the other of allowing the infiltration of Islamic extremists.

On February 17, 1989, the five North African chiefs of state—including Mauritania—met at Marrakech to sign a treaty creating the Union of Arab Maghreb. Various institutions were set up, including a council of the North African chiefs of state, a council of foreign ministers, and a court of justice. There have been a number of meetings of the North African foreign ministers over the years, but Morocco refuses to take part in Maghreb summits until its partners recognize its sovereignty over Western Sahara.

Although this westernmost corner of Africa appears isolated, it is politically an integral part of the Arab world. From the outset, Arab nationalists and states nourished the Moroccan independence movement against the European colonial powers. Since independence, the kingdom has maintained close ties with the Middle East, while preserving its specific tolerant and open interpretation of Islam. This has not been easy.

Initially, Morocco was dependent on Egypt for Arabic teachers but was wary of the spread of Nasserite Socialism and later the rigid Islamist doctrine of Muslim Brothers. At the same time, Libya openly supported the radical leftwing Moroccan opposition to the monarchy. The Moroccan establishment also looked with suspicion on Baathism—Arab nationalist Socialism—as practiced in Syria and Iraq. These political concerns discouraged the expansion of contacts with the Middle East and slowed the process of Arabization in Morocco.

Morocco, however, has a best friend in the Arab world: the kingdom of Saudi Arabia. The strategic alliance between the two monarchies was born in the early 1960s against their common enemy, Gamal Abdel Nasser, and his left-wing pan-Arabism. It was revived in 1979 against the Shiite revolution of Ayatollah Khomeini. It was nurtured in the 1980s by Morocco's struggle against Saharan nationalists backed by Socialist and republican Algeria and in the early 1990s by the first Gulf War against Saddam Hussein. And now, since September 11, 2001, Rabat and Ryad have been allied with the United States in the war against Islamic terrorists.

The Arab kingdoms are linked by more than common adversaries. The petroleum giant has provided Morocco with badly needed oil, financing, investments, and jobs, while Morocco has reciprocated by sending technical cadres and security specialists to Saudi Arabia and offering the Saudis welcoming vacation sites. It was the Moroccan and Saudi monarchs who founded the Organization of the Islamic Conference in Rabat in 1969 in an effort to gain support for the Palestinian cause. The Saudis were said to have contributed billions of dollars in loans and grants for Morocco's war in the Sahara. During the Lebanese civil war in the mid-1970s, pleasure-seeking Saudi princes and businessmen invaded Morocco, buying hotels, villas, and palaces. Many of them stayed on to invest in real estate and the tourism industry. Out of concern over the growing influence of the Left in the universities in the early 1980s, King Hassan made Islamic studies obligatory and imported Saudi teachers and their rigid Wahhabi brand of Islam. When Europe began to close its borders in the 1980s, thousands of Moroccans headed for Saudi Arabia and other Gulf states to find work. In the early 1990s, Saudi king Fahd gave Morocco a grant of $50 million to combat the effects of a menacing oil spill from an Iranian tanker, which in the end did not reach the Moroccan coast. As a tribute to the brotherly relations between Morocco and Saudi Arabia, King Hassan used the money for the construction of the country's first English-language university at Ifrane, named Al Akhawayn, the Two Brothers.

With the death of King Hassan, the close personal relationship between the two monarchies seems to have diminished somewhat. The kingdoms are still bound by a broad range of interests, not the least being the American-led offensive against Islamic extremists. But the relations have been clouded by a number of minor incidents, slights, and snubs, which would not have happened in King Hassan's time. The first public falling out took place during the summer of 2002, when Moroccans arrested three Saudi citizens for belonging to an Al Qaeda cell and plotting terrorist attacks. Reportedly, the Saudis learned about the case through the press.

The cooling of relations only increased after the May 16, 2003, terrorist attacks and the revelations of Wahhabi links to the local terrorist groups identified as Salafiya Jihadia. Although King Mohammed avoided attacking the Wahhabis, he has denounced "foreign" schools of Islam that seek to weaken the unity of Morocco's Malekite school. The trust between the followers of the two schools of Islam has been eroded.

Peace Mediator

Despite considerable criticism from Islamic circles abroad, the late King Hassan carved out a special role as a peace maker on the Arab-Israeli question, enjoying good relations with both sides. When he was still crown prince, Moulay Hassan had permitted the exodus of Moroccan Jews after independence, winning the respect of international Jewish organizations, the Moroccan-Jewish community in Israel, and the United States. On the other hand, King Hassan was proud of his Islamic credentials as a founder of the Organization of the Islamic Conference and head of the Jerusalem Committee to defend Arab interests in the Holy City.

Considering himself empowered as a mediator by the two parties, the Moroccan king invited Israeli leaders, including Yitzhak Rabin and Moshe Dayan, to Morocco for secret discussions. These meetings were said to have laid the groundwork for Anwar Sadat's historic journey to Jerusalem in 1977 and the Camp David peace talks. In 1986, King Hassan met openly with Shimon Peres in the mountain resort of Ifrane to try to resurrect the peace process.

In his memoirs, King Hassan speaks with pride at having brought the Palestine Liberation Organization together with the Central Intelligence Agency in Morocco. He gives few details of the encounter except that it involved "my friend" General Vernon Walters, then deputy director of the CIA. The PLO representative, who is not identified, promised that his organization would not strike American interests from then on. The king recalls that later General Walters had to admit that "the Palestinians keep their word," and the contacts between the PLO and the CIA continued.[16]

King Hassan proved his mettle as an ally of the United States during the 1991 Gulf War, which was overwhelmingly opposed by the Moroccan public and press. The king dispatched a unit of Moroccan troops to take part in the allied force against Iraq—but in deference to Moroccan opinion, he stressed that the Moroccan mission was to help defend Saudi Arabia and not to fight against the Iraqis. He also permitted a mass march in Rabat with angry slogans against Israel and the American bombing of Baghdad.

Meanwhile, Hassan II pursued his discreet efforts to promote the Arab-Israeli understanding, and among his close contacts was Israeli foreign minister David Levy, who is of Moroccan origin. After the signing of the Oslo Peace Accords in 1993, Rabin publicly recognized the Moroccan king for his role in the peace process. The following year, Rabat and Tel Aviv opened liaison offices, which functioned as informal embassies until 2000, when all of the Arab states severed ties with Israel over the degradation of the situation on the West Bank and Gaza. It took all of the monarch's political skills to balance prolonged efforts in favor of the Israeli-Palestinian peace process with the rising anger of the Moroccan public against the West, above all the United States, and what is widely seen as its unfair bias toward Israel.

King Hassan's final act as a peace maker was his own funeral. At the service, Israeli president Eizer Weizman and Prime Minister Ehud Barak had the opportunity to meet with Palestinian chairman Yasser Arafat, Presidents Bouteflika of Algeria and Moubarak of Egypt, and other Arab leaders. President Bill Clinton declared that, with the death of Hassan II, the Middle East had lost "one of the greatest architects of peace."

Early on, King Mohammed VI proclaimed his intention to pursue his father's conciliatory policies on the Israeli-Palestinian conflict. But he has played a less active role on the Middle East scene, and his absence has been conspicuous at various Arab summits. It must be stressed that the situation in the Middle East has not been propitious for peace making.

At home, neither the king nor his government came out in support of the policies of Israeli prime minister Ariel Sharon or the interventions of American president George W. Bush in the Middle East. However, the Moroccan authorities acted to contain anti-American and anti-Israeli demonstrations during the Israeli siege of Palestinian leader Yasser Arafat, the American bombardment of Afghanistan, and the Anglo-American assault on Iraq. The Moroccan press was free to voice its opposition to American and Israeli policies and did so with vehemence. But on several occasions, King Mohammed intervened to warn against blatant anti-Semitism in the Islamist newspapers.

Through this difficult period, Morocco retained its image, cultivated over the years by the monarchy and successive governments, whether led by conservatives, technocrats, or Socialists: the image of a tolerant, moderate Islamic kingdom moving slowly toward democracy and modernity and firmly anchored to the West.

Most Moroccans and the rest of the world were so persuaded of the truth of this image that little attention was paid to a warning in February 2003 purportedly from none other than Osama Bin Laden that pointed to Morocco as one of several Muslim nations with an "apostate" leadership. In a taped message to his followers, broadcast on Arab television, Bin Laden was quoted as saying: "Muslim people must be mobilized to liberate themselves from the apostate regimes enslaved to America, including Jordan, Morocco, Nigeria, Pakistan, the land of the two holy mosques [Saudi Arabia], and Yemen."

Kingdom at the Crossroads

13

May 16, 2003, is one of those defining dates that rearrange a country's landscape. Everything becomes clearer: the divisions in society, the country's strengths and vulnerabilities, the threats and choices.

The unthinkable happened that mild Friday evening in May. Twelve fanatical Moroccans blew themselves to bits, along with thirty-three random victims and any lingering illusions that this country could escape the rage of Islamic extremists. It was the first suicide bombing ever reported in North Africa—even after more than a decade of sectarian violence in Algeria.

The terrifying explosions rang out from the heart of Casablanca shortly after 10 P.M., and it sounded like car bombs going off all over the city center. Casablancans flocked in disbelief to the explosion sites, where people frantically searched for friends and loved ones among the mangled bodies, cries of terror and pain, and mass of fragments of metal, chunks of concrete, and shattered glass.

Human bombs, armed with backpacks full of explosives, had attacked five Jewish and foreign targets almost simultaneously. Four Spaniards, two Frenchmen, an Italian, and twenty-six Moroccans, plus twelve terrorists— all Moroccans—were killed in the blasts, and another hundred persons were wounded.

One of the main bomb sites was the Cercle de l'Alliance Israelite, where a Moroccan watchman and a policeman died. The Jewish club, which had been closed for Shabbat, was badly gutted and the furnishings destroyed. Another target was the deserted Jewish cemetery on the edge of the old Arab *medina* where three Moroccan passersby were killed in the explosion.

The worst carnage occurred in the Casa de España, a Spanish restaurant popular with Moroccans, particularly on Friday bingo nights. The restaurant was crowded when two kamikazes slashed the throat of the guard, forced their way into the central patio, and exploded, killing themselves and a score of diners. Eyewitnesses recounted the horror of burned and mutilated bodies scattered amid the debris and survivors bleeding or without their limbs, struggling to get out of the inferno.

Another group of bombers blew themselves up in front of an Italian restaurant, Le Positano, owned by a Jewish family and located across the street from the Belgian consulate. Three persons were said to have been decapitated by the explosion, and the façade of the restaurant was badly damaged. The fifth target was the luxury Al Farah Hotel owned by Kuwaitis, which catered to Arab tourists, nongovernmental groups, and Israelis at times. A terrorist slashed the throat of the guard, and two explosions at the hotel entry shattered the large bay windows and destroyed the ceiling of the reception hall, causing a number of casualties.

The destruction might have been worse, but three of the original fifteen zealots had second thoughts and got rid of their backpacks before they exploded. The failed bombers were promptly apprehended and were said to have provided valuable information to the authorities about the terrorist network in Morocco.

The Moroccan security forces did what they do best: they set up roadblocks, cordoned off targeted areas, rounded up suspects, made numerous detentions, and carried out interrogations. This time, they had almost free rein to pursue their investigations. The politicians, press, and public were virtually unanimous in condemning the aggression by Islamic radicals, whose principal aim seemed to be to destabilize a society that they considered too open, too modern, too Western.

Two months later at their trial before a Casablanca court, the three surviving kamikazes appeared contrite and confused. They were in their twenties, barely literate, fervent Muslims who came from the desolate shantytown of Sidi Moumen on the outskirts of Casablanca. All claimed to have been forced to take part in the assault under threat by the group leader, an unknown zealot named Abdelfettah, who had died in the attack.

From the prisoners' glass cage, Mohamed Omari, twenty-three, a night watchman, insisted that he had gone along with the group only because he feared reprisals against his family. He denied belonging to Salafiya Jihadia but confessed that he had joined the group of Islamic radicals called the Righteous Path, led by Miloudi Zakaria. "It was then that I began to think about *jihad*," he said.

Omari recounted that fourteen volunteers had gathered at his house the day before the attack and watched an Arabic videocassette called *Paradise and Hell*, which showed the horrible fate in store for unbelievers and the pleasures reserved for martyrs. He admitted that the backpack bombs had been assembled in his home, but gave no details as to where the explosives had been obtained or who had paid for them.

Declaring that he hated Jews "because of all the evil they are doing to Palestinians," Omari told the court that he had believed his group was going to attack a meeting of Jews at the Hotel Farah. "But on reaching the hotel," Omari said, "I looked inside and saw only Muslim brothers, and so I threw away the backpack and ran." However, witnesses said that Omari's backpack had failed to explode, and he tried to set fire to a bottle of inflammable liquid, but was stopped by hotel guests.

Despite their show of remorse, the three survivors and a "suicide reservist" were sentenced to death. Miloudi Zakaria, head of the Righteous Path and the only Islamic ideologue to applaud the May 16 attacks, was sentenced to life in prison. Three radical Islamic theoreticians received thirty years, and seventy-eight other militants were convicted of links to the attacks or plans for similar actions and given heavy jail terms.

From the outset, Moroccan officials contended that the suicide bombings were the work of foreigners; the foot soldiers were Moroccan, but the commanders were abroad. Minister of the Interior Mustapha Sahel told journalists that the attacks "bear the signature of international terrorism." Although the security services continued to make sweeping arrests among radical Islamic groups in the weeks and months that followed, they were unable to come up with proof of links to Al Qaeda. There were no claims of responsibility for the atrocious deeds, no specific demands of the authorities, and no explanation for what the Muslim extremists hoped to achieve.

The small group of suicide bombers has in many ways changed the course of the kingdom. Their action has soured the public toward radical Islam and rendered moderate Islamists suspect. It has strengthened the hand of the modernists on controversial issues like women's rights. But it has also jeopardized the country's faltering progress toward democracy.

For the first time, the Moroccan public realized that Islamic extremism was a serious threat to the kingdom. Morocco could no longer claim to be an island of moderation, whose people are united around an enlightened monarch leading them to equity and well-being. The coordinated offensive by Islamic extremists revealed that a sector of the population is fiercely opposed to the regime's project for gradual progress toward a modern, Western-type democracy.

King Mohammed was outraged. Terrorists had taken advantage of the extensive public freedoms in Morocco and betrayed the country and the people, the king charged. It would not happen again, he warned. What he called "the era of laxity" was over.[1]

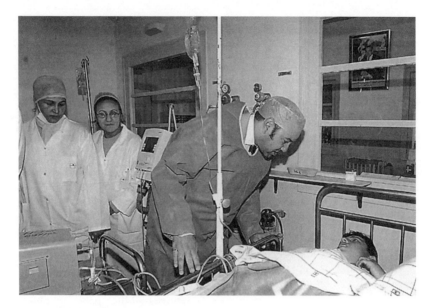

*King Mohammed VI, wearing a doctor's coat, visits a wounded
man after the May 16, 2003, Casablanca terrorist attacks.
(copyright Ali Linh/MAP)*

The Casablanca suicide bombings posed several key questions. How
deeply had Moroccan society been penetrated by radical Islamists with their
message of hatred, violence, and revolt? Where were the security services—
that widespread and repressive machine inherited from King Hassan's days,
which had already been reactivated for the war against terrorism? And how
would King Mohammed VI, who had tried to initiate a less authoritarian
way of governing, react to the brutal assault on the traditional Moroccan values of tolerance and coexistence among Muslims, Jews, and foreigners?

The Nation Speaks Out

The Casablanca attacks affected everyone, and almost everyone had something to say about the causes of the terrorist bombings and what to do about
Islamic extremism—in the press, in opinion polls, on the worldwide Web,
in seminars, and through their votes. As in the United States after September
11, 2001, a surge of patriotism was followed by heightened concern for law
and order. In this feverish atmosphere, only isolated voices warned against
witch hunts and a return to past human rights abuses.

"Everybody condemned the Casablanca attacks because this kind of suicide bombing is not Moroccan," explained an old Moroccan friend, who is a clerk in a Casablanca firm. He gave several causes for the attacks: the hopelessness of life in the *bidonvilles* where the terrorists came from, the official tolerance of local preachers who propagate hatred, television's promotion of suicide attacks in Russia and Israel, and the West's pro-Israeli double standard in the Middle East.

On May 25, more than a million people from the main political parties and nongovernmental organizations and a contingent of more than a thousand Moroccan Jews marched peacefully through downtown Casablanca under banners saying, "Don't Touch My Country." Organizers said it was the largest gathering since independence—and the main Islamist groups were not present. The Islamist Justice and Development party issued a communiqué supporting the demonstration, but some NGOs and political parties declared that Islamists were not welcome to march with groups that "defend a democratic society."

On the other hand, there was a wave of public sympathy for the tiny Jewish community of Casablanca, which appeared to be the primary target, although no Moroccan Jews were killed on May 16. King Mohammed met with Jewish community leaders at the badly damaged Jewish social club on the day after the attacks. Hundreds of Moroccan Muslims and Jews took part in a sit-in front of the Cercle de l'Alliance, carrying posters saying: "All Moroccans," "No to Terrorism, No to Intolerance."

"At first we were in a state of shock," said Boris Toledano, president of the Casablanca Jewish Community, which numbers about 2,500 out of a total of 4,000 Jews in Morocco (down from 300,000 at independence). He said the community had received reassurances and numerous messages of solidarity from Moroccan political parties, associations, and ordinary citizens.[2]

The independent daily *L'Economiste* asked viewers on its Website: should the PJD be banned? The newspaper reported that out of hundreds of responses, the majority favored the dissolution of the Islamist party on the grounds that political violence should not be tolerated—nor should those who condone it. Those who opposed a ban argued that the PJD had condemned violence and should not be closed in the name of democracy.[3] In another poll, 40 percent said the PJD should be banned, while 37 percent were against the banning.[4]

In the general mood of anxiety, the ever-vigilant Moroccan Association of Human Rights made public its annual review of the situation, concluding that there had been "a serious regression" in human rights since May 2002, including a return of kidnappings, disappearances, and torture. While condemning "the barbaric acts" committed in Casablanca, the association accused the government of profiting from popular concern to pass the antiterrorist law, "which is a major step backward." The human rights group also denounced other "regressive legislation," including the new Press Code and the Law on Associations. But theirs was an isolated voice in the broader clamor for security.

The Casablanca public showed extraordinary resilience in the wake of the May 16 assault. A few weeks after the tragedy, Casablancans were flocking to their favorite restaurants for lunch although it took a little longer to resume their active nightlife. "We were all shocked by the violence, particularly by the kamikazes," said Zeinab Benchakroun, a young mother of two who works for an insurance company. "Sure, we're scared of another attack, but we're not going to let it ruin our lives."

The initial emotional reaction was followed by public soul searching as to the causes of the suicide attacks. In a seminar in Rabat a month after the bombings, Driss Abbadi, professor of law at Mohammed V University, stressed that the root cause of the violence was poverty—12.5 million poor and 5.3 million living on less than ten *dirhams* or about $1 a day. "This latest violence involves economically vulnerable youths, desperate, frustrated delinquents, who have been recruited by religious extremists," Abbadi said.[5]

Also addressing the seminar, Simon Lévy, a dissident member of the Communist Party for Progress and Socialism, blamed the Left for failing to do anything to improve the lives of the masses. The left-wing parties, the labor unions, and the Socialist-led government of *Alternance* were responsible for the vacuum of leadership in the *bidonvilles*, which was being filled by Islamists, Lévy said. Another speaker, Rachid Belmokhtar, president of the elite Al Akhawayn University, acknowledged that the faulty education system was partly responsible for the suicide bombers. Emphasizing the "shameful" inequalities of education, he noted that while the children of the rich go abroad to study, there are still child maids in Morocco who can't go to school at all.

At a Berber studies group, Hassan Aourid, the royal spokesman, criticized intellectuals for accepting Islamist exhortations to murder as commonplace. Young Moroccans, he said, were attracted to the Islamist discourse because of a loss of confidence in politics and the political leadership and "imported ideas" like revenge against Israel and the United States. "To understand the spread of suicides, melancholia and depression," Aourid said, "it's necessary to look at the suicides in the Strait of Gibraltar ... those boatpeople who didn't have anything to lose except their lives."[6]

For a while it seemed that the nation was ready to come to grips with the deep underlying social, economic, and political problems that have nourished the young Islamic extremists. There was a general realization that Islamic extremism is not merely a security problem. In Morocco, as in other Muslim countries from Algeria and Egypt to Turkey and Pakistan, it is first of all the failure of Western-oriented governments to respond effectively to the problems of daily life that has favored the spread of political Islam. But also radical Islamic organizations, which have taken root in these disaffected Muslim societies, have benefited from American policies perceived to be anti-Islam, like support for the repressive regimes of the former shah of Iran and Israeli prime minister Sharon and the assaults against Afghanistan and Iraq.

The Silence of the Bidonvilles

"Before May 16, the women of Sidi Moumen didn't dare sing or listen to music or dance in their own homes," said Fauzia Assouli, national secretary of the Democratic League for Women's Rights. She recounted how these women were afraid to hold wedding feasts or even go out of the house alone. They had seen neighbors tried and executed by Islamic fanatics, and they lived in terror under the dictates of radical Islamists, long before Sidi Moumen attracted national attention for spawning the May 16 terrorists.[7]

"We knew the *bidonvilles* of Sidi Moumen were the fief of Islamic extremists, and that's why we had planned to take our caravan there to encourage the women to come out of their homes and talk about their problems," Assouli told me. By pure chance, the caravan was to have taken place on the weekend of May 17–18. It was postponed because of the terrorist attacks, but did happen a month later.

On June 14, the league set up tents in four of the *bidonvilles* and was able to contact some 8,000 women that weekend. The task force of doctors, lawyers, jurists, students, and activists of other NGOs organized workshops and forums, gave consultations, and held consciousness-raising sessions on women's rights. Assouli said the local religious leaders had indoctrinated men with the idea that woman—mother, wife, or daughter—was "Satan, the enemy." Since the caravan, some women from Sidi Moumen have come for help to the league's Women's Information and Observation Center in downtown Casablanca, she stressed.

The commune of Sidi Moumen boasts the largest conglomeration of *bidonvilles* in the country with an estimated population of 220,000 living in ugly cement or wood shacks with tin roofs. None of the political parties, not even the mainstream Islamist parties, had offices there but they would rent premises at election time. Nor did the main nongovernmental organizations have a permanent presence there. But radical Wahhabi associations were active in the area, according to local journalists.

Barely a month after the attacks, a new national left-wing association,

Democracy and Modernity, organized a conference with the commune of Sidi Moumen on "the role of civil society and young people." The gathering of representatives from civic organizations, students, parents, artists, and other intellectuals rejected all forms of Islamic extremism and discussed ways to help young people become active participants in a modern society threatened by terrorism and violence.

Ironically, the first government agency to move into Sidi Moumen after May 16 was a police station, with services to handle traffic accidents, identification documents, and patrol the neighborhood.

"The main problem of the *bidonvilles* is the vacuum, the absence of social, political, or human support groups," said Mohamed Belam, whose family has lived in the *bidonville* of Sidi Othmane since 1954, and whose aunt resides at Sidi Moumen, not far away. In 1981, the Belams scraped together 10,000 *dirhams* ($1,000), which they paid to be included on the list for public housing, but they are still waiting.[8]

A quiet, neatly groomed man of thirty-one, Belam is studying for his doctorate in mathematics at Casablanca's Hassan II University. He hopes to become a professor but realizes it won't be easy to get a job. "You have to know people . . . and who does a guy from the *bidonvilles* know?" He escaped

Mohammed Belam (left) visits his mother and brother in the family's neat, crowded home in the Sidi Othmane bidonville after the May 16 attacks. The suicide bombers came from a neighboring shantytown.

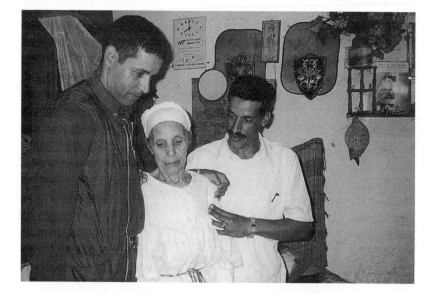

Sidi Othmane a couple of years ago when he got married and now lives with his wife and child in a one-room flat, thanks to his wife, who works as a seamstress in a sweatshop. In the summer, when school is out, he does odd soldering jobs to make ends meet.

"That's our historical monument," Belam smiled as we passed Sidi Othmane's fortress-like cinema. He recalled that, at three *dirhams* (thirty cents) a seat, movies were prohibitively expensive when he was growing up, working as a shoemaker's assistant and as a freelance house painter to help with family expenses. Leading me through the maze of alleyways to his family home, Belam pointed out the public fountain, public toilets, and public transportation—donkeys. Some 3,800 families, or about 20,000 people, live in this *bidonville*, mostly in shacks of wood and cardboard, concrete or cinder blocks, with tin roofs held down by stones.

Belam's mother raised five sons in the two-room house which she now shares with her son Saïd, his wife, and their two young children. Saïd, forty, a professional painter and plasterer, had moved to Tangier, where he made a decent living. But in 1995, he fell from a third floor, breaking his jaw, a leg, and an arm. His certificate of indigence covered six months in the hospital, but would not pay for an operation. His leg healed on its own, leaving him with a limp and unable to do heavy work. While he was laid up for two years, his wife worked, but the money ran out, and so they came home to Sidi Othmane.

The Belam residence is better than most because Saïd has made improvements: a hard floor with chunks of marble from a construction site, a Turkish toilet, and a makeshift balcony for the children's bedroom. They have electricity and even sewers, which the *bidonville* residents fought for and finally got in 2001. Saïd admits that going to the public fountain is an inconvenience because of the long lines, so usually he waits until midnight to get water. The family's only luxury is a large television set that takes up most of the living room; it was purchased in association with ten neighbors at 100 *dirhams* ($10) a month.

Mohammed Belam recalls that "the bearded ones" came into the *bidonvilles* in 1997, bringing some hope. At first, they offered odd jobs and other assistance, but when they began to recruit small children, people became alarmed. Residents of Sidi Moumen warned the police about the *intégristes*, but the police said things were under control. "In fact, the only time we saw a policeman at Sidi Moumen, he would be waiting behind a tree to catch cyclists without a helmet and then pocket the fine," Belam remarked wryly.

Belam has clear ideas as to what should be done about the Islamic extremists in the *bidonvilles*—and it is not to wipe out the shantytowns or the Islamists. "What is needed is reeducation and severity with wrongdoers," he stressed. Pointing out that 80 percent of the *bidonvilles'* inhabitants are illiterate, he said that people must be taught to read and be responsible. And, he stressed, all thieves must be punished—robbers, hospital personnel, policemen.

"We don't need a change of government or a change of system but a change of mentality, so people no longer think only of themselves," Belam said with a shrug, indicating that he thought there was little chance of this happening. Both he and his brother admitted they had voted blank in the last legislative elections because they don't trust the political parties.

It was this feeling of alienation that I sensed in the *bidonvilles*, especially from people like the Belams who had gotten out for a time. No wonder the Islamic radicals had found easy recruits for the suicide bombings, with their promises of paradise. More than tearing down and replacing entire communities of unhealthy, defective lodgings, the challenge of the *bidonvilles* is essentially how to give their inhabitants a voice, a feeling of belonging to the society.

The Hardliners

"Morocco will not go the way of Algeria; that's a certainty," a senior Moroccan security official, who asked not to be identified, asserted with conviction. What he meant was that Morocco would not let Islamist extremists get out of control, nor would the government carry out a policy of systematic repression, which has engendered a vicious cycle of violence in Algeria.

In the wake of the May 16 cataclysm, most Moroccans seemed to accept the need for strong security measures to quash the increasing violence of radical Islamic groups. General Hamidou Laanigri, head of the Direction de la Surveillance du Territoire—the Moroccan equivalent of the FBI—who had been vilified for magnifying the Islamic terrorist threat, now appeared vindicated.

Mr. Security, as the large, affable Laanigri is known, was the man responsible for dismantling the Al Qaeda sleeper cell in Casablanca in the spring of 2002 and later arresting a group of Islamic fanatics known as the Righteous Path, who were accused of murder and other crimes. The trouble is that when the cases came to court, there was little evidence of crime, aside from questionable confessions, and so even the Al Qaeda suspects received relatively light sentences of ten years in prison.

Some skeptical voices in the independent press had accused General Laanigri of "paranoia" and "fabricating plots." Now they faulted the security services for incompetence in not averting May 16. "Where were these security services, these thousands of agents, whose chiefs boasted of controlling the population?" asked Khalid Jamai in *Le Journal*, calling for investigations into failures of the security services.[9]

It was a question I was to hear again and again from businesspeople, human rights advocates, and ordinary citizens. How was it that the security services, known for their zeal and efficiency, were not aware of what was happening in Casablanca?

"We did know the *jihadists* were planning something, but the real problem is—when do you clamp down?" retorted the security official who had requested anonymity. He said it was the same problem other police services face in the war against terrorism, the problem of proof. If they wait until the suspects are ready to place the bomb, it is often too late.

The new antiterrorism law has facilitated the task of the police because it introduced the concept of preventive action, the official stressed. The legislation had been presented to parliament in December 2002, remained blocked until the May 16 attacks, but was passed a few days later.

In several off-the-record conversations with high-level security cadres during the summer of 2003, I learned that Moroccan intelligence services had been tracking radical Islamists for six years, ever since some 250 *jihadists* had returned from Afghanistan. The young *jihadists* began to form cells in the main cities around the country, but there was no central command. "It was like a corporate holding," one official commented.

They were all inspired by Salafiya Jihadia—a synthesis of the militant political creed of the Muslim Brothers and the religious rigor of Wahhabism, according to the security sources. The Brotherhood was a secretive, anti-Western association founded in 1928 by Egyptian revolutionary Hassan al Banna, which spread across the Arab world to become the first mass Islamist movement in modern times. Wahhabism, as I have noted, is a fundamentalist, intolerant form of Islam, developed at the end of the eighteenth century by Sheikh Muhammad Ibn Abd Al-Wahhab, linked to the ruling Al Saud dynasty of Saudi Arabia.

The security officials claimed that recent arrests were specifically targeted. They said the brunt of the police action had been directed against Salafiya Jihadia for advocating the violent overthrow of the monarchy and its replacement by a radical Islamic regime. Yassine's Al Adl wal Ihsane, which excludes violence, was not a target, the sources stressed, although some *jihadists* "had passed through the sheikh's movement."

The *jihadists* and their local ideologues—many of whom have been arrested—openly consider Osama Bin Laden a hero, Moroccan security sources stressed. The more virulent militants took up banditry. If a cell de-

cided on a *jihad*, the self-proclaimed leader would issue a *fetwa*, and all means were valid, including murder, robbery, and selling drugs to "benefit the *jihad*."

Other measures taken by the police included the closing of a hundred Wahhabi schools and the seizure of thousands of books and cassettes that propagated the Wahhabi doctrine. "We will suppress all traces of Wahhabism in this country," one official said.

The minister of justice, Mohamed Bouzoubaa, announced in August 2003 that a total of 1,042 suspects, including 2 Frenchmen and a British citizen, had been arrested in connection with the May 16 events. Most of them were said to belong to Salafiya Jihadia or its factions, and 11 were identified as belonging to the Al Qaeda network.

Never before had Moroccan justice worked with such speed and efficiency. The courts turned out verdicts like an assembly line. By early October, there were sixteen death sentences, dozens of lengthy prison terms, and almost no acquittals. Most suspects pleaded innocent to the charges and claimed their confessions had been extracted through torture. The convictions were mainly for belonging to Salafiya Jihadia and allegedly planning to carry out terrorist attacks similar to those of Casablanca in other cities.

A major weakness of the state's case was the fact that the principal defendants denied the existence of Salafiya Jihadia. Independent Islamic experts agreed, emphasizing that Salafiya Jihadia was a trend—not an organization. Some journalists covering the trials said it was like going back to *les années de plomb*—mass arrests and numerous convictions on nebulous charges of plotting against the state.

Only this time most Moroccans failed to protest against the severe sentences and police abuses. Protest was clearly not politically correct when the country seemed under siege. By and large, the Left and women, who have been directly targeted by radical Islamists, approved of the strong police measures. Devout conservatives also favored stiff sanctions against Islamic extremists, who they said had "distorted" the message of Islam. As for the moderate Islamists, they had been generally cowed into approving whatever the regime did or at least not standing up in protest.

Moroccan hardliners do not go so far as to espouse the Algerian policy of "eradication," that is, the physical elimination of Islamic extremists, which has only encouraged more violence. But there is the same odd alliance of security forces, the democratic Left, and women activists, who have led the fight against radical Islam in Algeria, Turkey, and elsewhere.

An important sector of the Left is persuaded that even the "moderates" of the PJD must be excluded from political life. Women's groups and Socialists, in particular, argue that the PJD, through its rhetoric of intolerance of Western influences, was in part responsible for the spread of Salafiya Jihadia. Driss Ben Ali, president of the Alternatives association, said openly that the PJD was guilty of spreading "the ideology of hate" and should be eliminated from politics. But he emphasized that Morocco must heed the lessons of Algeria and not respond to hatred with security measures only but proceed with necessary social reforms.

One outspoken foe of Islamic extremists, Mohamed El Gahs, secretary of state for youth and managing editor of the Socialist newspaper *Libération*, told a meeting of the party's young militants that Morocco has been divided into two camps since May 16: "*Salafi* terrorism" and "pro-life solidarity, tolerance, and democracy." Another Socialist journalist, Jamal Berraoui, has written in *Libération* that the security services must be given all necessary means and public support "to root out this cancer."

Leading women's organizations, which had long opposed cooperation with the Islamists, felt vindicated. Latifa Jbabdi, a left-wing activist and president of the Union of Feminine Action, declared, "We must no longer tolerate intellectual terrorism and even less, give into it." In an interview with the progovernment daily *Le Matin du Sahara*, Jbabdi said that *intégristes* had used "intellectual terrorism" to intimidate or prevent women from obtaining their basic rights. They had gone so far as to issue *fetwas* to condemn women to death and incite violence and crime against them. They even attacked young girls with knives to force them to wear veils.[10]

At the end of July, King Mohammed cast his own bombshell onto the scene. General Laanigri was transferred from the DST—Morocco's FBI—to become director general of the Department of National Security. Questions were rampant: was this punishment for letting May 16 happen or for the return to the old practices of human rights abuses? Or was it a promotion for being right about the danger of Islamic extremists?

The most plausible explanation for the security changes came from *TelQuel*'s Driss Ksikes, who wrote that "the optimists" who interpreted General Laanigri's new job as a way of bringing him to heel, were mistaken. Noting that the general was succeeded at the DST by two of his close aides, Ksikes stressed that the move could be seen as an attempt to improve coordination of the security services. It was, he said, a lesson learned from "our American mentor"—meaing U.S. Secret Services who have largely influenced Laanigri.[11]

This view was confirmed by diplomatic sources, who said that the transfer of Laanigri was designed to produce more transparency and cohesion in the police. They stressed that the king trusted Laanigri.

Under strong man Laanigri, there was no let-up in the crack-down on suspected Islamic extremists. By the time of the Madrid train attacks of March 11, 2004—blamed mainly on Moroccans—the official Moroccan tally had risen to 5,000 persons arrested on suspicion of terrorism and 1,500 tried and jailed—and the raids and detentions were continuing.

Vigilance and Mobilization

Since the May 16 suicide bombings, King Mohammed VI has demonstrated that his main priority is national security and the enemy is Islamic extremism. Democracy would have to come later. Mohammed VI has clearly opted for Hassan II's sweet-and-sour strategy, cracking down on dissidence and tightening public liberties, while accelerating economic development. King Mohammed, however, emphasizes the need for social improvements and has won the support of sectors of the population that had opposed his father—Socialists, Communists, and women.

In his first speech after the Casablanca attacks, King Mohammed lashed out against the suicide bombers and their chiefs as "ignoble villains who in no way can claim to be Moroccans or genuine Muslims." While reiterating his goals of democracy and modernity, the king emphasized: "The hour of truth has come and [it is] the end of the era of laxity regarding those who exploit democracy to undermine the authority of the state and those who sow the thorns of ostracism, fanaticism, and discord."[12]

On the king's orders, the security services made sweeping arrests among the known radical preachers and their followers. Before May 16, there had been considerable criticism in the independent press and human rights circles of the emphasis on security concerns and the alignment with the U.S. war on terrorism. Afterward, most of the political establishment came out in support of the regime's firm measures against terrorism even at the sacrifice of some individual freedoms.

Parliament unanimously approved the stringent new antiterrorism law, which rolled back certain public liberties. Earlier, the same bill had been criticized as abusive by all of the political parties. The law provided stiff penalties, including the death sentence, for terrorism-related crimes, from the possession and transport of arms and explosives to falsifying documents and extortion. The authorities have been given greater latitude to make searches, telephone taps, and mail and electronic surveillance. The period of preventive detention has increased from forty-eight to ninety-six hours and can be renewed twice.

King Mohammed reiterated his tough new stance against Islamic extremism in his Throne Speech on July 30, 2003, denouncing imported doctrines as "alien to Moroccan tradition." The monarch emphasized that for fourteen centuries, Moroccans have practiced the flexible Malekite rite of Islam, under the leadership of their own Commander of the Faithful and independent of the caliphate and Eastern rites. Therefore, he stressed, the country "cannot tolerate" the importation of foreign doctrines "incompatible with Moroccan identity." Reaffirming his position as Commander of the Faithful, consecrated by the *beia* and confirmed by the constitution, the king declared there could be no other religious reference for the nation and no party or group could present itself as a representative of Islam.[13]

Later, I questioned a senior government official about how Morocco could reconcile imposing the "uniformity of the Malekite rite" with its democratic ambitions. I was told that the king's declaration should be seen as a prohibition of other religions or schools of Islam, such as Wahhabism, to make propaganda in this country. There was no public reaction to the king's harsh words, but it was generally acknowledged that these were extraordinary times and required strong measures. Moroccans were not about to question firm action taken to defend the national rite against "criminals" who committed acts of terrorism in the name of religion and the ideologues who preached "foreign" doctrines advocating violence.

There was also little protest when the courts handed down multiple death sentences and scores of lengthy jail terms for persons implicated in the May 16 terrorist attacks. Nor were there many complaints when prominent radical clerics received twenty- to thirty-year prison sentences for "incitation to murder and participation in the preparation of terrorist acts."

A delegation from the International Federation of Human Rights, however, sounded the alarm after its investigation into human rights against the background of the fight against terrorism. While condemning the terrorist attacks, the federation noted the discrepancy between the official statistics of 2,000 arrests and the 5,000 cited by local human rights sources. Patrick Baudouin, a lawyer and former president of the federation, said the delegation had received numerous complaints of ill treatment and torture during the police investigation and was specifically concerned about the unexplained deaths of two suspects in custody. Noting the "unusual haste" of the trials, the human rights team pointed to the weak defense by court-appointed lawyers and questioned the value of confessions "made under threat or after inhuman treatment."[14]

Emphasizing the need for firm security measures, the king declared that the "real battle" is against underdevelopment and ignorance. The terrorist attacks focused attention on the explosive situation in Morocco's urban slums. It was no coincidence that the suicide bombers were jobless youths living in the shantytown of Sidi Moumen on the outskirts of Casablanca.

Shortly after the Casablanca attacks, the government announced ambitious social reforms, clearly aimed to diminish the influence of Islamists in areas where they had made significant inroads. The Ministry of Social Habitat made public a major housing program for Casablanca with a special focus on Sidi Moumen. A project costing $820 million would include 64,000 low-cost dwellings, two hospitals, ten schools, three mosques, three football fields, a youth center, and other amenities. King Mohammed went personally to lay cornerstones of future low-cost housing developments in several slums in the Casablanca area. With uncommon frankness, the monarch recalled that he had warned against the spread of these unhealthy slums in August 2001, but since then the *bidonvilles* had proliferated.

During the summer of 2003, the palace also demonstrated its concern over the youth problem. The World Youth Congress, held at Casablanca in August, took on new importance after the terrorist attacks. The gathering of a thousand young people from some 150 countries and 300 NGOs was seen as a vote of confidence in Casablanca. It provided King Mohammed with a platform to address his favorite theme: the role of Morocco as "a bridge between continents and civilizations, a living model of religious and cultural coexistence." Warning that the economic disparities between the north and south could be used to spread extremism, the monarch called for a general mobilization to reduce "the plague of poverty."[15]

On the national front, King Mohammed announced the creation of a permanent commission to give new impetus to the reforms under the National Education Charter and review all programs and curricula. In what amounted to an admission of failure of past reforms, the king stressed that the system must be ready by the 2004–2005 school year to provide new generations with "a modern and quality education."

In an immediate action, the secretary of youth, El Gahs, organized a program of "Vacations for All," clearly aimed at potential recruits for radical Islam. More than 100,000 young people, mostly from poor families, benefited from two-week holidays at the seashore or in the mountains, plus civics lessons.

The king and his government also came under new pressure to carry out economic reforms. The staid business monthly *Economie et Entreprises* mocked the prime minister for declaring it was necessary to determine "the profound cause" that had transformed young Moroccans into human bombs. "Jettou knows full well the answer. . . . It's the economy[,] stupid," wrote publisher Hassan M. Alaoui. "There's a social powder keg that feeds all this hatred against fellow Moroccans, against the State and against Morocco. Poverty, unemployment, inequality before the law and opportunities, the disdain of the bourgeoisie, and despair are elements that produce the enemies of the nation. . . . The keystone lies in development."[16]

King Mohammed had repeatedly stressed the need for economic development to resolve the problem of the unemployed urban youths, a fertile field for Islamic activists. In the wake of the Casablanca bombings, the monarch personally launched several major economic projects in the underdeveloped northern and eastern regions. Much publicity was given to the start of work on the new $1.2 billion Tangier-Mediterranean project to be built by a French construction firm with mostly Arab financing; it was expected to provide 22,200 construction jobs and work for as many as 110,000 people in the port, duty-free zone, and industrial area.

Hastily, as if to reassure the country that the events of May 16 had not shaken the government's resolve, Prime Minister Jettou presented a glowing report to parliament on the state of the kingdom in early July, after his first eight months in office. Reaffirming the government's commitment to democracy and the rule of law, the prime minister outlined in detail the social and economic measures taken or under way. Contracts were signed with investors for some $740 million in the first semester of 2003, or three times the amount in 2002, creating 9,000 new jobs. He also spoke of an ambitious public works program, the construction of low-cost housing, a campaign against the illiteracy which affects half the population, and a program to overhaul the country's health care system.[17]

Jettou's words fell on the ears of a disbelieving public, which had heard similar promises at election times in the past (municipal and senate votes were scheduled for the following month), with little or no follow-up. Why should this time be different?

Aftershocks

The country was slowly recovering from the May 16 disaster when several aftershocks occurred. Early in July, a young man broke into a popular campsite at Agadir, brandishing a knife, and wounding seven patrons—all Moroccans—in the bar, before killing himself. What would have been considered an unfortunate local incident in normal times took on national proportions and was seen as a new chapter in a violent Islamic moralizing campaign.

King Mohammed, who had been particularly distressed over the attacks against Jewish targets in Casablanca, took several pro-Israeli initiatives during the summer of 2003 that surprised many ordinary Muslims and angered the Islamists. In his palace at Tangier, the king granted a much-publicized audience to Israel's new grand rabbi, Shlomo Moshe Amar, a fifty-five-year-old native of Casablanca. The Rav Shlomo Amar blessed the king as the descendant of the Moroccan sultans, who had always protected their Jewish subjects.

Soon afterward, Israel's foreign minister, Sylvan Shalom, was received with honors and granted a royal audience. After presenting a letter to the king from Prime Minister Ariel Sharon, the Israeli minister announced that relations between the two countries, which had been severed in 1994 over the Israeli repression of the *intifada*, might be soon restored. A week later, King Mohammed telephoned Prime Minister Sharon, but the conversation remained confidential.

Although the royal gestures were intended as a renewal of Morocco's traditional role as a Middle East peace maker, they touched a sensitive nerve in public opinion. Moderate Islamists of the PJD reacted indignantly to the moves at a time when Israeli leader Sharon had hardened his positions and the U.S.-sponsored "road map" appeared all but dead. Calling the Morocco-Israeli rapprochement "inopportune," *TelQuel*'s publisher, Ahmed Benchemsi, speculated that the contacts could be a diplomatic maneuver to win help from the Jewish lobby in Washington to defend Morocco's position on Western Sahara.[18] Some critics went so far as to suggest that the Israeli visits may have inspired the subsequent killing of two Moroccan Jews.

Still recuperating from May 16, the fragile Jewish community was stunned when one of its members was murdered in Casablanca on September 11, 2003—the date was hardly coincidental. Albert Rebbibo, fifty-five, a respected wood merchant in Casablanca's Al Korea market, was closing the metal shutters of his shop at lunchtime when he was accosted and killed by two masked gunmen. There were numerous witnesses, and police rapidly identified the suspects as militants of Salafiya Jihadia. In what turned into a national tribute, government officials and leaders of civil society attended the funeral service for Rebbibo.

Two days later, another Moroccan Jew in the central city of Meknès was stabbed to death near his home. The second victim, Elie Aferyat, seventy-eight, was reportedly engaged in money lending and had a number of enemies. Initially, his case was said to be a common crime, but later it too was linked to Islamic extremists.

While the two incidents appeared unrelated, the Jewish community was terrified, and some members openly talked of packing their bags. The independent press questioned if this was the end of another Moroccan myth: the age-old peaceful coexistence between the Muslim and Jewish communities.

Shortly afterward, the security services announced the arrest of eight members of the shadowy organization the Moroccan Islamic Combatant Group, said to be linked to Al Qaeda. Few details were released, but the clandestine group was suspected of being behind the May 16 attacks and the murder of the two Moroccan Jews.

Spanish investigative journalist Antonio Baquero, who had access to Moroccan and Spanish intelligence, reported that the Moroccan Combatant suspects had confessed receiving orders "to put an end to [the] Jewish presence in Morocco." Baquero provided details on the shadowy organization, said to have been created by Moroccan radical Mohamed al Garbouzi in 1998 in the terrorist camps in Afghanistan, with the personal approval of Osama Bin Laden. Al Garbouzi, described as "the undisputed leader" of the Moroccan Combatants, was wanted by Interpol and was believed to be living in London.[19]

The Moroccan Islamic Combatant Group was to resurface less than a year later, when it was accused of being the lead operator in the Madrid bombings. This time, Spanish security services tried to track down the group's chief, Al Garbouzi, but he had reportedly disappeared from his London base.

One of the most disturbing terrorist actions planned for the Moroccan capital in the summer of 2003 didn't happen. Disturbing, because the targets were members of the royal family and a fashionable shopping center; disturbing, too, for the fact that the confessed suicide bombers were two fourteen-year-old sisters. The twins had been raised by a single mother in an environment of prostitution, drugs, and physical abuse. Recruited by a well known *intégriste*, the girls had donned headscarves and were told to distribute tracts attacking the Moroccan regime as un-Islamic. Their inflammatory discourse at the local mosque soon attracted the attention of the police, who had kept religious circles under close surveillance since May 16. Arrested before they could put their plans into effect, the twins and another girl of the same age were accused of "taking part in a criminal association that was preparing to commit terrorist acts." Tried under the new antiterrorist law, the twins were found guilty and sentenced to five years in prison—the first four in a juvenile corrections center—while their friend was acquitted.

That summer was troubled by another violent incident, apparently unrelated to Islamic extremism, but with far-reaching implications. A shoot-out between rival drug gangs in a nightclub at the northern resort of Kabila would not have attracted national attention except for the fact that it took place near the royal residence where the king spends holidays. Zealous police services made a number of arrests, including that of a young drug lord, Mounir Erramach, who reportedly talked. As a result, five magistrates of the Court of Appeals in the northern city of Tetouan, a score of high-level officers from the police, army, gendarmerie, national intelligence, customs, and several businessmen were brought before a special court on corruption charges. According to press reports, this network of officials was implicated in drug trafficking—not only hashish but cocaine—and more recently the smuggling of firearms to Islamic extremists.

The court case however dragged on, with little headway in proving the involvement of the officials in drug smuggling. Observers believed that the Erramach case would go the way of earlier attempts to clamp down on officials linked to the traffic of drugs—nowhere. After months of media attention, Erramach and another lead suspect received three-year prison terms, while most of the agents were acquitted. But in the spring of 2004, the Tetouan Court of Appeals sentenced the drug lord and an accomplice to twenty years in prison. It seemed the authorities were finally ready to take the drug trafficking problem seriously.

What had changed was that Spanish investigations into the Madrid train bombings had confirmed links between the drugs and terrorist networks—both mostly made up of Moroccans. The suspected bombers were found to have paid for explosives through sales of hashish and other drugs.

The Islamist Camp

One of the most difficult problems facing King Mohammed and the ruling establishment in the wake of May 16 was how to deal with the mainstream Islamists, who oppose violence but are committed to regime change and the establishment of *Sharia*, or Islamic law.

Even under a master politician like former King Hassan, the Islamist question had not been resolved but merely contained. His divide-and-rule policies of pitting Islamists against the Left and then against each other had actually encouraged the growth of the Islamist movement.

On coming to power, King Mohammed had hoped to win over Sheikh Yassine by setting him free after eleven years of house arrest. But the recalcitrant sheikh refused to recognize the king as Commander of the Faithful, and so his movement remained illegal. Furthermore, Yassine has refused to take part in the democratic process, claiming that elections are rigged.

Like his father, Mohammed VI favored the "moderate" Islamists of the PJD, even inviting the party's theoretician, Ahmed Raissouni, to the palace to give a lecture during the holy month of Ramadan. As the moderates gained strength, their discourse became more virulent and at times indistinguishable from Yassine's followers. In fact, the PJD led the opposition forces which defeated the government's plan to improve women's rights. But it was only when the PJD made a strong showing in the national legislative elections that the establishment began to worry about its moderates.

A key player in the palace's revised Islamic policy is Ahmed Toufiq, named minister for Islamic affairs in November 2002. An eminent historian and former director of the National Archives, Toufiq is a Sufi, a soft-spoken man of dialogue. He considers violent incidents like May 16 "political not social or religious" and notes that "young people in the United States, Japan, everywhere can be manipulated by extremists."[20]

Toufiq told me that he has embarked on a program to counter the influence of Islamic radicals, which includes the training of preachers and stricter criteria for the choice of *imams*. It also involves better regulation of Koranic schools and private institutions providing religious education "to avoid excesses." By way of guidance, the ministry has begun publishing a *Bulletin for Imams and Preachers*. "We warn them they must be responsible for their statements and speak of ethical principles—not attack persons," he said. "Mosques should not be used for propaganda."

The minister is also working to improve communications. He plans to set up libraries in annexes of a hundred mosques, offering not only religious books but scientific and cultural works. The main innovation is a greater use of television: daily programs of commentaries on the Koran and the sayings of the Prophet, reports on religious activities, and debates on current issues like secularism, modernity, and the role of women. Special telephone lines will be set aside for the public to ask questions of religious authorities.

"The challenge we face is how to adapt our religious traditions to modern reality," Toufiq said, emphasizing that this would entail a dialogue between "extremists" and "moderates." It was the first time I heard an official make such a daring suggestion in this increasingly polarized society.

The Casablanca attacks of May 16 had a major impact on all Islamist organizations, including the moderates. Initially it seemed that public anger against *intégristes* might spill over to Islamists in general for betraying Morocco's peaceful and tolerant image. And while the security services directed their wrath against Islamic zealots and their followers, it was inevitable that moderate Islamists should fall into the net.

To my surprise, the main Islamist organizations were not cowering in fear of public hostility or the harsh crack-down. On the contrary, both the PJD and Sheikh Yassine's Justice and Charity have emphasized their disapproval of the authors of the attacks and presented themselves as alternatives to Islamic extremism.

The sheikh's spokesperson, Nadia Yassine, was worried about the anti-Islamist backlash but spoke optimistically. The events of May 16 had a negative influence on the Islamic movement as a whole because the public is afraid and doesn't want to be associated with "Islamic terrorists," Yassine noted. But she thought that in the long run, the clamp-down on Islamic extremists would be "positive" for Al Adl wal Ihssane.[21]

"The people behind the May 16 tragedy were Wahhabis, initially encouraged by the state to counter my father's movement," Yassine asserted:

> Our people at Sidi Moumen were aware of their penetration. The Wahhabis were very visible with their tunics and *khol* [natural eyeliner], but we had no idea what they were planning. They manipulated young people—victims of illiteracy, poverty, and despair—offering them the gate to paradise. Behind them is an international Arab organization, seeking to destabilize the country [apparently a reference to Wahhabism].

Yassine said members of Justice and Charity have been arrested merely for belonging to an illegal association—"It's the administration's way to pressure our association to become legal, implying recognition of the king as *Amir al Mouminine*." There were signs, she noted, that once legalized, the association could be asked to provide youth leaders and monitors to "serve as a brake to extremists."

"They will realize that we're the loyal opposition and against destabilization. Already they understand our program for political change is based on spirituality, acts of faith, and [is] close to the Sufi program," Yassine said brightly. She had personal proof of a change in official attitude. For the first time, she had been given a passport to go to Budapest at the end of May to take part in a forum of the Mediterranean Studies Association.

Abdelilah Benkiran of the PJD took a similar line. His party had nothing to do with the Casablanca attacks, which were the work of the Salafiya Jihadia movement, he insisted. In fact, he claimed no knowledge of the links between the Salafists of the Wahhabi school and the young *jihadists*, who had appeared after the war in Afghanistan a decade ago.[22]

On the contrary, he stressed the positive role that the moderate Islamists have exercised over the past ten to twenty years as "a stabilizing force," saying they could have done more had they been given a free hand. The Movement for Unification and Reform (the main component of the PJD) used to have social activities in poor neighborhoods, but these were stopped by the authorities. "Unfortunately we didn't have an audience in Sidi Moumen," Benkiran said. "If we had been there, May 16 would never have happened."

He also indicated that in light of the stringent security measures, his movement was not prepared to go back into the *bidonvilles* in a big way, lest it be considered a provocation. We met in the modest office of the Islamist daily *Attajdid*, which he had taken over when the former managing editor fell into disgrace that spring. Ahmed Raissouni, leader of the Movement for Unification and Reform, had committed the unpardonable sin of questioning the role of the king as Commander of the Faithful. "It was an error," Benkiran said, insisting that the PJD didn't question the king's position.

Benkiran admitted that the Islamists had also erred in opening the pages of *Attajdid* to Islamic radicals, like the controversial preacher Abdelbari Zemzmi. "We didn't approve of his discourse of hatred, but there was lots of autonomy in the newspaper, and we were learning," Benkiran explained lamely. But he stressed that such errors could not justify the hostile campaign in the media against the PJD, the actions of the authorities against men with beards, and the efforts by "the radical Left" to ban the party.

With relatively few casualties, the mainstream Islamists managed to ride out the May 16 crisis and present themselves as important players on the political scene, not to be confused with the Islamic radicals but rather as a possible answer to Islamic extremism. This became evident in the elections that were held barely four months after the Casablanca attacks.

Lessons of the Polls

Municipal and communal elections in the fall of 2003 were much more than an opportunity to choose mayors and local councils. They were a chance to test the mood of young people because the voting age had been lowered to eighteen from twenty, which meant a potential million and a half new young voters. It was also the first opportunity to gauge the influence of the Islamist vote after May 16. After their strong showing in the national elections a year earlier, the PJD had been slated to win the main cities in the local elections. But the terrorist attacks were expected to produce a strong public backlash against Islamist candidates.

There was no Islamist sweep in the voting on September 12, 2003. In fact, the PJD came in eleventh out of the twenty-six parties taking part in the elections. Wary of appearing threatening, the PJD had deliberately downplayed its presence at the polls, presenting candidates in only 18 percent of the districts. (It is said the PJD's "self-limitation" was encouraged by the palace.) Even so, the PJD came in third in Casablanca, a former left-wing stronghold, and performed well in the cities and towns where it had presented candidates.

The two mainstream parties, the Istiqlal and the Socialist Union of Popular Forces, led with 17 percent and 15 percent of the vote, respectively. There was no resounding majority. Voter participation at 54 percent was better than the 52 percent of the legislative elections the year before—but hardly the boost expected from the new youth vote and the national rallying after May 16. Abstention was high in urban areas, running about 65 percent.

Another blow for the progressives was the pitiful score of women—only 127 councilwomen elected out of a total of 23,286 council seats, or .5 percent. The political parties had pledged to give a fair place to female candidates, but there were no quotas, and women candidates were either not presented or put at the bottom of the lists.

In the wrangling over mayorships, the two leading parties were the big losers. The Socialist Union lost its traditional fief of Rabat because of rivalry with the Istiqlal. The Istiqlal was defeated in Casablanca by Islamists in an alliance of smaller parties. The Islamists actually won in Meknès and some towns.

Elections to renew one-third of the upper house, held soon afterward in the professional and economic chambers and labor unions, confirmed the splintering of the political scene and the decline of the Socialists. The voting was marked by the old vices of opportunism, money, and manipulation. The rural-based Popular Movement won with 15 percent, followed by the Istiqlal with 14 percent, while the Socialist Union, hurt by the split with its labor union, came in eleventh, with under 3 percent.

In the Saharan capital of Laayoune, where the population had hoped to see movement toward the government's plans for "advanced autonomy," nothing had changed. Local elections proved to be the same old game of tribal influences. The turnout was the highest in the country with voters shepherded to the polls. A total of thirty-nine parties participated because every tribal faction wanted to be represented. The parties failed to present specific programs, and the victorious candidates were entrenched tribal chiefs. "The message is that Morocco is still the same, and people are tired of it," remarked a Saharan observer.

Not long after the elections, the dedicated monarchist Dr. Abdelkrim Khatib declared that at eighty-four, he was ready to retire as leader of the Islamist Justice and Development party. Khatib's departure was a double blow: for the palace, which had relied on him to control the hotheads in the Islamist movement, and for the Islamists, who looked to him as a bulwark against the regime's anti-Islamist hardliners.

Saad Eddine el Othmani, the forty-eight-year-old psychiatrist of Berber origin who was to replace Dr. Khatib, told me after the elections that the PJD had voluntarily "limited our participation in an effort to allay public fears of another Algerian situation." Emphasizing that Morocco needs investors and tourism, El Othmani, who has a long, narrow face and a trim mustache and beard, declared: "If we had won, the press would have presented the victory as an Islamist takeover; we do not want to be a factor of destabilization."[23]

Following the Socialists' weak performance in the elections for the municipalities and the upper house, Abderrahmane Youssoufi announced his resignation as party leader. King Mohammed praised Youssoufi for his "rectitude, fidelity, sincerity and moral honesty, probity and abnegation," and said he would continue to be called on to defend the higher interests of the nation. But Youssoufi's departure from the political scene marked the end of an era because he was the last of the "historical leaders" of the nationalist movement. The voters had shown it was time to move on.

When I met with the former prime minister during the spring of 2004, he was living quietly in retirement in a comfortable apartment in a middle-class neighborhood of Casablanca. He showed no bitterness over the obstacles that his government had faced, but rather, expressed satisfaction that many reforms they had initiated—in education and training, investment laws, labor code, land reform, the status of women, liberalizing state controls over radio and television—were being implemented by the Jettou government.

However, Youssoufi was openly concerned over the advances of the Islamist movement and suggested various reasons for its expansion. He noted that in the 1997 legislative elections, the PJD was a small party, whose popularity increased enormously with its show of solidarity for the Palestinian *intifada*. When the Socialists entered the government and things didn't happen fast enough for the Moroccan public, the Islamists took the place of the political opposition. By the 2002 national elections, the PJD had become a large party with broad public following. At the same time, many Moroccans who had gone to Afghanistan to fight the Communists had returned to form militant Islamic organizations. The Casablanca terrorist attacks were directly linked to the worsening situation in the Middle East. Most people had believed that the Islamists would be isolated and the party weakened after the May 16 tragedy, but the municipal elections of September 2003 proved them to be as strong as before, if not stronger.

"The Islamists are a political movement using religion for their own purpose," Youssoufi asserted. He emphasized that they aimed to disrupt Morocco's traditional diplomacy—as part of the Muslim world, while maintaining close relations with the West. "We have done everything possible to pursue and develop this policy of balances, but the Western world must realize that the Palestinian question is the central point that affects the entire region."[24]

It was increasingly clear that the main Islamic challenge facing Morocco was not the small bands of fanatics bent on destroying symbols of so-called Western corruption and the Jewish presence, but rather the "moderate" Islamists, who were gaining ground on every unkept promise of the government and the perceived anti-Islamic policies of Morocco's Western allies.

Royal Advances and Regressions

The first major test facing the palace in the post–May 16 era was the women's issue. The question on many minds was, in light of the new threat from Islamic radicals, would the king and the political establishment have the courage to make real changes in the *Moudawana*, known as one of the most conservative civil codes in the Muslim world? The royal commission had been laboring over a revision of the code for two and a half years behind closed doors, and had reached a stalemate by the summer of 2003. Impatient over the delays, the monarch ordered the commission to produce its report by that September. Meanwhile, word leaked out that the commission was revising its position to favor the women's demands for equal rights, in the wake of May 16.

Denouncing a new plot against the Moroccan family, the Islamist daily *Attajdid* accused anti-Muslim circles of taking advantage of the Casablanca attacks to push through a civil code that would jeopardize Morocco's Islamic identity. In front of some mosques, demonstrators attacked the "Satanic plan" as being antifamily and anti-Islam. But this time, the establishment appeared less willing to listen to the PJD and other Islamic militants.

To general astonishment, the royal commission came down solidly on the side of progress in the new Family Code. Presenting the reforms to parliament in October 2003, King Mohammed stressed that the new code was designed to "lift the iniquity weighing on women, protect children's rights, and preserve the dignity of men."[25]

The most significant alterations in the law were to place families under the "joint responsibility of both spouses"—not just men—and to free adult women from the obligatory control of male guardians. Although polygamy and repudiation were not actually banned, as the women's movement had demanded, much stricter limitations would be imposed. Other reforms included increasing the marriage age for girls to eighteen (the same as boys) from fifteen, facilitating divorce procedures for women, and introducing divorce by mutual consent. The reform also stipulated that a couple could make an agreement on the separation of common property acquired during the marriage.

The main lines of the new code, which was overwhelmingly approved by the parliament, looked very much like the Youssoufi government's plan that had been so vehemently criticized by religious and conservative circles a few years before. Only now the text was carefully couched in Islamic references.

The Islamist PJD, which had led the opposition to earlier attempts to reform the Moudawana, announced its support of the new Family Code as "a pioneer project of reform, in the interest of women and the family." Times were obviously different after May 16, and the Islamists were anxious to demonstrate their moderation and tolerance.

The revised Family Code was enthusiastically welcomed by the women's movement as satisfying most of the demands for which they had fought for so long. Leila Rhiwi, coordinator of Printemps de l'Egalité, which had spearheaded the movement for reform, said the new code was a victory for women, but she cautioned that the fight was not over; men still had the right to repudiate their wives and divorce without paying alimony. For Rhiwi and other activists, the main threat was in the implementation. "How can you expect a judge who has worked for years in a patriarchal frame to be progressive and impartial?" feminist lawyer Khadija Rouggany demanded.[26]

"Mohammed VI has engaged in a revolution, which is only the beginning of a long march that will see back-sliding, interruptions and opposition, both implicit and explicit," wrote the crusty columnist Khalid Jamai. "But what is inescapable is that finally a more egalitarian, more just and more harmonious society will emerge that will be able to contribute to our development and defense against fanatics of all kinds."[27]

Foreign praises for the landmark reform poured in from the European Union, Arab university women, and other groups. President George W. Bush hailed the king for "responsible and courageous leadership."[28] French president Jacques Chirac, visiting Morocco at the time, called the Family Code "a notable development on the road to democracy."[29]

In the glow of this applause, the palace moved to settle other troublesome human rights issues. After lengthy talks between the king's delegate in the Ministry of the Interior, Fouad Ali al Himma, and leaders of the Truth and Justice Forum, it was agreed to set up a Commission for Equity and Reconciliation to bring closure to the file on human rights violations of the 1970s and 1980s. The mission of the new body was to investigate forced disappearances, find the burial sites of persons who had died in custody, and provide compensation for victims of arbitrary imprisonment. Composed of respected human rights advocates, the commission was given eleven months to complete its work and report on its conclusions and recommendations. Omar Azziman, head of the government's Human Rights Council, stressed that the new commission would be "extrajudicial"; there would be no question of "rancor, vengeance, or penal action." It was clear the new body would not be a South African–type Truth and Justice Commission.

Fouad Abdelmoumni, vice president of the Moroccan Association for Human Rights, declared that the Commission for Equity and Reconciliation "lacked credibility because it established the impunity of criminals and came at [a] time when violations of human rights are continuing on a massive scale."[30]

Although the new commission appeared to be a positive step, it was another half-measure, characteristic of the late King Hassan's rule, an attempt to get rid of an unpleasant situation without getting to the roots of the problem. It also split the human rights community between those who believe it is better to obtain some satisfaction on past violations and those who continue to hold out for truth and justice.

On January 7, 2004, the same day that the new Commission for Equity and Reconciliation took office, it was announced that the king had granted royal pardon to thirty-three political prisoners, including a human rights activist, a score of Islamists, and seven journalists. It was an implicit recognition that Mohammed VI was sensitive to international pressures, particularly in the case of newspaper editor Ali Lmrabet, who was serving a three-year jail term for insulting the monarch.

Amid celebrations for the prisoners' release, some skeptics noted that there were no guarantees that the regime was ready to comply with international standards on human rights. In fact three weeks later, the forces of order forcibly broke up peaceful demonstrations with customary brutality, in front of parliament in Rabat. The police beat up Abdelhamid Amine, president of the Moroccan Association of Human Rights; a leading movie producer, Nabil Ayouche; and others, who were protesting against the U.S.-Morocco free trade agreement and its probable impact on the price of medicines. In Casablanca, families of boatpeople who had drowned off Cadix were harshly dispersed and prevented from holding a sit-in at the Spanish consulate to demand the return of the bodies.

Several months later, Reporters without Borders denounced the sentencing of a Tangier journalist to ten months in prison for libel against a cabinet minister; the report alleged that the minister was homosexual. And Norway's Foreign Office protested against the expulsion of two Norwegian journalists, who had openly set up an appointment with a Saharan nationalist. The glow of a new era in human rights had begun to fade.

At the end of February 2004, the country faced a new ordeal. An earthquake struck the northern region of Al Hoceima in the Rif Mountains, taking the lives of some 600 persons, wounding 1,000, and leaving 15,000 people homeless. Measuring 6.5 on the Richter scale, it was the worst earthquake since Agadir in 1960 and brought to light the difficult access to the mountainous region but also a dysfunctional leadership and conflicts between the administration and military authorities. After the initial shocks, an atmosphere of revolt set in with villagers accusing the government of abandoning them yet again, local officials of profiteering, and criminals of looting the foreign aid.

"The problem is that there are two governments," a senior official told me privately. It was announced that the king and his entourage would visit the quake site on the afternoon of the tragedy, and so the prime minister and members of his government had deferred going to the zone. Meanwhile, the world press and national and international relief agencies rushed to the chaotic scene.

Unlike his father who had flown immediately to Agadir and taken charge, King Mohammed had been discouraged from visiting the devastated area because of the tremors, which continued for several days and presented a security risk. Thus, neither the monarch nor the prime minister nor other key cabinet ministers showed up during the first few days, with the result that no one was in charge. Royal aides and the military acted to control the situation while local authorities, foreign governments, and NGOs tried to get help to the isolated villages as quickly as possible. Despite the obstacles, foreign aid workers said that the Moroccan mobile health teams and sanitation centers had done a remarkable job, and local associations had provided an effective distribution network.

When King Mohammed appeared five days after the catastrophe, he skillfully turned around an ugly situation by setting up his court in a tent, visiting the stricken villages, and making generous promises of aid. Some doubting Rifains recalled that the king had declared the Rif a national priority when he visited the area in 1999. But nothing had been done in this forsaken region, which lives mainly from cannabis and emigrants' checks. Rifains tended to blame an ineffective government and corrupt local officials for the inaction. Now the king announced what was called a "Marshall Plan for the Rif": roads, electricity, water, and earthquake-proof housing. The locals welcomed the news but could be forgiven for questioning whether there would be follow-up this time.

One of the most difficult dilemmas facing the king was how to respond to American pressures to join the Greater Middle East Initiative. A week after the Rif earthquake, Marc Grossman, U.S. under-secretary of state for political affairs, arrived at Al Hoceima to win the king's backing for the Bush administration's plans for democratizing the region. Addressing the press, the American diplomat praised the reforms undertaken by Morocco and declared: "We want to work with Morocco and others to advance the reform agenda that is coming from the region."[31]

At the same time, the White House announced that that President Bush had designated Morocco as a "major non-NATO U.S. ally" in recognition of the kingdom's "steadfast support in the global war on terror." Other Muslim countries, like Pakistan, Kuwait, Egypt, and Jordan, share this privileged status, which makes it easier to buy American arms. As expected, Algeria and the Saharan nationalists of POLISARIO reacted negatively to the designation, warning that it would lead to a new arms race in the region.

Morocco's political press was unanimously hostile to the American Middle East initiative. The Socialist daily *Libération* wrote that the overall Arab response to Washington's plans for Middle East reform was rejection. Recalling the dark history of U.S. relations with Arab countries, the liberal *Rissalat Al-Oumma* stressed that Washington aimed to serve its own strategic interests by imposing democracy on the Arab world. The conservative Istiqlal party's organ, *Al Alam*, noted that the North African states had kept silent on the American proposal because they don't consider themselves directly concerned. The Islamist daily *Attajdid* curtly suggested that instead of drafting unreal projects, the Bush administration should cease its decision-making and occupation in Iraq and press Ariel Sharon to end his assaults on the Palestinians.

King Mohammed promised to give careful consideration to the American proposal, but stressed the urgent need to resolve the Arab-Israeli conflict. It was clear that the monarch, who has persistently sought Washington's support on the Western Saharan issue, was reluctant to alienate his superpower ally and a key member of the UN Security Council. But as Commander of the Faithful, it was difficult to sign on to the American initiative, seen by Moroccans and most Muslims as an attempt to distract attention from the basic problems in the Middle East: the Palestine question and, now, Iraq.

Madrid and Beyond

The Madrid bombings on March 11, 2004, placed Morocco squarely in the middle of the global war being waged by Islamic radicals. Moroccans watched with horror the televised scenes of the mutilated bodies, bleeding survivors, and widespread wreckage from the explosions on the Madrid commuter trains. Then followed reports that the suspected terrorists were not Basque separatists but Islamic radicals—and most of them Moroccans. It was like reliving the Casablanca nightmare all over again, only far worse.

A dozen terrorists had planted backpacks full of explosives on four trains during the morning rush hour and detonated the explosions by cellular phones, taking the lives of 201 people and wounding about 1,800. By chance, two bombs failed to go off, and the police seized a mobile phone and a prepaid phone card, which led investigators to a telephone shop owned by a thirty-year-old Moroccan, Jamal Zougam. Described as deeply religious, Zougam had been questioned earlier by Spanish judge Baltasar Garzón in connection with the September 11, 2001, terrorist attacks in the United States but had been released for lack of evidence. This time, the Spanish police searched Zougam's apartment and seized radical Islamic documentation, including videos of guerrilla training camps and telephone numbers of Al Qaeda militants.

A representative of Al Qaeda's Al Ansar group in Europe named Abu Dujana Al Afgani claimed responsibility for the train attacks in a video found near a Madrid mosque on March 13. Two weeks later, the same person sent a letter to a Spanish newspaper warning that the group would turn Spain "into an inferno," if Madrid didn't withdraw its troops from Iraq and Afghanistan. At the same time, the police found explosives, which had failed to explode, on the Madrid-Seville high-speed rail line.

Spanish authorities announced that their investigations were focused on the Moroccan Islamic Combatant Group, based in Spain and believed to have ties with Al Qaeda. This was the same organization accused by Moroccan security officials of engineering the Casablanca attacks. The Spanish arrested Zougam and a score of other Moroccans and issued warrants for more Moroccans and a Tunisian, Serhane Ben Abdelmajid Fakhet, thirty-seven, identified as the spiritual leader of the group. Later, the police traced some suspects through cell phones and prepaid telephone cards to an apartment in a Madrid suburb, where they blew up themselves—and a police officer— before they could be arrested. One of the seven suspects was said to be the Tunisian fugitive Fakhet, a real estate agent married to a Moroccan. Another body was identified as Jamal Ahmidan, thirty-three, a Moroccan drug trafficker who had allegedly financed the terrorist cell through the sale of hashish and other drugs.

In the wake of this "collective suicide," the Spanish interior minister, Angel Acebes, announced that the terrorist cell responsible for the train attacks had been largely dismantled and the suspects were either dead or in jail. The main question, according to Acebes, was whether the Madrid operation was controlled by leadership from abroad. He specified that Spanish investigators were working with colleagues in seven countries, including Morocco, France, England, and Germany.

In Morocco, government spokesman Nabil Benabdallah expressed solidarity with Spain over the terrorist attacks, and top Moroccan security officials flew to Madrid to offer help with the investigation. Privately, Moroccan officials suggested that if communications with Spain had been better, the March 11 disaster might have been averted. They pointed out that Rabat had warned Madrid the previous year that Jamal Zougan was a "dangerous element" linked to Al Qaeda and had asked for his extradition, to no avail. Similarly, Rabat had asked London for the extradition of the Moroccan Islamic Combatant leader Al Garbouzi, but the British had refused.

"Now, maybe people will listen to us," a Moroccan security source said ruefully.

Ironically the Madrid tragedy resulted in a significant improvement in Spanish-Moroccan relations. Spain's new prime minister, José Luis Rodriguez Zapatero, went out of his way to repair misunderstandings on issues like fishing and immigration. Soon the two neighbors were cooperating not only in the war against terrorism but also had sent a joint peacekeeping mission to Haiti. In early 2005, Spain's King Juan Carlos and Queen Sofia paid a state visit to Morocco to cement the reconciliation, and the reception couldn't have been warmer. Besides effusive words of friendship, the two kings gave an important boost to the old dream of a twenty-four-mile rail tunnel under the Strait of Gibraltar and agreed to call on the European Union for help in financing the 3 billion Euros project.

Meanwhile, Morocco's independent press reported that the Madrid investigations had revealed the extent of Moroccan involvement with international terrorism. Referring to "the interminable lists" of Moroccans implicated in terrorist actions around the world, *Le Journal* said that Morocco had lost its idyllic image as a haven for a tolerant Islam: "Increasingly Morocco looks like a reservoir for Bin Laden's secret agents."[32]

The Casablanca attacks and the Madrid bombings did show that Islamic extremism is much broader and much deeper among Moroccans than anyone had believed. Mohammed VI has opted for the stick-and-carrot approach to the challenges facing the nation, which former King Hassan had used so effectively to achieve stability. But the problems that have fostered Islamic radicals—the tremendous social and economic disparities, ingrained corruption, and absence of democratic accountability—have not gone away.

The question posed with increasing urgency is whether these problems can be resolved by massive security sweeps, severe jail sentences, enlightened royal decrees, and piecemeal reforms, or do they require a new vision and profound structural changes?

Epilogue: The Challenges

*W*hen the shy, socially sensitive Crown Prince Mohammed became king in 1999, Moroccans were given a second chance to attain their dreams of progress and democracy, born with independence nearly a half century before. After enduring the prolonged despotic regime of Hassan II, the nation came together under the leadership of his son Mohammed VI and a coalition of the main political parties, backed by a broad array of civic groups. With support from powerful friends like France and the United States, the country appeared poised for take-off at the dawn of the twenty-first century.

During King Mohammed's first five years of reign, the atmosphere of public freedoms improved markedly, and measures were taken to modernize the economy, correct human rights abuses of the past, and advance the legal status of women. At the same time, Mohammed VI has pursued King Hassan's Western-oriented foreign policy, reinforcing Morocco's close political and economic relations with the United States and Europe and conciliatory positions on the Middle East.

But the opportunity for meaningful change has been partly squandered. Morocco is still ruled by the *Makhzen* (the word originally meant the sultan's treasury), a shadowy power structure around the king, which includes senior security officials, the royal cabinet, royal advisers, and a fluid palace entourage of prominent families and dignitaries—in addition to the central government—all accountable only to the king. Symptomatic of the king's failure to bring about change is the hand-kissing ritual in the royal court. Early on Mohammed VI showed his aversion to the servile gesture. But tradition triumphed, and in official ceremonies, most people bow deeply and kiss the monarch's hand.

Actual governance depends on the king, who is usually on the move around the country, traveling abroad, or simply swamped by the demands for his attention. Cabinet meetings are often delayed or canceled by the monarch; ministers must obey His Majesty's beck and call; ambassadors and other key nominations have to wait for a royal decree; and any important decisions must receive the sovereign's imprimatur.

The main political parties and labor unions, which had spearheaded the opposition to the arbitrary dictates of King Hassan and the *Makhzen* for nearly four decades, have been incorporated into a regime of consensus. In agreeing in 1998 to head the government of *Alternance* without the necessary powers to carry out his program, Socialist leader Abderrahmane Youssoufi took a major risk. His Socialist Union of Popular Forces, which obtained a narrow victory in legislative elections and lost heavily in municipal elections, seemed to have lost its credibility as the leading force for reform in the eyes of the nation. The Islamists, who remained in opposition to the impotent government, offered Moroccans hope for change, but that hope was partially tarnished by the violent acts of Islamic radicals.

Morocco has undergone a stunning shock over the discovery within its borders of clandestine radical organizations that advocate murder and destruction to achieve their goal of an Islamic state. The devastating suicide bombings of May 16, 2003, were seen not only as attacks on Jews and foreigners but as a warning to the ruling establishment that basic changes must be made to correct the immense social and economic inequities. They were also a warning to the political elite, aspiring to achieve Western-style parliamentary democracy, that there is a sector of society seeking to restore an Islamic state and Islamic law, by violence if necessary.

The preponderance of Moroccan suspects in the Madrid train bombings of March 11, 2004 constituted another warning that, despite the massive crack-down on suspected Islamic extremists, Moroccan radicals are alive and operating well beyond Morocco's borders.

The surprise for me was not that Moroccan Islamic groups have resorted to violence against a system which they consider impious, unjust, and alien, but that it hadn't happened sooner, as in Algeria and Egypt. The Casablanca suicide bombings were an attack on "enemies of Islam" but also a cry of despair, even more extreme than the acts of thousands of boatpeople who risk death each year in trying to cross the dangerous Strait of Gibraltar to get to Europe. The Madrid bombings on the other hand were essentially a sign of hatred for Spain, a country that had closely allied itself with the United States in what most Moroccans see as a wrongful war against fellow Muslims.

It is clear that Morocco's largely Muslim population has been affected, if somewhat belatedly, by the global resurgence of Islam. As in other Muslim countries, it has been the failure of development-oriented governments to respond effectively to the flagrant problems of poverty, slums, illiteracy, and corruption that has favored the spread of political Islam. It is no coincidence that the main Islamist political parties in Turkey and Morocco are both called parties of Justice and Development—because this is what Muslims everywhere are seeking.

Most Moroccans, including the mainstream Islamist organizations, who adhere to the relatively open and tolerant Malekite school of Islam, have condemned the terrorist acts by Islamic radicals. However, Saudi Arabia's inflexible, xenophobic Wahhabi interpretation of Islam has made inroads in Morocco in recent years as has a violent Islamic sect known as Salafiya Jihadia, born in the wars of Afghanistan. Islamic zealots have consolidated their foothold in the broad Muslim community by propagating "moralization" campaigns and preaching against the American-led wars in Afghanistan and Iraq, and the American failure to bring about a just settlement of the Palestinian question.

Demonstrating that he is not intimidated by Islamic radicals, King Mohammed has reacted firmly with sweeping security measures, tighter controls over Islamic affairs, and sharing antiterrorist intelligence with the country's main Western partners: France, Spain, and the United States.

These measures seem to have been counterproductive, however. The number of Islamic radicals—said to be a few hundred in 2003—has soared with the crack-down on Islamic activists. More than 5,000 people were arrested in the year following the Casablanca attacks, and 2,000 of these have been implicated in terrorism-related activities, according to the Moroccan minister of justice. The 2004 Madrid train bombings brought a new surge of detentions in Morocco, international arrest warrants, and charges that Al Qaeda was behind the terrorist network.

Amnesty International reported in November 2003 that after "a positive trend" toward improved human rights over the previous decade, there had been "a sharp rise in cases of torture or ill treatment." Amnesty told the UN Committee against Torture in Geneva that it has recorded in the past two years scores of cases of ill treatment of Islamists implicated in violent acts, Sahraouis favoring independence, and civil society activists.[1]

As time passed the situation only worsened. In October 2004, Human Rights Watch issued a severe report, denouncing a regression in public liberties since May 16, 2003, under the new antiterrorist legislation. The seventy-page document praised the establishment of the Commission of Equity and Reconciliation but pointed to the limitations of its mandate and power.[2]

At the same time Transparency International reported a "worsening" of corruption in Morocco, noting that the kingdom, which had achieved 45th place (out of a total of 146 countries) had now regressed to 77th position, along with Egypt and Mali.[3]

With their harsh crack-down on Islamists and other dissidents, the Moroccan authorities risk rolling back the main achievement of King Mohammed's reign—the improvement in human rights—by reverting to the abuses of the past.

Voices of Change

Even before the Casablanca suicide bombings, a number of Moroccan academics, journalists, and political groups were seeking new answers to the challenges posed by Islamic extremism. Despite royal taboos, these voices have begun to question the palace's strategy of confronting radical Islam with repression and uncoordinated social improvements. Hardly revolutionary, these critics contend that profound changes in the system are urgently needed to avoid another explosion.

Abdelhak Serhane, fifty-two, is a psychologist and author whose novels are a ringing indictment of contemporary Moroccan society, poverty, corruption, and injustice. A few months before May 16, Serhane had published in *Le Journal* a merciless analysis entitled "Morocco of Illusions," warning against Islamic violence. Free elections, he wrote, were meaningless to the hundreds of thousands of Moroccans living in *bidonvilles*, the jobless graduates, the illiterates, and the unemployed workers. He charged that Moroccan democracy was illusory because all power was in the hands of the king, and despite denunciations of numerous financial scandals, those responsible still enjoyed broad impunity.

Currently a professor of French literature at Lafayette University in Louisiana, Serhane had come home to Morocco for the holidays during that uneasy summer of 2003. When we met over coffee at a Casablanca hotel, he expressed concern that the king appeared to be headed in the same direction as Hassan II and making the same errors. "He doesn't understand that the archaic system of allegiances, multiple centers of power around the throne, and royal intervention is incompatible with freedom, democracy, modernity, and a state of law," Serhane said. In a lengthy conversation, he stressed the gravity of the developments:

> May 16 was a strong signal by young Moroccans to the monarchy and the establishment that they must act urgently to improve the situation. Usually terrorists attack foreigners; this was Moroccans attacking Moroccans and so the problem is Moroccan, a problem of immense despair.

It's not by arresting half the population that they are going to re-solve the problem of Islamism in Morocco. The authorities must con-front the problem in a responsible and serious fashion, starting by re-vising the primary school books, which teach children that those who don't say their prayers will be condemned to death. The state must abandon its policy of condoning violent sermons by Islamic zealots while arresting journalists for speaking out against abuses. Above all, the leadership must strike against the causes of extremism, such as poverty, ignorance, exclusion of the majority, disinterest of young people, corruption, injustice, and lack of civic responsibility.

Morocco must confront its past history with responsibility and without passion. The reign of Hassan II was a tragedy in every way, and the young generations are paying for the consequences of this policy of undermining the structures of freedom, democracy, and de-velopment. A lawless state can only give birth to despair and hatred, and this was what the criminal attacks of May 16 demonstrated. It was not so much about Islamism but rather the atmosphere of des-titution, the lack of political visibility, and the hopelessness of young people, who see their horizons blocked and their lives lost in demon-strations, hunger strikes, and waiting. The more courageous will die in the treacherous waters of the Mediterranean trying to escape to Spanish shores and the dream of millions of Moroccans.[4]

The independent press is undoubtedly the main force for change, and one of the most influential voices in the French-language press is Ahmed Benchemsi's *TelQuel*, or *As It Is*. The slight, soft-spoken Benchemsi is not a crusader but believes the role of his weekly news magazine is "to show Mo-roccan realities behind the public declarations of intentions and the mysti-fications." Over mineral water at Rick's Cafe in the spring of 2004, he said that the freedoms of press and speech had improved substantially since Mo-hammed VI came to power: "There are no taboos now except the private lives of the king and the royal family—which don't interest me."[5]

Benchemsi's irreverent features have shown up the theatrics of Casa-blanca's stock market, the unrecognized importance of the informal econ-omy, the undemocratic practices of political parties, the ineffectiveness of the government, social hypocrisy on child labor, even misleading policies on Western Sahara. Rather than make frontal assaults, his criticism is generally good-humored and constructive.

A year after the May 16 tragedy, Benchemsi published a cover story on "Citizen Action," how young people of Casablanca's slums have set up asso-ciations and drafted projects to improve their neighborhoods. "The poten-tial is there, the ideas abound, all they lack is money," Benchemsi wrote.[6] Acting on *TelQuel*'s report, the Moroccan Businessmen's Confederation agreed to finance forty-one of the fifty projects, and Prime Minister Jettou said the government would fund the rest.

That winter of 2004–2005, the independent press tested the boundaries with articles critical of the monarchy. *TelQuel* caused a furor with its cover on "The Salary of the King." According to official statistics, the monarch earns $40,000 a month, plus $250 million yearly for the royal court of 1,100 people. *Le Journal Hebdomodaire* followed with its cover showing an empty throne and the title: "What's the King Doing?" Noting the monarch's prolonged holiday and absence from important events, Aboubakr Jamai reported increased concern over the worsening economy and demanded urgent constitutional reform. Unconditional royalists accused the weeklies of sensationalism and plotting against the monarchy, and warned that the press could lose the freedom it had gained under King Mohammed.

The most persistent voice for change comes from civil society. The beleaguered Moroccan Association for Human Rights (AMDH), which celebrated its twenty-fifth anniversary in 2004, has never wavered in its struggle for basic freedoms, as set forth in the Universal Declaration of Human Rights. President Abdelhamid Amine, sixty, is a mild-mannered, bespectacled agricultural engineer, who eschews the limelight. Amine has a long history of activism as a student militant and labor unionist, and he spent twelve years and three months in prison for allegedly plotting against the monarchy and the security of the state. On his release, Amine was reintegrated into the Ministry of Agriculture, resumed his union activity, and joined the political bureau of the Human Rights Association.

Whenever it comes to defending women's and workers' rights, press freedoms, and even the rights of terrorist suspects, Amine and other association militants are ready to go to the trenches. In fact, the human rights activist was badly beaten by the police early in 2004 in a demonstration by artists and members of the medical profession against the American free trade association.

The AMDH's seventh congress, held in April 2004, praised the Moroccan state for improvements in public freedoms but noted that these "fragile advances" had been reversed by "the serious regression" in the state of human rights since the terrorist attacks of May 16, 2003. Specifically, the congress criticized the authorities for adopting "the security approach" in the fight against terrorism instead of tackling the profound causes which are found in "the lack of democracy in a global sense, poverty, and exclusion of the majority of citizens."[7]

"We're against the Islamist project for society, which amounts to fascism, but we defend their rights," Amine stressed in an interview in the association's headquarters in a shabby five-floor walk-up in downtown Rabat. The association, which has 6,000 members nationwide, lives on dues and gifts from activists but has received aid from the European Union to set up a center for information and documentation.[8]

What the association wants is a democratic constitution—one drafted by representatives of the people and not a product of the palace as in the past, Amine said. The present constitution, he said, was contrary to basic human rights because it did not provide for the real separation of powers or an independent judiciary and did not recognize the possibility of control of the government by the governed.

The main political parties, with the Socialists in the lead, have been an important force for change in the past. They continue to argue for constitutional reform but have not brought enough pressure to make it happen. As part of the governing majority, the parties seem unwilling to confront the palace.

On the other hand there are demands for real change from within the moderate Islamist movement. At its fifth national congress in the spring of 2004, the Party for Justice and Development (PJD) reaffirmed its attachment to Islam, the monarchy, and the territorial integrity of the state. But a few days before the congress, a popular PJD leader, Mustapha Ramid, publicly questioned the prerogatives of the king and demanded changes in the constitution. His views were not included in the party's political report but were not renounced.

"History shows us that the monopoly of power by leaders is at the origin of revolts and tensions," Ramid wrote in a commentary in the Arabic weekly *As-Sahifa al-Ousbouiya*. Sounding much like critics on the Left, Ramid suggested that "to preserve its role as arbiter," the royal institution should be spared the daily tasks of governing. "It would be advisable to found a political regime based on the delegation of authority to a government represented by the parliamentary majority and the expression of the will of the people," he said.[9]

"I don't demand the cancellation of Article 19," Ramid, a member of parliament, told me in a meeting in the PJD's chambers, referring to the clause in the constitution that loosely describes the royal prerogatives. "The king's powers should be limited by the constitution. The king is arbiter; his powers of governing should be eased and the government made responsible before the people."[10]

Describing himself as an Islamic Democrat, the forty-five-year-old bearded lawyer emphasized that his party had condemned the terrorist attacks of September 11, May 16, and March 11 and was against "the tyrant" Saddam Hussein. "But the United States doesn't have the right to invade Iraq and should play an even-handed role in Palestine," Ramid declared. "If one day the

United States ceases its unfair policies in the Middle East, the terrorists won't have an impact on the population."

Ramid admitted that the Ministry of the Interior had exerted pressure on the PJD leadership to have him removed from his position as chief of the party's parliamentary group. "I decided to resign because I didn't want to be a cause of conflict," he said, but he remains an active member of the group's leadership.

After our interview, Ramid suggested that I should hear the story of his next visitor, whose husband appeared to be a victim of the current anti-Islamist witch hunt. Fatima Merroun was a black-shrouded British woman in her late thirties from Wales, who spoke a halting Arabic and had come to ask the Islamist deputy for help in obtaining the release of her husband, the father of their three young children.

Abdelatif Merroun, forty-two, who had lived in London for twenty years and has dual British and Moroccan nationality, was arrested at Casablanca airport on June 20, 2003, his wife told us in a matter-of-fact manner. After a five-minute trial, he was sentenced on September 26 to five years in prison on charges of links to the radical theologian Mohamed Fizazi.

"Abdelatif is a devout Muslim, not a fanatic and doesn't belong to any association," Mrs. Merroun stressed. Her husband, who had been employed by Air Canada, had met Fizazi once by chance at London's Heathrow Airport in 1998, when his superior had told him to help "an old man from Morocco get on the plane." She said that last year Merroun was working in Dubai on a three-month contract as a bus driver, when he learned that the secret police had gone to his mother's home in Tangier looking for him. He decided to return to Morocco to clear his name because he said he had done nothing wrong.[11]

At first, Merroun had simply disappeared, his wife recounted. The police denied that he had been arrested or that he had even arrived in Casablanca. The British consulate could do nothing because he had not entered Morocco with his British passport. Mrs. Merroun finally located her husband in the Salé prison and hired a defense lawyer to no avail because the court refused to hear proof of his innocence.

"What can I do now? How can a man be charged for a crime in another country? How can I find out what is the evidence against him?" the wife asked Ramid. She had already written to British prime minister Tony Blair, talked to the Moroccan Security Services and the Ministry of Justice, and contacted the Supreme Court, international human rights organizations, and the press.

The Islamist deputy, who appeared genuinely moved, said that the PJD has repeatedly denounced the "regression in human rights, the kidnappings, and arbitrary arrests," but there was nothing they could do about her specific case. "The only thing you can do now is write to the king and ask him for a royal pardon," Ramid said apologetically.

Her bitterness was palpable. How could she ask for pardon for nothing? she said to me later, admitting that she almost wished her husband had done something to deserve this. And I thought: that's a good way to make radicals.

Ironically some of the strongest voices for a transformation of Moroccan society are found in the *Amazigh* movement. The *Amazighs* are dispersed and do not have a political organization yet. Nor does Morocco have a volatile concentration of Berberism like Kabylie in Algeria. The kingdom's Berber-speaking regions, like the Rif and the High Atlas, are more remote and have not undergone the social transformation of Kabylie. Also, the Moroccan monarchy, while resisting the Berbers' political claims, has adopted a pragmatic approach to the question by supporting Berber-led royalist parties of the Popular Movement and promoting the Berber cultural movement. As Michael Brett and Elizabeth Fentress note in their historical work, *The Berbers*: "No doubt the Moroccan Monarchy has its eye upon Algeria, seeking to avoid the mistakes of Algiers in provoking a wave of Berber opposition at a time when Islamism offers a more radical challenge to the direction of the state."[12]

Initially, Berbers had placed high hopes for change in the Royal Institute of *Amazigh* Culture set up by the king in 2002. Its first dean, Mohammed Chafik, is a respected scholar and author of the 2001 Berber Manifesto, which demands recognition of the *Amazigh* language on a par with the national idiom of Arabic. Chafik had enjoyed privileged relations with the palace but retired in the fall of 2003 for health reasons. His replacement, Ahmed Boukous, is a well-known linguist and a hard worker, but he has been unable to cut through the bureaucratic impediments, and the royal institute has come under criticism from *Amazigh* militants.

Meryam Demnati, a member of the royal institute who has been working on the project to create a standard written Berber language based on the ancient *Tifinagh* script, acknowledged that she was discouraged because there had been no time or means to train *Amazigh* teachers properly or to produce a single teaching manual before the school year began. They had managed to open 300 *Amazigh* schools nationwide in the 2003–2004 school year but had to use local teachers and three different manuals in the three regional dialects.

"The *Amazigh* movement is in crisis because of a lack of leadership, but the Amazigh identity is developing in every Berber-speaking town or village, in the mountains and rural areas," said Demnati, who does not seek regime change but changes in society.[13]

When we last met over mint tea in my Rabat hotel, Demnati told me she has had to fight "double discrimination," as an *Amazigh* activist and as a feminist bringing up two sons alone in a man's world. "Reforming the *Moudawana*—Islamic family law—will not change the degrading situation lived by women in Morocco—in *Amazigh* as well as Arab societies," she emphasized. "One must separate state and religion and treat this as a human rights issue. The *Amazigh* man must understand one important thing: as long as the *Amazigh* woman is marginalized, the *Amazigh* community as a whole is in danger."

Demnati openly describes herself as a secularist in this country, where Islam is the state religion, the king is the Commander of the Faithful, and the word "secularism" is generally equated with apostasy. On the Berber Website www.Kabyle.com, Demnati has written: "For us secular *Imazighen* [plural of *Amazigh*], secularism means . . . above all the existence of a modern society and a state of law where the logic of democratic individualism and human rights prevail . . . a society that does not accept ideologies of religious fanaticism and dogmas of hatred."[14]

Late in 2004, a group of Berber militants threw down the gauntlet with the publication of a "charter of *Amazigh* claims for a constitutional revision." Their demands were no less than revolutionary: the enshrinement of

Prince Moulay Hicham in the garden of his office in Rabat talks about his vision of the future of his country.

Amazighte in the Constitution, linguistic equality, regionalization of the centralized state, and secularism.[15]

A leading proponent of change in the antiquated power structure is the king's outspoken cousin Prince Moulay Hicham. The prince talked to me at length about the impact of May 16 on Morocco and the implications of March 11 during a meeting in the spring of 2004 in his office at his mother's villa in Rabat. He noted positive developments but did not hide concern over the deteriorating situation in his homeland:

> King Mohammed acceded to the throne with an extraordinary reservoir of good will and hope. There was a widespread belief that the monarchy would now lead the way to a new balance of Moroccan society and politics via thoroughgoing institutional and constitutional reform. But since then, there has been continued stagnation and a growing sense of disappointment and hopelessness. One has the impression that a unique opportunity was lost for the monarchy and the country. Now the king has put himself on the frontline by disregarding the results of national elections and naming his confidant as prime minister. This leaves no buffer to shield the monarch from the failures of government or the assaults of the opposition, whether secular or Islamic.
>
> The changes in the Family Code are a concrete plus for the monarchy because it appears as a modernizing force, in that it succeeded where the secular parties had failed. But the new Family Code should not hide the lack of real economic and constitutional reforms.
>
> The events of May 16 shattered any assumptions we might have had about the social peace or political consensus in our country. We are now rudely confronted with the fact that large sectors of our people are mired in destitution and poverty. We know that there is a sense of hopelessness that extends even to educated youth who despair of their future. We can no longer avoid the need to do something about this. We know that these conditions are the breeding grounds for individuals and small groups who can turn to violence, confused by violent *jihadist* ideologies that claim Islam as their basis, and resentful of the wealth and comfort surrounding them in the lives of their elite compatriots as well as the images of an omnipresent globalized media.
>
> Al Qaeda is not a centralized headquarters, but a kind of brand name that has been licensed to, or pirated by, any number of autonomous cells and "franchises" that have local roots and local leaders in many places throughout the Islamic world. Morocco, includ-

ing the Moroccan *émigré* population of Europe, is now one of those sites. For a myriad of reasons—poverty, despair, loss of hopeful prospects at home, difficulty of integration, loss of dignity in the face of discrimination in host countries, continued anger at the U.S.-supported Israeli repression of Palestinian aspirations, the general Islamization of Arab-Muslim politics and ideology, and so on—Moroccans at home and abroad are susceptible to recruitment by murderous *jihadists*. And there are Moroccans, some who trained in the original anti-Soviet *jihad* in Afghanistan, who are willing and ready to lead this effort, without the need for explicit orders from some mythical Al Qaeda headquarters. All of this is exacerbated by the lack of any hopeful project at home.

In this sense, the Madrid bombings can be understood as a geographical displacement and political extension of the Casablanca bombings of May 16, 2003. After May 16 in Morocco, more than 2,000 people were arrested from across the spectrum of Islamic tendencies, and in the past year, we've heard any number of different stories, with no definitive solution and murky results. After the Madrid bombings, the Spanish police arrested about forty people, eighteen of whom have been charged in the attacks. Those who could not be charged were released, while the Spanish government did all it could to make it clear that it is not blaming Morocco or Moroccans in general.

There are symptoms of political and social problems that the security forces cannot cure. They point precisely to the need for a wide, frank political discussion that engages a large social front—traditional political parties, civil society groups, pacific Islamists—to confront the unresolved problems of poverty, democracy, and modernization.

Political movements inspired by Islam have become a strong force in our region of the world and will likely be with us for some time. Most of them are peaceful, committed to legal political contestation, and as horrified by the violence as everyone else. The challenge for us is to engage these groups within a genuinely representative political process that encourages recognition and respect for movements with different ideological motivations. The more secular political movements have to stand forcefully and respectfully on the strength of their own political and social agendas. I am hopeful that there are enough shared concerns among the more secular and Islamic political movements to support a consensus regarding an agenda of democracy and modernization.[16]

Even in circles of power, there is talk of the need for constitutional revisions. For example, a leader of the pro-palace Constitutional Union (UC) party, Mohamed M'hamedi Alaoui has called for a new constitution. Among the amendments proposed by Alaoui are the reinforcement of the king's religious and moral authority as Commander of the Faithful and enhancement of the powers of the prime minister, who should come from the party that wins the elections. Coming from one of the main parties, such a proposal would be considered an act of provocation, but from the small, royalist UC it could be a trial balloon.

For an independent opinion on the constitutional issue, I met with Rkia El Mossadeq, one of the country's leading authorities and the first Moroccan woman to obtain her doctorate from Paris's respected School of Political Sciences.

"I want a state of law and the supremacy of the constitution, but there have been deviations of interpretation since 1983," El Mossadeq, professor of constitutional law, political institutions, public freedoms, and human rights at the University of Fez, told me. A youthful, intense woman, El Mossadeq emphasized that what is needed is not a new constitution but "the rehabilitation of the present charter and readjustment of political practices." The basic problem, she said, is that "the implicit powers" of the king have increased over the years at the expense of the explicit powers as defined by the constitution.[17] She said that the controversial Article 19, which loosely defines the monarch's powers, states:

> The king, Commander of the Faithful, Supreme Representative of the Nation, Symbol of its unity, guarantor of the perpetuity and continuity of the State, is watchful over the respect for Islam and the constitution. He is the protector of the rights and freedoms of citizens, social groups and collectivities. He guarantees the independence of the Nation and the territorial integrity of the kingdom within its authentic borders.

In her book *The Labyrinths of Democratic Transition*, the constitutionalist points to various anomalies over the years that have resulted from an implicit interpretation of the royal powers. Among the examples cited are the insistence of the king—both the late King Hassan and King Mohammed VI—on naming key cabinet ministers (like interior, foreign affairs, justice), which should be a prerogative of the prime minister; the monarch's decision to prolong the mandate of parliament by two years in 1989; the royal decision (at the request of the main parties) to name a commission to draft election laws in 1992; the use of the title of Commander of the Faithful to justify the transfer of the reform of the personal status code from parliament to the palace in 1992; and the king's invocation of Article 19 to name a commission to control elections in 1997.[18] More recently, she noted, the king had referred to Article 19 to set up a Diwan al Madhalim, or ombudsman, at the end of 2001, when the government had already prepared a bill on this matter to have been submitted to parliament for discussion and passage.

"What we have is continuity of an autocratic regime, not a transition to democracy," El Mossadeq said, adding that it was urgent to restore the supremacy of the constitution because of the threat of the Islamists who seek to impose the *Sharia*. "In view of the absence of a supreme constitutional order, governing all institutions including the monarchy, the constitution is subjected to tactical considerations. The prime example of such tactics is the participation in parliament of Islamists, who hold that the *Sharia* takes precedence over all national or international juridical orders."

These are just a few voices of change, people who believe that Morocco's ills cannot be cured without fundamental alterations in what remains an authoritarian system behind a democratic façade. Their complaints are indicative of different sectors of opinion, which hold that things are not right in the kingdom. My hope is that the king ventures beyond his coterie of yes-people to listen to voices like these and solicit their help in confronting the enormous challenges ahead.

The Ides of May

Morocco in early May 2004 was radiant with excitement. Everyone seemed obsessed with the kingdom's candidacy to host the World Soccer Cup in 2010. It was the fourth time Morocco had presented its bid, and this time the chances were said to be good. Multicolored flags adorned Rabat—and people said it was to celebrate winning the honor of hosting the games. The center of the capital looked like a construction site with pavements and gardens uprooted and the main Avenue Hassan II cut off to traffic—and everyone concluded it must be work to prepare for the Cup.

There was a collective hope that if Morocco won the Cup, all problems would be resolved, including the stagnant development, lack of jobs, *bidonvilles*, woefully inadequate public transportation and health services, not to mention the threat from Islamic radicals.

TelQuel's Benchemsi issued a warning that even if Morocco should become the center of the world for one month in 2010, this would not launch the kingdom on the road to development. "It's a cheap dream they've offered us," he wrote. "What we need is a real dream, a grand project that depends on us this time, a genuine mobilizing force." Whatever the outcome of the World Cup bid, he stressed that Moroccan enthusiasm needed to be channeled into an important national venture: "Mohammed VI hasn't found his [project], but the day that happens, the face of the kingdom will be transformed."[19]

On the morning of May 15—decision day—Casablanca was charged with anticipation. The streets were nearly deserted as people crowded into cafes to watch televised reports of the ceremony in Zurich. When the head of the International Soccer Federation announced that the victor was South Africa, people in the cafes sat for a few moments in crushed silence. Then they soberly returned to their humdrum lives.

Commemorations of the first anniversary of the May 16 terrorist attacks on the following day were a pale anticlimax. What had been billed as a united national stand against terrorism turned out to be small groups of citizen activists in the main cities who called for peace and threatened terrorists with the slogan "Don't touch my country."

In Casablanca, various civic groups made brief pilgrimages to the sites of the bombings, but there was little enthusiasm and less public interest. A national youth network brought some 300 young people from around the country to Casablanca's new May 16 Park. There they observed a minute of silence at the marble monument to the Spanish, French, Italian, and Moroccan victims of the suicide bombings, unveiled three weeks earlier by King Mohammed and Spanish prime minister José Luis Rodriguez Zapatero. Several demonstrators admitted that they didn't know why they were there. The police firmly kept what little public there was out of the park "for security reasons." A father and his two sons brandished a banner saying "No to Terrorism" in English, perhaps for the benefit of the handful of foreign mourners.

Where was the impassioned show of solidarity of barely a year ago? The desultory public reaction could not be blamed completely on Morocco's loss of the 2010 Soccer Cup. The palace and the political parties were not visible in the demonstrations, and the Islamists, who are very good at organizing protest demonstrations, were unwanted. The fledgling civic associations were new at this kind of organization. One demonstrator, a young medical student, gave me a plausible explanation for the public apathy: "Most Moroccans want to forget the horror and just hope it never happens again."

Moroccan journalists who went to Sidi Moumen reported that one year after the May 16 events, there was the same desolation, the same filth and poverty that had spawned the fourteen kamikazes. Yet, King Mohammed VI had gone to Sidi Moumen two weeks after the suicide attacks and personally launched several public housing projects to replace the *bidonville*. Emphasizing that no concrete results could be seen, the independent weekly

*A Moroccan family, with "No to Terrorism" signs, demonstrates
on the first anniversary of the Casablanca attacks.*

Maroc-Hebdo said: "If nothing else has changed, at least there's stricter police surveillance, some mosques have been closed and those that remain are
closely controlled."[20]

Noting that even the United States had formed a commission to investigate the failures of the system after September 11, *Le Journal*'s fiery columnist
Khalid Jamai stressed that no commission had been named to look into May
16, no parliamentary investigation launched, no officials questioned or held
responsible for security failures. Refuting claims by the authorities that the
Casablanca attacks were the work of Al Qaeda, Jamai wrote: "The May 16 attacks are a purely national product whose causes are found intra-muros. . . .
The 16th of May is the result of specific socio-economic conditions, an inadequate education system, wrongful religious policy, the failure of political parties, an obsolete system of government and an inappropriate media
policy."[21]

There were even suggestions that the Moroccan public had deliberately
boycotted the commemorations, by way of protest against policies that have
done nothing to alleviate the causes of Islamic revolt.

Nothing seemed to be going right during the spring of 2004. The terrorist threat had not abated; the economic take-off had not happened; there was

no let-up of protests by the unemployed; illegal immigration continued. And Morocco had lost its chance to host the World Cup. Even the forces of nature were conspiring against the kingdom: there was a devastating earthquake in the north and a dangerous outbreak of locusts in the south, which threatened to develop into a plague by the end of the year and spread across all of northern Africa and eastward to the Red Sea.

Royal Agenda

They could call him the "Teflon king." The Moroccan public generally attributes the kingdom's woes, even the locusts, to failures of the government, and all advances or good fortune, like rain, are credited to the king.

King Mohammed, forty-one, who completed the first five years of his reign in July 2004, undoubtedly remains the most popular figure in the country. This is obvious from the enthusiasm of the crowds on his frequent tours of the country and the affection with which ordinary people speak of "the young king."

The king has indeed made a promising start toward resolving some of the most delicate problems facing the country with the creation of a liberal, if not perfect, new Family Code; a Commission for Equity and Reconciliation to investigate the regime's past abuses; and the Royal Institute for *Amazigh* Culture.

At the same time, Mohammed VI has reacted firmly to the first major threat to his rule from Islamic extremists. The security forces have made widespread arrests among well-known zealots and their followers. The police have closed numerous "pirate" mosques, seized large quantities of radical Islamic literature, and purged school manuals of passages that could incite violence.

The courts have dealt severely with suspects, handing down numerous death sentences and scores of prison terms of thirty years to life for persons convicted of involvement in terrorist acts or planning future attacks. Various human rights groups have expressed concern over torture allegations, hasty trials, and convictions based on confessions without proof of guilt.

As a sign that he is aware that the security response is not enough, King Mohammed has launched a project to restructure the religious domain. From his palace at Casablanca at the end of April 2004, the monarch announced a multidimensional strategy aimed "to give a new stimulus to the religious sector and protect it from extremism and terrorism."[22] Under this reform, the Ministry of Islamic Affairs was given the task of bringing the country's 32,232 mosques under closer supervision and modernizing the

400 religious schools in mostly rural zones. The Councils of *Oulema* would be enhanced, rejuvenated, decentralized, and for the first time would include women. The religious scholars would be entrusted with a new mission: to contact young people, who are vulnerable to the influences of Islamic radicals.

King Mohammed has also publicly recognized the social frustrations and anger behind the Islamic militants. The monarch has announced numerous new social and economic projects and laid countless inaugural stones. In some cases, like the Rif, he has made return visits to ensure that his orders are carried out.

What has not happened is any change in the autocratic system of governance. Mohammed VI has repeatedly articulated a vision of Morocco as a democratic, progressive, and modern state, with the people united in their Islamic faith under his leadership as Commander of the Faithful. But the monarch has shown no willingness to relinquish his absolute powers over the executive, parliament, judiciary, or mosque. On the contrary, since the appearance of radical Islamic groups, he has reinforced his control over the system. In fact, on the eve of the visit by the king and queen of Spain to Morocco in early 2005, Mohammed VI told the Spanish daily *El Pais* that there was no possibility of Morocco becoming a European-type parliamentary monarchy because of its "specificities and obligations." But he stressed that the constitition could be changed.[23]

The country had been stricken by a political malaise since the election fiasco of 2003. There was widespread criticism of Prime Minister Jettou's government for inaction—even by the semiofficial press—accompanied by persistent rumors of a cabinet reshuffle. The king was reportedly dissatisfied with some ministers and their failure to carry out his instructions.

Finally, in June 2004, the palace announced a "technical readjustment" of the cabinet, designed to enable the government to better carry out the king's priorities. Jettou was retained as prime minister, and the new cabinet was reduced to thirty-five ministers and secretaries of state, down from thirty-nine. But it remained an unwieldy body composed of six divergent political parties, plus technocrats and minus Islamists. The main cabinet posts were still directly responsible to the king. Although some good, competent people were brought into the new cabinet, it suffered from the same problem as its predecessors: the lack of cohesion and authority to improve the administration's efficiency, excite public opinion, and advance the country on the road to democracy.

In one of his first speeches, King Mohammed said that he had "a different concept of authority" from that of his father. Now, however, Mohammed VI looks increasingly like his father, dominating the government and relying on his security services to control dissent. But King Mohammed lacks his father's political experience and acumen and is more dependent on his advisers. Some royal aides are extremely competent, others less so, but all of them answer only to the throne.

The strongman of King Mohammed's entourage is the deputy secretary of the interior, Fouad Ali Al Himma. A former schoolmate of the king, the prematurely balding Al Himma does not seek the limelight but seems to enjoy his position as the main power behind the throne. In the name of the king, he deals with the key issues from human rights and political parties to the Sahara. Discreet and efficient, he has only one boss—the king.

Among the most high-profile and able counselors to the king is André Azoulay, who regularly represents the monarch at international economic and cultural forums. I first met Azoulay, a Jewish Moroccan, left-wing journalist, in the early 1960s. He went on to become a successful banker in Paris and an activist in the cause of Arab-Jewish reconciliation. In 1991, Hassan II invited Azoulay to return to Morocco and help lay the groundwork for the reforms which opened up the archaic, autocratic regime. When he came to the throne, King Mohammed asked Azoulay to stay on as a counselor, charged with economic and financial dossiers. I had seen Azoulay several times since, particularly as the prime mover behind the International Film Festival of Marrakech and the Festival of *Gnaoua* Music of Essaouira. In early May 2004, I asked for an interview to get his views on the Islamic terrorist attacks of Casablanca and Madrid.

"What is remarkable is that, with all the hatred in the Middle East beamed at us daily by television, the gentleness of the Moroccan way of life and the spirit of reconciliation have survived," Azoulay said, on receiving me in his office at the royal palace in Rabat.[24]

His Majesty's counselor, lean and elegant, acknowledged that he had been personally attacked for his Jewish religion by some Moroccan newspapers and in anti-Israeli demonstrations. And he appeared even more concerned about the recent poll by the Pew Research Center, which found that 92 percent of Moroccans had a negative opinion of Jews.

"Morocco hasn't changed," Azoulay insisted, pointing out that when the poll was taken, Moroccans were furious over Israeli prime minister Sharon's aggressive policies. He explained that gangs of *intégristes*—Islamic radicals—had penetrated schools and mosques with pamphlets calling for violence and hate, and at first, few people had reacted against them. Among the activists who have been fighting against all forms of intolerance for years, Azoulay stressed, is the new minister of social solidarity, Abderrahim Harouchi, head of a private association for civic responsibility and development. Now, the king's counselor said, many Moroccans have rejected the extremes and formed groups like the Moroccan Organization against Hatred and Racism, whose leaders include Simon Lévy, head of the Jewish Museum of Casablanca, and Nourredine Ayouch, president of the Zakoura Education Foundation.

Azoulay spoke optimistically of the first World Congress of *Imams* and Rabbis for Peace, set for the end of May—an initiative worthy of the late King Hassan. Fifty of the most important *imams* and the same number of prominent rabbis were to meet at the Middle Atlas resort of Ifrane near Fez, under the auspices of King Mohammed. The congress had been organized by the Swiss-based foundation Hommes de Parole, with support from the Islamic Education and Scientific Organization, whose center is in Rabat. "We have to be creative and create a new dynamic for understanding," Azoulay told me. (A few days later, the organizers announced in Paris that the Moroccan congress of religious leaders had been postponed because "the degradation of the situation in Gaza, in the Arab 'Palestinian' territories and in Iraq had dangerously altered the climate of serenity indispensable for the success [of the encounter]." By telephone, Azoulay stressed that the meeting had not been canceled, only put off until a more opportune time. The *imams* and rabbis did meet early in 2005, but in Belgium not Morocco.)

Azoulay was upbeat about the reforms engendered by Mohammed VI, emphasizing that it wasn't easy for the young monarch to build his own identity, following the towering figure of Hassan II. He described King Mohammed's rule as one of "continuity and change . . . different but coherent." Insisting that the monarch has a clear vision of his priorities, Azoulay said: "He knows where to go and when, and all the major decisions are his, not those of his advisers."

Asked what he considered to be the main achievements of King Mohammed's first five years, Azoulay responded without hesitation: the new Family Code, social reforms, and creating a favorable investment climate, "which means jobs." He stressed that foreign investments had increased to $3 billion in 2004, as compared to $2 billion in the previous year and $600 million in 1995. "Nothing is more vital than jobs," Azoulay concluded, reminding me that urban unemployment still stands at 20 percent.

Another visible member of the royal entourage is Hassan Aourid, the palace spokesman and a Berber scholar. His Tarik Ibn Zyad Center is making a significant contribution to Berber research and also regularly organizes lectures on controversial subjects like "The Monarchy and Political Islam in Morocco" with leading Moroccan and international experts. Aourid contends that the "clash of civilizations" is a clash within Islam and calls for "a new vision of Islam."[25]

In the tense spring of 2004, Aourid announced the establishment of a foundation to honor eighty-seven-year-old Jewish author Edmond Amran El Maleh, whose works celebrate Morocco's Arabic, Berber, and Jewish cultural heritage. It was a strong show of royal support for a multiethnic society at a time when the Islamists seemed to be gaining ground.[26]

There were other signals that the king wanted to liberalize the regime, starting with the stultifying royal protocol. On the first birthday of Crown Prince Hassan III, the king broke with tradition to receive journalists from the French magazine *Paris Match* at his home. In the thirteen-page cover story on "Mohammed VI *en famille*," the royal couple, wearing Western clothes, appeared like any other doting parents. The Moroccan public learned that their sovereign and his wife, Princess Salma, had moved out of his bachelor quarters at Salé—too small for raising a child—at the end of 2003 and have taken up residence at Dar Essalam, a vast property of orange trees, date palms, cedars, jacaranda, and bougainvillea on the outskirts of the capital, where his grandfather King Mohammed V had lived.[27]

The monarch refused to give a balance sheet for his rule thus far, emphasizing that he was "still at the beginning of what I want to achieve for Morocco." Among "the great advances of which I am rather proud," the king cited the new *Moudawana*, establishing equal rights of men and women.

But all was not smooth sailing for the royal reforms.

Plaudits continued to pour in for the progressive Family Code, but by February 2005, difficulties appeared in implementation. Fawzia Assouli, a leader of the Democratic League for Women's Rights, said that the main problem was conservative judges and notaries unfamiliar with the new laws.

The King's Commission for Equity and Reconciliation did hold public hearings in the winter of 2004–2005, which was hailed as a unique happening in the Muslim world. Two hundred victims of torture, arbitrary detention, and other violations gave heartrending testimony on abuses by the state, from independence to King Mohammed's accession to the throne in

King Mohammed and his wife, Princess Lalla Salma, celebrate the first birthday of Crown Prince Hassan III. (Azzouz/MAP)

1999. A total of 22,000 cases have been filed with the commission and are to serve as the basis for compensation and a report on that dark period.

Royal efforts to contain the truth process, however, seemed doomed. Human rights activists argued that the presentations did not go far enough, because the victims were barrred from identifying their abusers and the present period was excluded. Several newspapers dared to reveal names of officials implicated in the crimes. The Association for Human Rights organized alternative hearings in the spring of 2005, in which witnesses were free to name their torturers and denounce official misdeeds, even under the current king. Advocates of truth and justice vowed they would not turn the page on the past until the officials responsible for the abuses—some of whom remain in positions of authority—were brought to justice.

Despite the king's push for economic development and jobs, official forecasts for 2005 were for a gloomy 2.6 percent growth—nowhere near the 6 percent needed to absorb unemployment.[28] Agricultural production was expected to decline because of inclement weather, and predictions for textile and other exports were not bright. As the deficit rose to 3.9 percent of the GDP, there were reports that the International Monetary Fund might have to reimpose a Structural Adjustment Plan, like the plan that had caused so much social unrest in the 1980s.

King Mohammed's Morocco is not the same as his father's kingdom. Events under Mohammed's reign have demonstrated that Morocco is part of the contemporary globalization of political Islam and, not to be underestimated, the inclusion on Osama Bin Laden's list of impious countries.

For this reason, King Mohammed is under much greater pressure than was his father to deal with the Islamist challenge. Since the deadly terrorist attacks in Casablanca of May 16, 2003, Moroccan security services have acquired greater ascendancy empowered with new antiterrorist laws. At the same time, the king has attempted to regain control over the religious sector with better supervision of religious education and the mosques.

In view of new pan-Islamic pressures, King Mohammed has had to handle with extreme care Morocco's budding partnership with the United States, which is widely seen as an enemy of the Arabs and Islam. Since September 11, Washington has repeatedly pointed to Morocco as a moderate Islamic country opposed to terrorism, in a generally hostile Muslim world. First there was enhanced cooperation in the war on terror. Then, in the spring of 2004, the Bush administration designated Morocco as a "major non-NATO ally." And Morocco, a non-NATO nation, was invited to host important NATO exercises off its Atlantic coast in the summer of 2004.

For its part, Rabat has been generally receptive to the American advances because it shares concerns over Islamic radicals but also in hopes of gaining

Washington's support for Moroccan claims to Western Sahara. With the growing public opposition to American policies in the Middle East, however, some Moroccan officials feel that relations with the superpower are getting too close for comfort. A sign of this concern was Morocco's refusal, along with Egypt and Saudi Arabia, to attend the G-8 meeting of leading industrial nations in Georgia in June 2004 to discuss the Greater Middle East Initiative.

The landmark U.S.-Morocco free trade agreement was finally signed on June 15, 2004, in a ceremony in Washington, but not by the two heads of state, as had been expected. King Mohammed chose that day to begin a five-nation tour of Africa, dispatching his chief negotiator to do the honors in Washington. Marking the occasion, Robert B. Zoellick, the U.S. trade representative, said the accord would be beneficial to the two countries and glowingly portrayed Morocco as "a bright light of reform and moderation in the Islamic world."[29]

Early in 2005, Morocco's ambassador to Washington, Aziz Mekouar, began touring the main cities in the United States to attract trade and investments under the new free-trade pact. Emphasizing that Dell Computer and Motorola have begun operations in Morocco, the ambassador called for investments in high tech, agriculture, and financial services. His main selling points were Morocco's location as a trading hub, a free-trade accord with the European Union, a well-established market economy, and modernizing policies.

Bowing to public pressure, Morocco did not send peacekeeping forces to Iraq. But at the United Nations in September 2004, Morocco's foreign minister, Mohamed Benaissa, and U.S. secretary of state Colin Powell announced that Morocco would host the first "Forum for the Future" for reform in the Middle East and North Africa at the end of the year. The forum was the offspring of Washington's controversial Greater Middle East Initiative and brought together the G-8 with political, civic, and business leaders from the region.[30]

Morocco's Islamist PJD immediately condemned the forum as "not acceptable" for excluding some Arabs, like Syria and Libya, and including Israel.[31] The outspoken Abelhamid Amine, head of the Moroccan Human Rights Association, called the forum "an offense to the Moroccan people" in view of U.S. policy in the Middle East.[32]

Not much was achieved except an agreement to meet again. In the end, of the twenty-seven countries in the region, only Israel and the Sudan did not receive invitations. And Morocco, as co-host with the United States, counted on a sympathetic ear in Washington when the problem of Western Sahara next came up.

Morocco has come under increasing international pressure to tackle the poisonous Saharan issue with new sensitivity and imagination. The UN secretary general, Kofi Annan, warned that the UN peace keepers would be pulled out of Western Sahara if no agreement were reached between Morocco and the POLISARIO front by the end of February 2005. Showing his impatience, Annan declared that after spending thirteen years and more than $600 million, it was clear that "the United Nations was not going to solve the problem without requiring that one or both of the parties do something they would not voluntarily do."[33]

At the United Nations in New York in the fall of 2004, the secretary general's new special representative for Western Sahara, Alvaro de Soto, told me that he did not expect a breakthrough in the near future because there was no political will to work out a compromise. "We continue to adhere to the right of people emerging from colonial status to exercise self-determination; this is unquestionably the case of Western Sahara, as generally accepted for decades," Under-Secretary-General de Soto, a veteran peacemaker, declared. "Unfortunately efforts so far to enable the people to exercise their rights remain elusive. We will continue, however, to look for opportunities to break the deadlock."[34]

In late January 2005, Secretary General Annan said he was still prepared to help the parties reach a mutually acceptable solution to the Sahara question and reiterated his appeal to POLISARIO to release the remaining 410 Moroccan military prisoners (about 600 have been gradually let go, some held for more than two decades). Earlier, POLISARIO had freed two Moroccan military prisoners in critical condition, and one of them died shortly afterward. A month later, a Moroccan captain and a soldier escaped from a POLISARIO jail and accused their captors of savage torture.

The question is, can King Mohammed provide the courageous leadership needed on that deadlocked Saharan problem that he has demonstrated on other delicate issues?

Looking Ahead

Morocco has made significant strides in social and economic development and democratic rights since independence a half century ago. It is because the kingdom has so much to its credit that it can be held to higher standards than other countries in the region.

Most Moroccans I have come to know—Socialists, conservatives, Islamists, and the nonpartisan majority—have opted for the goals of democracy, modern development, and economic justice, while maintaining their Muslim identity. They are tired of delays, artifices, half-measures, and unkept promises and will exert increasing pressure on their leaders to listen to their demands and do something about them.

King Mohammed could be a significant force for profound change if he charts a clear course toward his stated goals of democracy and moderniza-tion. He must start by shaking up the sluggish system. The old practices of rule by nepotism, cronyism, and privilege must give way to considerations of competence, efficiency, dynamism, and the rule of law.

While retaining his central role as national symbol and arbiter, the monarch must give the political forces the power to govern democratically through a freely elected parliament and a government reflecting the people's will and responsiblity to the nation. Specifically, the administration must be empowered to achieve long-term solutions to the grinding problems of un-employment, illiteracy, *bidonvilles*, and abysmal health care. What is required is a firm, systematic approach to social and economic problems, not merely a series of well-intentioned gestures. The authorities must tackle official cor-ruption from top to bottom, unlike previous campaigns, which have only scratched the surface. On the gnawing Saharan problem, the Moroccan ad-ministration should convince the Saharans, including POLISARIO, that it is to their advantage to accept broad autonomy in a Morocco moving toward democracy. But of course the authorities will have to demonstrate to the na-tion as a whole that they are serious about the democratic agenda.

The palace has pushed a badly needed reform of political parties. But the legislation was drafted by the ministry of the interior, not by the elected leg-islators. Some changes are positive, like obligatory transparency on party fi-nances. The trouble is the ministry of interior has the power to authorize and dissolve all parties at will.

For their part, the political parties should work to regain the confidence of the electorate, renewing their leadership, bringing in more women and young people, and developing their grassroots action. There should also be a regrouping of political trends to achieve a working majority and real alter-natives of ideological choices. The small parties on the far Left have merged to form the Rally of the Democratic Left but have been unable to attract the main Socialist Party. The three branches of the rural Popular Movement have come together and could very well unite for the next national elections in 2007. The union feared by most political circles would be that of the PJD and Sheikh Yassine's Justice and Charity Association, but their divergences are as important as those of the non-Islamist parties.

Above all, the ruling establishment must come to terms with the Islamists in all of their diversity. What is urgently needed is for the Commander of the Faithful to publicly embrace all sectors of the population as long as they op-pose violence and are committed to respecting the laws of the land. This could serve as a condition for the legalization of Yassine's movement and other Islamic groups and their integration into public life.

The main Islamist organizations, both the PJD and Sheikh Yassine's Al Adl wal Ihssane, should come out forcefully against those extremists who take innocent lives in the name of religion. Their voices could be heard by people who have lost faith in "official religion."

On the other hand, the pro-Western elite, who preach democracy, must recognize the right of Islamists to take part in the life of the country, if they agree to obey the law.

And tolerance must be restored. For example, when the tsunami swept across South Asia, it didn't strike Morocco but caused a political upheaval at the beginning of 2005. A commentator for the Islamist daily *Attajdid* declared that the tsunami was divine punishment for sex tourism and a warning to Morocco. Waves of protests followed, with mainstream Moroccans denouncing Islamists as obscurantists—and Islamists brandishing the flag of freedom of the press. The tsunami seemed forgotten in the emotional exchanges.

Morocco's friends can encourage the democratic transition, but no outsider should dictate democratic reforms. Europe—above all France, Spain, and Germany—and the United States can help by applauding democratic advances and firmly denouncing abuses. They must treat Morocco fairly as an economic partner and engage with the broad spectrum of civil society, including women's groups and Islamists, not just the ruling elite.

The United States is currently at a disadvantage because of widespread anger over its Middle East policies and would do well to let Europeans take the lead in helping with political and even economic modernization. The United States would gain by concentrating investments in high-tech and humanitarian fields like health and education, which are badly in need of reform. At least, Morocco's foreign partners should coordinate their support rather than plunge into cutthroat rivalry. And whether this cooperation is called the Barcelona Process, the Forum for the Future, or something else, it must respect local Muslim sensitivities.

The king, the political establishment, and civil society face a deadline to demonstrate their democratic bona fides—2007, the date for the next parliamentary elections. If progress has not been made toward giving average Moroccans hope for a better life, the feeling that they have a stake in the future of the kingdom and its management, in sum, conviction that the country is finally engaged on the route to democracy, the Islamist alternative—be it moderate or radical—will be waiting.

In the throes of the local elections of September 2003, Mohammed Guessous, a long-time Socialist activist and professor of social sciences, remarked wryly: "Don't forget it took Europe 200 years to consolidate its democracy."[35]

But in this age of electronic speed and satellite images, Moroccans are clamoring for justice, accountability, and hope—and they want change now.

Notes

Chapter 1

1. Hassan II, with Eric Laurent, *La Mémoire d'un roi* (Paris: Librairie Plon, 1993), 22.

2. Malika Oufkir, *Stolen Lives*, trans. Ros Schwartz (New York: Hyperion, 2001): 35–36.

3. King Mohammed's speech to regional authorities, Royal Palace, October 12, 1999.

4. King Mohammed's first Throne Speech, July 30, 1999.

5. Interview with Prime Minister Abderrahmane Youssoufi, November 16, 1999.

6. King Mohammed on forty-sixth anniversary of exile of royal family in 1953.

7. Conversation with Bachir Ben Barka, November 27, 1999.

8. Scott Mac Leod, "The King of Cool," *Time* (June 26, 2000): 27–28.

9. Roxanne Roberts and Kimberly Palmer, "Morocco's King of Hearts," *Washington Post*, June 22, 2000.

10. Interview with Prince Moulay Hicham ben Abdallah el Alaoui, February 16, 2002.

11. Hicham ben Abdallah el Alaoui, "To Be a Citizen in the Arab World," *Le Monde Diplomatique* (July 1995): 11.

12. Moulay Hicham el Alaoui, "Deadly Waiting in Morocco," *Le Monde* (June 27, 2001): 1.

13. Interview with Moulay Hicham, February 16, 2002.

14. Conversation with Nadia Yassine, June 13, 2002.

15. Ahmed R. Benchemsi, "The Fight against Terrorists: On the Efficiency of Torture," *TelQuel* (January 27–February 11, 2004).

Chapter 2

1. Paul Bowles, Too Far from Home (Hopewell, N.J.: ECCO, 1993), 677.
2. Mark Twain, *The Innocents Abroad* (New York: Library of America, 1984), 61.
3. Bowles, *Too Far from Home*, 677.
4. William Burroughs, "Letter to Allen Ginsberg [June 16, 1954]," in *The Letters of William Burroughs*, ed. Oliver Harris (New York: Penguin, 1994), 215.
5. Owen Bowcott, "Morocco Losing Forests to Cannabis," *Guardian*, December 16, 2003.
6. Conversations with Khalid Taouil, Moroccan journalist, in Fez, February 18 and 19, 2001.
7. Interview with Mohamed Baghdadi, supervisor at American Language Center, Fez, February 19, 2001.
8. Conversations with David Amster, director of American Language Center, Fez, February 18 and 19, 2001.
9. Interview with Asmae el Mahdi, head of Initiative for the Protection of Women's Rights, Fez, February 18, 2001.
10. Interview with Haddou Ohdouch, student from Imilchil, February 19, 2001.
11. Interview with Souheil Ben Barka, head of the Moroccan Cinema Center, Rabat, July 20, 2001.
12. Edith Wharton, "To Bernard Berenson [Fez, October 2, 1917]," in *The Letters of Edith Wharton*, ed. R. W. B. Lewis and Nancy Lewis (New York: Scribner's, 1988), 401–3.
13. Conversations with former U.S. ambassador to Rabat Frederick Vreeland, October 18 and 23, 2001.
14. Conversation with Amine Bennouna, head of Marrakech office of Noor Web, February 22, 2001.
15. Conversation with Adolfo de Velasco, social mentor and antique dealer, Marrakech, February 22, 2001.

Chapter 3

1. John Waterbury, *The Commander of the Faithful: The Moroccan Political Elite: A Study in Segmented Politics* (New York: Columbia University Press, 1970), 33–34.
2. Abdallah Laroui, *Esquisses historiques* (Casablanca: Centre Culturel Arabe, 1992), 22.
3. André Chouraqui, *Histoire de Juifs en Afrique du Nord* (Paris: Hachette, 1985), 18.
4. Charles-André Julien, *Histoire de l'Afrique du Nord: des origines à la conquête arabe (647 ap.J.-C.)* (Paris: Payot, 1972), 147.
5. Nevill Barbour, *Morocco* (London: Thames and Hudson, 1965), 43–44.
6. Jamil Abun-Nasr, *A History of the Maghrib in the Islamic Period* (Cambridge: Cambridge University Press, 1987), 215.
7. Albert Ayache, *Le Maroc* (Paris: Sociales, 1956), 81.
8. Waterbury, *Commander of the Faithful*, 38–39.

9. Interview with Allal el Fassi, head of the Istiqlal party, Rabat, 1962.

10. Alal Al-Fasi (Allal el Fassi), *The Independence Movements in Arab North Africa* (Washington, D.C.: American Council of Learned Societies, 1954), 116.

11. Conversation with *Agence France Presse* correspondent Bertrand Bellaigue, Chuelles, France, August 1, 2002.

12. Elliot Roosevelt, *As He Saw It* (New York: Duell, Sloan and Pearce, 1946), 109–12.

13. Marvine Howe, *One Woman's Morocco* (London: Barker, 1956), 101–4.

14. Conversations with Prince Moulay Hassan, fall of 1952.

15. Conversations with Abderrahim Bouabid, Istiqlal leader, fall of 1952.

16. Conversations with M'hamed Douiri, assistant director of mines, spring of 1953.

17. Conversation with Prince Moulay Hassan, July 1953.

18. Stephane Bernard, *The Franco-Moroccan Conflict, 1943–56* (New Haven, Conn.: Yale University Press, 1968), 160–61.

19. Conversation with Elinor Canedy, manager of Radio Maroc's American program, September 1953.

20. Douglas E. Ashford, *Political Change in Morocco* (Princeton, N.J.: Princeton University Press, 1961), 78.

21. Conversations with Mehdi Ben Barka, founder of the National Union of Socialist Forces, summer of 1955.

22. Bernard, *Franco-Moroccan Conflict*, 293.

23. Stephen O. Hughes, *Morocco under King Hassan* (Reading, U.K.: Ithaca Press, 2001), 61.

24. Conversation with Abderrahim Bouabid, August 1955.

25. Rom Landau, *Mohammed V: King of Morocco* (Rabat: Morocco Publishers, 1957), 97.

26. Ibid., 98.

27. Ibid., 100.

28. Conversation with Prince Moulay Hassan, spring of 1956.

Chapter 4

1. King Mohammed V's Throne Speech, November 18, 1955, in *Réalisations et Perspectives: 16 Novembre 1955–18 Novembre 1957* (Rabat: Ministry of Information and Tourism, Kingdom of Morocco, 1957), 8.

2. Ignace Dalle, *Les Trois Rois* (Paris: Fayard, 2004), 181–85.

3. Conversations with Prince Moulay Hassan, winter of 1956.

4. Conversation with Ben Barka, spring of 1957.

5. Conversation with Prince Moulay Hassan, December 1957.

6. Conversation with Abderrahmane Youssoufi, January 1960.

7. Correspondence from Mehdi Ben Barka, spring of 1960.

8. Hassan II, with Eric Laurent, *La Mémoire d'un roi* (Paris: Librairie Plon, 1993), 69–74.

9. John Waterbury, *The Commander of the Faithful: The Moroccan Political Elite: A Study in Segmented Politics* (New York: Columbia University Press, 1970), 289–98.

10. Hassan II, *Mémoire*, 81.

11. Stephen O. Hughes, *Morocco under King Hassan* (Reading, U.K.: Ithaca Press, 2001), 153.

12. Ahmed Boukhari, *Le Secret: Ben Barka et le Maroc: Un Ancien Agent des Services Spéciaux Parle* (Neuilly-Sur-Seine, France: Lafon, 2002), 174–76.

13. Jamil Abun-Nasr, *A History of the Maghrib in the Islamic Period* (Cambridge: Cambridge University Press, 1987), 418.

14. Hughes, *Morocco*, 160.

15. Hassan II, *Mémoire*, 160.

16. Ibid., 168, 170.

17. Hughes, *Morocco*, 206.

18. Will D. Swearingen, *Moroccan Mirages: Agrarian Dreams and Deceptions, 1912–1986* (Princeton, N.J.: Princeton University Press, 1987), 189.

19. Hassan II, *Mémoire*, 293–96.

20. Conversation with M'hamed Douiri, July 9, 1995.

21. Interview with Abderrahmane Youssoufi, leader of Socialist opposition, Casablanca, July 4, 1995.

Chapter 5

1. John P. Entelis, "Political Islam in the Maghreb: The Nonviolent Dimension," in *Islam, Democracy, and the State in North Africa*, ed. John P. Entelis (Bloomington and Indianapolis: Indiana University Press, 1997), 56.

2. King Mohammed VI interview with Anne Sinclair, *Paris Match*, November 8, 2001, 44.

3. King Mohammed VI's address on "Muslim World Image in Western Press: Between Fairness and Bias," *Maghreb Arabe Presse*, January 9, 2002.

4. Abdallah Laroui, *Esquisses historiques* (Casablanca: Centre Culturel Arabe, 1992), 41.

5. Hassan II, with Eric Laurent, *La Mémoire d'un roi* (Paris: Librairie Plon, 1993), 242.

6. Abdellatif Agnouche, "'The Command of the Faithful' from Hassan II to Mohammed VI," *L'Indépendant Magazine* (December 13–15, 2002): 3–5.

7. Interview with Mohamed Darif, head of Department of Public Law, University of Hassan II, September 19, 2003.

8. François Burgat and William Dowell, *The Islamic Movement in North Africa* (Austin: Center for Middle Eastern Studies, University of Texas, 1993), 177.

9. Darif, "Islamic Youth: A New Version," *La Gazette du Maroc*, June 16, 2003, 14.

10. Darif interview, September 19, 2003.

11. Interview with Fathallah Arsalane, October 30, 2001.

12. Mohamed Tozy, "Who Are the Islamists in Morocco ?" *Le Monde Diplomatique* (July–August 2002): 46–47.

13. Emad Eldin Shahin, "Secularism and Nationalism: The Political Discourse of Abd al-Salam Yassin," in *Islamism and Secularism in North Africa*, ed. John Ruedy (London: Macmillan, 1994), 129.

14. Interviews with Nadia Yassine, spokeswoman for Sheikh Yassine, November 1995.

15. Nadia Yassine, *Toutes voiles dehors* (Casablanca: Le Fennec, 2003), 9.

16. Interview with Nadia Yassine, June 27, 2003.

17. Interview with PJD's Benkiran, July 3, 2002.

18. Abdellatif el Azizi, "A Sharia Tailored to Fit," *Maroc-Hebdo International*, December 20–26, 2002, 15.

19. Conversation with leaders of Al Badil Hadari, Amine Ragala and Mustapha Moatassim, July 10, 2003.

20. Poll, "Moroccans Believe Bin Laden Innocent," *Al Ahdath Al Maghribia*, October 29, 2001; reprinted in *Le Journal*, November 3, 2001, 13.

21. Interview with Islamic scholar Mohamed Tozy, September 21, 2000.

22. Interview with Najat Ikhich, head of the Moroccan League for Women's Rights, June 30, 2003.

23. Abdelkébir Alaoui M'Daghri, interview, "In Morocco, the Danger Doesn't Come from Islamists," *Maroc-Hebdo International* (June 28–July 4, 2002): 4–5.

24. Khalid Jamai, "The Affair of the 'Al Qaeda Cell': Bullshit," *Le Journal Hebdomadaire*, June 22–28, 2002, 8–9.

25. Abdellatif Mansour, "Moroccan Taliban," *Maroc-Hebdo*, August 2002.

26. Interview with Benkiran, July 3, 2002.

27. Interview with Tozy, September 24, 2002.

Chapter 6

1. Interview with Princess Lalla Aicha, 1956.

2. Douglas E. Ashford, *Political Change in Morocco* (Princeton, N.J.: Princeton University Press, 1961), 399–401.

3. Fatima Sadiqi, "Women and Linguistic Space in Morocco," *Women and Language* 26, no. 1 (Spring 2003): 35–43.

4. Nouzha Skalli, parliamentarian at Convergences 21 seminar in Rabat, June 21, 2003.

5. Nadia Yassine, *Toutes voiles dehors* (Casablanca: Le Fennec, 2003), 297–300.

6. "Plan for the Integration of Women in Development" (Rabat: Secretariat of the Family, Children and Social Protection, 1999), 18–19.

7. Driss Ksikes,"Why the Veil Is Gaining Ground," *TelQuel* (November 2–8, 2002): 17–25.

8. Conversation with Hinde Taarji, journalist and author, October 10, 2001.

9. Conversation with Bahia Amrani, publisher of *Le Reporter*, July 14, 2002.

10. Interview with Aicha Zaimi Sakhri, publisher of *Femmes du Maroc*, October 12, 2001.

11. Amina Talhimet, editorial, *Libération,* December 24, 2002.

12. Interview with Amina Benkhadra, July 18, 2001.

13. Interview with Hakima Moktari, Islamist social worker, July 4, 2003.

14. Interview with Bassima Hakkaoui, PJD deputy, September 17, 2003.

15. Interview with Noureddine Ayouch, head of the Zakoura Foundation, July 9, 2002.

16. Interview with Irene Natividad, organizer of the Thirteenth Global Summit of Women at Marrakech, June 28–30, 2003.

17. Mohammed VI, Message to Global Summit of Women, June 28, 2003.

18. Yasmina Baddou, secretary for family and social affairs, address to Global Summit of Women, June 29, 2003.

19. Interview with Aicha Ech-Chenna, head of Solidarité Feminine, September 21, 2000.

20. Interview with Fattouma Benabdenbi, July 25, 2001.

21. Interview with Leila Rhiwi, leader of Printemps de l'Egalité, July 5, 2003.

22. Interview with Aicha Belarbi, November 21, 1999.

23. Conversation with Najia Zirari, journalist and activist in the women's movement, November 15, 1999.

24. King Mohammed VI, speech on the 46th Anniversary of "the Revolution of the King and People" (date the royal family was sent into exile), August 20, 1999.

25. Interview with Nadia Yassine, November 21, 1999.

26. Interview with Prime Minister Abderrahmane Youssoufi, September 14, 2000.

27. Interview with Amina Lemrini, September 16, 2000.

28. Conversation with Youssoufi, September 16, 2000.

29. Interview with Bassima Hakkaoui, September 17, 2003.

30. Interview with Nouzha Skalli, congresswoman and a founder of the Democratic Association of Moroccan Women, July 15, 2002.

31. M'hamed Boucetta, interview with *Libération,* March 10, 2003.

32. Conversation with Mernissi, June 15, 2002.

33. Interview with Nouzha Guessous-Idrissi, June 16, 2003.

Chapter 7

1. Driss Ksikes quotes linguist Mohamed Dahbi, "Darija: Notre vraie langue nationale," *TelQuel* (June 15–21, 2002): 20.

2. Interview with Ali Ben Bachir Hassani, July 13, 2001.

3. Interview with M'hamed Douiri, July 14, 2001.

4. Ignace Dalle, *Maroc 1961–1999: L'espérance brisée* (Paris: Maisonneuve et Larose, 2001), 50.

5. Interview with Ibrahim Akhiat, October 4, 2002.

6. Interview with Mohammed Achaari, July 27, 2001.

7. Interview with Mohamed Chafik, June 14, 2002.

8. Interview with Ahmed Assid, *Amazigh* poet and militant, October 9, 2002.

9. Chafik Laabi, quoting PJD deputy secretary general Saad Eddine el Othmani, "Sharp Battle of Alphabets on the *Amazigh* Question," *La Vie Economique*, January 16, 2003, 4.

10. Interviews with Meryam Demnati, *Amazigh* poet and militant, June 25 and September 15, 2003.

11. Belkacem Lounes, president of *Amazigh* World Congress, "Action against Moroccan Minister of National Education," *Le Monde Amazigh*, May 2004.

12. World *Amazigh* Congress, "The *Amazigh*s of Morocco: A People Depicted as a Minority," www.amazighworld.org, November 15, 2004.

13. Daniel J. Schroeter, "Jews among the Berbers," in *Juifs parmi les Berbères: Photographies d'Elias Harrus* (Paris: Musée d'art et d'histoire du Judaisme, 1999), 16–19.

14. Lawrence Rosen, *The Culture of Islam* (Chicago: University of Chicago Press, 2002), 76–87.

15. Interview with Mohammed Guessous, member of the Commission for the National Charter on Education, October 9, 2002.

16. Interview with Hassan Najmi, October 5, 2002.

17. Interview with Ahmed Assid, October 9, 2002.

18. Ahmed Aydoun, *Musiques du Maroc* (Casablanca: EDDIF, 2001), 145–56.

19. Richard Parker, *Islamic Monuments in Morocco* (Charlottesville, Va.: Baraka, 1981), 26–27.

20. Afrol News, "Mazagan, Morocco Honoured as 'Outstanding,'" www.afrol.com, July 5, 2004.

21. Michel Thévoz, "Extraordinary Creativity," *Maroc-Hebdo* (December 20–26, 2002): 32–33.

22. Conversation with Karima Faouzi, October 8, 2002.

23. Conversation with Latifa Tijani, artist and activist in the women's movement, September 13, 2003.

24. Interview with Lahcen Zinoun, June 17, 2003.

25. Quoted in Jean-Pierre Tuquoi, "A Moroccan Film Target of Censors and Islamists," *Le Monde*, January 22, 2003.

26. Dr. Saad Eddine el Othmani, vice secretary general of the PJD, "Rectification," February 20, 2003.

27. Chafik Laabi, "What Do the Islamists Want?" *La Vie Economique* (January 24–30, 2003).

28. Abdelmounaim Dilami, Editorial, *L'Economiste* (January 17, 2003).

29. Omar Dahbi, "PJD: Threat against Festivals," *Aujourd'hui le Maroc*, June 22, 2004.

Chapter 8

1. Interview with Governor Driss Benhima, Casablanca, June 22, 2002.

2. Interview with Saad Bendidi, August 3, 2001.

3. Guilain P. Denoeux, "Morocco's Economic Prospects: Daunting Challenges Ahead," *Middle East Policy* 8, no. 2 (June 2001): 78.

4. Aboubakr Jamai, "2003: The Test Year," *Le Journal Hebdo,* January 31, 2004.

5. Interview with Khalil Nouara, October 11, 2001.

6. Interview with Eric Stoclet, October 10, 2001.

7. Will D. Swearingen, *Moroccan Mirages: Agrarian Dreams and Deceptions, 1912–1986* (Princeton, N.J.: Princeton University Press, 1987), 183–89.

8. Interview with Najib Akesbi, professor at the Hassan II Institute of Agronomy and Veterinary Studies, July 3, 2003.

9. Najbi Akesbi at Convergences 21 seminar, June 21, 2003.

10. Hassan M. Alaoui, "A Generation of Parasites," *Economie et Entreprises* (December 2002).

11. Special report, "The Luxury Business Boom," *Economie et Entreprises* (December 2002): 93–100.

12. *Association Ifarkhane Tizi 2000,* report on conditions in Tizi N'Choug (2000).

13. Conversations with Bouchra Hassoune, October 16–17, 2001.

14. Conversation with Rachid Mindilli, October 16, 2001.

15. Conversations with Amina Aït Ezzaouyt, Tizi N'Choug, October 16–17, 2001.

16. Interview with Fathallah Oualalou, September 15, 2003.

Chapter 9

1. Conversation with Ahmed Sanoussi, July 20, 2003.

2. Abdellah Hammoudi, *Master and Disciple: The Cultural Foundations of Moroccan Authoritarianism* (Chicago: University of Chicago Press, 1997), 25.

3. Christine Daure-Serfaty, *Lettre du Maroc* (Paris: Stock, 2000), 30.

4. Douglas E. Ashford, *Political Change in Morocco* (Princeton, N.J.: Princeton University Press, 1961), 271.

5. Khalid Jamai, "Unions and Parties: 'Incestuous' Relations," *Le Journal* (June 16–22, 2000): 17.

6. Interview with Nizar Baraka, October 3, 2002.

7. Interview with Prime Minister Youssoufi, November 17, 1999.

8. Conversation with Prime Minister Youssoufi, July 8, 2001.

9. Stephen Smith and Jean-Pierre Tuquoi, "Morocco: Waiting for Mohammed VI," *Le Monde* (July 13, 2001): 12.

10. Conversation with Prime Minister Youssoufi, July 8, 2001.

11. Conversation with Abdelatif Jebro, July 9, 2001.

12. Interview with Aboubakr Jamai, July 30, 2001.

13. Interview with Prince Moulay Hicham, July 2, 2003.

14. National Union of the Moroccan Press, "Three Regional Journalists Also Arrested," *Le Reporter,* June 19, 2003.

15. Interview with Ahmed Reda Benchemsi, May 15, 2004.

16. Interview with Prime Minister Youssoufi, September 25, 2002.

17. Interview with Kamal Labib, September 23, 2002.

18. Interview with Driss Jettou, minister of the interior and future prime minister, October 8, 2002.

Chapter 10

1. Report, "The Association Movement," *Libération*, July 20, 2001.
2. Interview with Mustapha Chafii, November 5, 2001.
3. Interview with Abdelaziz Bennani, July 12, 1995.
4. Interview with Mohamed el Boukeli, July 2, 2003.
5. Lawrence Rosen, *The Culture of Islam* (Chicago: University of Chicago Press, 2002), 13.
6. Interview with Sion Assidon, July 24, 2001.
7. Conversation with Salah El Ouadie, July 31, 2001.
8. Interview with Driss Benzekri, July 22, 2001.
9. Interview with Prime Minister Youssoufi, July 8, 2001.
10. Interview with Abraham Serfaty, July 30, 2001.
11. Interview with Khadija Rouissi, October 12, 2001.
12. Conversation with Mouhcine Ayouche, a leader of the leftist OADP and the General Confederation of Moroccan Businesses, July 28, 2001.
13. Conversation with Fatema Mernissi, July 21, 2001.
14. Interview with Najat Mjid, July 24, 2001.
15. Houda Benbouya, "Hakima Himmich: The AIDS Epidemic Takes a Dangerous Turn," *L'Economiste*, July 8, 2004.
16. Interview with Leila Benhima Cherif, July 16, 2002.
17. Conversation with Leila Benhima Cherif at International Women's Summit, Marrakech, June 29, 2003.
18. Interview with Meriem Othmani, July 8, 2002.
19. Interview with Noureddine Ayouch, July 9, 2002.
20. Interview with Leila Tazi, July 4, 2002.
21. Conversation with Ali Amahan, counselor to the minister of culture, July 20, 2001.
22. Conversation with Jamila Hassoune, head of the Caravanes Civiques, July 20, 2001.
23. Interview with Abdelali Benameur, November 26, 1999.
24. Interview with Ali Belhaj, November 25, 1999.
25. Interview with Ali Bouabid, July 17, 2001.
26. Interview with Hassan Belguerda, November 4, 2001.
27. Seminar organized by the UN Population Fund for some sixty women's NGOs, fall of 1995.
28. Interview with Bassima Hakkaoui, September 17, 2003.
29. Conversation with Leila Chaouni, July 25, 2001.
30. Conversation with Nadia Yassine, June 27, 2003.

Chapter 11

1. King Mohammed VI, speech delivered in Laayoune, March 6, 2002.

2. Lloyd Cabot Briggs, *Tribes of the Sahara* (Cambridge, Mass.: Harvard University Press, 1960), 211–36.

3. Tomás García Figueras, *Marruecos (La acción de España en el norte de Africa)* (Tetuan: Marroquí, 1955), 327–30.

4. Tony Hodges, *Western Sahara: The Roots of a Desert War* (Westport, Conn.: Hill, 1983), 68.

5. Allal el Fassi, quoted by Douglas E. Ashford, *Political Change in Morocco* (Princeton, N.J.: Princeton University Press, 1961), 179.

6. King Mohammed V, quoted by Hodges, *Western Sahara*, 88.

7. King Hassan II, quoted by Hodges, *Western Sahara*, 174.

8. International Court of Justice, "Advisory Opinion: Western Sahara," October 16, 1975.

9. Tomás Bárbulo, *La historia prohibida del Sahara Español* (Barcelona: Destino, 2002), 92.

10. Hodges, *Western Sahara*, 153.

11. Interview with Abderrahim Bouabid, February 1977.

12. Declaration by Mohamed Abdelaziz, February 27, 1977.

13. Bachir Mustapha, press conference, February 27, 1977.

14. Interview with Mohamed Salem Ould Salek, early March 1977.

15. Hodges, *Western Sahara*, 356.

16. Bachir Mustapha's press conference, February 27, 1977.

17. King Mohammed VI, speech on anniversary of the Green March, November 6, 2002.

18. Interview with Ambassador William L. Swing, June 20, 2002.

19. Interview with Abdelatif Guerraoui, governor of Western Sahara, June 21, 2002.

20. Interview with Governor Hamid Chabbar, Laayoune, June 20, 2002.

21. Conversation with Alaouate Edaha, Wahada *bidonville*, June 23, 2002.

22. Interview with Zouin Rabiaa, June 23, 2002.

23. Interview with Ahmed Kher, June 23, 2002.

24. Conversations with Alia Erguibi, Laayoune, June 19–23, 2002.

25. Conversation with Daoudi el Batoul, June 22, 2002.

26. Conversations with Mohamed Laghdef, June 19 and 20, 2002.

Chapter 12

1. Remarks by President Bush and Morocco's King Mohammed VI, "Bush Meets with Moroccan King Mohammed VI in Washington," Washington File, U.S. Department of State, April 2, 2002.

2. "King Mohammed VI Expresses Morocco's Solidarity with Iraq," *Le Matin du Sahara*, March 20, 2003.

3. Nabil Benabdallah, Moroccan government spokesman, *Le Matin du Sahara*, March 20, 2003.

4. Abderrahmane Youssoufi, "Direct Expression," *Libération*, May 12, 2003.

5. Hassan II, with Eric Laurent, *La Mémoire d'un roi* (Paris: Librairie Plon, 1993), 19, 20.

6. Richard B. Parker, *North Africa: Regional Tensions and Strategic Concerns* (New York: Praeger, 1984), 31, 32.

7. Ambassador Edward M. Gabriel, address to the Council on Foreign Relations, September 15, 1999.

8. Interview with James Bednar, September 18, 2003.

9. Interview with Minister of Finances Fathallah Oualalou, September 15, 2003.

10. Ambassador Margaret Tutwiler, interview by Imad Bentayeb, Redouane Ghadouna, and Maria Hammouchene, *Finances News Magazine*, December 2002.

11. Pierre Vermeren, *Le Maroc en transition* (Paris: La Découverte, 2001), 151–59.

12. Abderrahmane Youssoufi, "Direct Expression," *Libération*, May 12, 2003.

13. King Mohammed VI, quoted by *MAP*, December 22, 2002.

14. French president Jacques Chirac's speech at dinner offered by King Mohammed at Fez, *MAP*, October 9, 2003.

15. Spanish position paper, "Differences between the Question of Gibraltar and the Status of Ceuta and Melilla," obtained in Rabat, September 2003.

16. Hassan II, *Mémoire*, 229–30.

Chapter 13

1. King Mohammed VI, post–May 16 speech, *MAP*, May 29, 2003.

2. Interview with Boris Toledano, June 20, 2003.

3. Survey, "Should the PJD Be Banned?" *L'Economiste*, July 11, 2003.

4. Poll on May 16 events, "The Casablanca Attacks: An Opinion Poll," *Al Ahdath al Maghribia*; synopsis in *L'Economiste*, June 11, 2003.

5. Driss Abbadi, law professor; Simon Lévy, head of the Jewish Museum; and Rachid Belmokhtar, president of Al Akhawayn University, at Convergences 21 seminar, Rabat, June 21, 2003.

6. Abdellatif El Azizi quotes Hassan Aourid, "Contradictions and Social Cracks," *Maroc-Hebdo*, July 12, 2003.

7. Interview with Fauzia Assouli, June 30, 2003.

8. Interview with Mohammed Belam, graduate student from a Casablanca *bidonville*, June 30, 2003.

9. Khalid Jamai, "Chronicle," *Le Journal*, June 28, 2003.

10. Latifa Jbadi, interview in *Le Matin du Sahara*, July 14, 2003.

11. Driss Ksikes, "The Future after May 16: From the Sword to the Rosary," *TelQuel*, August 9, 2003.

12. King Mohammed VI, post–May 16 speech, *MAP*, May 29, 2003.

13. King Mohammed VI, Throne Speech, *MAP*, July 30, 2003.

14. Laetitia Grotti quotes Patrick Baudouin, "They Too Have Rights," *TelQuel*, August 9, 2003.

15. King Mohammed VI, message to World Youth Congress, Casablanca, *MAP*, August 19, 2003.

16. Hassan M. Alaoui, editorial, *Economie et Entreprises*, June 2003.

17. Prime Minister Driss Jettou, *MAP*, July 10, 2003.

18. Ahmed Benchemsi, "Morocco/Israel," *TelQuel*, September 5, 2003.

19. Antonio Baquero, "Al Qaeda's Moroccan Tentacle," *El Periódico de Catalunya*, October 3, 2003.

20. Interview with Ahmed Toufiq, September 19, 2003.

21. Interview with Nadia Yassine, June 27, 2003.

22. Interview with Abdelilah Benkiran, June 26, 2003.

23. Interview with Saad Eddine el Othmani, September 16, 2003.

24. Interview with former Prime Minister Youssoufi, Casablanca, May 14, 2004.

25. King Mohammed VI, speech to parliament, *MAP*, October 10, 2003.

26. Leila Rhiwi and Khadija Rouggany quoted in Maria Daif, "Feminists: What Next?" *TelQuel*, October 26, 2003.

27. Khalid Jamai, "Tribune and Debate," *Le Journal Hebdomadaire*, October 18, 2003, 6.

28. President George W. Bush, "Praise of Mohammed VI," *MAP*, October 24, 2003.

29. President Jacques Chirac, "Reaction to the Moudawana," *MAP*, October 11, 2003.

30. Fouad Abdelmoumni, "The State Would Be Credible Only If It Publicly Presents Its Excuses," *Le Journal Hebdomadaire*, October 25, 2003, 13.

31. Statement by Under-Secretary of State Marc Grossman, U.S. State Department, March 3, 2004.

32. Ali Amar, "The Moroccans of Al Qaeda," *Le Journal Hebdomadaire*, March 27, 2004.

Epilogue

1. Amnesty International, "Morocco/Western Sahara: Briefing to the Committee against Torture," UN Committee against Torture, Geneva, November 11, 2003.

2. Human Rights Watch, "Morocco: Counter-Terror Crackdown Sets Back Rights Progress," downloaded from http://hrw.org/english/docs/2004/10/21/morocc9522_txt .htm.

3. Transparency International, "Media Criticizes 'Worsening' of Corruption in Morocco," *Arabic News*, October 22, 2004.

4. Interview with Abdelhak Serhane, June 19, 2003.

5. Interview with Ahmed Benchemsi, May 15, 2004.

6. Benchemsi, "May 16: One Year Later," *TelQuel* (May 15–21, 2004): 30–31.

7. Final communiqué of the Seventh Congress of the Moroccan Association for Human Rights, April 11, 2004.

8. Interview with Abdelhamid Amine, May 10, 2004.

9. Mustapha Ramid, "The Main Characteristics of the Construction for Morocco's Constitution," *As-Sahifa al-Ousbouiya*, April 1, 2004.

10. Interview with Mustapha Ramid, May 12, 2004.

11. Interview with Fatima Merroun, May 12, 2004.

12. Michael Brett and Elizabeth Fentress, *The Berbers* (Oxford: Blackwell, 1996), 276.

13. Interview with Meryam Demnati, May 13, 2004.

14. Demnati, "Secularism: A Social Ethic," www.Kabyle.com, downloaded May 4, 2004.

15. "Charter of Amazigh Claims for a Constitutional Revision," *Le Journal Hebdomadaire*, October 30–November 4, 2004.

16. Interview with Prince Moulay Hicham at his Rabat office, May 7, 2004.

17. Interview with Rkia El Mossadeq, May 13, 2004.

18. Rkia El Mossadeq, *Les labyrinthes de la transition démocratique* (Casablanca: Najah el Jadida, 2001), 26–29.

19. Ahmed R. Benchemsi, "Desperate Search for a Dream," *TelQuel*, May 8–14, 2004.

20. Chifaa Nassir, "Sidi Moumen: One Year Later," *Maroc-Hebdo International*, May 21–27, 2004.

21. Khalid Jamai, "May 16: One Year Later," *Le Journal Hebdomadaire*, May 29–June 4, 2004.

22. King Mohammed VI, speech, Casablanca, April 30, 2004.

23. King Mohammed VI, interview with *El Pais*, reproduced by *Le Matin du Sahara*, January 17, 2005.

24. Interview with André Azoulay, May 11, 2004.

25. Hassan Aourid, "Dialogue entre monde musulman et Occident," *Le Matin du Sahara*, November 16, 2003.

26. Aourid quoted in "Creation in Rabat of the Edmond Amran El Maleh Foundation," *Le Matin du Sahara*, June 14, 2004.

27. Caroline Pigozzi, "Mohammed VI: Happiness in Broad Daylight," *Paris Match* (May 13–19, 2004): 44–54.

28. High Planning Commission, "Forecast: Growth for 2005 Will Be 2.6 Percent," *Le Matin du Sahara*, February 13, 2005.

29. Robert B. Zoellick, "Free Trade Can Change the Middle East," *International Herald Tribune*, June 14, 2004.

30. Mouaad Rhandi, "Will the Greater Middle East Be Built in Morocco?" *Le Journal Hebdo*, October 16, 2004.

31. Ibid.

32. Abdelhamid Amine, "Interview with the Secretary General of the AMDH," *As-Sahifa Al-Ousbouiya*, October 6, 2004.

33. United Nations Secretary General Kofi Annan, "Western Sahara: 13 Years and $600 Million Later, Peace Nowhere in Sight," allAfrica.com, April 28, 2004.

34. Interview with Alvaro de Soto, the special representative of the UN secretary general for Western Sahara, United Nations, New York, October 29, 2004.

35. Conversation with Mohammed Guessous, September 12, 2003.

Glossary

Transliteration

Since most Moroccans use the French transliteration of Arabic and Berber proper names, places, and common words, I have chosen the French rather than the English usage. For example, I have used the common French transliteration for the name of the ruling Alaouite dynasty (not Alawite), *oulema* (rather than *ulama*) for Islamic scholars, and *beia*, not *bay'a*, for the pledge of allegiance. Only in instances where the English version is widely accepted have I employed an English transliteration, like sherif rather than the French *cherif*, and for certain Middle Eastern names, such as Muhammad Abduh, the Egyptian scholar and founder of the Salafiya Islamic reform movement.

Ahidous: Berber line dance of the Middle Atlas, with chanting and improvised poetry.

Ahouach: Berber group dance of the south, with women in a circle or lined up facing men.

Amazigh: Berber word for *Berber*, pertaining to the original people of North Africa.

Amazighte: Berber culture.

Amir al Mouminine: Commander of the Faithful, the title assumed by the king of Morocco as spiritual ruler.

Baraka: Divine power or simply good luck.

Beia: Ceremony of allegiance.

Bled al Makhzen: Territory controlled by the state.

Bled as Siba: Dissident or uncontrolled territory.

Burnous: Hooded cloak, usually of wool, worn by men.

Caid: Tribal chief.

Chira: Marijuana concentrate.

Couscous: Wheat-based staple food in North Africa, similar to rice in China.

Dahir: Royal decree.

Darija: Moroccan Arabic enriched with Berber, French, and Spanish terms.

Dirham: Moroccan currency.

Diwan al Madhalim: Royal ombudsman.

Djellaba: Long loose overcoat worn by men and women.

Djemaa or Jemaa: Community council or assembly.

Douar: Rural hamlet.

Eid: Holiday after the month of fasting, Ramadan.

Emir (also **amir**): Leader, prince, or commander.

Fantasia: Traditional show of group horsemanship; a simulation of battle.

Fetwa or fatwa: Opinion by a religious leader.

Fkih: Scholar in Islamic law.

Gnaoua: Descendants of slaves from sub-Saharan Africa whose music resembles blues.

Goumier: Moroccan auxiliary soldier serving with the French colonial army.

Hadith: Saying of the Prophet Mohammed or about him and his opinions.

Haik: Sheetlike wrap that covers the whole body, worn by some country women.

Haj: Muslim pilgrimage to Mecca that every believer must make at least once.

Hammam: Moorish bath.

Harem: Private section of the house for women and children, which only close male relatives may visit.

Hedya: Gift-giving ceremony.

Hijab: Clothing that covers a woman's body according to stipulations in the Koran.

Imam: Prayer leader.

Imazighen: Free people, meaning *Berbers* in the Berber language.

Intifada: People's uprising.

Jihad: Sacred struggle or crusade.

Kasbah: Fortress.

Khol: Oily type of natural eyeliner used by some traditional women and religious men.

Kif: Dried, crushed leaves of cannabis or marijuana whose use and production is condoned but whose trade is illegal.

Ksar (*pl.* ksour): Fortified village.

Lalla: Title of respect, similar to Lady.

Maghreb: In Arabic, the West, which has come to mean North Africa.

Makhzen: Arabic word for treasury, which has come to mean the power of the state.

Malekite: One of the four main schools of Islam and that which is observed by most Moroccans.

Marabout: Extremely devout person or saint and, by inference, a saint's tomb.

Medersa: Islamic school.

Medina: Old part of a city.

Moudawana: Civil code or family law.

Moujahid: Muslim combatant

Moulay: Title of respect, like lord.

Muezzen: Man who chants the call to prayer five times a day.

Muslim: Any person who submits to the will of Allah, or God.

Oulema: Religious scholars who interpret Islamic law.

Pasha: Governor at time of the protectorates.

Pateras: Boatpeople.

Salafi: Islamic reform movement.

Salafiya Jihadia: Islamic extremists.

Sharia: Islamic law.

Sheikh: Religious leader.

Sherif: Descendant of the Prophet Mohammed, plural shorfa.

Shoura: Consultation.

Sidi: Term of respect more than mister, in some instances, equivalent to lord or sir; -Si is abbreviation of Sidi.

Sidna: Our Lord, used to refer to the king or sultan.

Souk: Market.

Sufi: Member of a mystical religious order.

Sultan: Political ruler of the kingdom.

Tagine: Form of stew.

Tamazight: The main Berber dialect in Morocco and now refers to the Berber language.

Tifinagh: Original Berber script.

Umma: Global community of Muslims.

Wahhabi: Strict fundamentalist movement in Islam, founded in Saudi Arabia in the late eighteenth century and still practiced and propagated by the Saudis.

Zaouia: Religious brotherhood organized around a sanctuary, similar to a monastery.

Bibliography

Abu-Lughod, Janet. *Rabat: Urban Apartheid in Morocco*. Princeton, N.J.: Princeton University Press, 1980.

Abun-Nasr, Jamil M. *A History of the Maghrib in the Islamic Period*. Cambridge: Cambridge University Press, 1987.

Africanus, Leo [Al Hassan ibn Mohammed al Wezaz al Fasi]. *The History and Description of Africa and of the Notable Things wherein Contained*, trans. John Pory. 3 vols. London: Haklyut Society, 1896.

Akharbach, Latifa, and Narjis Rerhaye. *Femmes et politique*. Casablanca: Le Fennec, 1992.

Alaoui, Mohamed Ben El Hassan. *La Coopération entre l'Union Europeenne et les pays du Maghreb*. Paris: Nathan, 1994.

Al-Fasi, Alal. *The Independence Movements in Arab North Africa*, trans. Hazem Zaki Nuseibeh. Washington, D.C.: American Council of Learned Societies, 1954.

Ashford, Douglas E. *Political Change in Morocco*. Princeton, N.J.: Princeton University Press, 1961.

Ayache, Albert. *Le Maroc*. Paris: Sociales, 1956.

———. *Etudes d'histoire sociale Marocaine*. Rabat: Okad, 1997.

Aydoun, Ahmed. *Musiques du Maroc*. Casablanca: Eddif, 2001.

Balfour, Sebastian. *Deadly Embrace: Morocco and the Road to the Spanish Civil War*. New York: Oxford University Press, 2002.

Barbour, Nevill. *Morocco*. London: Thames and Hudson, 1965.

Bárbulo, Tomás. *La historia prohibida del Sahara Español*. Barcelona: Destino, 2002.

Bellaigue, Bertrand C. *Du mellah aux rives du Jordain*. Paris: Publibook, 2002.

Ben Barka, Abdelkader. *El Mehdi Ben Barka: Mon frère*. Paris: Laffont, 1966.

Ben Barka, Mehdi. *Option révolutionnaire au maroc: Ecrits politiques*. Paris: Maspero, 1966.

Benjelloun-Laroui, Latifa. *Les bibliothèques au Maroc*. Paris: Maisonneuve and Larose, 1990.

Ben Jelloun, Tahar. *This Blinding Absence of Light*, trans. Linda Coverdale. New York: New Press, 2002.

Bennouna, Mehdi. *Héros sans gloire: echec d'une révolution 1963–1973*. Casablanca: Tarik, 2002.

Bernard, Stephane. *The Franco-Moroccan Conflict, 1943–56*. New Haven, Conn.: Yale University Press, 1968.

Berque, Jacques. *French North Africa: The Maghrib between the Two World Wars*, trans. Jean Stewart. London: Faber and Faber, 1967.

Boukhari, Ahmed. *Le Secret: Ben Barka et le Maroc: Un ancien agent des services spéciaux parle*. Paris: Lafon, 2002.

Boutaleb, Abdelhadi. *Pour mieux comprendre l'Islam*. Casablanca: Afrique Orient, 2001.

Bowles, Paul. *The Sheltering Sky*. New York: ECCO, 1978.

———. *The Spider's House*. Santa Barbara, Calif.: Black Sparrow, 1993.

———. *Too Far from Home*. Hopewell, N.J.: ECCO, 1993.

Brett, Michael, and Elizabeth Fentress. *The Berbers*. Oxford: Blackwell, 1996.

Briggs, Lloyd Cabot. *Tribes of the Sahara*. Cambridge, Mass.: Harvard University Press, 1960.

Brown, Kenneth L. *People of Salé: Tradition and Change in a Moroccan City 1830–1930*. Manchester, England: Manchester University Press, 1976.

Burgat, François, and William Dowell. *The Islamic Movement in North Africa*. Austin: Center for Middle Eastern Studies, University of Texas, 1993.

Burke, Edmund, III. *Prelude to Protectorate in Morocco: Precolonial Protest and Resistance*. Chicago: University of Chicago Press, 1976.

Burroughs, William. *Interzone*. New York: Penguin, 1990.

Choukri, Mohamed. *For Bread Alone*, trans. Paul Bowles. London: Owen, 1973.

Chouraqui, André. *Between East and West*. Philadelphia: Jewish Publication Society of America, 1968.

———. *Histoire de Juifs en Afrique du nord*. Paris: Hachette, 1985.

Chraibi, Driss. *Le Passé simple*. Paris: Denoel, 1954.

Combe, Julie. *La Condition de la femme Marocaine*. Paris: L'Harmattan, 2001.

Combs-Schilling, M. Elaine. *Sacred Performances: Islam, Sexuality and Sacrifice*. New York: Columbia University Press, 1989.

Cooley, John Kent. *Baal, Christ and Mohammed: Religion and Revolution in North Africa*. London: Murray, 1967.

Cunninghame-Graham, R. B. *Mogreb-el-Acksa*. London: Heinemanne, 1898; reprint, London: Century, 1988.

Dalle, Ignace. *Maroc 1961–1999: L'éspérance brisée*. Paris: Maisonneuve and Larose, 2001.

———. *Les trois rois: La monarchie Marocaine de l'indépendence a nos jours*. Paris: Fayard, 2004.

Daoud, Zakia, with Maati Monjib. *Ben Barka*. Paris: Michallon, 1996.

Daure-Serfaty, Christine. *Tazmamart: Une prison de la mort au Maroc*. Paris: Stock, 1992.

———. *Lettre du Maroc*. Paris: Stock, 2000.

Ech-Channa, Aicha. *Miseria: Témoignages*. Casablanca: Le Fennec, 2000.

Eickleman, Dale F. *Moroccan Islam*. Austin: University of Texas Press, 1976.

El Maleh, Edmond A. *Mille ans un jour.* Grenoble: La Pensée Sauvage, 1986.

Elmandjra, Mahdi. *Première guerre civilisationnelle.* Casablanca: Toubkal, 1992.

El Ouadie, Salah. *Le marié.* Casablanca: TARIK, 2001.

Entelis, John P. *Culture and Counterculture in Moroccan Politics.* Boulder, Colo.: Westview, 1989.

Entelis, John P., ed. *Islam, Democracy, and the State in North Africa.* Bloomington and Indianapolis: Indiana University Press, 1997.

Esposito, John L. *The Islamic Threat: Myth or Reality?* New York: Oxford University Press, 1992.

Fernea, Elizabeth Warnock. *A Street in Marrakech.* 1976. Reprint, Prospect Heights, Colo.: Waveland, 1988.

Gallagher, Charles F. *The United States and North Africa: Morocco, Algeria and Tunisia.* Cambridge, Mass.: Harvard University Press, 1963.

García Figueras, Tomás. *Marruecos (La acción de España en el norte de Africa).* Tetuán: Marroquí, 1955.

Geertz, Clifford, Hildren Geertz, and Lawrence Rosen. *Meaning and Order in Moroccan Society: Three Essays in Cultural Analysis.* Cambridge: Cambridge University Press, 1979.

Gellner, Ernest, and Charles Micaud, eds. *Arabs and Berbers: From Tribe to Nation in North Africa.* Lexington, Mass.: Lexington Books, 1972.

Gershovich, Moshe. *French Military Rule in Morocco: Colonialism and Its Consequences.* London: Cass, 2000.

Hahn, Lorna. *North Africa: Nationalism to Nationhood.* Washington, D.C.: Public Affairs Press, 1960.

Halstead, John P. *Rebirth of a Nation: The Origins and Rise of Moroccan Nationalism 1912–1944.* Cambridge, Mass.: Harvard University Press, 1969.

Hammoudi, Abdellah. *Master and Disciple.* Chicago: University of Chicago Press, 1997.

Harris, Oliver, ed. *The Letters of William Burroughs, 1945–1959.* New York: Penguin, 1993.

Harris, Walter. *The Morocco That Was.* London: Eland, 1984.

Hassan II, with Eric Laurent. *La Mémoire d'un roi.* Paris: Librairie Plon, 1993.

———. *Le Génie de la modération: Réflexions sur les vérités de l'Islam.* Paris: Librairie Plon, 2000.

Hodges, Tony. *Western Sahara: The Roots of a Desert War.* Westport, Conn.: Hill, 1983.

Hoshen, Sarah Harel. *Juifs parmi les Berberes,* ed. Elias Harrus. Paris: Musée d'Art et d'Histoire du Judaisme, 1999.

Hourani, Albert. *A History of the Arab Peoples.* London: Faber and Faber, 1991.

Howe, Marvine. *The Prince and I.* New York: Day, 1955.

———. *One Woman's Morocco.* London: Barker, 1956.

Hughes, Stephen O. *Morocco under King Hassan.* Reading, U.K.: Ithaca Press, 2001.

Ibn Battuta, Muhammad. *Travels in Asia and Africa 1325–1354,* trans. H. A. R. Gibb. London: Routledge, 1983 (orig. 1929).

International League for the Rights and Liberation of Peoples. *Western Sahara and the Struggle of the Sahraoui People for Self-Determination: Dossier.* Rome: Leberit, 1978.

Julien, Charles-André. *L'Afrique du nord en marche.* Paris: Julliard, 1972.

———. *Histoire de l'Afrique du nord: des origines à la conquête arabe (647 AP.J-C).* 2 vols. Paris: Payot, 1952.

———. *Le Maroc face aux imperialismes 1415–1956.* Paris: JA, 1978.

Khair-Eddine, Mohammed. *Agadir.* Paris: Seuil, 1967.

———. *Une vie, un rêve, un people, toujours errants.* Paris: Seuil, 1978.

Lacouture, Jean, and Simone Lacouture. *Le Maroc à l'épreuve.* Paris: Seuil, 1958.

Landau, Rom. *The Sultan of Morocco.* London: Hale, 1951.

———. *Mohammed V: King of Morocco.* Rabat: Morocco Publishers, 1957.

Laroui, Abdallah. *The History of the Maghrib,* trans. Ralph Manheim. Princeton, N.J.: Princeton University Press, 1977.

———. *Les Origines du nationalisme Marocain.* Paris: Maspero, 1977.

———. *Esquisses historiques.* Casablanca: Centre Culturel Arabe, 1992.

———. *Islamisme, modernisme, liberalisme.* Casablanca: Centre Culturel Arabe, 1997.

Laskier, Michael M. *North African Jewry in the 20th Century.* New York: New York University Press, 1994.

Layadi, Fatiha, and Narjis Rerhaye. *Maroc: Chronique d'une démocratie en devenir.* Casablanca: EDDIF, 1998.

Lewis, Percy Wyndham. *Journey into Barbary.* Santa Barbara, Calif.: Black Sparrow, 1983.

Lewis, R. W. B., and Nancy Lewis, eds. *The Letters of Edith Wharton.* New York: Scribner's, 1988.

Marzouki, Ahmed. *Tazmamart: Cellule 10.* Paris: Gallimard, 2000.

Maxwell, Gavin. *Lords of the Atlas: The Rise and Fall of the House of Glaoua 1893–1956.* London: Arrow, 1991.

Mayne, Peter. *The Alleys of Marrakesh.* London: Murray, 1953.

Mernissi, Fatema. *Beyond the Veil.* Cambridge, Mass.: Schenkman, 1975.

———. *Islam and Democracy: Fear of the Modern World.* Reading, Mass.: Addison-Wesley, 1992.

———. *Dreams of Trespass: Tales of a Harem Girlhood.* Reading, Mass.: Addison-Wesley, 1994.

———. *Les Aït-Débrouille: ONG rurales du Haut Atlas.* Casablanca: Le Fennec, 1997.

———. *Scheherazade Goes West.* New York: Washington Square Press, 2001.

———. *Le harem politique, le prophète et les femmes.* Paris: Editions Complexe, 1992.

Ministry of Information and Tourism. *Réalisations et perspectives: 16 Novembre 1955–18 Novembre 1957.* Rabat: Kingdom of Morocco, 1957.

Montagne, Robert. *Révolution au Maroc.* Paris: France Empire, 1953.

———. *The Berbers: Their Social and Political Organization,* trans. David Seddon. London: Cass, 1973.

Munson, Henry, Jr. *Religion and Power in Morocco.* New Haven, Conn.: Yale University Press, 1993.

Oufkir, Malika, with Michele Fitoussi. *Stolen Lives,* trans. Ros Schwartz. New York: Hyperion, 2001.

Parker, Richard B. *North Africa: Regional Tensions and Strategic Concerns.* New York: Praeger, 1984.

———. *Islamic Monuments in Morocco*. Charlottesville, Va.: Baraka, 1981.

Perrault, Gilles, and Christine Daure-Jouvin. *Notre ami le roi*. Paris: Gallimard, 1990.

Roosevelt, Elliot. *As He Saw It*. New York: Duel, Sloan, and Pearce, 1946.

Rosen, Lawrence. *The Anthropology of Justice: Law as Culture in Islamic Society*. Cambridge: Cambridge University Press, 1989.

———. *The Culture of Islam: Changing Aspects of Continuing Muslim Life*. Chicago: University of Chicago Press, 2002.

Ruedy, John, ed. *Islamism and Secularism in North Africa*. London: Macmillan, 1994.

Sadiqi, Fatima. *Women, Gender and Language in Morocco*. Leiden: Brill, 2002.

Sarne, Daniel. *L'Affaire Ben Barka*. Paris: La Table Ronde, 1966.

Sauzey, François *Mohammed VI*. Paris: L'Atelier de l'Archer, 2000.

Serhane, Abdelhak. *Messaouda*. Paris: Seuil, 1983.

Smith, Stephen. *Oufkir: Un destin Marocain*. Paris: Calmann-Lévy, 1999.

Stevens, Edmund. *North African Powder Keg*. New York: Howard McCann, 1955.

Swearingen, Will D. *Moroccan Mirages: Agrarian Dreams and Deceptions, 1912–1986*. Princeton, N.J.: Princeton University Press, 1987.

Szulc, Tad. *The Secret Alliance*. London: Macmillan, 1997.

Taarji, Hinde. *Les Voilées de l'Islam*. Paris: Balland, 1990.

———. *30 jours en Algérie: Journal d'une Marocaine*. Casablanca: EDDIF, 1998.

Terrasse, Henri. *History of Morocco*, trans. Hilary Tee. Casablanca: Atlantides, 1952.

Tozy, Mohammed. *Monarchie et Islam politique au Maroc*. Paris: Presses de Sciences Politiques, 1999.

Tuquoi, Jean-Pierre. *Le dernier roi: Crépuscule d'une dynastie*. Paris: Grasset, 2001.

Twain, Mark. *The Innocents Abroad*. New York: Library of America, 1984.

Vermeren, Pierre. *Le Maroc en transition*. Paris: La Découverte, 2001.

———. *Histoire du Maroc depuis l'indépendance*. Paris: La Découverte, 2002.

Villiers, Marq de, and Sheila Hirtle. *Sahara: A Natural History*. New York: Walker, 2002.

Waterbury, John. *The Commander of the Faithful: The Moroccan Political Elite: A Study in Segmented Politics*. New York: Columbia University Press, 1970.

Westermarck, Edward. *Ritual and Belief in Morocco*. 2 vols. London: Macmillan, 1926.

Yassine, Abdessalam. *Islamiser la modernité*. Casablanca: Al Ofok Impressions, 1998.

Yassine, Nadia. *Toutes voiles dehors*. Casablanca: Le Fennec, 2003.

Zartman, I. William. *Morocco: Problems of New Power*. New York: Atherton, 1964.

Zartman, I. William, ed. *Man, State and Society in the Contemporary Maghrib*. London: Pall Mall, 1973.

———. *The Political Economy of Morocco*. London: Praeger, 1987.

Index